D0762357

Assessment Issues in Child Neuropsychology

Critical Issues in Neuropsychology

ASSESSMENT ISSUES IN CHILD NEUROPSYCHOLOGY
Edited by Michael G. Tramontana and Stephen R. Hooper

HANDBOOK OF CLINICAL CHILD NEUROPSYCHOLOGY
Edited by Cecil R. Reynolds and Elaine Fletcher-Janzen

MEDICAL NEUROPSYCHOLOGY: The Impact of Disease on Behavior
Edited by Ralph E. Tarter, David H. Van Thiel, and Kathleen L. Edwards

NEUROPSYCHOLOGICAL FUNCTION AND BRAIN IMAGING
Edited by Erin D. Bigler, Ronald A. Yeo, and Eric Turkheimer

Assessment Issues in Child Neuropsychology

Edited by

Michael G. Tramontana

Bradley Hospital
East Providence, Rhode Island
and Brown University
Providence, Rhode Island

and

Stephen R. Hooper

Clinical Center for the Study of Development and Learning
University of North Carolina School of Medicine
Chapel Hill, North Carolina

Plenum Press • New York and London

Library of Congress Cataloging in Publication Data

Assessment issues in child neuropsychology / edited by Michael G. Tramontana and
Stephen R. Hooper.
    p.   cm. —(Critical issues in neuropsychology)
    Includes bibliographies and index.
    ISBN 0-306-42898-9
    1. Developmental disabilities—Diagnosis. 2. Neuropsychological tests for children.
I. Tramontana, Michael G. II. Hooper, Stephen R. III. Series.
    [DNLM: 1. Child Development Disorders—diagnosis. 2. Neuropsychological Tests—
in infancy & childhood. 3. Neuropsychology—in infancy and childhood. WS 340
A8453] RJ131.A789   1988
618.92'8588—dc19
DNLM/DLC   88-22399
for Library of Congress   CIP

© 1988 Plenum Press, New York
A Division of Plenum Publishing Corporation
233 Spring Street, New York, N.Y. 10013

Printed in the United States of America

To Maryanne and our son, Michael Joseph, and to our
anticipated new arrival

          M.G.T.

To my family

          S.R.H.

Contributors

GLEN P. AYLWARD, Division of Developmental and Behavioral Pediatrics, Departments of Pediatrics and Psychiatry, Southern Illinois University School of Medicine, Springfield, Illinois

RUSSELL A. BARKLEY, Department of Psychiatry, University of Massachusetts Medical Center, Worcester, Massachusetts

ERIN D. BIGLER, Austin Neurological Clinic, and Department of Psychology, University of Texas at Austin, Austin, Texas

THOMAS A. BOYD, Cleveland Metropolitan General Hospital, and Case Western Reserve University School of Medicine, Cleveland, Ohio

ROBERT T. CONNOR, Kennedy Institute, Johns Hopkins School of Medicine, Baltimore, Maryland

MICHAEL A. CRARY, Departments of Communicative Disorders and Neurology, University of Florida Health Science Center, Gainesville, Florida

RAYMOND S. DEAN, Neuropsychology Laboratory, Ball State University, Muncie, Indiana, and Indiana University School of Medicine

DOROTHY EDGELL, Department of Psychology, Jack Ledger Child and Adolescent Psychiatric Unit, Arbutus Society for Children, Victoria, British Columbia, Canada

JANE M. FLYNN, Gundersen Medical Foundation, LaCrosse, Wisconsin

JEFFREY W. GRAY, Neuropsychology Laboratory, Ball State University, Muncie, Indiana

NANCY J. HAAK, Departments of Communicative Disorders and Neurology, University of Florida, Gainesville, Florida

STEPHEN R. HOOPER, Department of Psychiatry, University of North Carolina School of Medicine, and Clinical Center for the Study of

Development and Learning, University of North Carolina, Chapel Hill, North Carolina

GEORGE W. HYND, Departments of Educational Psychology and Psychology, University of Georgia, Athens, Georgia, and Department of Neurology, Medical College of Georgia, Augusta, Georgia

JOEL LEVY, Department of Psychology, Texas Institute for Rehabilitation and Research, Houston, Texas

G. REID LYON, Departments of Neurology and Communication Science and Disorders, University of Vermont, Burlington, Vermont, Gundersen Medical Foundation, and Department of Special Education, St. Michael's College, Winooski, Vermont

LOUISA MOATS, Associates in Counseling and Education, East Thetford, Vermont

GRANT L. MORRIS, Department of Psychology, University of Northern Colorado, Greeley, Colorado

NAOMI NIEVES, Kennedy Institute, Johns Hopkins School of Medicine, Baltimore, Maryland

FRANCIS J. PIROZZOLO, Department of Neurology, Baylor College of Medicine, and Neurology Service, Houston VA Medical Center, Houston, Texas

ANTHONY H. RISSER, Department of Neurology, University of Wisconsin Medical School, Mount Sinai Medical Center, Milwaukee, Wisconsin

MICHAEL G. TRAMONTANA, Bradley Hospital and Department of Psychiatry and Human Behavior, Brown University, East Providence, Rhode Island

KYJTA K. S. VOELLER, Department of Neurology, University of Florida Health Science Center, Gainesville, Florida

W. GRANT WILLIS, Department of Psychology, University of Rhode Island, Kingston, Rhode Island

Foreword

Neuropsychology has its roots in clinical neurology. Reading case descriptions by 19th century neurologists, such as Wernicke's painstakingly detailed examinations of patients with the "aphasic symptom-complex," makes it obvious that neuropsychology is not a new discipline. Even the marriage with psychology is not new; the neurologist Arnold Pick, for example, was fully conversant with the developments in contemporary psychological as well as linguistic research. However, the primary focus of 19th and early 20th century psychology was on "general psychology," and only a small number of psychologists ventured into what then was called "differential psychology" (the psychology of individual differences) including a few who became attached to neurological research and rehabilitation units after World War I. It remained until World War II for psychologists to establish a more solid working relationship with neurology.

What psychology had to offer to neurology was its experimental skill, the development of a sophisticated methodology, and, for clinical work, the development of psychometrics. On the whole, the marriage between the two disciplines has been fruitful, leading to new insights, models, and discoveries about brain-behavior relationships, documented in several textbooks which appeared in rapid succession since the 1960s. In clinical practice, neuropsychology has been inventive in some respects, in others merely introducing psychometric rigor to already existing neurological examinations.

As described in greater detail in this book, developmental neuropsychology is of even more recent origin. Yet again, to a large extent this is not a new field, but one which pediatric neurology and several allied disciplines like neonatology, teratology, and embryology have developed over the course of the century. In addition, developmental psychology and developmental linguistics have developed a solid core of information and theory, emphasizing a "psychobiological approach" for many years. Integration of these many sources of knowledge into a neuropsychological framework has been attempted for individual topics during the last twenty years and as integrated overviews only in recent years.

I think it is important to remember and acknowledge, as well as to integrate existing knowledge into developmental neuropsychology rather than treat this field as *terra nova*. This book is a first critical appraisal of the clinical application of child neuropsychology focusing on assessment issues. It is to the credit of the editors and authors that they present assessment issues not in isolation, but in the context of basic knowledge about developmental neuropsychology, its history, and its neighbor disciplines. The book is not restricted to the critical evaluation of traditional assessment methods, but includes a coverage of basic neurodevelopmental considerations, a comparison with pediatric, radiologic and electrodiagnostic sources of information, different models of neuropsychological inference, and the implications of assessment for treatment. It then moves on to the major topics of assessment of attention, memory, functional laterality, language, and to more specific areas such as infancy, early childhood, and learning disabilities. The successful integration of these diverse areas is a major accomplishment of this book.

One recurrent problem is, of course, the practice of drawing on assessment techniques developed for the adult patient, and extending these methods downward. Within certain age limits and for some areas of function, this may be satisfactory. However, most techniques "bottom out" at age 5 or 6, i.e., at an age before the child becomes aquainted with the test-taking attitude required in school. The preschool child has not yet acquired these attitudes, and does not deliver a consistent performance.

More serious yet is the problem of developmental changes. To expect the same tests to measure the changing component skills in the young child which gradually develop into complex adult performance is hazardous and disregards the accumulated knowledge of child development. Hence, new and age-appropriate measuring instruments need to be developed and linked to neuropsychological theory. Most of the authors in this book consider these problems carefully for their area of assessment and suggest ways in which existing methods can be used in a neuropsychological framework; others find areas which are not covered sufficiently and recommend a new design and a drastic re-development of assessment methodology.

Finally, the limited behavioral repertoire of the infant, toddler, or young child, allows fewer and fewer standardized psychological measurements compared to what can be used with the adolescent and adult. Observations of "baby holds rattle" or responses to light, sound, and touch stimuli take the place of tests. Yet, observing the richness of the Brazelton examination in newborns gives us an inkling of what is to come as the child grows up. As Aylward describes in this book, the expansion of this basic repertoire should be examined carefully in the light of developmental neuropsychological theory.

A considerable portion of this book focuses on learning disabilities. This rather complex area perhaps takes up so much of our interest because it started as a neurological theory, suggested by Pringle Morgan in 1896, as a "congenital" parallel to the aquired "word-blindness" as described by James Hinshelwood and others. Although theories about the forms and causes of learning disabilities have changed, and evidence which substantiates the claim to neurological damage or dysfunction has been found only recently, the neuropsychological focus has been present throughout the century. In contrast, developmental neuropsychology has been quite slow in exploring mental retardation, another area of important neuropsychological inquiry which was discussed in a position paper by Benton in 1974. Perhaps because of the very different social and educational demands of the mentally retarded, research in this field has developed in relative isolation, although a majority of this population suffers from brain abnormalities. Only recently have some special syndromes, e.g., Turner's, fragile X, and Down's syndrome attracted specific neuropsychological research.

Although the development of systematic neuropsychological assessment methods for children remains the primary target of this book (and, I am certain, of many future discussions arising from it), the future development of such procedures should not exclude traditional assessments, especially in the area of emotional, social and other adjustment areas. Tramontana and Hooper's introduction and Bigler's and Hooper's chapters make this point, but it is important to stress that emotional disorders as well as cognitive disorders may arise from brain abnormalities so often that the inclusion of an assessment of the adaptive status of the child is almost mandatory unless neuropsychological assessment is viewed as ancillary to other assessments.

It is also essential to see the child as it develops in its own special environment, not just as a biological organism. For this reason, a careful exploration of the influences and attitudes of family, neighborhood and school, of resource availability, socio-economic status, and resourcesfulness of the parents often will explain some of the adjustment problems and even some of the cognitive and language problems of a given child.

What emerges as the field of clinical child neuropsychology, then, is a multifaceted composite. Neuropsychological assessment, almost by definition, is not likely to account for more than a portion of the variance presented by children. This portion is further reduced by the lack of direct correspondence between lesion area and type of deficit as we have come to expect from early studies of adults with clearly circumscribed damage, especially in gunshot and shrapnel victims. As outlined by Risser and Edgell as well as by other authors in this book, brain lesions in children are rarely clearly defined and circumscribed, nor do they show direct cause-effect relationships even if age at onset is taken into account. A look at Nichols and Chen's effort in 1981 to tease out the longitudinal effects of pregnancy, delivery and early childhood factors in a population of 53,000 participants provides an appreciation of the small magnitude of variance which can be explained by such antecedent variables as smoking and convulsions of the mother during pregnancy, low fetal heart rate and placental weight, head circumference at 12 months, and the Bayley Motor Scales at 8 months among many others.

Progress in the neuropsychological assessment of the child often has been preceded by the development of new research methods, such as unique methods for determining lateralization in infancy. This process no doubt will continue in the future. Yet, as we look for tools for clinical neuropsychological assessment we also must be guided by what the editors describe as ecological validity in addition to construct and diagnostic validity, i.e., by what the assessment contributes to the choice, delivery and monitoring of treatment, and long-term prediction of outcome. This is a difficult and lengthy task because it includes a consideration of different treatment options and their effectiveness. Only a few authors, such as Rourke and Bakker in the field of learning disabilities, have addressed this task (also described by Lyon, Moats, and Flynn in this book). Ultimately, however, the development of neuropsychology as a *clinical* discipline cannot survive unless it provides answers to these questions.

Given the magnitude of the task of neuropsychological and related assessments, one must marvel at the progress already shown in these chapters. It is too early to say that child neuropsychological assessment has come of age, but perhaps it has reached puberty.

Otfried Spreen

Victoria, B. C., Canada

Preface

Recent years have witnessed the emergence of child neuropsychology as a growing subspecialty within clinical neuropsychology. The collective efforts in this field over the last 15 years or so have been truly impressive. They have succeeded in drawing attention not only to the special roles that neuropsychological assessment can play in the clinical evaluation of children, but also to the important differences in brain-behavior relationships that must be considered in evaluating children versus adults. Much remains to be learned concerning the effects of brain dysfunction in childhood, but the work to date has served to create a distinct base of knowledge that is sure to grow.

The specialized nature of this field would not be apparent, however, if one were only to inspect the current tools that are used in the neuropsychological assessment of children. Indeed, these largely represent downward extensions of adult neuropsychological methods, most of which lack a clear linkage with existing knowledge on the neuropsychology of the developing brain. The range of well-validated assessment methods designed specifically for children is quite limited, especially for the very young. New developments are needed, as the available methods generally have not kept pace with the evolving aims and ever-widening applications of child neuropsychological assessment.

The present volume is devoted specifically to an in-depth examination of assessment issues in child neuropsychology. Other key volumes within the field have served to establish the importance of child neuropsychology and its potential contributions to the study and evaluation of children with disordered brain function. It is time to pause and take critical inventory of the current status of assessment in this field. This is vitally important, as the future progress of child neuropsychology will depend greatly on the availability of appropriate tools for assessing brain-behavior relationships as they unfold in childhood. The intent of this volume is not simply to lament over present shortcomings, but rather to help outline constructive ways in which progress can be achieved. It is easy to criticize present assessment procedures, but it is important that this be balanced by a genuine appreciation for the conceptual and practical complexities involved in the neuropsychological assessment of the developing child. Emphasis is given not only to identifying critical areas in need of further development, but also to providing informed opinions as to which of the current methods offer particular promise in assessing various aspects of child neuropsychological functioning.

This volume consists of 14 chapters divided into four parts. Parts I and II provide an overview of assessment in child neuropsychology, both in terms of the general approaches to assessment that are currently available as well as important conceptual issues that apply to the field as a whole. These are followed by a special topics part (III) in which each chapter focuses on a specific aspect of child neuropsychological assessment. There were many more potential topics than possibly could have been included in this section. We chose to emphasize certain aspects of functioning that require particular consideration in childhood, including attention, memory, functional laterality, and language development. The assessment of learning disabilities is covered extensively, mainly because it represents an area that has been the subject of intensive neuropsychological inquiry. This is balanced by a careful consideration of infant and early childhood assessment—a topic that, by contrast, has received relatively little attention in child neuropsychology. The final part (IV) of the book offers an integration of the problems and prospects identified, highlighting crucial avenues in which a concerted effort in future work will be especially needed.

The book is written at an advanced level and assumes that the reader has some familiarity with basic brain-behavior relationships. It is intended primarily for advanced students and professionals in the fields of neuropsychology, clinical psychology, and school psychology. Its content also should be pertinent to professionals in other disciplines involved in the study or care of children with brain dysfunction, including neurologists, child psychiatrists, pediatricians, speech and language pathologists, and special educators. Moreover, the emphasis on addressing assessment issues in a fashion which integrates research in developmental neuropsychology should serve to provide useful guidelines for researchers and practitioners alike.

We wish to extend our sincere appreciation to a number of individuals whose efforts helped us greatly in the completion of this book. We are indebted especially to both Roseanne Rabideau and Elaine Nardolillo for their superb assistance throughout the various stages of editing and organizing chapter manuscripts. The dedication and countless hours that they gave went well beyond the call of duty, and will be remembered always. We also owe a special note of thanks to Maryanne Tramontana for her patience and generosity in creating a very supportive atmosphere on those many occasions when our work on this book extended late into the night.

Michael G. Tramontana
Stephen R. Hooper

Contents

Part I: INTRODUCTION

Chapter 1
Child Neuropsychological Assessment:
Overview of Current Status 3
Michael G. Tramontana and *Stephen R. Hooper*

Introduction 3
Historical Trends in Assessment 5
Current Approaches in Child Neuropsychological Assessment 9
  Fixed-Battery Approaches 9
  Other General Approaches 16
  Special-Purpose Measures 20
Applications 21
  Neurological Disorders 21
  Systemic Illness 23
  Psychiatric Disorders 24
  Learning Disabilities 26
  Rehabilitation and Assessing Recovery of Function 27
Conceptual and Practical Issues 28
Summary 32
References 32

Part II: GENERAL ISSUES IN CHILD NEUROPSYCHOLOGICAL
ASSESSMENT

Chapter 2
Neuropsychology of the Developing Brain: Implications for
Neuropsychological Assessment 41
Anthony H. Risser and *Dorothy Edgell*

Introduction 41

Principles of Neural Development 42
    Proliferation and Migration 43
    Differentiation 44
    Myelination 47
    Functional Organization 49
    Summary 51
Abnormalities in Neural Development 51
Developmental Neuropsychological Implications 56
Conclusions 59
References 60

Chapter 3

The Role of Neuropsychological Assessment in Relation to Other
Types of Assessment with Children 67

Erin D. Bigler

Introduction 67
Pediatric Neurological Exam (PNE) 68
    Basic Components 68
    The Nature of Findings 70
    Mental Status Characteristics of Neurologically Impaired
        Children 74
    Relationship between Pediatric Neurological Exam and
        Neuropsychological Assessment 75
Neuroradiological Tests 75
Electrodiagnostic Tests 80
    Relationship between Electrodiagnostic Findings and
        Neuropsychological Assessment 82
Psychological Assessment 84
    Intellectual Assessment versus Neuropsychological Assessment
        with Children: What's the Difference? 86
Conclusions 87
References 88

Chapter 4

Neuropsychological Diagnosis with Children: Actuarial and
Clinical Models 93

W. Grant Willis

Diagnostic Models 94
    Data–Diagnosis Contingency 94
    Consideration of Data 95
    Relative Importance of Data 96
Actuarial Models 97
    Methods 97

Base–Rate Considerations 98
Validity of Diagnostic Criteria 100
Stability and Generalizability of Actuarial Rules 101
Clinical Judgment 102
Interpretive Strategies 103
Debiasing Techniques 105
Assessment Design and Decision Rules 106
Summary 107
References 108

Chapter 5
From Assessment to Treatment: Linkage to Interventions with
Children 113
G. Reid Lyon, Louisa Moats, and Jane M. Flynn

Introduction 113
Neuropsychological Assessment: Purposes and Measurement
    Characteristics 115
Relating Assessment to Treatment: Models and Studies 119
Standardized Assessment Batteries: Implications for Treatment ... 119
    The Halstead-Reitan: Linkages to Treatment 119
    The Luria-Nebraska: Linkages to Treatment 122
    The K-ABC: Linkages to Treatment 122
Selected Assessment Batteries: Linkages to Treatment 123
    Empirical Subtype Intervention Studies: The Lyon Research
        Program 125
    Clinical Subtype Intervention Studies: The Bakker Research
        Program 131
    Direct Assessment Intervention Studies: The Flynn Research
        Program 132
Some Final Thoughts, Conclusions, and Directions 135
    Professional Preparation and Experience 135
    Developmental Issues in Assessment 136
    The Need for Dynamic Assessment 137
    The Need for Continued Classification Research 138
References 139

PART III: SPECIAL TOPICS IN ASSESSMENT

Chapter 6
Attention 145
Russell A. Barkley

Introduction 145

Importance of Attention in Child Neuropsychology 146
Components of Attention 148
Assessment of Attention 153
Behavior Rating Scales 153
Psychometric Tests and Laboratory Measures 159
Direct Observational Measures 167
Discussion 169
Summary 170
References 171

Chapter 7

Clinical Assessment of Memory in Children: A Developmental
Framework for Practice 177
Thomas A. Boyd

Introduction 177
Current Status of Memory Assessment with Children 179
Models of Memory Development in Childhood 185
Information-Processing Models 186
Interactionist Models of Memory 188
Suggestions for a Children's Memory Battery: General Format 195
Suggestions for a Children's Memory Battery: Types of Tasks 196
Clinical Relevance of the Models 199
Conclusions 200
References 201

Chapter 8

Assessing Functional Laterality 205
Jeffrey W. Gray and Raymond S. Dean

Introduction 205
Methods of Laterality Assessment 206
Perceptual Asymmetry Techniques 207
Electrophysiological Measures 210
Lateral Preference Measures 211
Unimanual Performance Measures 214
Applications with Learning-Disabled/Language-Impaired
Children 215
Clinical Implications 218
References 219

Chapter 9

Infant and Early Childhood Assessment 225

Glen P. Aylward

The Status of Neuropsychological Assessment in Infancy and
    Early Childhood 225
Conceptual Issues in Early Neuropsychological Assessment 227
    Differences in Assessing School-Age versus Younger
        Children 227
    Consistency of Dysfunction 229
    Classification of Early Neuropsychological Findings 231
Assessment Instruments 234
    Newborn/Neonatal 235
    Infancy 235
    Early Childhood 235
    Useful Findings 239
Directions 239
Appendix 245
References 246

Chapter 10

Questions of Developmental Neurolinguistic Assessment 249

Michael A. Crary, Kyjta K. S. Voeller, and *Nancy J. Haak*

Introduction 249
Basics of Language Development 250
    Prelinguistic Communication 251
    Lexical Expansion Stage 252
    Grammatical Expansion Stage 253
    A Comment on Styles of Language Processing 254
Relation of Neurological Maturation to Acquisition of Language
        Skills 254
    Neuroanatomic Maturation 254
    Hemispheric Functions 256
Language Assessment at Present—What's Covered,
        What's Not? 261
    Prelinguistic Assessment (0 to 12+ Months) 262
    Lexical Expansion Assessment (12 to 24+ Months) 263
    Grammatical Expansion Assessment (2 to 4+ Years) 264
    Summary of Present Assessment Capabilities 269
Guidelines and Questions Regarding Developmental
        Neurolinguistic Assessment 269

A Concluding Example 273
References 274

Chapter 11

Learning Disabilities Subtypes: Perspectives and Methodological
Issues in Clinical Assessment 281
George W. Hynd, Robert T. Connor, and Naomi Nieves

Introduction 281
Early Conceptualizations of Learning Disabilities 282
    Clinical Case Reports and Observations 282
    What's in a Name? 283
Defining Learning Disabilities 284
    The Public Forum and PL 94-142 284
    Acknowledging the Neurological Etiology 284
Multifactor Research 285
    Perspectives on the Single Factor Research 285
    Early Subtyping Studies 286
    Some Directions in Subtyping Research: Multivariate
        Classification Approaches 287
    Neurolinguistic Subtyping 300
Neuroanatomical–Linguistic Perspectives 301
    The Wernicke–Geschwind Model 301
    Clinical Implications for Process-Based Assessment 304
Conceptual Framework for Clinical Evaluation 305
Conclusions 307
References 308

Chapter 12

The Prediction of Learning Disabilities in the Preschool Child: A
Neuropsychological Perspective 313
Stephen R. Hooper

Introduction 313
The Importance of Early Prediction of Learning Disabilities 314
    Extent of the Problem 315
    Minimizing Educational Failure 316
    Minimizing Social–Emotional Difficulties 316
    Effects of Environmental Influences 317
    Summary 318
The Prediction of Learning Disabilities: Current Status 318
    Recent Reviews of the Literature 318
    Exemplary Studies 321

Summary 323
Issues and Directions 324
 Neurodevelopmental Theory 325
 Neuropsychological Constructs and Preschool Prediction 328
 Related Issues in the Prediction of Learning Disabilities 330
Conclusions 331
References 332

Chapter 13

Electrophysiological Assessment in Learning Disabilities 337

Grant L. Morris, Joel Levy, and Francis J. Pirozzolo

Introduction 337
 Anatomical Correlates of Learning Disorders 338
 Neuroimaging Methods 340
Electrophysiological Techniques and Findings 343
 Electroencephalography 343
 Evoked Potentials 352
Conclusions 362
References 363

Part IV: COMMENT

Chapter 14

Problems and Prospects in Child Neuropsychological
Assessment 369

Michael G. Tramontana

Index 377

I

Introduction

Child Neuropsychological Assessment
Overview of Current Status

MICHAEL G. TRAMONTANA and STEPHEN R. HOOPER

INTRODUCTION

There has been a tremendous growth of interest in child neuropsychology as a distinct subspecialty within the broader field of clinical neuropsychology. Whereas it was not too long ago that one could find only selected chapters dealing with children in some of the major texts within the field (e.g., Filskov & Boll, 1981; Reitan & Davison, 1974), there are now entire volumes devoted exclusively to the topic (Gaddes, 1985; Hynd & Obrzut, 1981; Hynd & Willis, 1988; Ivan, 1984; Obrzut & Hynd, 1986a, 1986b; Rourke, 1985; Rourke, Bakker, Fisk, & Strang, 1983; Rourke, Fisk, & Strang, 1986; Rutter, 1983; Spreen, Tupper, Risser, Tuokko, & Edgell, 1984). Likewise, there has been a proliferation of symposia, workshops, and journal articles covering various aspects of neuropsychological research and practice with children. All of this certainly attests to the emergence of child neuropsychology as a focus of vigorous interest and inquiry.

Various factors have been cited as responsible for this increased interest and activity in child neuropsychology. Hynd, Snow, and Becker (1986), for example, underscored two factors that they saw as particularly

MICHAEL G. TRAMONTANA • Bradley Hospital and Department of Psychiatry and Human Behavior, Brown University, East Providence, Rhode Island.   STEPHEN R. HOOPER • Department of Psychiatry, University of North Carolina School of Medicine and Clinical Center for the Study of Development and Learning, University of North Carolina, Chapel Hill, North Carolina important. The first had to do with the passage of the Education for All Handicapped Children Act (Public Law 94-142, *Federal Register*, 1976) and, among other things, its calling national attention to the fact that a significant percentage of children suffer from learning disabilities and other developmental handicaps presumed to have a neurodevelopmental etiology. This, in turn, served to accentuate an important role for neuropsychological assessment both in the identification of specific neurodevelopmental disorders and in helping to devise appropriate educational plans. Another factor cited by Hynd *et al.* concerns the increased prevalence of children surviving neurological trauma. Advances in medical care have brought about a dramatic increase in the survival of children whose conditions (or their treatment) have a potentially adverse impact on the developing brain (e.g., very low birthweight associated with prematurity, iatrogenic effects of childhood cancer treatment). Thus, whereas mortality has decreased, there has been a relative increase in morbidity. This has created a greater need for the careful assessment of the extent, pattern, and developmental significance of possible neuropsychological sequelae in these survivors of serious childhood illness.

Along with this increased demand for child neuropsychological assessment has come the growing realization of important differences in brain–behavior relationships between children and adults. Not only do children differ in the types of brain insult commonly experienced, they also differ with respect to the specificity of behavioral effects manifested, the pattern and course of (re)acquisition of function after injury, the modifying effects of ongoing developmental change, and the extent to which deficits sometimes can be delayed or "silent" until later developmental periods (Almli & Finger, 1984; Boll & Barth, 1981; Chadwick & Rutter, 1983; Rourke *et al.*, 1983). Developmentalists argue that a child should never be viewed as simply a scaled-down version of an adult. Likewise, an appropriate assessment of brain–behavior relationships in children cannot be based simply on scaled-down versions of assessment methods used with adults.

Unfortunately, many of the available assessment tools in child neuropsychology largely represent downward extensions of adult neuropsychological models and methods, many of which lack any clear linkage with the neuropsychology of the developing brain. There is more to the development of appropriate assessment procedures for children than simply gathering norms on adult tests for children of different ages (although even this would be welcome in many instances). It also means more than simply reducing the length or complexity of test procedures to make them more practical for use with children. The measures themselves, as well as their organization within an overall assessment strategy, must be tailored to elucidate brain–behavior relationships as they unfold at different points in a child's development. It is important that the field does not rush to meet the increased demand and new challenges it now faces armed only with assessment tools borrowed from work with adults. New challenges will require new approaches if the field of child neuropsychology is to prosper and continue to grow.

This volume is devoted to underscoring important assessment issues in child neuropsychology. In this chapter we will provide a general overview of historical trends within the field, the current approaches to assessment, their clinical applications, and some of the key conceptual and practical issues involved in the neuropsychological assessment of children. We hope thus to set the stage for selected issues and topics to be pursued at greater depth in subsequent chapters in this volume.

HISTORICAL TRENDS IN ASSESSMENT

The history of assessment in child neuropsychology can be distinguished into four distinct but overlapping stages of development. These are similar to, but generally have lagged behind, the stages of development that have characterized adult neuropsychology.

The first stage, the *single-test approach*, dominated the field from about the mid-1940s to the mid-1960s. It was characterized by the use of general, all-purpose measures for diagnosing brain damage or "organicity." The approach was guided by the belief that brain damage, regardless of its extent, location, or pathological process, manifested itself in a unitary fashion—whether it was in terms of a loss of abstraction abilities, perceptual-motor skills, or other factors. The goal was to differentiate brain-damaged children from normals, and it was thought that a single well-chosen measure could achieve that end. The issue of *how* brain dysfunction was being manifested really did not matter because the interest was more in the global differentiation of cases. Examples of tests used in this fashion (although not necessarily with the encouragement of their authors) included the Bender Visual Motor Gestalt Test (Bender, 1938; Koppitz, 1964), the Visual Retention Test (Benton, 1963), and the Memory for Designs Test (Graham & Kendall, 1960).

The problems with the single-test approach have been well documented. For example, Herbert (1964) conducted a thorough review of the tests in use up to the early 1960s and concluded that none achieved a sufficient differentiation of brain-damaged and normal children to justify its clinical use with individual cases. Even if there were such a justification, there still would remain the issue of whether anything really is gained by simply being able to classify a child as brain-damaged or not. The single-test approach did have the historical significance of introducing psychologists into the role of making inferences regarding brain dysfunction. However, by today's standards, most neuropsychologists would

regard the continued reliance on this approach as constituting mal-
practice.

Next came the *test battery/lesion-specification stage* of neuropsychological assessment. Ernhart and Graham are credited as being
among the first to apply a battery of psychological tests in assessing the
developmental outcomes of a heterogeneous group of children with documented brain damage (Ernhart, Graham, Eichman, Marshall, & Thurston,
1963; Graham, Ernhart, Craft, & Berman, 1963). They found that brain-
damaged children manifested deficits on verbal and conceptual measures
as well as on perceptual-motor tasks. Also, whereas no single measure
yielded a satisfactory discrimination of brain-damaged children, use of
the entire test battery did. This underscored the variability of brain
damage, and the need for a test battery covering a broad range of functions
to capture its effects. Shortly thereafter, Reitan and his colleagues (Reed,
Reitan, & Klove, 1965) reported on the successful discrimination of brain-
damaged children and normals using the Halstead-Reitan Neuropsychological Battery (HRNB). This battery (and its variants) quickly came to be
the predominant assessment approach of this period, at least in North
America.

There was another significant aspect to this stage of development in
neuropsychology. The work with adults had shown that test batteries
such as the HRNB not only provided a valid discrimination of brain-
damaged and normal subjects but also were reasonably accurate in distinguishing among brain-damaged patients who differed in terms of the
extent, location, and other characteristics of their lesions (see Reitan &
Davison, 1974). Indeed, neuropsychological test batteries achieved an
equal, if not superior, discrimination of lesion characteristics in comparison with many of the other neurodiagnostic methods available at the
time (Filskov & Goldstein, 1974). Inspired by this success with adults,
similar efforts were made with children, albeit with unimpressive results.
In the absence of significant hemimotor signs, even attempts to lateralize
early cerebral lesions on the basis of neuropsychological test performance
remains a controversial and poorly validated enterprise at best (Chadwick
& Rutter, 1983).

Both of the above stages constituted what Rourke (1982) has referred
to as the *static phase* of development in clinical neuropsychology. The
emphasis was on the detection and localization of brain lesions. The
approach (either with single tests or test batteries) was empirical, atheoretical, and geared heavily toward establishing cutoff scores and rules of
inference for the purpose of maximizing hit rates in categorical diagnosis.
These applications were quite appealing at the time because of the void
that existed in noninvasive neurodiagnostic technology until about the
mid-1970s.

This gave way to the *functional profile stage*, or what Rourke (1982) has referred to as the *cognitive phase* of neuropsychological assessment. Controversy over the validity of neuropsychological batteries to localize brain lesions in children, coupled with the rapid development of other noninvasive neurodiagnostic methods, resulted in a gradual de-emphasis on using neuropsychological tests for making inferences regarding brain lesions. The emphasis shifted more to the role of neuropsychological assessment in specifying the behavioral effects of cerebral lesions. The goal was to differentiate between spared and impaired abilities, functional strengths and weaknesses, and so forth. The concern was not only on the extent of impairment but also on the pattern of deficit and the underlying components of impaired performance. It represented the "re-psychologizing" of neuropsychology, in that the emphasis was on assessing the psychological aspects of neurological insults and anomalies. Of all the available neurodiagnostic methods, neuropsychological assessment had a unique and complementary role to play in determining the mental and behavioral effects of brain injury, in identifying functional assets and deficits for the purpose of treatment planning, and in evaluating subsequent change.

A particularly important aspect of this period involved the neuropsychological study of children with learning disabilities. Just as the field of neuropsychology, in general, had moved away from unitary concepts and single-test measures of brain dysfunction, so too the study of learning disabilities progressed from single-factor research to multivariate research and the identification of *subtypes* of disabled learners (see Chapter 11, this volume). Neuropsychological test profiles, along with statistical clustering techniques, were used in identifying more homogeneous groupings of children having distinguishable patterns of disability. The work was not exclusively descriptive and empirical but also entailed theory building and model testing. This was important not only because it involved the extension of neuropsychological assessment into the realm of syndrome definition but also because it represented a major line of neuropsychological research focused on children. Furthermore, it promoted a closer linkage between assessment and treatment, in that the differentiation of learning disabilities into subtypes provided at least a theoretical basis for the specification of differential approaches to treatment.

Although this stage of development represented a shift in the goals of neuropsychological assessment, there were no dramatic changes or innovations in the types of tests and measures being used. Basically, many of the same measures that originally had been validated on their ability to discriminate brain damage were being used now for the purpose of neuropsychological description and functional analysis. True, the existing methods usually allowed for the assessment of a broad range of brain function, but many of the measures never were designed to achieve a detailed analysis of the underlying components of complex deficits. This limited the specificity of neuropsychological description, and quite possibly the degree of meaningful differentiation that could be achieved in empirical studies of subtypes of neuropsychological disability.

The field now appears to have entered yet another stage of development, with its chief characteristic being an emphasis on *ecological validity*. Issues identified in the previous stage continue to be addressed, but now there is an added demand to relate assessment findings to an individual's everyday functioning (Chelune & Edwards, 1981). Parents of brain-impaired children and other consumers of neuropsychological services want to be provided with more than just a delineation of the child's deficits. They want to know precisely what these will mean in terms of the child's everyday functioning and future potential. The emphasis is not only on description but on making prescriptive statements regarding the types of treatments and environments that will maximize adaptive functioning.

Rourke (1982) has referred to this as the *dynamic phase* of development in neuropsychological assessment, with the goal being to evaluate the individual's current neuropsychological functioning in relation to the specific environmental demands and developmental tasks that must be faced. Rourke *et al.* (1986) have incorporated this thinking in their model of a treatment-oriented approach to the neuropsychological assessment of children. According to the model, behavioral predictions and treatment plans should be based on a careful consideration of "the interaction that obtains between brain lesion(s) and the child's ability structure as this impacts on adaptive behavior" (p. 251). This entails not only assessing brain–behavior relationships within the child but also relating these to the unfolding developmental demands of the child's immediate and long-range environments. However, a potential limitation has to do with the actual power of existing neuropsychological measures to reflect important aspects of everyday functioning. As Rourke *et al.* have pointed out, the use of brief, homogeneous, narrow-band tests—although internally consistent and stable—may be of little use in assessing the child's capacity to meet complex environmental demands.

The foregoing overview has highlighted some of the major historical trends in assessment that have characterized child neuropsychology. We have seen the goals of assessment shift from a static emphasis on diagnosing brain lesions to more of a focus on neuropsychological description and the analysis of functional deficits, and, more recently, to an emphasis on neuropsychological prescription that is relevant to everyday functioning. Neuropsychologists will continue to make important contributions to diagnosing brain damage and delineating its effects, but in a fashion that operates more from a biopsychosocial framework. The emphasis now is on ecological validity, and the relationship between assessment results and the individual's capacity to deal with important tasks of daily life. This is one area in which the current status of neuropsychological assessment with children actually appears to be somewhat ahead of work with adults. That is, the major attention given to the neuropsychological assessment of learning disabilities certainly has dealt with the child's adaptive capacity (and future potential) in an important real-life context, namely, school. However, as already noted, new developments are needed in assessment measures, themselves, because these generally have not kept pace with the evolving aims and ever-widening applications of neuropsychological assessment.

CURRENT APPROACHES IN CHILD NEUROPSYCHOLOGICAL ASSESSMENT

Fixed-Battery Approaches

A fixed-battery approach in neuropsychological assessment is one that aims to provide a comprehensive assessment of brain function using an invariant set of validated test procedures. The composition of the battery is not tailored to the presenting characteristics of the individual patient being assessed nor to the specific clinical hypotheses to be addressed. Rather, the emphasis is on administering as many of the designated procedures as the patient's condition will permit. Individual variability is thought to be captured reasonably well so long as the battery has been designed to tap a broad range of human capabilities. Moreover, the use of a fixed battery across patients provides a standard data base on which different clinical groups can be compared.

To date, fixed batteries such as the Halstead-Reitan Neuropsychological Battery (HRNB) and the Luria-Nebraska Neuropsychological Battery (LNNB) have represented the most commonly used approaches in neuropsychological assessment (Hynd et al., 1986). A detailed review of these batteries is beyond the scope of this chapter, but some of the more pertinent features of each are discussed below. The reader may wish to refer to other available sources for a more thorough description of the composition and validation of the HRNB (Boll, 1981; Reitan & Davison, 1974) and the children's revision of the LNNB (Golden, 1981, 1987). Also, Hynd et al. (1986) have provided an excellent critical review of the validity and utility of both of these batteries in child neuropsychological assessment.

Halstead-Reitan Neuropsychological Battery (HRNB)

Reitan and his colleagues developed two versions of the HRNB for use with children: the Reitan-Indiana Neuropsychological Test Battery for

Children (ages 5 to 8) and the Halstead Neuropsychological Test Battery for Children (ages 9 to 14). For convenience, both of these versions of the battery, along with the supplemental tests that commonly are included, will be referred to simply as the HRNB.

The HRNB for older children is a downward extension of the adult version of the battery and includes the following procedures: Lateral Dominance Examination, Aphasia Screening Test, Category Test (168 items), Tactual Performance Test (six blocks), Sensory-Perceptual Examination (including Tactile Finger Recognition, Tactile Form Recognition, and Fingertip Number Writing), Grip Strength Test, Finger Oscillation Test, Trail-Making Test, Speech-Sounds Perception Test (three-choice format), and the Seashore Rhythm Test. The HRNB for younger children consists of modified versions of the tests in the older children's battery, but the Trail-Making Test, the Speech-Sounds Perception Test, and the Seashore Rhythm Test are excluded. Six additional tests are included that are suited specifically for use with younger children: Marching Test, Color Form Test, Progressive Figures Test, Matching Pictures Test, Target Test, and Individual Performance Test. Usually each version of the battery is supplemented by the appropriate Wechsler scale for assessing intelligence and by a standardized test of academic achievement. Performance on the HRNB is evaluated in terms of Reitan's four methods of inference— i.e., level of performance, pattern of performance, right–left differences, and pathognomonic signs. For the older children's battery, these methods of inference have been operationalized in an actuarial system of rules for neuropsychological diagnosis (Selz & Reitan, 1979). Based on norms for 9- to 14-year-olds, each rule converts raw scores on the various HRNB measures to scaled scores ranging from 0 to 3. However, the system uses only a single set of norms for all children in this age range. Additional normative data for 5- to 14-year-olds have been provided by Knights (1966) as well as Spreen and Gaddes (1969).

The HRNB has been found to discriminate effectively between normal children and those with documented brain damage. This has been demonstrated both with 5- to 8-year-olds (Klonoff, Robinson, & Thompson, 1969; Reitan, 1974) and with 9- to 14-year-olds (Boll, 1974; Reed et al., 1965). In each of these studies, brain-damaged children performed more poorly on most of the test variables constituting the HRNB, with their deficits spanning both verbal-conceptual and perceptual-performance abilities. Interestingly, test variables drawn from the Wechsler Intelligence Test for Children were consistently among the most discriminating measures.

In general, attempts to localize brain injury in children with the HRNB have met with little success (Chadwick & Rutter, 1983). Perhaps this is because children, unlike adults, are more likely to experience generalized as opposed to focal brain damage (Kolb & Whishaw, 1980). Also, secondary pathological changes may serve to produce more generalized neuropsychological features even among children with seemingly focal lesions (Hynd et al., 1986). Or it simply may be that the neuropsychological deficits associated with localized brain damage are less specific in children than in adults (Chadwick & Rutter, 1983). In any event, many of the customary "rules" for localizing lesions in adults cannot be applied to children. For example, differences between Wechsler Verbal IQ and Performance IQ do not provide a valid means of lateralizing brain damage to either the left or the right hemisphere in children with early lesions; if anything, a pattern of lower Performance IQ than Verbal IQ seems to be characteristic of children with generalized brain damage (Boll & Barth, 1981). Overall, in the absence of lateralized sensory or motor signs, there is little evidence to support the validity of the HRNB in lateralizing childhood cerebral lesions.

In contrast to the groups of children considered so far, children with learning disabilities have presumptive, as opposed to documented, evidence of brain dysfunction. One would expect them to show less overall impairment than a group of children with known brain damage, and to pose more of a diagnostic challenge for a test battery to identify. Using the HRNB, Selz and Reitan (1979) achieved an overall accuracy of about 73% in correctly classifying 9- to 14-year-old children as normal, learning-disabled, or brain-damaged. Misclassifications were almost entirely in the direction of false negatives, because their system of rules for neuropsychological diagnosis tended to underestimate dysfunction in both the learning-disabled and brain-damaged groups. Not surprisingly, the learning-disabled children showed an intermediate level of impairment in comparison with the other two groups; the hit rate rose to 87% when the learning-disabled group was excluded and the remaining subjects were classified as either brain-damaged or normal. Using a test battery based largely on the HRNB, Rourke and his colleagues likewise have shown that learning-disabled children can be distinguished reliably on the basis of their neuropsychological results. Perhaps more importantly, different subtypes of learning disability have been distinguished on the basis of differential patterns of neuropsychological performance (e.g., Rourke & Finlayson, 1978).

There has been very little investigation into either the construct validity of the individual measures of the HRNB or on the factorial composition of the battery as a whole. Crockett, Klonoff, and Bjerring (1969) conducted a factor analysis of the younger children's version of the HRNB administered to a sample of normal children. The factors that accounted for the most variance included: (1) a perceptual-analytic factor (15.5%), (2) motor speed (8.3%), and (3) verbal concept formation (6.9%). Although Wechsler IQ scores were not included in the analysis, the Block Design and Object Assembly subtests were the variables that contributed most strongly to Factor I, whereas the Vocabulary subtest had the highest rank of the variables loading on Factor III.

Several studies have examined the interdependence between intelligence, as assessed on the Wechsler Intelligence Scale for Children-Revised (WISC-R), and performance on the older children's version of the HRNB (Klesges, 1983; Seidenberg, Giordani, Berent, & Boll, 1983; Tramontana, Klee, & Boyd, 1984). Taken together, the results of these studies have indicated substantial overlap between general intelligence and overall performance on the HRNB (e.g., r = .59 in the Tramontana *et al.* study). The greatest influence of IQ has been found on the tests tapping more complex skills and problem-solving abilities, language functions, and auditory-perceptual analysis. In contrast, measures of basic tactile perception, motor strength and speed, and right–left hand differences have not been found to be affected by IQ and thus appear to represent the more distinctive and nonredundant aspects of functioning assessed by the HRNB. Moreover, there is some indication that the overlap between general intelligence and performance on the HRNB is *greater* in brain-damaged children than among normals (Boll & Reitan, 1972).

Critique. The HRNB clearly has been the dominant approach to child neuropsychological assessment for over the last 20 years. It has been used in research on childhood brain dysfunction not only by Reitan and his colleagues but also in some fashion by many other investigators. Reitan certainly must be credited for pioneering a rigorous clinical approach to neuropsychological diagnosis through the use of a standard battery of tests. The strict emphasis on standardization has had the benefit of promoting replicability and comparability of findings across clinicians and researchers alike. It also has provided a standard data base on which different clinical groups can be compared.

The HRNB provides a reasonably accurate means of distinguishing brain-damaged, learning-disabled, and normal children. To date, however. there is little evidence to support its validity in localizing early brain lesions or in specifying other lesion characteristics in brain-damaged children. Its discriminative power appears to be limited to fairly broad diagnostic categories that, to some degree, can be differentiated on the basis of intelligence testing alone. It has been shown to overlap substantially with IQ, with its nonredundant contributions to assessment mainly involving measures of basic motor and sensory-perceptual abilities. Given this, comparable accuracy probably could be achieved in discriminating brain-damaged, learning-disabled, and normal children simply through the use of standard measures of intelligence and academic achievement supplemented by selected tests of motor and sensory-perceptual abilities.

Consistent with the goals of neuropsychological assessment at the time of its development, the composition of the HRNB was based heavily on the selection of tests sensitive to brain damage. Although the battery permits a broad differentiation of spared and impaired abilities, its composition does not lend itself readily to conducting a more detailed analysis of a child's functional capabilities. Some tests require such a complex interplay of abilities that it often is difficult to distinguish the precise components of deficient performance. Language skills are assessed rather crudely, and the response format for the Speech-Sounds Perception Test is such that results often can be confounded by a child's reading or spelling difficulties. Memory is not assessed adequately, and other important areas of a child's functioning, such as attention, are not assessed at all. No test battery can be expected to cover everything, but the range and specificity of coverage should be better for a test battery as time-consuming to administer as the HRNB.

Luria-Nebraska Neuropsychological Battery–Children's Revision (LNNB–CR)

Golden (1981) introduced a downward extension of the LNNB for children ranging from 8 to 12 years of age. The selection of test items was determined by administering the standard adult version of the battery (Golden, Hammeke, & Purisch, 1980) to normal children of above-average ability. Items that proved to be too difficult were eliminated, some new items were added, and other modifications in administration and scoring were made to adapt the battery for use with children. This resulted in a battery consisting of 149 test items (versus 269 in the adult version) on which normative data then were obtained from a sample of 125 normal children (25 for each age level from 8 to 12).

The LNNB-CR is organized in terms of 11 summary scales similar to those in the adult version: Motor, Rhythm, Tactile, Visual, Receptive Speech, Expressive Speech, Writing, Reading, Arithmetic, Memory, and Intellectual Processes. Also, like the adult version, these are supplemented by three second-order scales: the Pathognomonic (consisting of 13 items in the battery that provide the best discrimination of brain damage), and the Left Sensorimotor and Right Sensorimotor scales (based on items on the Motor and Tactile scales performed with the contralateral hand). Each item in the battery is scored on a 3-point system (0 to 2), with higher scores being indicative of impairment. Item scores are summed within each scale, with each total then converted to a T score (mean = 50, standard deviation = 10). The usual rule for classifying a child as impaired is based on the presence of elevations on at least two of the summary scales that exceed a critical level cutoff adjusted for the child's age (Gustavson et al., 1984). This is computed by the regression formula: $82.02 - (.14 \times \text{Age in months})$. Modified criterion rules have been recommended for maximizing the discrimination of neuropsychological impairment in special populations, including children with learning disabilities (Geary, Jennings, Schultz, & Alper, 1984) or psychiatric disorders (Tramontana & Boyd, 1986).

In addition to examining the level and pattern of scale elevations on the LNNB-CR, interpretation is based on a careful analysis of performance on the individual items making up the battery. In compairson with the HRNB, the test items on the LNNB-CR are relatively simple and are geared more toward assessing the component skills underlying broader dimensions of function. It is this feature of the battery that is thought to incorporate Luria's (1966, 1973) emphasis on the qualitative analysis of component skill deficits. However, the reliability of this level of analysis is questionable in that the assessment of specific component skills generally rests on very few test items. This is more of a problem on the LNNB-CR than on the adult version of the battery because of the reduction of nearly half of the total item pool.

The LNNB-CR has been found to discriminate effectively between brain-damaged children and normal controls (Gustavson et al., 1984; Sawicki, Leark, Golden, & Karras, 1984; Wilkening, Golden, MacInnes, Plaisted, & Hermann, 1981). In the Gustavson et al. study, the presence of two or more scales above critical level cutoff yielded a correct classification rate of 79% for brain-damaged children, 89% for normals, and an overall hit rate of 85%. To date, however, there is little evidence as to the validity of the LNNB-CR in distinguishing different lesion characteristics in brain-damaged children. It does discriminate effectively between learning-disabled children and normals, but, in controlling for IQ, its discriminative power tends to be limited to the Expressive Speech, Writing, and Reading scales (Geary & Gilger, 1984; Nolan, Hammeke, & Barkley, 1983). It appears to be less sensitive to factors underlying math deficits than reading or spelling deficits in learning-disabled children (Nolan et al., 1983), and its capacity to discriminate the severity of learning disability is eliminated once IQ and overall academic achievement level are controlled (Snow, Hynd, & Hartlage, 1984).

A number of studies have found the LNNB-CR to add significantly to the discrimination obtained through the WISC-R alone. The overlap between the two measures appears to be greater among brain-damaged children than in either children with psychiatric disorders or normal controls (Sweet, Carr, Rossini, & Kaspar, 1986). Among children with psychiatric disorders, impairment on the LNNB-CR has been found to be associated with differences in brain density as assessed through computed tomography (Tramontana & Sherrets, 1985), as well as in the severity of behavioral disturbance (Tramontana et al., in press), with neither set of findings being attributable to differences in IQ alone. It provides a better prediction of academic achievement for this population than WISC-R IQ, whether examined separately or in conjunction with behavioral and demographic factors (Tramontana, Hooper, Curley, & Nardolillo, 1988). This is surprising, given that overall results on the WISC-R and LNNB-CR have been found to correlate quite strongly in this population (−.69), with the correlations between IQ and every LNNB-CR scale being significant and ranging from −.35 to −.66 (Tramontana et al., 1984). Besides the fact that specific neuropsychological deficits may contribute to learning impediments, the enhanced ability of the LNNB-CR to predict academic achievement on a standard measure such as the Woodcock-Johnson Tests of Achievement can be attributed to its inclusion of a screening of basic academic skills on the Writing, Reading, and Arithmetic scales (Hooper & Tramontana, 1987).

Factor-analytic studies have been conducted examining both within-scales factors (Gustavson, Wilkening, Hermann, & Plaisted, 1982; Karras et al., 1987) and across-scales factors on the LNNB-CR (Karras et al., 1987; Snow & Hynd, 1985). In the Karras et al. study, which was based on a mixed sample of 719 children, a total of 11 factors were extracted from the 149 items of the LNNB-CR: (1) general academic skills, (2) spatial organization, (3) spatially based movement, (4) motor speed, (5) drawing quality, (6) drawing speed, (7) rhythm perception and reproduction, (8) somatosensory function, (9) basic receptive language, (10) simple expressive speech, and (11) abstract verbal thinking. This was different from the factor structure that has been described for the HRNB (Crockett et al., 1969). Specifically, the inclusion of a General Academic Skills factor, together with the greater number of discrete factors that constitute the LNNB-CR, points toward the presence of important differences in the composition of these two batteries.

Nonetheless, the overall results of the HRNB and LNNB-CR have been found to correspond very highly, with a 91% rate of agreement in identifying neuropsychological impairment in brain-damaged children (Berg et al., 1984) and as much as 86% agreement in children with psychiatric disorders (Tramontana, Sherrets, & Wolf, 1983). In the Tramontana et al. (1983) study, however, differences in the results of the two batteries were apparent at a closer level of inspection. For example, Speech-Sounds Perception on the HRNB did not correlate significantly with the Receptive Speech scale of the LNNB-CR; also, the two batteries yielded discrepant appraisals of right–left hand differences.

Critique. A good deal of research on the LNNB-CR has been generated in the relatively short time since its introduction as an experimental instrument in 1981. It appears to discriminate brain dysfunction in children about as well as the HRNB, and, at least for general classification purposes, the two batteries yield highly comparable results. This has important practical implications, given that the LNNB-CR takes about half the time to administer. There is some indication that it adds to the discriminant validity achieved by the WISC-R alone in children manifesting milder forms of brain dysfunction. However, in the case of children with learning disabilities, the discrimination probably is no better than what would be achieved when standard measures of intelligence and academic achievement are combined. As with the HRNB, the nonredundant contributions to assessment by the LNNB-CR mainly appear to involve its measures of sensory-perceptual and motor abilities.

An attractive feature of the LNNB-CR is the relative simplicity and range of coverage of its test items, which allow for more of an analysis of component skill deficits. The item format lends itself rather nicely to providing a detailed specification of functional strengths and deficits. However, this very positive feature is weakened by a number of psychometric problems exhibited by the present form of the battery. There simply are too few items tapping specific component skills for these to be assessed reliably, and the inclusion of items on a given summary scale is based largely on nominal factors rather than statistical confirmation of internal consistency. The present norms are rather weak (based on only 25 subjects for each year level) and cover a limited age range. Also, what is essentially a pathognomonic-sign approach to scoring items on the LNNB-CR places a major constraint on the degree of variation possible in assessments of change.

Probably the chief weakness of the LNNB-CR is its lack of a firm grounding in developmental neuropsychology. For example, Hynd et al. (1986) have criticized the battery for its exclusion of items assessing frontal lobe function based on Golden's (1981) assumption that the frontal lobes do not begin to reach functional maturation until adolescence. This is contrary to available evidence (e.g., Passler, Isaac, & Hynd, 1986) that suggests that frontal lobe functions develop in a stepwise fashion, with some functions being developed by about 6 to 7 years of age and others continuing to mature into adolescence. Even Luria (1973), whose theory guided the construction of the LNNB-CR, has suggested that prefrontal cortical zones begin to develop at about 4 years of age. Moreover, developmental considerations hardly could have been taken into account in the omission of test items specifically assessing attention and learning—these being critical aspects of functioning to assess in the developing child who has sustained brain injury. Contrary to Golden's (1981) original claims, the construction of the LNNB-CR does not appear to have been based on a careful consideration of developmental factors. Like the HRNB, it simply represents a downward extension of a test battery primarily designed for adults.

Other General Approaches

Three other general approaches to neuropsychological assessment will be considered briefly in this section: (1) eclectic test batteries, (2) qualitative approaches, and (3) process-oriented approaches. There are major differences among these in the rationale and guiding principles of assessment, and in the relative emphasis given to quantitative versus qualitative methods of analysis. However, they all share in the conviction that an effective neuropsychological assessment cannot be based on a restricted or fixed set of test procedures as exemplified by the HRNB and LNNB-CR.

Eclectic Test Batteries

This approach strives to preserve the quantitative nature of neuropsychological assessment by selecting standardized tests that, when taken together, cover a broad range of neuropsychological functions. There generally is at least an implicit outline of the relevant functions and abilities that should be assessed routinely. However, any of a variety of available tests may be selected to quantify the extent of deficit in each of the functional areas of interest. The psychometric properties of individual tests (e.g., adequacy of norms) as well as their complementarity when embedded in a battery are usually important factors guiding specific test selection.

For example, Smith (1975) presented the rationale for the selection of tests in the Michigan Neuropsychological Test Battery, which includes the WISC-R, Visual Organization Test, Raven's Coloured Matrices, Benton Visual Retention Test, Purdue Pegboard, Symbol Digit Modalities Test, Peabody Picture Vocabulary Test, Color Naming/Recognition, and Memory for Unrelated Sentences. From a somewhat different perspective, Gaddes (1985) provided an outline of the Victoria Battery, which includes recommended measures for assessing a child's functioning in each of the following areas: intelligence, visual-spatial-constructional abilities, auditory perception, tactile perception, sensorimotor integration, body image, motor function, cerebral dominance, memory, language, educational achievement, and personality. Many other examples of eclectic batteries for children could be cited, but the foregoing should give some idea of the possibilities that exist.

Qualitative Approaches

Rather than an emphasis on quantifying the extent of deficit, qualitative approaches are concerned more with determining *how* the individual passes or fails a particular task. For example, although a child may recall a memory item accurately, it is extremely important from a qualitative perspective to understand what strategies the child used to remember. Did the child utilize cues based on the verbal, visual, or multimodal aspects of the task? Were contextual ones (e.g., main themes or key words) employed? Perhaps rehearsal, chunking, verbal labeling, or other mnemonic strategies were utilized to some degree. These kinds of data are extremely important not only in distinguishing the precise nature of underlying neuropsychological dysfunction but also in identifying effective treatment strategies that can be used in helping the child to compensate for deficits in particular skills.

Qualitative approaches are less concerned with test standardization or in comparing an individual's performance against general norms than with conducting a careful idiographic analysis of performance for each case. Almost any task may be used or modified in such a way as to facilitate an in-depth analysis of where and how a particular individual's performance breaks down. Informal testing procedures typically are used, but even standardized tests can be utilized from a qualitative perspective so long as the emphasis is on observing how the individual performs instead of focusing only on the test scores that are obtained.

Probably the most recognized approach to qualitative assessment is exemplified in the work of Luria (1966, 1973) as described by Christensen (1975). There are three major parts to Luria's Neuropsychological Investigation. The first part consists of an initial evaluation of the individual's functioning utilizing a hypothesis-testing approach. Based on the patient's initial performance, the second part employs a more individualized set of tasks to explore suspected deficits more fully. Finally, once the qualitative information is obtained, the results are formulated according to Luria's theory of functional systems. Christensen organized the various examination tasks used by Luria into 11 major areas of function. Golden et al. (1980) later used these as the original pool of items from which the summary scales of the LNNB were developed.

Process-Oriented Approaches

These approaches represent a hybrid of quantitative and qualitative methods in neuropsychological assessment. For example, in the Boston Process Approach (Milberg, Hebben, & Kaplan, 1986) the emphasis is on understanding the qualitative nature of the behavior assessed by psychometric tests. It draws selectively from a core set of standardized tests for the purpose of gaining a quantified overview of the patient's general pattern of spared and impaired functions. Depending on the initial results, the examination thereafter is guided by clinical hypothesis-testing aimed at pinpointing the precise nature of the individual's deficits. This is achieved through the use of various "satellite tests," which may consist of standardized tests, the addition of new components to published tests, or a set of tasks designed specifically for each patient. The possibilities are limited only by the examiner's knowledge of available tests and his/her creativity in designing new tasks for assessing particular deficit areas.

Using a similar logic, Wilson (1986) has presented a branching hypothesis-testing model of neuropsychological assessment designed specifically for preschool-aged children. An initial selection of measures is used for a general assessment of complex cognitive functions. On the basis of these results, additional measures are selected for a further assessment of specific functional areas. These are organized according to a scheme of neuropsychological constructs that includes language (auditory integration, auditory cognition, short-term auditory memory, semantic retrieval), visual functions (visual-spatial, visual cognition, short-term visual memory), and motor functions (fine-motor, graphomotor). Wilson provides an extensive listing of tests currently available for use with preschool-aged children that can be drawn upon in assessing these various aspects of neuropsychological functioning.

General Critique

There are distinct advantages associated with each of the approaches to neuropsychological assessment considered in this section. Eclectic batteries preserve the quantitative nature of neuropsychological assessment but are not bound to any particular tests or measures in achieving that end. Rather, the emphasis is on selecting tests that are best suited to assess particular abilities, which, taken together, span a broad range of function. Tests may be substituted as better ones become available, and specific tests may be added or deleted in adapting the battery to different applications. Moreover, the approach lends itself nicely to neuropsychological description if tests are selected deliberately so that they are aligned with well-defined areas of ability. Qualitative approaches offer maximum flexibility and a richness of clinical data that surpasses what possibly could be obtained through the use of standardized tests alone. The emphasis on identifying the cognitive strategies available to the patient provides an obvious linkage between assessment and treatment planning. Of all the approaches considered, it is the one that is most dependent on the skills and conceptual framework of the individual examiner. Process-oriented approaches attempt to integrate quantitative and qualitative methods of assessment, taking the best from both worlds so to speak. Also, as in qualitative approaches, the emphasis in process-oriented approaches on careful case study serves to play an important role in theory building.

However, a major problem with each of these approaches is that there has been insufficient validation research on which to judge their adequacy. The absence of standardization in qualitative approaches is incompatible with conducting independent appraisals of reliability and validity. Many American neuropsychologists would argue that standardization and quantification are defining features of neuropsychological assessment, and that qualitative approaches are more characteristic of methods in behavioral neurology. An eclectic battery may utilize well-validated individual tests, but little is known about the validity and utility of the battery as a whole. Indeed, this would be difficult to assess if the composition of the battery were subjected to constant change. There also is the problem of making comparisons among the measures within a battery that may differ in terms of their normative base, test construction, and other factors. Even if they were more carefully researched, it is doubtful that the present examples of eclectic batteries would not share some of the problems identified with the HRNB and LNNB-CR. The flexible nature of test selection in process-oriented approaches is thought to result in greater diagnostic efficiency, but this is yet to be demonstrated. As Rourke *et al.* (1983) have pointed out, a flexible or individualized approach would be at least as time-consuming as a fixed battery if an assessment of comparable breadth is to be achieved. Also, a fixed-battery approach serves to assure a consistently comprehensive assessment that is not biased by either referral complaints or the child's initial presentation.

The differences among the various approaches to neuropsychological assessment seem to have gotten overstated sometimes for the sake of academic argument. In practice, there probably are relatively few neuropsychologists who are purists with respect to one approach or another, and a melding of approaches probably is quite common. This makes good sense because the different perspectives can be combined in a complementary fashion in an effort to maximize both breadth and depth of assessment. A fixed battery of procedures that is brief, but nonetheless spans a broad range of abilities, helps to assure a consistently comprehensive assessment that can produce comparable results across times, patient groups, and different research settings. It provides a *horizontal analysis* of general functioning that, along with qualitative observation, can be used in tailoring an in-depth or *vertical analysis* of specific functional areas based on a more flexible selection of tests. Process-oriented approaches achieve this to some extent, but the validity of initial screening decisions may be compromised by the absence of a fixed set of procedures that could assure a consistently broad-based assessment for all cases.

Special-Purpose Measures

In addition to the general, all-purpose approaches to neuropsychological assessment that we have discussed, there are a host of individual measures and specialized test batteries available to assess more specific aspects of neuropsychological functioning in children. Examples include Benton's Motor Impersistence Battery and other special-purpose tests (Benton, Hamsher, Varney, & Spreen, 1983), the Goldman, Fristoe, and Woodcock (1974) Auditory Skills Battery, the children's version of the California Verbal Learning Test (Delis, Kramer, Kaplan, & Ober, 1986), and the Wisconsin Card Sorting Test (Heaton, 1981), to name only a few.

Some measures have been validated on the basis of their prediction of specific types of childhood outcomes, as, for example, the Florida Kindergarten Screening Battery, which appears to provide an effective means of identifying children at risk for reading disabilities (Satz & Fletcher, 1982). There also are instruments for assessing specific features in selected populations. For example, the Glascow Coma Scale (Teasdale & Jennett, 1974) can assess level of consciousness in cases of traumatic brain injury, and the Rancho Los Amigos Levels of Cognitive Functioning Scale (Hagen, 1981) provides a useful means of gauging overall recovery of function in rehabilitation settings.

The above examples are mentioned only to give some idea of the special-purpose measures currently available in child neuropsychology. The available tools for assessing critical aspects of functioning in children, such as attention, learning and memory, cerebral dominance, and language functions, will be dealt with more extensively in Part III of this volume.

APPLICATIONS

As was apparent in the discussion of historical trends in assessment, the goals of child neuropsychological assessment have evolved to encompass a broad range of clinical applications. In general, these include: (1) aiding in the detection of brain dysfunction for the purpose of differential diagnosis, (2) providing a precise specification of the behavioral effects of known brain injury, (3) helping to identify the specific underlying dimensions of dysfunction in particular handicaps, (4) using assessment data to help formulate effective treatment strategies, (5) helping to assess the child's prognosis and risk for certain developmental outcomes, and (6) conducting ongoing assessments of functional change over the course of development and in response to particular interventions. The precise form and relative importance of these different applications of neuropsychological assessment depend, to some extent, on the particular clinical population under consideration. Here we will consider important applications in four different but overlapping clinical populations, including children with neurological disorders, systemic illness, psychiatric disorders, and learning disabilities. We also will touch upon applications in pediatric rehabilitation and in assessing (re)acquisition of function after brain injury.

Neurological Disorders

There are literally dozens of neurological disorders in childhood that may require a careful neuropsychological assessment. These include genetic disorders (e.g., Turner's syndrome), structural abnormalities of the brain (e.g., agensis of the corpus callosum, hydrocephalis), traumatic injuries, and a variety of neuropathological processes including anoxic episodes, viral and bacterial encephalitis, toxicity (e.g., carbon monoxide poisoning, lead poisoning), metabolic disorders, demyelinating diseases such as multiple sclerosis, neuromuscular disorders such as muscular dystrophy, and, more rarely in children, tumors (e.g., medulloblastomas, craniopharyngioma, cerebellar astrocytomas) and cerebral vascular accidents. Although case studies have appeared in the literature depicting neuropsychological findings for selected childhood neurological disorders (e.g., Rourke et al., 1983), the effects of most insults to the immature nervous system are only beginning to be understood. Suffice it to say that the precise effects depend on a complex interplay involving the type of injury, individual variables, and environmental factors.

One area in which neuropsychological methods have been used extensively is in children with seizure disorders. This is an important group of disorders to assess, not only because they are among the most prevalent neurological disorders of childhood (Meighan, Queener, & Weitman, 1976) but because their frequent chronicity carries the potential for continued impact throughout a child's life. There is no such thing as a "typical" neuropsychological profile for seizure-disordered children (Boll & Barth, 1981), although, as a group, their overall cognitive abilities tend to fall toward the lower end of the normal range (Bolter, 1984), they tend to be at greater risk for learning difficulties (Yule, 1980), and they tend to show a higher incidence of psychopathology than the general population (Dreisbach, Ballard, Russo, & Schain, 1982; Rutter, Graham, & Yule, 1970). The variability among children with seizure disorders certainly underscores the importance of careful individual assessment.

Childhood head injury is another example of an important area for neuropsychological assessment. There are many factors to consider in evaluating the child with a head injury, including the specific nature of the injury and its resultant process (e.g., shearing, contre coup), age at onset, premorbid cognitive and emotional functioning, duration of impaired consciousness, and the rate of posttraumatic recovery. The effects of a closed head injury tend to be less localized than in the case of brain tumors or cerebral vascular accidents, with deficits spanning a wide variety of functions (Chadwick, Rutter, Brown, Shaffer, & Traub, 1981). As with adults, the first 6 months postinjury seems to be the time when neuropsychological deficits are most prominent in children (Levin & Eisenberg, 1979), with the bulk of recovery occurring during the first year (Brink, Garrett, Hale, Woo Sam, & Nickel, 1970). However, neuropsychological changes have been observed to occur over a much longer period, which sometimes may extend up to 5 years (Klonoff, Low, & Clark, 1977). Besides the child's general adjustment, educational functioning is one of the most important areas to be monitored. The child's social-emotional adjustment also appears to be a critical dimension to assess because children with accidental head injuries appear to be at higher risk for developing psychiatric difficulties (Brown, Chadwick, Shaffer, Rutter, & Traub, 1981).

Some neurological disorders may require neurosurgical intervention, as in the case of partial lobectomies or complete hemispherectomies for the treatment of severe seizures. Probably the most common neurosurgical intervention in childhood involves the insertion of a shunt for the treatment of hydrocephalis. Hydrocephalic children successfully treated by shunt insertion have been reported to show difficulties in attention (Hurley, Laatsch, & Dorman, 1983), memory (Cull & Wyke, 1984), and visual-motor functions (Soare & Raimondi, 1977). One study also found academic lags and poor impulse control, but a relative sparing of verbal fluency, motor coordination, and verbal naming abilities (Fennell et al., 1987). Difficulties may result from the actual insertion of the shunt, and secondary complications sometimes may contribute to severe impairment in cognitive and adaptive functioning. Further, the neuropathology of hydrocephalis, which may include fiber stretching, delays in myelination, and interference with thalamocortical connections as well as limbic structures (Spreen et al., 1984), can result in a rather varied neuropsychological picture in these children. It is important that the effects of this disorder as well as its treatment be assessed individually, with careful follow-up assessment of functions associated with so-called "silent" brain regions that normally would not emerge until later developmental periods.

Systemic Illness

Interest in the neuropsychological functioning of children with systemic illness has shown considerable growth recently (e.g., Hynd & Willis, 1988). There are a variety of pediatric illnesses that can impact negatively on the developing nervous system, including defects in specific organ systems (e.g., pulmonary disease, congenital heart disease, renal dysfunction), metabolic disorders (e.g., elevated blood phenylalanine, defects in amino acid metabolism, lipid storage diseases, and mucopolysaccharidosis), autoimmune disorders, and infections (e.g., meningitis, cytomegalovirus, Reye's syndrome). Evidence regarding the neuropsychological sequelae of such childhood illnesses has begun to emerge.

For example, Holmes and Richman (1985) examined the cognitive profiles of children with insulin-dependent diabetes and found that children with early disease onset (7 years of age or younger) and a chronic course (5 years or more) were more likely to show reading and memory difficulties. They also tended to have a lower Performance IQ on the

WISC-R, but this appeared to be due largely to slow response time rather than to a specific deficit in visual-spatial abilities. Similar findings have been obtained by other researchers (Ryan, Vega, & Drash, 1985; Ryan, Vega, Longstreet, & Drash, 1984). However, interacting factors apparently must be considered as well; i.e., Rovet, Gore, and Ehrlich (1983) found that whereas females with diabetes onset prior to 3 years of age tended to experience deficits in visual-motor functioning, their male counterparts did not.

A major area in which neuropsychological assessment can play a crucial role is in pediatric oncology. For example, acute lymphocytic leukemia (ALL) accounts for 35% of all malignancies of childhood, with approximately 40% of these cases becoming disease-free survivors (George, Aur, Mauer, & Simone, 1979). An important question concerns the possible iatrogenic effects of the various treatments required to stabilize these children medically. The evidence is inconclusive, but there is some indication that children with ALL who receive intracranial radiation and chemotherapy (Methotrexate) may suffer a variety of posttreatment neuropsychological deficits (Goff, 1982; Waber, Sollee, Wills, & Fischer, 1986) and are more likely to be later diagnosed as having learning disabilities (Elbert, Culbertson, Gerrity, Guthrie, & Bayles, 1985).

As was noted before, advances in medical care have brought about a dramatic increase in the survival of children with serious illnesses. This has created a greater need for the careful assessment of possible neuropsychological sequelae associated with these diseases or their treatment. Ongoing neuropsychological assessment may contribute effectively to monitoring improvement, stability, or deterioration in the child's functioning, and may indicate the need for other kinds of intervention (e.g., special education). Its utility in assessing children with various pediatric illnesses is only beginning to be realized.

Psychiatric Disorders

There is strong evidence that brain dysfunction in childhood is associated with an increased risk for psychiatric disorder. The risk is much greater than for children with other types of physical handicap (Seidel, Chadwick, & Rutter, 1975), and the relationship appears to hold both for children with documented brain damage (e.g., Brown et al., 1981; Rutter et al., 1970) and for those with so-called soft neurological signs (e.g., Shaffer et al., 1985). Among children with accidental head injuries, the risk is compounded by factors such as psychosocial adversity and any pre-existing tendencies toward behavioral or emotional disturbance (Brown et al., 1981). The relationship is not trivial, given that the effects appear to persist and influence the child's long-range behavioral adjustment (Breslau & Marshall, 1985; Shaffer et al., 1985).

Conversely, there is a relatively high rate of neuropsychological dysfunction among children with psychiatric disorders, even when cases with known brain damage are excluded (Tramontana, Sherrets, & Golden, 1980). Tramontana and Sherrets (1985) found that neuropsychological abnormality in such cases actually corresponded to differences on various indices of brain density as revealed by CT results, which was a remarkable finding in view of the exclusion of cases having documented neurological involvement. Moreover, the presence of neuropsychological deficits has been found to be associated with more extensive behavior problems among younger boys with psychiatric disorders, regardless of factors such as IQ, socioeconomic status, and whether the deficits could be linked specifically with a history of brain injury (Tramontana et al., in press). Thus, the presence of neuropsychological deficits in childhood appears to constitute an important index of increased psychiatric risk.

A number of studies have begun to examine whether there are distinguishing neuropsychological features associated with specific forms of child psychopathology, including autism (e.g., Fein, Waterhouse, Lucci, & Snyder, 1985), attention deficit disorder (e.g., Chelune, Ferguson, Koon, & Dickey, 1986; Passler, Isaac, & Hynd, 1986), and depression (e.g., Wilson & Staton, 1984). In a comprehensive review of this research, Tramontana and Hooper (in press) concluded that there was little evidence of specificity with respect to the type or pattern of brain dysfunction associated with different forms of child psychopathology. Although there were some promising leads, the greater weight of evidence suggested a largely nonspecific, indirect relationship between brain dysfunction and psychopathology in childhood. There is absolutely no evidence to support earlier thinking (e.g., Wender, 1971) regarding the existence of a behavioral stereotype among children with brain dysfunction, consisting of symptoms such as hyperactivity, inattention, and impulsivity. Symptoms such as these do not distinguish children with either documented brain damage (Brown et al., 1981; Rutter et al., 1970) or soft neurological signs (Shaffer et al., 1985) because they appear to be common features of psychiatric disorders in general, regardless of whether neurological abnormality is present (Rutter, 1977). If anything, it appears that internalizing rather than externalizing symptoms are more distinctively tied to brain dysfunction in childhood, with symptoms such as anxiety, withdrawal, and depression being among the more common outcomes associated with a history of chronic handicap (Breslau & Marshall, 1985; Shaffer et al., 1985). Child neuropsychologists may play an important role in determining more precisely how this process unfolds so that it might be redirected more positively, if not prevented.

There are a number of issues surrounding valid neuropsychological diagnosis with this population that require special consideration. These have been discussed extensively by Tramontana (1983). Briefly, it is important to apply more conservative rules for diagnosing neuropsychological impairment in children with psychiatric disorders because there appears to be a greater likelihood of false-positive errors in diagnosis with this population. Following this line of thinking, Tramontana and Hooper (1987) were able to distinguish adolescent psychiatric referrals with and without documented brain damage at a 76% rate of overall accuracy, which was a substantial improvement over the results obtained with the use of standard cutoffs for defining impaired performance.

There also has been some work examining the use of brief screening procedures in identifying child psychiatric cases who are likely to show significant abnormalities on a comprehensive neuropsychological assessment. Tramontana and Boyd (1986) derived a regression formula, based on the WISC-R and Aphasia Screening Test (AST), for predicting impaired/nonimpaired overall performance on standard test batteries such as the HRNB and LNNB-CR in child psychiatric referrals. This approach capitalized on the common use of the WISC-R in clinical settings, on the substantial overlap that has been found between the WISC-R and the results of a comprehensive neuropsychological test battery (Tramontana et al., 1984), and on the brevity and efficiency of the AST in identifying verbal and spatial-motor deficits (Wolf & Tramontana, 1982). Application of the regression formula in a cross-validation study (Boyd, Tramontana, & Hooper, 1986) yielded a hit rate of about 80% in correctly predicting impaired/nonimpaired neuropsychological status. Although not a substitute for a full neuropsychological assessment, procedures such as these may help clinicians in identifying child psychiatric cases for whom a comprehensive neuropsychological assessment is indicated.

Learning Disabilities

As was noted before, the study of learning disabilities has been one of the most intensive areas of investigation in child neuropsychology. The explicit presumption of central nervous system dysfunction in current definitions of learning disability (Hammill, Leigh, McNutt, & Larsen, 1981) has served to underscore the important role of neuropsychological assessment in this field. Neuropsychological assessment can contribute effectively both in the identification of specific underlying dimensions of dysfunction in particular learning handicaps and in the formulation and evaluation of specific educational plans. The work in learning disabilities—which has dealt with the child's adaptive capacity (and future potential) in the real-life context of school—has taken an exemplary lead in relating neuropsychological assessment to questions of ecological validity. Much remains to be learned, but major advances have been achieved in the area of syndrome definition and subtype analysis, and in the identification of developmental precursors of learning disabilities, possible neuroanatomical and neurophysiological factors, as well as relevant aptitude x treatment interactions. These topics are dealt with extensively in subsequent chapters in this volume. They are mentioned here for the sake of highlighting this very important area of application in child neuropsychology.

Rehabilitation and Assessing Recovery of Function

Child neuropsychologists are relative newcomers to the field of pediatric rehabilitation. The professional disciplines involved in providing rehabilitation services to brain-injured children typically have included physical therapists, occupational therapists, speech and language pathologists, special educators, physicians, social workers, and perhaps behavioral psychologists. Child neuropsychologists now are entering this arena in increasing numbers, bringing with them a unique combination of skills. The child neuropsychologist's background in neurocognitive functions, mechanisms of recovery of function, and child development and psychopathology, together with skills in behavioral treatment and psychotherapy, certainly serves to enhance the range of expertise represented on the pediatric rehabilitation team. Roles may include not only assessment and treatment consultation but also the actual delivery of treatment services, particularly with respect to cognitive, neuromuscular, behavioral, social-emotional, and family intervention components (Incagnoli & Newman, 1985). Furthermore, with the recent explosion in computerized cognitive rehabilitation software, neuropsychologists have taken the lead in calling for standards regarding their marketing, clinical utility, and usage (Kay, Becker, Bleiberg, & Long, 1986). Current thinking suggests that many of these cognitive retraining packages are useful, but that their application should be restricted to use by trained clinicians as part of a more comprehensive treatment program (Adamovich, Henderson, & Auerbach, 1985).

A key role for neuropsychological assessment is in the monitoring of the child's (re)acquisition of function after brain injury. There is a complex interplay of factors that influence the actual recovery patterns and developmental progress of children who suffer early brain lesions (Chelune & Edwards, 1981). Systematic knowledge regarding the prognostic significance of different types of early brain lesions is only beginning to emerge (e.g., Dennis, 1985a, 1985b). The factors affecting the child's prognosis certainly are more complex than suggested simply by the concept of plasticity and the enhanced potential for recovery of function that presumably characterizes the immature brain.

There are many clinical examples of children with seemingly catastrophic brain injuries who somehow manage to survive and do reasonably well, whereas others with comparatively minor injuries may be impeded by significant handicaps. Craft, Shaw, and Cartlidge (1972) showed the importance of monitoring developmental progress by documenting that even mildly brain-injured infants, who were described as fully recovered, continued to manifest cognitive, behavioral, and sensorimotor deficits several years following their injury. Whereas deficits involving motor function tend to be relatively stable over time, cognitive functioning may show considerable variability from infancy through early childhood (Aylward, Gustafson, Verhulst, & Colliver, 1987). Moreover, as Rourke et al. (1983) have pointed out, deficits involving so-called "silent" brain regions may not become apparent until later developmental stages. The child may develop normally at first but later may appear to "grow into a deficit" when faced with new developmental demands. All of this underscores the importance of ongoing neuropsychological assessment in monitoring the child's developmental progress. Early prognostic formulations must be viewed as tentative, at best, and subject to revision on the basis of periodic reassessment of the child's actual functioning.

Neuropsychological assessment also can play a key role in helping to formulate treatment plans, monitor treatment progress, and adjust the child's rehabilitation program as needed. Rourke et al. (1986) have provided a general framework for integrating neuropsychological assessment in the treatment planning process. To date, however, little is known regarding the prescriptive significance of different patterns of neuropsychological data in the actual selection of treatments. Treatment options tend to be selected on the basis of theory (e.g., Luria, 1966, 1973), personal experience, or practical issues such as the availability of particular therapeutic resources. There has been very little research that could serve to link neuropsychological assessment and treatment more directly. This is a critical new frontier for child neuropsychology that is greatly in need of systematic inquiry. Issues involved in bridging the gap between assessment and treatment are discussed more fully in Chapter 5, this volume.

CONCEPTUAL AND PRACTICAL ISSUES

We have seen that the effects of brain damage tend to be less specific in children than in adults (Chadwick & Rutter, 1983). Because brain damage primarily seems to impair new learning and achievement, decrements in general intelligence often are among the chief manifestations of early childhood brain injury (Boll & Barth, 1981; Rourke et al., 1983). Hynd et al. (1986) have suggested that the effects of brain damage begin to take on a more specific character, resembling those seen in adults, when injuries are sustained after the functional organization of the cerebral hemispheres has become fairly well established, at about 5 to 7 years of age. Nonetheless, there is considerable overlap or redundancy between standard measures of intelligence and current test batteries used for assessing neuropsychological functioning in children (Seidenberg et al., 1983; Sweet et al., 1986; Tramontana et al., 1984). What, then, defines neuropsychological assessment and distinguishes it from simply a general assessment of a child's mental abilities? Is it something intrinsic to the procedures, themselves, that constitute neuropsychological tests? Or is it the conceptual perspective that is brought to bear when interpreting performance data on measures of whatever type?

Certainly, many of the standard instruments available for assessing children's abilities, such as the WISC-R or McCarthy Scales of Children's Abilities (McCarthy, 1972), or an instrument like the Kaufman Assessment Battery for Children (Kaufman & Kaufman, 1983), which permits a differentiation of sequential and simultaneous processing abilities, can be used quite effectively in evaluating a child's neuropsychological functioning (Wilson, 1986). This is especially true when the use of such instruments is accompanied by careful qualitative observations of the child's performance. However, most of these tests were neither developed from a neuropsychological perspective nor designed to facilitate neuropsychological inferences regarding a child's functioning. Procedural modifications usually must be included to facilitate hypothesis-testing, such as introducing certain cues or altering the response mode on a task once the standard administration of the test is completed. There is no question that this can be an effective means of neuropsychological assessment, provided that the process is guided by a clear conceptual framework of developmental brain–behavior relationships. However, the process would be more efficient if the basic composition of the tests in question were aligned more closely with relevant aspects of neuropsychological functioning.

Thus, in contrast to standard cognitive testing, the tests or measures making up a neuropsychological assessment are selected, designed, or adapted to facilitate the conceptualization of a child's performance in terms of known or hypothesized brain–behavior relationships. Although virtually any measure of a child's abilities may be used in making neuropsychological inferences, some measures are better than others in revealing specific aspects of neuropsychological functioning. It is this feature, not simply their sensitivity to childhood brain damage, that is a defining characteristic of neuropsychological tests. Moreover, to be considered as components of a comprehensive neuropsychological assessment, the tests must be embedded within an overall assessment strategy that is organized according to current knowledge of brain–behavior relationships and the process by which these unfold over the course of development. The latter feature is particularly critical in child neuropsychological assessment in in that a given test or measure (e.g., name writing) may tap very different functions at different points in a child's development.

Various conceptual frameworks have been proposed for organizing the clinical assessment of brain–behavior relationships in childhood (e.g., Rourke et al., 1986; Wilson, 1986). These are important in that they serve to anchor the assessment in terms of well-defined neuropsychological constructs. To date, however, these achieve only a partial incorporation of a developmental perspective into the assessment process. Applying a developmental perspective in neuropsychological assessment means more than simply assuring that the tests and measures are appropriate for the age range of children being assessed. It also entails more than utilizing measures that are sensitive to the child's increasing competence over time. It involves understanding how brain functions develop normally, as well as under various pathological conditions. A child not only grows more competent with age but also develops new and more efficient strategies for solving problems. This is a fundamental tenet of developmental psychology, and it is also reflected in Luria's (1966, 1973) ontogenetic theory of functional systems. When applied to child neuropsychology, this perspective requires that a conceptual framework for assessment indicate not only what areas of function should be assessed but how these should be assessed at different points in development. It requires, quite frankly, a more complete and dynamic understanding of normal and abnormal brain development than the field currently can provide. Much remains to be learned regarding the neuropsychology of the developing brain and its implications for clinical assessment (see Chapter 2, this volume).

Besides the issue of developmental change, there are a host of other factors that can obscure and complicate the assessment of brain–behavior relationships in children. These include: (1) problems in specifying the precise time of onset for various forms of brain pathology, (2) the absence of a referential baseline of premorbid functioning in cases of early brain damage, (3) the sometimes blurred distinction between neurodevelopmental anomalies and normal variations in the rate and pattern of acquisition of function, (4) the extent to which deficits sometimes can be delayed or "silent" until later developmental periods, (5) the absence of a standard nosology for classifying childhood neurodevelopmental disorders, (6) the interacting effects of various nonneurological attributes within the child that may serve to compound or mitigate the effects of brain dysfunction, and (7) the impact of environmental factors, including the family, in shaping the child's outcomes. In addition, there are a number of practical complications that often may occur in assessing the brain-impaired child, including problems in maintaining behavioral compliance and sustained attention for prolonged periods of assessment. Also, the younger child may be unable to provide a reliable subjective report of deficits, and the circumstances in which these are more or less likely to be problematic. Reports of parents and teachers often are crucial in providing accounts of the child's abilities outside of the testing situation. Although some of the above issues may apply in the evaluation of adults, they are far more likely to arise as complicating factors in the neuropsychological assessment of children.

Nowhere are the age-specific constraints on assessment more apparent than in the evaluation of children during the first 3 or 4 years of life. Perhaps this is why, with few exceptions, the bulk of research and practice in child neuropsychology has dealt almost exclusively with children 5 years of age and older. The relatively limited response repertoire of infants or toddlers that can be used in assessing their abilities, together with the degree to which performance is state-dependent, places major constraints on formal neuropsychological assessment (see Chapter 9, this volume). This is largely an uncharted territory for neuropsychologists that, up to this point, mainly has involved the work of developmental psychologists and pediatric neurologists. At present, there is little resemblance between what is done in assessing brain function in infancy or early childhood (which tends to rely heavily on the evaluation of reflexes, sensorimotor development, and other developmental milestones) and what ordinarily would constitute a neuropsychological assessment in later years. The extent to which there is continuity in the neuropsychological meaning of the assessment data obtained over these developmental periods is an open question.

Finally, consideration must be given to the unique challenges that arise in the assessment of children with special handicapping conditions such as sensory loss, physical deformities, motor disabilities, and language impairment. The nature of the handicap as well as its impact on the child's general functioning must be assessed, but care must be taken to devise an appropriate assessment strategy that will yield a balanced picture of the child's overall abilities. It would be inappropriate to utilize tasks that unduly tax the child's specific handicap, and then go on and use these results to draw conclusions about the child's more general functioning. For example, the assessment of nonverbal abilities in a language-impaired child would be biased if this were based on tasks that depended heavily on the comprehension of spoken instructions. Conducting a comprehensive assessment that effectively works around the child's handicap and maintains his or her motivation to perform requires a great deal of skill, ingenuity, and patience on the part of the examiner. It also requires a knowledge of any unique neurodevelopmental features associated with specific handicaps. For example, a blind child is likely to show delays in sensorimotor development, and may use different cognitive strategies in performing certain tasks than a sighted child. Although inconclusive, there also is evidence to suggest that children with a specific sensory loss in early life may develop an atypical pattern of cerebral organization of function (e.g., Gibson & Bryden, 1984). Differential neuropsychological features may be associated with other types of handicap as well. This is an

important area of application in child neuropsychology, one that ultimately may prove to require a highly specialized background of knowledge and skill.

SUMMARY

This chapter has provided a general overview of child neuropsychological assessment. We began by tracing the major historical trends in
assessment that have characterized the field, culminating with the present
emphasis on using neuropsychological methods prescriptively in identifying factors that could maximize the brain-impaired child's capacity to
deal effectively with important tasks of daily life. Next, we considered the
current approaches to neuropsychological assessment, outlining their respective strengths and weaknesses, their similarities and differences, as
well as possible ways in which the various approaches might be combined in an efficient and complementary fashion. We then discussed
important applications of neuropsychological assessment in treatment
planning and in monitoring (re)acquisition of function, and highlighted
its potential contributions in the assessment of selected clinical populations, including children with neurological disorders, systemic illness,
psychiatric disorders, and learning disabilities. Last, we addressed some
key definitional issues that pertain to neuropsychological assessment, the
need for conceptual guidance from a developmental framework of brain–
behavior relationships, and some of the common complications that can
arise in the neuropsychological assessment of children. Although our
coverage in this chapter was selective, and undoubtedly a number of
important topics were omitted (e.g., mental retardation), we believe that it
nonetheless provides a reasonably thorough overview of the current status of the field. With this, the stage now should be set for selected issues
and topics in child neuropsychological assessment to be pursued at greater depth in the subsequent chapters of this volume.

REFERENCES

Adamovich, B. B., Henderson, J. A., & Auerbach, S. (1985). Cognitive rehabilitation of closed
    head injured patients. San Diego, CA: College-Hill Press.
Almli, C. R., & Finger, S. (1984). Early brain damage. Orlando, FL: Academic Press.
Aylward, G. P., Gustafson, N., Verhulst, S. J., & Colliver, J. A. (1987). Consistency in the
    diagnosis of cognitive, motor, and neurologic function over the first three years. Journal
    of Pediatric Psychology, 12, 77–98.
Bender, L. (1938). A visual motor gestalt test and its clinical use (Research Monograph No.
    3). New York: American Orthopsychiatric Association.
Benton, A. L. (1963). The Revised Visual Retention Test: Clinical and experimental applica-
    tions. New York: Psychological Corporation.

Benton, A. L., Hamsher, K., Varney, N. R., & Spreen, O. (1983). *Contributions to neuropsychological assessment: A clinical manual.* New York: Oxford University Press.

Berg, R. A., Bolter, J. F., Ch'ien, L. T., Williams, S. J., Lancaster, W., & Cummins, J. (1984). Comparative diagnostic accuracy of the Halstead-Reitan and the Luria-Nebraska Neuropsychological Adult and Children's Batteries. *Clinical Neuropsychology. 6*(3), 200–204.

Boll, T. J. (1974). Behavioral correlates of cerebral damage in children aged 9–14. In R. M. Reitan & L. A. Davison (Eds.), *Clinical neuropsychology: Current status and applications* (pp. 91–120). New York: Wiley.

Boll, T. J. (1981). The Halstead-Reitan Neuropsychology Battery. In S. B. Filskov & T. J. Boll (Eds.), *Handbook of clinical neuropsychology* (pp. 577–607). New York: Wiley.

Boll, T. J., & Barth, J. T. (1981). Neuropsychology of brain damage in children. In S. B. Filskov & T. J. Boll (Eds.), *Handbook of clinical neuropsychology* (pp. 418–452). New York: Wiley.

Boll, T. J., & Reitan, R. M. (1972). Comparative ability interrelationships in normal and brain-damaged children. *Journal of Clinical Psychology, 28,* 152–156.

Bolter, J. F. (1984). *Neuropsychological impairment and behavioral dysfunction in children with chronic epilepsy.* Unpublished doctoral dissertation, Memphis State University.

Boyd, T. A., Tramontana, M. G., & Hooper, S. R. (1986). Cross-validation of a psychometric system for screening neuropsychological abnormality in older children. *Archives of Clinical Neuropsychology, 1,* 387–391.

Breslau, N., & Marshall, I. A. (1985). Psychological disturbance in children with physical disabilities: Continuity and change in a 5-year follow-up. *Journal of Abnormal Child Psychology, 13,* 199–216.

Brink, J., Garrett, A., Hale, W., Woo Sam, J., & Nickel, V. (1970). Recovery of motor and intellectual function in children sustaining severe head injuries. *Developmental Medicine and Child Neurology, 12,* 565–571.

Brown, G., Chadwick, O., Shaffer, D., Rutter, M., & Traub, M. (1981). A prospective study of children with head injuries: III. Psychiatric sequelae. *Psychological Medicine, 11,* 63–78.

Chadwick, O., & Rutter, M. (1983). Neuropsychological assessment. In M. Rutter (Ed.), *Developmental neuropsychiatry* (pp. 181–212). New York: Guilford Press.

Chadwick, O., Rutter, M., Brown, G., Shaffer, D., & Traub, M. (1981). A prospective study of children with head injuries: II. Cognitive sequelae. *Psychological Medicine, 11,* 49–61.

Chelune, G. J., & Edwards, P. (1981). Early brain lesions: Ontogenetic-environmental considerations. *Journal of Consulting and Clinical Psychology, 49,* 777–790.

Chelune, G., Ferguson, W., Koon, R., & Dickey, T. (1986). Frontal lobe dysinhibition in attention deficit disorder. *Child Psychiatry and Human Development, 16,* 221–234.

Christensen, A. L. (1975). *Luria's neuropsychological investigation.* New York: Spectrum.

Craft, A., Shaw, D., & Cartlidge, N. (1972). Head injuries in children. *British Medical Journal, 4,* 200–203.

Crockett, D., Klonoff, H., & Bjerring, J. (1969). Factor analysis of neuropsychological tests. *Perceptual and Motor Skills, 29,* 791–802.

Cull, C., & Wyke, M. A. (1984). Memory function of children with spina bifida and shunted hydrocephalus. *Developmental Medicine and Child Neurology, 26,* 177–183.

Delis, D. C., Kramer, J. H., Kaplan, E., & Ober, B. A. (1986). *The California Verbal Learning Test: Children's Version.* New York: Psychological Corporation.

Dennis, M. (1985a). Intelligence after early brain injury: I. Predicting IQ scores from medical variables. *Journal of Clinical and Experimental Neuropsychology, 7,* 526–554.

Dennis, M. (1985b). Intelligence after early brain injury: II. IQ scores of subjects classified on the basis of medical history variables. *Journal of Clinical and Experimental Neuropsychology, 7,* 555–576.

Dreisbach, M., Ballard, M., Russo, D. C., & Schain, R. J. (1982). Educational intervention for children with epilepsy: A challenge for collaborative service delivery. *Journal of Special Education, 16*, 111–121.

Elbert, J. C., Culbertson, J. L., Gerrity, K. M., Guthrie, L. J., & Bayles, R. (1985, February). *Neuropsychological and electrophysiologic follow-up of children surviving acute lymphocytic leukemia*. Paper presented at the annual meeting of the International Neuropsychological Society, San Diego.

Ernhart, C. B., Graham, F. K., Eichman, P. L., Marshall, J. M., & Thurston, D. (1963). Brain injury in the preschool child: Some developmental considerations. II. Comparison of brain-injured and normal children. *Psychological Monographs, 77*(Whole No. 574), 17–33.

Fein, D., Waterhouse, L., Lucci, D., & Snyder, D. (1985). Cognitive subtypes in developmentally disabled children: A pilot study. *Journal of Autism and Developmental Disorders, 15*, 77–95.

Fennell, E. B., Eisenstadt, T., Bodiford, C., Rediess, S., de Bijl, M., & Mickle, J. (1987, February). *The assessment of neuropsychological dysfunction in children shunted for hydrocephalus*. Paper presented at the Fifteenth Annual Meeting of the International Neuropsychological Society, Washington, D.C.

Filskov, S. B., & Boll, T. J. (Eds.). (1981). *Handbook of clinical neuropsychology*. New York: Wiley.

Filskov, S. B., & Goldstein, S. G. (1974). Diagnostic validity of the Halstead-Reitan Neuropsychological Battery. *Journal of Consulting and Clinical Psychology, 42*, 383–388.

Gaddes, W. H. (1985). *Learning disabilities and brain function: A neuropsychological approach* (2nd ed.). New York: Springer-Verlag.

Geary, D. C., & Gilger, J. W. (1984). The Luria-Nebraska Neuropsychological Battery-Children's Revision: Comparison of learning disabled and normal children matched on full scale IQ. *Perceptual and Motor Skills, 58*, 115–118.

Geary, D. C., Jennings, S. M., Schultz, D. D., & Alper, T. G. (1984). The diagnostic accuracy of the Luria-Nebraska Neuropsychological Battery-Children's Revision for 9 to 12 year old learning disabled children. *School Psychology Review, 13*, 375–380.

George, S. L., Aur, R. J. A., Mauer, A. M., & Simone, J. V. (1979). A reappraisal of the results of stopping therapy in childhood leukemia. *New England Journal of Medicine, 300*, 269–273.

Gibson, C. J., & Bryden, M. P. (1984). Cerebral laterality in deaf and hearing children. *Brain and Language, 23*, 1–12.

Goff, J. R. (1982). *Memory deficits and distractibility in survivors of childhood leukemia*. Paper presented at the annual meeting of the American Psychological Association.

Golden, C. J. (1981). The Luria-Nebraska Children's Battery: Theory and formulation. In G. W. Hynd & J. E. Obrzut (Eds.), *Neuropsychological assessment and the school-age child: Issues and perspectives* (pp. 277–302). New York: Grune and Stratton.

Golden, C. J. (1987). *Manual for the Luria-Nebraska Neuropsychological Battery-Children's Revision*. Los Angeles, CA: Western Psychological Services.

Golden, C. J., Hammeke, T. A., & Purisch, A. D. (1980). *Manual for the Luria-Nebraska Neuropsychological Battery*. Los Angeles: Western Psychological Services.

Goldman, R., Fristoe, M., & Woodcock, R. W. (1974). *Manual for the Goldman-Fristoe-Woodcock Auditory Skills Test Battery*. Circle Pines, MN: American Guidance Service.

Graham, F. K., Ernhart, C. B., Craft, M., & Berman, P. W. (1963). Brain injury in the preschool child: Some developmental considerations: I: Performance of normal children. *Psychological Monographs, 77*(Whole No. 573), 1–16.

Graham, F. K., & Kendall, B. S. (1960). Memory-for-Designs-Test: Revised general manual. *Perceptual and Motor Skills Monograph* (Supplement, No. 2-VII), *11*, 147–188.

Gustavson, J. L., Golden, C. J., Wilkening, G. N., Hermann, B. P., Plaisted, J. R., MacInnes, W. D., & Leark, R. A. (1984). The Luria-Nebraska Neuropsychological Battery-Children's Revision: Validation with brain-damaged and normal children. *Journal of Psychoeducational Assessment, 2*, 199–208.

Gustavson, J. L., Wilkening, G. N., Hermann, B. P., & Plaisted, J. R. (1982). *Factor analysis of the children's revision of the Luria-Nebraska Neuropsychological Battery.* Unpublished manuscript.

Hagen, C. (1981). Language disorders secondary to closed head injury: Diagnosis and treatment. *Topics in Language Disorders, 1,* 73–87.

Hammill, D. D., Leigh, J. E., McNutt, G., & Larsen, S. C. (1981). A new definition of learning disabilities. *Learning Disability Quarterly, 4,* 336–342.

Heaton, R. K. (1981). *Manual for the Wisconsin Card Sorting Test.* Odessa, FL: Psychological Assessment Resources.

Herbert, M. (1964). The concept and testing of brain damage in children: A review. *Journal of Child Psychology and Psychiatry, 5,* 197–216.

Holmes, C. S., & Richman, L. C. (1985). Cognitive profiles of children with insulin-dependent diabetes. *Journal of Developmental and Behavioral Pediatrics, 6,* 323–326.

Hooper, S. R., & Tramontana, M. G. (1987). *The relationship between neuropsychological variables and academic achievement in child psychiatric patients.* Paper presented at the 95th Annual Convention of the American Psychological Association, New York.

Hurley, A. D., Laatsch, L. K., & Dorman, C. (1983). Comparison of spina bifida, hydrocephalic patients, and matched controls on neuropsychological tests. *Zeitschrift für Kinderchir, 17,* 65–70.

Hynd, G. W., & Obrzut, J. E. (Eds.). (1981). *Neuropsychological assessment and the school-age child: Issues and procedures.* New York: Grune and Stratton.

Hynd, G. W., Snow, J., & Becker, M. G. (1986). Neuropsychological assessment in clinical child psychology. In B. Lahey & A. Kazdin (Eds.), *Advances in clinical child psychology* (Vol. 9). New York: Plenum.

Hynd, G. W., & Willis, W. G. (1988). *Pediatric neuropsychology.* New York: Grune and Stratton.

Incagnoli, T., & Newman, B. (1985). Cognitive and behavioral interventions. *International Journal of Clinical Neuropsychology, 7,* 173–182.

Ivan, L. P. (Ed.). (1984). *Pediatric neuropsychology.* St. Louis: Warren H. Green.

Karras, D., Newlin, D. B., Franzen, M. D., Golden, C. J., Wilkening, G. N., Rothermel, R. D., & Tramontana, M. G. (1987). Development of factor scales for the Luria-Nebraska Neuropsychological Battery-Children's Revision. *Journal of Clinical Child Psychology, 16,* 19–28.

Kaufman, A. S., & Kaufman, N. L. (1983). *Manual for the Kaufman Assessment Battery for Children.* Circle Pines, MN: American Guidance Service.

Kay, G. G., Becker, B., Bleiberg, J., & Long, C. J. (1986, August). *Cognitive rehabilitation software: Therapy or adjunct? A call for standards.* Paper presented at the Annual Meeting of the American Psychological Association, Washington, D.C.

Klesges, R. C. (1983). The relationship between neuropsychological, cognitive, and behavioral assessments of brain functioning in children. *Clinical Neuropsychology, 1,* 28–32.

Klonoff, H., Low, M. D., & Clark, C. (1977). Head injuries in children with a prospective 5-year follow-up. *Journal of Neurology, Neurosurgery and Psychiatry, 40,* 1211–1219.

Klonoff, H., Robinson, G. C., & Thompson, G. (1969). Acute and chronic brain syndromes in children. *Developmental Medicine in Child Neurology, 11,* 198–213.

Knights, R. M. (1966). Normative data on tests for evaluating brain damage in children from 5 to 14 years of age (Research Bulletin No. 20). London, Ontario: University of Western Ontario.

Kolb, B., & Wishaw, I. Q. (1980). *Fundamentals of human neuropsychology.* San Francisco: W. H. Freeman.

Koppitz, E. M. (1964). *The Bender Gestalt Test for Young Children.* New York: Grune and Stratton.

Levin, H. S., & Eisenberg, H. M. (1979). Neuropsychological impairment after closed head injury in children and adolescents. *Journal of Pediatric Psychology, 4,* 389–402.

Luria, A. R. (1966). *Higher cortical functions in man.* New York: Basic Books.

Luria, A. R. (1973). *The working brain.* New York: Basic Books.

McCarthy, D. (1972). *Manual for the McCarthy Scales of Children's Abilities.* New York: Psychological Corporation.

Meighan, S. S., Queener, L., & Weitman, M. (1976). Prevalence of epilepsy in children of Multnomah County, Oregon. *Epilepsia, 17,* 245–256.

Milberg, W. P., Hebben, N., & Kaplan, E. (1986). The Boston process approach to neuropsychological assessment. In I. Grant & K. M. Adams (Eds.), *Neuropsychological assessment of neuropsychiatric disorders* (pp. 65–86). New York: Oxford University Press.

Nolan, D. R., Hammeke, T. A., & Barkley, R. A. (1983). A comparison of the patterns of the neuropsychological performance in two groups of learning disabled children. *Journal of Clinical Child Psychology, 12,* 13–21.

Obrzut, J. E., & Hynd, G. W. (1986a). *Child Neuropsychology: Theory and Research.* (Vol. 1). New York: Academic Press.

Obrzut, J. E., & Hynd, G. W. (1986b). *Child Neuropsychology: Clinical Practice.* (Vol. 2). New York: Academic Press.

Passler, M., Isaac, W., & Hynd, G. W. (1986). Neuropsychological development of behavior attributed to frontal lobe functioning in children. *Developmental Neuropsychology, 1,* 349–370.

Reed, H. B. C., Reitan, R. M., & Klove, H. (1965). Influence of cerebral lesions on psychological test performance of older children. *Journal of Consulting Psychology, 29,* 247–251.

Reitan, R. M. (1974). Psychological effects of cerebral lesions in children of early school age. In R. M. Reitan & L. A. Davison (Eds.), *Clinical neuropsychology: Current status and applications* (pp. 53–90). New York: Wiley.

Reitan, R. M., & Davison, L. A. (Eds.). (1974). *Clinical neuropsychology: Current status and applications.* New York: Wiley.

Rourke, B. P. (1982). Central processing deficiencies in children: Toward a developmental neuropsychological model. *Journal of Clinical Neuropsychology, 4,* 1–18.

Rourke, B. P. (1985). *Neuropsychology of learning disabilities: Essentials of subtype analysis.* New York: Guilford Press.

Rourke, B. P., Bakker, D. J., Fisk, J. L., & Strang, J. D. (1983). *Child neuropsychology: Introduction to theory, research and practice.* New York: Guilford Press.

Rourke, B. P., & Finlayson, M. A. J. (1978). Neuropsychological significance of variations in patterns of academic performance: Verbal and visual-spatial abilities. *Journal of Abnormal Child Psychology, 6,* 121–133.

Rourke, B. P., Fisk, J. L., & Strang, J. D. (1986). *Neuropsychological assessment of children: A treatment-oriented approach.* New York: Guilford Press.

Rovet, J., Gore, M., & Ehrlich, R. (1983). Intellectual and behavioral deficits associated with early onset diabetes mellitus. *Diabetes, 32* (Supplement 1), 17.

Rutter, M. (1977). Brain damage syndromes in childhood: Concepts and findings. *Journal of Child Psychology and Psychiatry, 18,* 1–21.

Rutter, M. (Ed.). (1983). *Developmental neuropsychiatry.* New York: Guilford Press.

Rutter M., Graham, P., & Yule, W. (1970). *A neuropsychiatric study in childhood* (Clinics in Developmental Medicine Nos. 35–36). London: Spastics International Medical Publications/Heinemann Medical Books.

Ryan, C., Vega, A., & Drash, A. (1985). Cognitive deficits in adolescents who developed diabetes early in life. *Pediatrics, 75,* 921–927.

Ryan, C., Vega, A., Longstreet, C., & Drash, A. (1984). Neuropsychological changes in adolescents with insulin-dependent diabetes. *Journal of Consulting and Clinical Psychology, 52,* 335–342.

Satz, P., & Fletcher, J. M. (1982). *Florida Kindergarten Screening Battery.* Odessa, FL: Psychological Assessment Resources.

Sawicki, R. F., Leark, R., Golden, C. J., & Karras, D. (1984). The development of the pathognomonic, left sensorimotor, and right sensorimotor scales for the Luria-Nebraska Neuropsychological Battery-Children's Revision. *Journal of Clinical Child Psychology, 13*(2), 165–169.

Seidel, U. P., Chadwick, O., & Rutter, M. (1975). Psychological disorders in crippled children: A comparative study of children with and without brain damage. *Developmental Medicine and Child Neurology, 17,* 563–573.

Seidenberg, M., Giordani, B., Berent, S., & Boll, T. J. (1983). IQ level and performance on the Halstead-Reitan Neuropsychological Test Battery for Older Children. *Journal of Consulting and Clinical Psychology, 51,* 406–413.

Selz, M., & Reitan, R. M. (1979). Rules for neuropsychological diagnosis: Classification of brain function in older children. *Journal of Consulting and Clinical Psychology, 47*(2), 258–264.

Shaffer, D., Schonfeld, I., O'Connor, P. A., Stokman, C., Trautman, P., Shafer, S., & Ng, S. (1985). Neurological soft signs. *Archives of General Psychiatry, 42,* 342–351.

Smith, A. (1975). Neuropsychological testing in neurological disorders. In W. J. Friedlander (Ed.), *Advances in neurology* (Vol. 7). New York: Raven Press.

Snow, J. H., & Hynd, G. W. (1985). Factor structure of the Luria-Nebraska Neuropsychological Battery-Children's Revision. *Journal of School Psychology, 23,* 271–275.

Snow, J. H., Hynd, G. W., & Hartlage, L. C. (1984). Difference between mildly and more severely learning-disabled children on the Luria-Nebraska Neuropsychological Battery-Children's Revision. *Journal of Psychoeducational Assessment, 2,* 23–28.

Soare, P. L., & Raimondi, A. J. (1977). Intellectual and perceptual-motor characteristics of treated myelomeningocele children. *American Journal of Diseases of Children, 131,* 199–204.

Spreen, O. J., & Gaddes, W. H. (1969). Development norms for 15 neuropsychological tests age 6–15. *Cortex, 5,* 171–191.

Spreen, O. J., Tupper, D., Risser, A., Tuokko, H., & Edgell, D. (1984). *Human developmental neuropsychology.* New York: Oxford University Press.

Sweet, J. J., Carr, M. A., Rossini, E., & Kaspar, C. (1986). Relationship between the Luria-Nebraska Neuropsychological Battery-Children's Revision and the WISC-R: Further examination using Kaufman's factors. *International Journal of Clinical Neuropsychology, 8,* 177–180.

Teasdale, G., & Jennett, B. (1974). Assessment of coma and impaired consciousness. *Lancet, 11,* 81–84.

Tramontana, M. G. (1983). Neuropsychological evaluation of children and adolescents with psychopathological disorders. In C. J. Golden & P. J. Vicente (Eds.), *Foundations of clinical neuropsychology* (pp. 309–340). New York: Plenum.

Tramontana, M. G., & Boyd, T. A. (1986). Psychometric screening of neuropsychological abnormality in older children. *International Journal of Clinical Neuropsychology, 8,* 53–59.

Tramontana, M. G., Hooper, S. R., & Nardolillo, E. M. (in press). *Behavioral manifestations of neuropsychological impairment in children with psychiatric disorders. Archives of Clinical Neuropsychology*

Tramontana, M. G., & Hooper, S. R. (1987). Discriminating the presence and pattern of neuropsychological impairment in child psychiatric disorders. *International Journal of Clinical Neuropsychology, 9,* 111–119.

Tramontana, M. G., & Hooper, S. R. (in press). Neuropsychology of child psychopathology. In C. R. Reynolds (Ed.), *Handbook of child clinical neuropsychology.* New York: Plenum.

Tramontana, M. G., Hooper, S. R., Curley, A. D., & Nardolillo, E. M. (1988, January). *Determinants of academic achievement in children with psychiatric disorders.* Paper presented at the Annual National Conference of the International Neuropsychological Society, New Orleans.

Tramontana, M. G., Klee, S. H., & Boyd, T. A. (1984). WISC-R interrelationships with the Halstead-Reitan and Children's Luria Neuropsychological Batteries. *International Journal of Clinical Neuropsychology, 6*, 1–8.

Tramontana, M. G., & Sherrets, S. D. (1985). Brain impairment in child psychiatric disorders: Correspondencies between neuropsychological and CT scan results. *Journal of the American Academy of Child Psychiatry, 24*, 590–596.

Tramontana, M. G., Sherrets, S. D., & Golden, C. J. (1980). Brain dysfunction in youngsters with psychiatric disorders: Application of Selz-Reitan rules for neuropsychological diagnosis. *Clinical Neuropsychology, 2*, 118–123.

Tramontana, M. G., Sherrets, S. D., & Wolf, B. A. (1983). Comparability of the Luria-Nebraska and Halstead-Reitan Neuropsychological Batteries for older children. *Clinical Neuropsychology, 5*, 186–190.

Waber, D., Sollee, N., Wills, K., & Fischer, R. (1986, February). *Neuropsychological effects of two levels of cranial radiation in children with acute lymphoblastic leukemia (ALL)*. Paper presented at the Fourteenth Annual Meeting of the International Neuropsychological Society, Denver, Colorado.

Wender, P. (1971). *Minimal brain dysfunction in children*. New York: Wiley.

Wilkening, G. N., Golden, C. J., MacInnes, W. D., Plaisted, J. R., & Hermann, B. P. (1981, August). *The Luria-Nebraska Neuropsychological Battery-Children's Revision: A preliminary report*. Paper presented at the meeting of the American Psychological Association, Los Angeles.

Wilson, B. C. (1986). An approach to the neuropsychological assessment of the preschool child with developmental deficits. In S. B. Filskov & T. J. Boll (Eds.), *Handbook of clinical neuropsychology* (Vol. 2). New York: Wiley.

Wilson, H., & Staton, R. D. (1984). Neuropsychological changes in children associated with tricyclic antidepressant therapy. *International Journal of Neuroscience, 24*, 307–312.

Wolf, B. A., & Tramontana, M. G. (1982). Aphasia Screening Test interrelationships with complete Halstead-Reitan test results for older children. *Clinical Neuropsychology, 4*, 179–186.

Yule, W. (1980). Educational achievement. In B. M. Kulig, M. Meinhardi, & G. Stores (Eds.), *Epilepsy and behavior*. Lisse, The Netherlands: Swets & Zeitlinger.

II

General Issues in Child
Neuropsychological Assessment

Neuropsychology of the Developing Brain

Implications for Neuropsychological Assessment

ANTHONY H. RISSER and DOROTHY EDGELL

INTRODUCTION

Childhood neuropsychological assessment contributes interpretative data on the relation between overt behavior and the functional systems of the child's brain. These data are obtained in the expectation that they will be useful in interpretating the significance of the child's manifest problems. The assessment provides a comprehensive analysis of test-delimited neuropsychological systems, such as language comprehension or visual short-term memory, and of the integrated functioning of these systems. Neuropsychological interpretation occurs in a diagnostic milieu that also might include clinical neurological, neuroimaging, electrophysiological, psychological, and educational data.

As with any psychological assessment, neuropsychological assessment is performed with an awareness of other important factors, such as the child's history, family environment, and expected normative psychosocial and biological development. Any mediating factor may influence behaviors manifested on assessment. There is a defining neuropsychological dimension of this interpretative context, however; namely, obtained data are viewed in light of knowledge about the central nervous system

ANTHONY H. RISSER • Department of Neurology, Mount Sinai Medical Center, University of Wisconsin Medical School, Milwaukee, Wisconsin.   DOROTHY EDGELL • Department of Psychology, Jack Ledger Child and Adolescent Psychiatric Unit, Arbutus Society for Children, Victoria, British Columbia, Canada.

(CNS) substrate, which is presumed to account to some extent for the obtained performances. The developmental neuropsychologist views data—both behavioral and neurological—that are transient, albeit characteristic features of evolving systems at the time of assessment. A three-part focus is created by this context for the analysis of neuropsychological findings: (1) as possible consequences of past occurrences, (2) as functions representing current status, and (3) as influences upon further development.

The major purposes for obtaining neuropsychological data include (1) exploring the cognitive and behavioral consequences of a known neurological insult to determine the extent of its impact, (2) exploring possible neurological processes that may underlie abnormal cognitive or behavioral manifestations to address possible cause, and (3) creating treatment or management plans. In all instances, the assessment requires knowledge of the developing brain as it relates to a performance characteristic or to a syndrome (i.e., a set of correlated characteristics). Although appropriate childhood neuropsychological assessments can be accomplished without special reference to underlying neural function (Taylor, Fletcher, & Satz, 1984), an elementary premise of neuropsychological practice is that relations between brain and behavior do exist, although they are not likely to be isomorphic in nature.

A formal neuropsychology of the developing brain—that is, one that can integrate features of neurological and psychological development—is a contemporary goal rather than an established feat (Benton, 1982). However, one need only compare compilations of contemporary empirical findings, such as this volume, with those of only a decade ago, such as Witelson's (1977) germinal evaluation of issues surrounding the development of hemispheric specialization, to realize how the scope and depth of our basic knowledge has changed. This advance has been particularly true for brain–behavior phenomena that encompass the first 2 years of life. To provide an outline that may be of use as a guide when examining the specific neurobehavioral topics of later chapters, this chapter provides a basic overview of the normal and pathological developing brain, with an emphasis on development from the prenatal period through the first years of life.

PRINCIPLES OF NEURAL DEVELOPMENT

Two dimensions define brain development. First, as individual cells are created in accordance with genetic instruction, they develop along predetermined parameters of growth. Second, aspects of this maturation show degrees of flexibility or plasticity in adaptive response to the environment (broadly defined) as cell populations evolve into committed functional systems. Growth in the developing brain proceeds along distinctive temporal-spatial dimensions—cell populations differing in their ultimate destinies mature through developmental stages at different times and in different regions of the brain. These stages are *proliferation, migration, differentiation,* and *myelination.*

Each stage will be introduced below; in the interest of brevity, proliferation and migration will be discussed together. Gross normative status at birth will be discussed in the section on differentiation. The *functional organization* of brain–behavior relations also will be introduced. The distinctions between stages are somewhat arbitrary, and others have employed different criteria to distinguish them. Kandel and Schwartz (1981), in their edited text on neural science, for example, separate aspects of neuronal development from aspects of transneuronal synaptic development. The reader is referred to works of general embryonic development (e.g., Thomas, 1968), developmental neurobiology (e.g., Jacobson, 1978; Lund, 1978; Williams & Caviness, 1984), and child neuropsychology (e.g., Rourke, Bakker, Fisk, & Strang, 1983; Spreen, Tupper, Risser, Tuokko, & Edgell, 1984) for discussions of neural development from several different perspectives.

Proliferation and Migration

The creation of embryonic cells by cell division results in the appearance of the neuroectoderm (a thickened, elongated central region of the embryonic disk) in the third gestational week. Neuroectodermal demarcation of brain-cell precursors from other embryonic cells evolves into the distinctive neural tube during the fourth week. Accelerated brain-cell creation occurs shortly thereafter, during the period of embryo-wide organ formation in the fourth and fifth weeks. The internal wall of the neural tube, which surrounds a fluid-filled cavity, is the birth site of neuroblasts (destined to become neurons) and glial-cell precursors. Where along this elongated wall, and when during this time period, a cell is created plays a critical role in the cell's ultimate destiny in the mature CNS. Different cell populations reside in specific regions of the expanding neural tube. The tube's anterior end bulges and bends at particular sites of extensive cell creation, such as the forebrain, midbrain, and hindbrain vesicles—precursor areas for cell populations destined to become the brain. Generally, neurons are created before glial cells, neurons found in the deeper layers of the cortex are created prior to those destined for superficial levels, and cerebellar neurons are created late in proliferation. Golgi class I neurons, which have large axons and form major pathways, generally proliferate before Golgi class II neurons (microneurons), which form connections within brain areas. Brain-cell proliferation slows by the end of the first trimester of pregnancy; most neurons have been created by the beginning of the final trimester.

Once a population of neuroblasts has stopped multiplying, its constituents migrate as true neurons outward from their birth sites. Young neurons migrate in sheets (laminae) of similar cells created at similar times toward specific zones of the outer layer of the neural tube, which eventually will become the multilayered cortical "gray matter" and the various subcortical nuclei. Axons that will enter or leave this outer layer on route to their target synaptic zones form an intermediate layer destined to become "white matter." Rakic (1981) has provided a detailed description of migratory mechanisms and their roles in configuring the cortex. The goal of migration is to emplace neurons at their mature functional sites, creating the gridwork for subsequent cellular differentiation and synapse formation.

Characteristic physical changes in the fetal brain during this time involve its regional distinctiveness: the rapid growth of the cerebral hemispheres, the initial appearance of sulcal and gyral landmarks, and cerebellar development. As early as the sixth gestational week, features such as the cortex and the internal capsule are evident. By the 23rd week, major sulcal and gyral landmarks on the cortical surface are evident (Chi, Dooling, & Gilles, 1977). Figure 1 presents sulcal development in relation to brain weight over the course of prenatal development.

Differentiation

Differentiation is a multifactorial growth period during which maturation of the structure of existing cells is accomplished. Differentiation permits cells to function as committed constituents of specific neural systems. The major components of differentiation include (1) formation of the dendritic field and distal axonal growth, (2) maturation of cell-body structures that are required for proper metabolic functioning, (3) creation and maturation of synaptic architecture and the establishment of functional transmission links, (4) maturation of enzyme and neurotransmitter synthesis and storage, and (5) selective retrogressive processes (e.g., neuronal death) to streamline the neural substrate. Differentiation of neuronal populations begins in earnest once they have migrated to their mature placement sites. Differentiation is a characteristic feature of fetal brain development, but it also continues beyond birth. Some elements of differentiation become life-span features of neurological maintenance. For example, synaptic differentiation is extensive during fetal development when synaptic turnover (i.e., creation and elimination) is great, but it also may continue as a modulating mechanism in response to change throughout the lifespan (Cotman & Nieto-Sampedro, 1982, 1984).

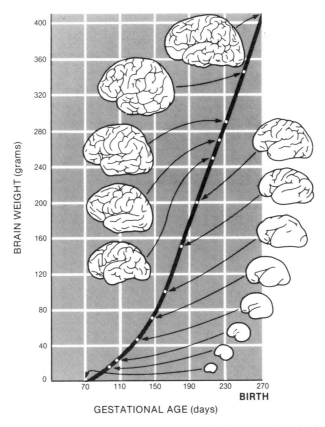

FIGURE 1. The relation between brain weight and the development of cerebral sulci. (Adapted from Lemire, Loeser, Leech, & Alvord, 1975.)

The destiny of a neuron population to become, for example, the substrate for brainstem nuclei, primary sensory or motor cortex, or the regions of association cortex, unfolds genetically during fetal proliferation. Subsequent neural growth is the result of differentiation, representing vast increases in the size and complexity of existing cells. It is during differentiation that neurons become active as committed members of specialized functional systems, as relevant synaptic connections between neurons become established and they begin to communicate. Activity may remain immature or poorly integrated for some time. This is particularly true for neurons that have axons yet to myelinate and for systems that continue to evolve in infancy and childhood prior to their ultimate commitment to subserve particular functions. Aspects of differentiation, such as the growth and pruning of synaptic spines on dendrites (receptive postsynaptic regions), appear to have a strong environmental component, occurring in response to the experience of the organism in its postnatal environment (e.g., Lund, 1978).

Until neuronal populations are committed to subserve certain functions, they may display some degree of plasticity to subserve other functions if required to do so. The mechanisms of brain–behavior plasticity and commitment remain to be established and are of key research concern. Basic neuroscientific models of CNS plasticity exist; the most successful has been the primate model of dorsolateral prefrontal cortical development (e.g., Goldman, 1979; Goldman & Galkin, 1978; Goldman-Rakic, Isserhoff, Schwartz, & Bugbee, 1983). The dorsolateral prefrontal cortex subserves specific higher cognitive and integrative abilities in primates. These abilities require time for adult performance levels to be attained and are subserved by subcortical regions prior to cortical commitment. Lesioning the dorsolateral prefrontal cortex in the adult monkey results in a characteristic behavioral deficit on delayed-response tasks that require the animal to remember the location of a salient stimulus, such as food, over brief time intervals (Jacobsen, 1936). Lesioning this region during either fetal development or postnatally until the first 2 months of life, however, does not result in a performance deficit when lesioned animals are subsequently tested as adults. This model's utility in understanding plasticity in the human brain with regard to behavioral implications derives from its analogous fit to higher cortical development in its relative timing, early-life experiential component, and requisite adult cortical commitment.

Once neurons have ceased proliferating, they become irreplaceable. As neurons continue to differentiate, their structure and their functional features also become unique. Although other neuronal populations may supplement or even assume the responsibilities of other neurons if required to do so (simple descriptions of proposed mechanisms have been presented by Gazzaniga, Stein, & Volpe, 1979), destroyed neurons cannot be replaced directly by a newly created population. The number of neurons created during proliferation is in excess of what is needed in the normal brain. This provides the evolving system with a degree of initial redundancy. During differentiation, this redundancy dissipates. A competition among neurons for limited aspects of their synaptic target zones results in a "weeding out" of those neurons that lose the competition either by not establishing synapses at the proper time or by somehow synapsing in improper fashion (Cowan, Fawcett, O'Leary, & Stanfield, 1984; Purves & Lichtman, 1980).

Although differentiation is the most ubiquitous of all growth stages, peak periods of differentiation occur at different times in different brain regions. Subcortical structures that maintain the vegetative state of the organism and cortical areas composed predominantly of Golgi class I neurons, such as sensorimotor cortex, differentiate early in the second trimester. Other areas, such as the cerebellum and the vast regions of microneuron-composed association cortex, continue to differentiate well beyond birth, concurrent with the substantial functional acquisitions in language and motor control that the infant achieves during the first 2 years of life. The neural differentiation that occurs in the context of mediating normal psychological learning remains an enigma, addressed speculatively in classic works such as that by Hebb (1949) and more recently by Bakker (1984).

Birth occurs while the majority of neuronal populations are still differentiating. As the *sine qua non* for further brain–behavior development, birth provides the evolving brain with the environmental context to guide subsequent maturation. The full-term newborn's brain is a functioning organ, although historically it was considered to be quiescent. A cardinal change in all developmental disciplines has been the relatively recent understanding of the functioning of the neonatal brain. This has entailed its recognition as more than the modest precursor to the adult brain. The neonatal brain has matured by birth to encounter the real-time ontogenetic adaptations it must make to ensure continued normative development, albeit predominantly through relatively more mature reflexive subcortical systems. These adaptations have been described by Oppenheim (1981) and Turkewitz and Kenny (1982). Examples of these adaptations are neonatal reflexes and modal sensory abilities. Many observed neonatal reflexes, once considered to be the primitive features of mature behavior, are now considered to be prenatal neurobehavioral adaptations to increase the probability that the fetus will be in the lower-risk, normal vertex birth position. Likewise, sensory abilities at any given time during development are attuned to adaptive ontogenetic requirements for different combinations of intramodal and intermodal performances, and are not simply the immature versions of adult sensory capabilities.

Myelination

Prior to myelination, neuronal communication is characterized by slow transmission rates and long refractory periods (Bronson, 1982). Although many neuronal populations are structurally mature prior to their myelination, true functional maturity occurs only after this process of exogenous axonal sheathing has occurred. The relative rates of myelination in different brain regions do serve as a rough index of the sequence in which components of the CNS reach functional adult levels (Yakovlev & Lecours, 1967), although a myelin sheath is not necessary for conduction of action potentials and some neuronal populations do not require myelination at all (Bronson, 1982; Purpura & Reaser, 1974). The population of glial cells that produce myelin have late proliferation periods and mature postnatally. The bulk of axonal myelination, therefore, occurs during infancy and early childhood. New glia and their myelin product are the prime factors (along with continued structural differentiation of neuron populations) that account for the dramatic postnatal growth in the size of the brain (Bronson, 1982). Brain weight at birth is approximately 350 g, about one-quarter of approximate adult weight. However, by age 2, brain weight is approximately 1300 g—close to the adult range of 1400–1500 g.

Myelination, like other dimensions of brain development, proceeds in a general temporal-spatial pattern. This was noted as early as 1901 by Flechsig. Yakovlev and LeCours (1967) and LeCours (1975) have provided a detailed description of human myelogenetic development (Figure 2). Beginning with the sensory and motor roots of the spinal cord and proceeding to axons of neurons in "primordial zones," such as the primary sensorimotor cortical areas, myelination starts prenatally and continues through early infancy. In the pyramidal tract, for example, the major efferents from the motor cortex begin to undergo myelination 1 month prior to birth and are essentially completed by the end of the first year of life. The slower, postnatal myelination of cortical-subcortical pathways, callosal fibers, and association cortex Golgi class II interneurons is related to the gradual emergence of language, cognitive, and motor skills from late infancy through middle childhood.

Better clinical appreciation of normal (and aberrant) patterns of mye-

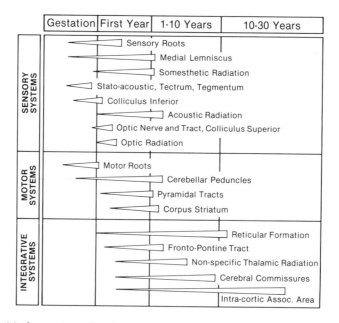

FIGURE 2. Myelogenetic cycles of regional maturation in the human brain. (Adapted from Yakovlev & LeCours, 1967.)

lination may be substantially enhanced by the introduction of magnetic resonance imaging (MRI) of the brain (Risser, 1984). MRI is the best available clinical imaging modality for visualizing white matter and gray-white matter delineation (Lee et al., 1986). MRI data samples have been providing atlaslike delineations of the course of normal (McArdle et al., 1987) and abnormal (Johnson et al., 1987) myelination from preterm birth through early childhood. This imaging modality should prove invaluable for correlational research comparing structural images and indices of brain development, such as myelination patterns, with neurobehavioral features in individual children.

Functional Organization

Postnatally, during periods of continued differentiation and myelination, brain development is paralleled by elaboration of the organism's adaptive behavioral repertoire. Exactly how structure and function are related is unclear, but it appears that the two are mutually dependent. Structural changes appear in many ways to produce modifications in behavior, whereas various dimensions of brain structure are shaped, to some degree, by behavioral experiences that may contribute to individual differences in brain–behavior patterns (e.g., Greenough & Juraska, 1979). The traditional topograpical representation of different structural areas on the lateral and medial surfaces of the brain and their related functions are illustrated by Brodmann's map of the cytoarchitecture of the cortex (Figure 3), which defines areas by cell structure and cellular layers. To the neuropsychologist, units of interest are composed by the functional integration of these regions. Components of functionally integrated units attain maturity at different rates and at different times during early development. As a result, assessment of children depends upon measures that take into account the pattern of structural and functional maturation at any given time in a changing, maturing brain.

The "behavioral geography of the brain" (Lezak, 1983, p. 41) reflects the discipline of adult behavioral neurology and is well presented in many neuropsychological resources (e.g., Walsh, 1978). One of several ways to approach this behavioral geography, which incorporates development, was presented by Luria (1973). As part of Luria's neuropsychological model of three functional units delineating the CNS (i.e., arousal, informational interaction, and programming units), three functional cortical zones may be distinguished and described ontogenetically. These are the primary, secondary, and tertiary zones.

Primary zones are modality specific and receive input from the senses or control motor activity. These zones are somatotopically arranged and possess an abundance of neurons in afferent cell layer IV. Their characteristic topographical organization and modality specificity

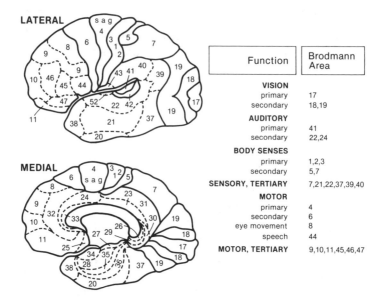

Function	Brodmann Area
VISION	
primary	17
secondary	18,19
AUDITORY	
primary	41
secondary	22,24
BODY SENSES	
primary	1,2,3
secondary	5,7
SENSORY, TERTIARY	7,21,22,37,39,40
MOTOR	
primary	4
secondary	6
eye movement	8
speech	44
MOTOR, TERTIARY	9,10,11,45,46,47

FIGURE 3. Brodmann's cytoarchitectonic areas of the brain. (From Elliott, 1969.)

are helpful diagnostically because lesions in these zones lead to fairly stereotypic deficits. According to Luria's developmental approach, these zones become fully functional by the end of the first year of life and form the basis for successful secondary zone expression. *Secondary zones* lie adjacent to primary ones and integrate modality-specific information into perceptive information. Afferent cell layers II and III predominate and are composed of associative microneurons. Lesions in these areas give rise to perceptual deficits that typically are restricted to specific modalities, but the deficits are less stereotypic. These areas become fully functional within the first 5 years of life and form the basis for successful tertiary zone expression. *Tertiary zones* are associative, supramodal areas encompassing the borders of parietal, temporal, and occipital zones as well as the vast prefrontal region with its abundant cortical and subcortical (e.g., thalamus) connections. These zones generally serve to integrate information across modalities and to control executive, purposive, and conative aspects of functioning. Supramodal regions become functional between the ages of 5 and 8, whereas the prefrontal region becomes functional later. Passler, Isaac, and Hynd (1985) suggested that this prefrontal development is dynamic, occurring in stages, with functional maturity by age 12.

Over the course of development, not only is a hierarchical relationship of zones expressed, but a lateralization of the functioning of these zones also is obtained between the two hemispheres. Lateralization of hemispheric functional specialization, of course, has held a predominant position in adult and developmental neuropsychological research, given compelling evidence for both structural and cognitive asymmetries (Bryden, 1982; Corballis & Morgan, 1978; Geschwind & Galaburda, 1985a, 1985b, 1985c). Conscious activity occurs through the integrated working of hierarchical and lateralized specialized zones within the three-unit functional system that is the CNS.

Summary

If made more elaborate, this selective overview of the most rapid and critical periods of growth observed in the developing brain would fall far afield of the overall focus of this volume. Yet it is during this period of normal brain development that the bulk of the neural framework for subsequent neuropsychological functioning is created. It is also here, perhaps, that a subclinical anoxic-ischemic episode or some microstructural or neurochemical anomaly may set the stage for a neuropsychological disorder, such as a specific learning disability or an attentional deficit, that may not be evident until later in childhood.

Proposals of the sort described above have a notable history (Knobloch & Pasamanick, 1966) and have been presented on the basis of selective neuropathological findings (Fuller, Guthrie, & Alvord, 1983; Towbin, 1971), but they remain speculative. Speculative relations of this type, tested on a case-study postmortem basis, have gained an invaluable documentational aid in Galaburda's cytoarchitectonic studies of the postmortem brains of dyslexic individuals (Galaburda & Eidelberg, 1982; Galaburda & Kemper, 1979; Galaburda, Sherman, Rosen, Aboitiz, & Geschwind, 1985). In group analyses, however, such speculative relations are usually found to account for only a very small portion of outcome variability. Naeye and Peters (1987), for example, found that the presence of fetal and perinatal hypoxia accounted for only 2% of IQ variation on the Wechsler Intelligence Scale for Children (WISC) at age 7. In sum, although at a tangent to the practical concerns of the clinician, explorations of the neural side of normal brain–behavior development do, and shall continue to, contribute to a fuller understanding of normal cognitive and behavioral development and provide a firmer basis for appreciating the significance of deviations from normal development.

ABNORMALITIES IN NEURAL DEVELOPMENT

An insult to brain tissue at any time may result in impairments in behavior, and these impairments may be permanent. Damage to the young CNS, however, may cause quantitatively and qualitatively different impairments (with differences in permanence) than would damage to the adult CNS. Although the bulk of the literature addressing this issue has been delineated in terms of age, it is now recognized that reference to the age of the CNS may be more confusing than helpful in seeking to understand those CNS mechanisms that account for differences in the developing versus the mature brain's response to injury. More precisely, damage to the functionally uncommitted brain may not be the same as damage to the committed brain (Goldman-Rakic et al., 1983). Relevant experimental evidence about the traditional role of age dates back to Stoltmann in 1876 (cited by Goldman-Rakic et al., 1983) and has generated two heuristic guidelines about the timing of a brain insult. It also has created an arena for critical debate about recovery of function following a brain insult (Isaacson, 1975; Schneider, 1979; St. James-Roberts, 1979).

The two guidelines that have emerged from this literature are the Kennard principle (Kennard, 1940, 1942) and the Dobbing hypothesis (Dobbing & Smart, 1974). The ablation studies in monkeys by Kennard (1942) led to the general conclusion that brain lesions early in life produced fewer deficits than similar lesions in later life. The Kennard principle states, therefore, that the degree of impaired function subsequent to brain damage is proportional to the age at which the injury occurred. The Dobbing hypothesis, tested extensively upon rat models of adult brain–behavior consequences of early-life malnutrition or irradiation (Dobbing & Sands, 1971), states that brain damage during development has its greatest impact upon those cell populations and/or individual growth parameters that show the greatest rate of development at the time of the insult. Insults occurring during cell proliferation limit the number of cells in the mature brain; insults during differentiation do not necessarily alter the number of cells in the brain but do influence cell size—a gross index of altered cellular architecture (Winick & Rosso, 1969).

Euphemistically, Kennard's principle suggests that earlier rather than later brain damage would be preferable in sparing function, whereas Dobbing's hypothesis suggests the opposite—later, rather than earlier, brain damage would be preferable to avoid permanent impairment. The fact that either may have relevance at different levels of analysis (e.g., cellular, systemic, behavioral) and in different contexts (e.g., language development, electrophysiology) points toward an underlying complexity that evades a simple explanation. The behavioral consequences of brain damage are made more complex by findings that suggest that plasticity at a structural level is not necessarily associated with improved function (Isaacson, 1975).

Perhaps the simplest statement that can be made from an integration of both rules is that brain damage during infancy and early childhood may prove less devastating in outcome than damage either during fetal development or in the mature brain. The timing of an insult to the developing brain will influence the nature and extent of any resultant deficit and the probability for the acquisition of the normal repertoire of abilities. Interference with neural development at a given time will have a characteristic influence on the normal status of different cell populations depending upon what stage(s) of growth they are experiencing. This will have a compounding impact upon the organism's ability to recover losses, develop further, and reach levels of ultimate maturity. Given the previously outlined stages of brain development, it is important to recognize that an early lesion is a fetal lesion, not necessarily one that occurs during infancy or childhood. This recognition has not always proved of benefit in neuropsychology for two reasons.

First, traditional examinations of age issues in neuropsychology have compared adult ("late") with child or infant ("early") lesions. Age is a comparison with practical value. For example, adult soldiers of different ages who suffered war-related brain injury showed different levels of resiliency to long-term behavioral losses (Teuber, 1975). In addition, children, like adults, usually have some degree of vocal and cooperative interaction with the trained assessor. Although the assessor may not use tests created from a developmental neuropsychological perspective, available adult neuropsychological tests have been revised, renormed, or reinterpreted to permit purposeful administration to young children and can be supplemented by the use of established child *psychological* instruments, such as the McCarthy ability scales (McCarthy, 1972). Examples of downwardly extended adult tests include the Halstead-Reitan Battery (Reitan & Davison, 1974), the Neurosensory Center Comprehensive Examination of Aphasia (Gaddes & Crockett, 1973), and the Token Test for Children (DiSimoni, 1978). Despite the practicality of using such "borrowed" tests, their interpretation remains that of how children perform on adult-derived tests rather than how children perform on tests that have been constructed to reflect purer developmental neuropsychological measures of age-relevant behaviors. How one can collect infant and preschool neuropsychological data, which are valuable both on their own and in making a comparison with adolescent and adult findings, remains a challenging investigational question (see Chapter 9, this volume).

Second, many of the truly early insults (e.g., lesions that occur during the prenatal periods of proliferation and migration) may result in spontaneous abortion or create individual cases that are not usually accessible to neuropsychologists. Prenatal lesions can have a devastating impact upon the integrity of the CNS. Survivors of such early insults are more frequently seen in neurological, rather than neuropsychological, practice and usually are left with severe mental and sensorimotor deficits. On the other hand, determining whether subtle prenatal insults may evade identification at onset but leave some discernible "thumbprint" on subsequent neuropsychological development awaits a suitable methodology for study.

Timing will never be the sole dimension of an insult to be considered in trying to appreciate its consequences. The nature, severity, and location of the insult, control over secondary aspects of the insult (e.g., increased intracranial pressure or seizures), and treatment all need to be considered, as is true for any neurological insult (Adams & Victor, 1985). However, timing of insult is the obvious defining developmental dimension. The significance of timing as an *isolated* dimension in altering development may be seen more clearly in a neuropathology laboratory than in a neuropsychology clinic. The general timing of an insult during neural migration provides an example in that it may alter the number of neocortical cell layers (e.g., Lund, 1978). These consequences range from schizencephaly (agenesis of entire regions, which can result from an insult during the second gestational month) to the mildest migratory defect (resulting from insults prior to the seventh month) in which all six neocortical layers are present, but deviant collections of cells (heterotopias) are found buried in white matter, not having migrated to their proper locations.

Timing, in a neuropsychological context, also is correlated with age-related, ontogenetic changes in the epidemiology of neurological insults across the life-span, the extent of the repertoire of neuropsychological abilities available to be assessed, the probability of functional restitution, and the availability of reliable and valid assessment devices (Boll & Barth, 1981; Chelune & Edwards, 1981; Pape & Fitzhardinge, 1981; Rourke et al.,

TABLE 1. Selective List of Possible Etiologic Agents, Neural Abnormalities, and Neuropsychological Consequences[a]

Etiologic agent	Neural abnormality	Neuropsychological consequence
Genetic	Microcephaly	Mental retardation
Nutritional	Regional agenesis	Learning disability
Traumatic	Migratory defect	Attentional disorder
Infectious	Axon/dendrite	Sensory loss
Metabolic	damage	Motor deficit
Intoxicant	Synaptic loss	Language deficit
Systemic disease	Synaptic aberrance	Speech deficit
Maternal disease	Tissue infarction	Memory disorder
Anoxic-hypoxic	Tissue ischemia	Emotional alteration
Neoplastic	Hemorrhage	Isolated defects
Environmental deprivation	Demyelination	Developmental delay
Idiopathic	Aberrant cell growth	Normal-range functioning
	Gliosis	
	Diffuse	
	Unidentifiable	

[a]Categories are not meant to be exhaustive in delineation or representative of any classification system.

TABLE 2. Selective List of Mediating
Variables Influencing the Impact of an
Etiologic Agent upon Neural Substrate and
Neuropsychological Functioning

Timing, nature, and severity of insult
Age at insult or gestational age at birth
Location, extent, velocity of lesion formation
Plastic, homeostatic, and defense features
Neural commitment
Functional plasticity
Genetic compliment
Diagnosis, treatment, and management
Control over secondary consequences of insult
Prevention

1983). In practice, however, only gross distinctions in timing (i.e., pre/
peri/postnatal) can usually be made for insults that place the child at risk
for altered behavioral development (Kopp, 1983; Kopp & Parmelee, 1979).

Table 1 presents a selective listing of etiologies, neural abnormalities,
and neuropsychological consequences; Table 2 presents a selective listing
of mediating variables that may relate to them. Neuropsychological syndromes are a consequence of neural abnormalities that, themselves, are
due to some underlying etiology. Variations in the outcome of both neuropsychological and neural consequences are due to multidimensional mediating variables that encompass systemic, behavioral, and educational
influences on development. Agents that impair the normal progression of
brain development are varied. Identification of agent etiology, when possible, is part of the medical diagnostic process, even if the diagnosis
occurs years after the insult and can be stated only in probabilistic terms.
Identifying the consequences of an insult on the neural substrate is a
feature of the neurological diagnostic process. Comprehensive descriptions of these identifiable consequences are provided in child neurology
texts (e.g., Menkes, 1985). Neuropsychological consequences span the
observable, assessable aspects of neuropsychological syndromes. General
descriptions of most of these syndromes are readily available—e.g.,
Robinson and Robinson's text (1976) on mental retardation, Gaddes
(1985) on learning disabilities, Barkley (1981) or Weiss and Hechtman
(1979) on hyperactivity.

Genetic diseases (i.e., hereditary and chromosomal aberrations) are
the most frequent causes of neural abnormalities, but, because they are so
often incompatible with continued embryonic or fetal development, only
a minority of such fetuses may actually reach birth. Defined sets of phys-

ical and intellectual features (e.g., Down's and Turner's syndromes) characterize many of the survivable genetic diseases (Robinson & Robinson, 1976). Although the predominant worldwide cause of acquired defective brain development and neurobehavioral morbidity is protein-calorie malnutrition and its attendant milieu of deprivation and infection (Pollitt & Thomson, 1977), the most frequent identifiable cause in industrialized societies is traumatic brain damage. Traumatic brain damage in late infancy and childhood is typically the result of head injuries caused by falls and motor vehicle or recreational accidents (Annegers, Grabow, Kurland, & Laws, 1980).

In an earlier era, perinatal brain trauma was a fairly frequent phenomenon. Although medical advances have resulted in a significant decrease in birth-related mechanical injury, other frequent perinatal causes of neural abnormalities usually result from the spectrum of risks associated with preterm and postterm births. This is particularly true for the very-low-birth-weight (VLBW; defined as a birth weight at or under 1500 g) premature newborn (Levene & Dubowitz, 1982). The VLBW neonate is at particular risk for periventricular and intraventricular hemorrhages from the germinal matrix and the choroid plexus (Goddard-Finegold, 1984). Other risks for the premature newborn include anoxic-ischemia, seizures, infections, and systemic disease. Generally, however, single factors are less important than combinations of complications in determining outcome. Although survival rates have improved, neurobehavioral morbidity is a frequent outcome. Performances of VLBW infants usually are poorer than normal-birthweight infants on neurobehavioral measures at follow-up (Kitchen et al., 1986).

DEVELOPMENTAL NEUROPSYCHOLOGICAL IMPLICATIONS

Many of the challenges in contemporary assessment occur because (1) an insult's nature and timing may be silent at its onset and on medical evaluation, making it an intangible influence on functioning, (2) neuropsychological problems may appear only once the child has "grown up" into a challenging academic environment, where the deficit is forced to reveal itself, (3) the neuropsychological consequences of a prior insult may dissipate via natural compensatory mechanisms and not manifest themselves as might be expected, (4) similar pathological events may lead to different disorders depending on mediators, such as the time of onset, and (5) it is not always possible to distinguish pathological from immature (i.e., still evolving) performances on evaluation.

Except in the context of addressing a referral of a child with a known neurological etiology, it is common for many neuropsychological problems to present themselves without an overt cause and without gross brain damage (children with learning problems being the archetypical example). Many neuropsychological problems may not have an etiology that can be identified from the child's history and performance data. These problems are neuropsychological manifestations of what seems to be a dysfunctional brain, in the absence of other, nonneuropsychological explanations that could provide a more valid, parsimonious understanding of the observed anomalies. Contemporary controversies exist over several basic neuropsychological explanations. Two controversies of relevance to developmental neuropsychological practice are (1) the validity of the concept of "soft" neurological signs, and (2) the value of comparative statements about the "dysfunctional" brain, such as deficit, delay, lag, or retardation in development, used to interpret poor neuropsychological performances.

Clinical concern exists over the ability to identify and attribute soft signs to disordered brain functioning (Shafer, Shaffer, O'Connor, & Stokman, 1983). Soft signs include dysdiadokinesia, mirror movements, dysgraphesthia, astereognosis, and choreiform movements. Soft signs may be a consequence of early acquired lesions due to obstetric difficulties (Prechtl & Stemmer, 1962). Conversely, they may represent normal genetic variants (Nichols & Chen, 1981), they may be generated by stress or be learned behaviors (Prechtl & Stemmer, 1962), or, finally, they may be transient phenomena observed during neurological maturation (Peters, Romaine, & Dykman, 1975). These hypotheses are all generally compatible with a developmental course in which soft signs become more difficult to elicit with increasing age.

The presence of soft signs is sometimes stated to be diagnostically helpful and to possess some predictive usefulness. Some studies have found that, in children of normal intelligence without focal neurological signs, the presence of soft signs is associated with cognitive dysfunction, learning difficulties, and behavioral disturbances (Shafer et al., 1986; Shaffer, O'Connor, Shafer, & Puris, 1983). The usefulness of soft signs as predictors of later neurological and psychiatric status has been the subject of longitudinal research (Sarazin & Spreen, 1986; Shafer et al., 1986; Shaffer, 1978; Stokman et al., 1986). These findings usually have reported persistent soft signs in male adolescents with accompanying behavioral disturbances. Other research findings, however, have been equivocal and contradictory. Some of the contradictions can be explained by misclassification, the reliability of measurement, the confounding effects of focal neurological findings or low levels of cognitive functioning, and biases in sampling created by relying upon clinic-referred children (Shaffer et al., 1983).

Despite the literature that documents their existence and correlates, soft signs are considered to be of minimal value. In general, the base rate of neurological soft signs in children who do not show problems is so high as to suggest that these phenomena are of only limited clinical value for screening and prediction. Although these are associated with learning and behavior problems, even on a long-term basis in certain children, they also are observed frequently in normal children without being correlated with cognitive deficits or maladaptive outcomes.

Assessing whether the term *dysfunctional* actually can be employed to implicate covert aberrant brain function, which can only be detected upon proper and sensitive (typically neuropsychological) evaluation, has a legitimate basis, despite its various controversies (Benton, 1975). Among the many available works, Taylor *et al.* (1984) provide a concise review of the concept of dysfunction in the evolution of developmental neuropsychology; a thoughtful paper by Denckla (1978), which addresses key conceptual concerns, is also of value. One realm of developmental neuropsychological research has been directed at determining the existence of brain–behavior relations in the absence of both overt brain damage and a recognized neurological etiology. Examples of this research include the search for biochemical explanations of minimal brain damage (Wender, 1971), structural hemispheric deviations from the range of normative findings in computed tomography (CT) (Haslam, Dalby, Johns, & Rademaker, 1981; Hier, LeMay, Rosenberger, & Perlo, 1978; LeMay, 1981) and in MRI imaging data of the brains of dyslexic children (Rumsey *et al.*, 1986), and the detailed cytoarchitectonic study of the brains of dyslexics at autopsy (e.g., Galaburda & Kemper, 1979).

Another aspect of concern is whether observed dysfunctions are truly evidence of neurological defects or instead are indicators of a developmental delay. The concept of delayed development infers that there is a slower *rate* of maturation of otherwise normal brain regions and behavioral manifestations of brain functioning (Satz, Taylor, Friel, & Fletcher, 1978). Mental retardation in the absence of a genetic or acquired structural etiology might be considered an example of delayed maturation in its most severe form. A maturational lag is based on the assumption that structure and function normally mature according to an identifiable pattern, are hierarchically organized, and develop sequentially by a system of associated and interrelated components. According to Rodier (1984), there is little evidence of a genuine delay (i.e., a retardation) in brain morphology. A brain that has sustained injury during development does not appear immature or "unfinished." Rather, the regions forming during the injury appear abnormal. The implication of a delay (i.e., that at some point in the future, development will eventually be finished) appears inappropriate to describe morphologically based dysfunctions.

The concept of delayed maturation has been questioned on the grounds that if a delay in function is due to a maturational lag, then psychological development should otherwise be normal, except for the fact that its timing is off (Knights & Bakker, 1976). However, a 12-year-old with a reading problem does not read as if he or she were 7 years old. Research with reading-disabled children suggests that learning strategies used by these children are not merely delayed but are truly aberrant, thus suggesting a deficit in skills rather than skill slowness. An early work by Witelson (1976), for example, posited an association between reading problems and inadequate hemispheric specialization for both linguistic and spatial functioning. The same finding appears true for children with language delays. In addition to a delay in language function, these children often are found to show deviant aspects of language function (Menyuk, 1978).

A key aspect in the debate about developmental delays is found in the learning disability follow-up literature. Studies have demonstrated that although learning-disabled readers may improve their skills somewhat over time, they continue to be disabled readers, never "catching up" to their peers in reading skills (Rutter, Tizard, Yule, Graham, & Whitmore, 1976; Satz & Sparrow, 1970; Satz, et al., 1978; Spreen, 1978). In fact, it is likely that the presence of delay itself may act as an influence upon the child, thus altering the form and quality of continued growth (Zigler, 1969). Conceivably, a developmental delay could result in faulty organization of cognitive skills, causing defective and aberrant levels of performance. On the other hand, the presence of a frank deficit does not imply that some gains cannot be anticipated over time or that aggressive intervention may not prove a significant aid in improving the child's abilities to approximate better adaptive functioning. Validation of an acceptable construct of delay will await the development of direct measures of *in vivo* brain maturation, and a clearer understanding of the relation between function and brain maturation.

CONCLUSIONS

Assessment of children to evaluate suspected neuropsychological deficits has proceeded for many years in the absence of a *formal* neuropsychology of the developing brain (Benton, 1982). A work by E. M. Taylor (1959), as one example, provided detailed instructions concerning the evaluation of psychological consequences of pediatric neurological insults, prior to the appreciation of the value of developmental neuropsychology that occurred during the 1970s. Further, many successful child neuropsychology clinics have been functioning for well over 15 years. Practical clinical demands cannot await the results of systematic basic research, but they can generate interest in executing such work. One prime goal of the emergent neuropsychology of the developing brain is to provide procedures and objective brain–behavior validations to increase both the efficiency and the effective scope of the neuropsychological assessment of the child (Spreen *et al.*, 1984). In the context of advanced imaging technologies (MRI and ultrasound), evolving neuropsychological and educational interventions, and a multidisciplinary professional community, all bodes well for the future of a developmental neuropsychology.

REFERENCES

Adams, R. D. & Victor, M. (1985). *Principles of neurology* (3rd ed.). New York: McGraw-Hill.

Annegers, J. F., Grabow, J. D., Kurland, L. T., & Laws, E. R. (1980). The incidence, causes, and secular trends of head trauma in Olmsted County, Minnesota, 1935–1974. *Neurology, 30,* 912–919.

Bakker, D. J. (1984). The brain as a dependent variable. *Journal of Clinical Neuropsychology, 6,* 1–16.

Barkley, R. A. (1981). *Hyperactive children: A handbook for diagnosis and treatment.* New York: Guilford Press.

Benton, A. (1975). Developmental dyslexia: Neurological aspects. *Advances in Neurology, 7,* 1–27.

Benton, A. (1982). Child neuropsychology: Retrospect and prospect. In J. de Wit & A. Benton (Eds.), *Perspectives in child study: Integration of theory and practice* (pp. 41–61). Lisse: Swets and Zeitlinger.

Boll, T. J., & Barth, J. T. (1981). Neuropsychology of brain damage in children. In S. B. Filskov & T. J. Boll (Eds.), *Handbook of clinical neuropsychology* (pp. 418–452). New York: Wiley Press.

Bronson, G. (1982). Structure, status and characteristics of the nervous system at birth. In P. Stratton (Ed.), *Psychobiology of the human newborn* (pp. 99–114). New York: Wiley Press.

Bryden, M. P. (1982). *Laterality: Functional asymmetry in the intact brain.* New York: Academic Press.

Chelune, G. J., & Edwards, P. (1981). Early brain lesions: Ontogenetic environmental considerations. *Journal of Consulting and Clinical Psychology, 49,* 777–790.

Chi, J. G., Dooling, E. C., & Gilles, F. H. (1977). Gyral development of the human brain. *Annals of Neurology, 1,* 86–93.

Corballis, M. C., & Morgan, M. J. (1978). On the biological basis of human laterality: I. Evidence for a maturational left-right gradient. *Behavioral and Brain Sciences, 2,* 261–336.

Cotman, C. W., & Nieto-Sampedro, M. (1982). Brain function, synapse renewal, and plasticity. *Annual Review of Psychology, 33,* 371–401.

Cotman, C. W., & Nietro-Sampedro, M. (1984). Cell biology of synaptic plasticity. *Science, 225,* 1287–1294.

Cowan, W. M., Fawcett, J. W., O'Leary, D. D. M., & Stanfield, B. B. (1984). Regressive events in neurogenesis. *Science, 225,* 1258–1265.

Denckla, M. B. (1978). Minimal brain dysfunction. In J. S. Chall & A. F. Mirsky (Eds.), *Education and the brain, 77th yearbook of the National Society for the Study of Education* (pp. 223–268). Chicago: University of Chicago Press.

DiSimoni, F. (1978). *The Token Test for Children, manual.* Hingham, MA: Teaching Resources Corp.

Dobbing, J., & Sands, J. (1971). Vulnerability of developing brain: IX. The effect of nutritional growth retardation on the timing of the brain growth spurt. *Biology of the Neonate, 19,* 363–378.

Dobbing, J., & Smart, J. L. (1974). Vulnerability of developing brain and behavior. *British Medical Journal, 30,* 164–168.

Elliott, H. (1969). *Textbook of anatomy.* Philadelphia: Lippincott.

Flechsig, P. (1901). Developmental (myelogenetic) localization in the cerebral cortex of the human subject. *Lancet, 2,* 1027–1029.

Fuller, P. W., Guthrie, R. D., & Alvord, E. C. (1983). A proposed neuropathological basis for learning disabilities in children born prematurely. *Developmental Medicine and Child Neurology, 25,* 214–231.

Gaddes, W. H. (1985). *Learning disabilities and brain function: A neuropsychological approach* (2nd ed.). New York: Springer-Verlag.

Gaddes, W. H., & Crockett, D. J. (1973). *The Spreen-Benton aphasia tests, normative data as a measure of normal language development* (Research Monograph No. 25). Victoria, BC: University of Victoria.

Galaburda, A. M., & Eidelberg, D. (1982). Symmetry and asymmetry in the human posterior thalamus. II. Thalamic lesions in a case of developmental dyslexia. *Archives of Neurology, 39,* 333–336.

Galaburda, A. M., & Kemper, T. L. (1979). Cytoarchitectonic abnormalities in developmental dyslexia: A case study. *Annals of Neurology, 6,* 94–100.

Galaburda, A. M., Sherman, G. F., Rosen, G. D., Aboitiz, F., & Geschwind, N. (1985). Developmental dyslexia: Four consecutive patients with cortical anomalies. *Annals of Neurology, 18,* 222–233.

Gazzaniga, M. S., Stein, D., & Volpe, E. T. (1979). *Functional neuroscience.* New York: Harper & Row.

Geschwind, N., & Galaburda, A. M. (1985a). Cerebral lateralization: Biological mechanisms, associations, and pathology. A hypothesis and a program for research. *Archives of Neurology, 42,* 428–459.

Geschwind, N., & Galaburda, A. M. (1985b). Cerebral lateralization: Biological mechanisms, associations, and pathology. A hypothesis and a program for research. *Archives of Neurology, 42,* 521–552.

Geschwind, N., & Galaburda, A. M. (1985c). Cerebral lateralization: Biological mechanisms, associations, and pathology. A hypothesis and a program for research. *Archives of Neurology, 42,* 634–654.

Goddard-Finegold, J. (1984). Periventricular, intraventricular hemorrhages in the premature newborn: Update on pathologic features, pathogenesis, and possible means of prevention. *Archives of Neurology, 41,* 766–771.

Goldman, P. S. (1979). Development and plasticity of frontal association cortex in the infrahuman primate. In C. L. Ludlow & M. E. Doran-Quine (Eds.), *The neurological bases of language disorders in children: Methods and directions for research* (NIH Publication No. 79-440) (pp. 1–16). Washington, DC: U.S. Government Printing Office.

Goldman, P. S., & Galkin, T. W. (1978). Prenatal removal of frontal association cortex in the fetal rhesus monkey: Anatomical and functional consequences in postnatal life. *Brain Research, 152,* 451–485.

Goldman-Rakic, P., Isserhoff, A., Schwartz, M. L., & Bugbee, N. M. (1983). The neurobiology of cognitive development. In M. M. Haith & J. J. Campos (Eds.), *Infancy and developmental psychobiology;* Vol. 2 of P. H. Mussen (Ed.), *Handbook of child psychology* (4th ed., pp. 281–344). New York: Wiley Press.

Greenough, W. T., & Juraska, J. M. (1979). Experience-induced changes in brain fine structure: Their behavioral implications. In M. E. Hahn, C. Jensen, & B. C. Dudek (Eds.), *Development and evolution of brain size* (pp. 295–320). New York: Academic Press.

Haslam, R. H. A., Dalby, J. T., Johns, R. D., & Rademaker, A. W. (1981). Cerebral asymmetry in developmental dyslexia. *Archives of Neurology, 38,* 679–682.

Hebb, D. O. (1949). *Organization of behavior.* New York: Wiley Press.

Hier, D. B., LeMay, M., Rosenberger, P. B., & Perlo, V. P. (1978). Developmental dyslexia: Evidence for a subgroup with a reversal of cerebral asymmetry. *Archives of Neurology, 35*, 90–92.

Isaacson, R. L. (1975). The myth of recovery from early brain damage. In N. R. Ellis (Ed.), *Aberrant development in infancy* (pp. 1–25). Potomac: Erlbaum.

Jacobsen, C. F. (1936). Studies of cerebral function in primates. *Comparative Psychological Monographs, 13*, 1–68.

Jacobson, M. (1978). *Developmental neurobiology* (2nd ed.). New York: Plenum Press.

Johnson, M. A., Pennock, J. M., Bydder, G. M., Dubowitz, L. M. S., Thomas, D. J., & Young, I. R. (1987). Serial MR imaging in neonatal cerebral injury. *American Journal of Neuroradiology, 8*, 83–92.

Kandel, E. R. & Schwartz, J. H. (1981). *Principles of neural science*. New York: Elsevier/North-Holland.

Kennard, M. A. (1940). Relation of age to motor impairment in man and subhuman primates. *Archives of Neurology and Psychiatry, 44*, 377–397.

Kennard, M. A. (1942). Cortical reorganization of motor function: Studies on series of monkeys of different ages from infancy to maturity. *Archives of Neurology and Psychiatry, 47*, 227–240.

Kitchen, W. H., Rickards, W. H., Ryan, M. M., Ford, G. W., Lissenden, J. V., & Boyle, L. W. (1986). Improved outcome to two years of very low birthweight infants: Fact or artifact. *Developmental Medicine and Child Neurology, 28*, 579–588.

Knights, R. M., & Bakker, D. J. (Eds.). (1976). *The neuropsychology of learning disorders: Theoretical approaches*. Baltimore: University Park Press.

Knobloch, H., & Pasamanick, B. (1966). Prospective studies on the epidemiology of reproductive casualty: Methods, findings, and some implications. *Merrill-Palmer Quarterly of Behaviour and Development, 12*, 27–43.

Kopp, C. B. (1983). Risk factors in development. In M. M. Haith & J. J. Campos (Eds.), *Infancy and developmental psychobiology*; Vol. 2 of P. H. Mussen (Ed.), *Handbook of child psychology* (4th ed., pp. 1081–1188). New York: Wiley Press.

Kopp, C. B., & Parmelee, A. H. (1979). Prenatal and perinatal influences on infant behavior. In J. Osofsky (Ed.), *Handbook on infant behavior* (pp. 29–74). New York: Wiley-Interscience.

LeCours, A. R. (1975). Myelogenetic correlates of the development of speech and language. In E. H. Lenneberg & E. Lenneberg (Eds.), *Foundations of language development: A multidisciplinary approach* (Vol. 1, pp. 121–135). New York: Academic Press.

Lee, B. C. P., Lipper, E., Nass, R., Ehrlich, M. E., deCiccio-Bloom, E., & Auld, P. A. M. (1986). MRI of the central nervous system in neonates and young children. *American Journal of Neuroradiology, 7*, 605–616.

LeMay, M. (1981). Are there radiological changes in the brains of individuals with dyslexia? *Bulletin of the Orton Society, 31*, 135–141.

Lemire, R. J., Loeser, J. D., Leech, R. W., & Alvord, E. C. (1975). *Normal and abnormal development of the human nervous system*. New York: Harper & Row.

Levene, M. I., & Dubowitz, L. M. S. (1982). Low-birth-weight babies long-term follow-up. *British Journal of Hospital Medicine, 24*, 487–491.

Lezak, M. (1983). *Neuropsychological assessment* (2nd ed.). New York: Oxford Press.

Lund, R. D. (1978). *Development and plasticity of the brain: An introduction*. New York: Oxford Press.

Luria, A. R. (1973). *The working brain: An introduction to neuropsychology*. Middlesex: Penguin Press.

McArdle, C. B., Richardson, C. J., Nicholas, D. A., Mirfakhree, M., Hayden, C. K., & Amparo, E. G. (1987). Developmental features of the neonatal brain: MR imaging: Part I. Gray–white matter differentiation and myelination. *Radiology, 162*, 223–229.

McCarthy, D. (1972). *McCarthy scales of children's abilities*. New York: Psychological Corporation.

Menkes, J. H. (1985). *Textbook of child neurology* (3rd ed.). Philadelphia: Lea & Febiger.

Menyuk, P. (1978). Linguistic problems in children with developmental dysphasia. In M. A. Wyke (Ed.), *Developmental dysphasia* (pp. 135–157). London: Academic Press.

Naeye, R. L., & Peters, E. C. (1987). Antenatal hypoxia and low IQ values. *American Journal of Diseases of Childhood, 141,* 50–54.

Nichols, P., & Chen, T. (1981). *Minimal brain dysfunction: A prospective study*. Hillsdale, NJ: Lawrence Erlbaum.

Oppenheim, R. W. (1981). Ontogenetic adaptations and retrogressive processes in the development of the nervous system and behavior: A neuroembryological perspective. In K. J. Connolly & H. F. R. Prechtl (Eds.), *Maturation and development: Biological and psychological perspectives* (pp. 73–101). Philadelphia: Lippincott.

Pape, K. E., & Fitzhardinge, P. M. (1981). Perinatal damage to the developing brain. In A. Milusky, E. A. Friedman, & L. Gluck (Eds.), *Advances in perinatal medicine* (Vol. 1, pp. 45–86). New York: Plenum Press.

Passler, M. A., Isaac, W., & Hynd, G. W. (1985). Neuropsychological development of behavior attributed to frontal lobe functioning in children. *Developmental Neuropsychology, 1,* 349–370.

Peters, J. E., Romaine, J. S., & Dykman, R. A. (1975). A special neurological examination of children with learning disabilities. *Developmental Medicine and Child Neurology, 17,* 63–78.

Pollitt, E., & Thomson, C. (1977). Protein-caloric malnutrition and behavior: A view from psychology. In R. J. Wurtman & J. J. Wurtman (Eds.), *Nutrition and the brain* (Vol. 2, pp. 261–304). New York: Raven Press.

Prechtl, H. F. R., & Stemmer, C. H. (1962). The choreiform syndrome in children. *Developmental Medicine and Child Neurology, 4,* 119–127.

Purpura, D. P., & Reaser, E. P. (1974). *Methodological approaches the study of brain maturation and its abnormalities*. Baltimore: University Park Press.

Purves, D., & Lichtman, J. W. (1980). Elimination of synapses in the developing nervous system. *Science, 210,* 153–157.

Rakic, P. (1981). Developmental events leading to laminar and areal organization of the neocortex. In F. Schmitt (Ed.), *The organization of the cerebral cortex* (pp. 7–28). Cambridge: M.I.T. Press.

Reitan, R. M., & Davison, L. A. (Eds.). (1974). *Clinical neuropsychology: Current status and applications*. New York: Wiley Press.

Risser, A. H. (1984, February). *Nuclear magnetic resonance imaging: A primer for the neuropsychologist*. Paper presented at the XIIth annual meeting of the International Neuropsychological Society, Houston, TX.

Robinson, H., & Robinson, N. (1976). *The mentally retarded child* (2nd ed.). New York: McGraw-Hill.

Rodier, P. M. (1984). Exogenous sources of malformations in development. In E. S. Gollin (Ed.), *Malformations of development: Biological and psychological sources and consequences* (pp. 287–313). New York: Academic Press.

Rourke, B. P., Bakker, D. J., Fisk, F. L., & Strang, J. D. (1983). *Child neuropsychology: An introduction to theory, research, and clinical practice*. New York: Guilford Press.

Rumsey, J. M., Dorwart, R., Vermess, M., Denckla, M. B., Kruesi, M. J. P., & Rapoport, J. L. (1986). Magnetic resonance imaging of brain anatomy in severe developmental dyslexia. *Archives of Neurology, 43,* 1045–1046.

Rutter, M., Tizard, J., Yule, W., Graham, P., & Whitmore, K. (1976). Research report: Isle of Wight studies 1964–1974. *Psychological Medicine, 6,* 313–332.

Sarazin, F. F-A. & Spreen, O. (1986). Fifteen-year stability of some neuropsychological tests in learning disabled subjects with and without neurological impairment. *Journal of Clinical and Experimental Neuropsychology, 8,* 190–200.

Satz, P., & Sparrow, S. (1970). Specific developmental dyslexia: A theoretical formulation. In D. J. Bakker & P. Satz (Eds.), *Specific reading disability: Advances in theory and method* (pp. 17–39). Rotterdam: Rotterdam University Press.

Satz, P., Taylor, H. G., Friel, J., & Fletcher, J. M. (1978). Some developmental and predictive precursors of reading disabilities: A six year follow-up. In A. Benton & D. Pearl (Eds.), *Dyslexia: An appraisal of current knowledge* (pp. 313–348). New York: Oxford Press.

Schneider, G. E. (1979). Is it really better to have your brain disease early? A revision of the "Kennard principle." *Neuropsychologia, 17,* 557–584.

Shafer, S. Q., Shaffer, D., O'Connor, P. A., & Stokman, C. J. (1983). Hard thoughts on neurological "soft signs." In M. Rutter (Ed.), *Developmental neuropsychiatry* (pp. 133–143). New York: Guilford Press.

Shafer, S. Q. Stokman, C. J., Shaffer. D., Ng, S. K-C., O'Connor, P. A., & Schonfield, I. S. (1986). Ten year consistency in neurological test performance of children without focal neurological deficit. *Developmental Medicine and Child Neurology, 28,* 417–427.

Shaffer, D. (1978). "Soft" neurological signs and later psychiatric disorder—A review. *Journal of Psychology and Psychiatry and Allied Disciplines, 19,* 63–65.

Shaffer, D., O'Connor, P. A., Shafer, S. Q., & Puris, S. (1983). Neurological soft signs: Their origins and significance for behaviour. In M. Rutter (Ed.), *Developmental neuropsychiatry* (pp. 144–164). New York: Guilford Press.

Spreen, O. (1978). *Learning disabled children growing up* (Final report to Health and Welfare Canada, Health Programs Branch). Ottawa: Health and Welfare Canada.

Spreen, O., Tupper, D., Risser, A., Tuokko, H., & Edgell, D. (1984). *Human developmental neuropsychology.* New York: Oxford Press.

St. James-Roberts, I. (1979). Neurological plasticity, recovery from brain insult, and child development. In H. W. Reese & P. Lipsitt (Eds.). *Advances in child development and behavior* (Vol. 14, pp. 253–319). New York: Academic Press.

Stokman, C. J., Shafer, S. Q., Shaffer, D., Ng, S. K-C., O'Connor, P. A., & Wolff, R. W. (1986). Assessment of neurological soft signs in adolescents: Reliability studies. *Developmental Medicine and Child Neurology, 28,* 428–439.

Taylor, E. M. (1959). *Psychological appraisal of children with cerebral defects.* Cambridge: The Commonwealth Fund.

Taylor, H. G., Fletcher, J. M., & Satz, P. (1984). Neuropsychological assessment of children. In G. Goldstein & M. Hersen (Eds.), *Handbook of psychological assessment* (pp. 211–234). New York: Pergamon Press.

Teuber, H-L. (1975). Recovery of function after brain injury in man. *Outcome of severe damage to the central nervous system, Ciba Foundation Symposium 34 (new series)* (pp. 159–186). Amsterdam: Elsevier.

Thomas, J. (1968). *Introduction to human embryology.* Philadelphia: Lea & Febiger.

Towbin, A. (1971). Organic causes of minimal brain dysfunction: Perinatal origin of minimal cerebral lesions. *Journal of the American Medical Association, 217,* 1207–1214.

Turkewitz, G., & Kenny, P. (1982). Limitations on input as a basis for neural organization and perceptual development: A preliminary theoretical statement. *Developmental Psychobiology, 15,* 357–368.

Walsh, K. W. (1978). *Neuropsychology: A clinical approach.* Edinburgh: Churchill Livingstone.

Weiss, G., & Hechtman, C. (1979). The hyperactive child syndrome. *Science, 205,* 1348–1354.

Wender, P. H. (1971). *Minimal brain dysfunction in children.* New York: Wiley-Interscience.

Williams, R., & Caviness, V. B. (1984). Normal and abnormal brain development. In R. E.

Tarter & G. Goldstein (Eds.), *Advances in clinical neuropsychology* (Vol. 2, pp. 1–62). New York: Plenum Press.

Winick, M., & Rosso, P. (1969). The effect of severe early malnutrition on cellular growth of human brain. *Pediatric Research, 3,* 181–187.

Witelson, S. F. (1976). Abnormal right hemisphere specialization in developmental dyslexia. In R. M. Knights & D. J. Bakker (Eds.), *The neuropsychology of learning disorders: Theoretical approaches* (pp. 233–256). Baltimore: University Park Press.

Witelson, S. F. (1977). Early hemisphere specialization and interhemisphere plasticity: An empirical and theoretical review. In S. J. Segalowitz & F. A. Gruber (Eds.), *Language development and neurological theory* (pp. 213–287). New York: Academic Press.

Yakovlev, P. I., & LeCours, A. R. (1967). The myelogenetic cycles of regional maturation of the brain. In A. Minkowski (Ed.), *Regional development of the brain in early life* (pp. 3–69). Oxford: Blackwell Scientific.

Zigler, E. (1969). Development versus difference theories of mental retardation and the problem of motivation. *American Journal of Mental Deficiency, 73,* 536–556.

The Role of Neuropsychological Assessment in Relation to Other Types of Assessment with Children

ERIN D. BIGLER

INTRODUCTION

Neuropsychological assessment represents an important aspect in the overall evaluation of the child with neurological disorder. The efficacy of neuropsychological findings, however, can be greatly enhanced by a better understanding of the interrelationship between neuropsychological testing and other aspects of the neurological and psychological evaluation. With recent advances in neurodiagnostics, particularly in the area of brain imaging and related assessment techniques, there is a greater abundance of clinical information that must be integrated with neuropsychological findings. This has resulted in further overlap between specialty areas in the clinical neurosciences and has furthered the need for one specialty to understand the significance of findings in the others. To that end, this chapter will attempt to relate and contrast neuropsychological test findings with other assessment practices.

First, the pediatric neurological exam will be reviewed. This has been a standard part of any neurological evaluation with children, and frequently it is the first examination undertaken with the child presenting neurobehavioral symptoms. Accordingly, it is important to understand the relationship between pediatric neurological exam findings and neuropsychological assessment. There has been a marked increase in the utilization of brain imaging and electrophysiological techniques in the as-

ERIN D. BIGLER • Austin Neurological Clinic, Austin, Texas, and Department of Psychology, University of Texas at Austin, Austin, Texas.

sessment of neurological disorders of children. The next two sections of the chapter will address these areas in relationship to neuropsychological assessment. Last, the unique role of neuropsychological assessment in the context of traditional psychological testing will be reviewed and discussed.

PEDIATRIC NEUROLOGICAL EXAM

Basic Components

The pediatric neurological exam (PNE) naturally varies with the age of the child. For the purpose of this chapter, the neurological exam outlined will be based on the child 4 years of age and older since it is at this age that the exam begins to take on the characteristics of the more formal, systematic exam of the adolescent or adult patient (Hartlage & Krawiecki, 1984). In general, the components of the exam include an evaluation of gait and station, motor and sensory function, reflex integrity, and physical development, along with a brief overview of mental status. These topic areas will be briefly reviewed below.

Station and Gait

Normal gait consists of smooth, effortless movement that is fluid, symmetric, and rhythmic (Brown, 1982). Leg position should be narrow-based and arm swing should be even. Such features also should be present when gait is stressed such as in tiptoe and heel walking, balancing, or running. Abnormal motor findings constitute a deviation from this. For example, spastic gait typically is characterized by the child who has a shuffling gait, with flexion at the knees and hips, along with increased adductor tone. These abnormal movements are greatly exaggerated when the child is asked to run or when gait is otherwise stressed. These can result from damage to the primary motor system at various levels or regions. Gait disturbance secondary to cerebellar involvement is quite different, with the prominent features being a wide-based, veering, and unsteady ataxic gait in which the child has great difficulty in controlling or adjusting to postural change (i.e., turning around). With peripheral motor involvement, gait disturbance typically takes the form of a waddling or steppage gait. The examination for disturbance in gait and station is made through direct inspection of the child performing various movements.

Motor Function

Muscle tone and strength are tested by the child's strength of grip and limb strength resistence in various positions of the extremities. Muscle tone is visually and tactually inspected, as well as the child's response to reflex assessment in upper and lower extremities. Hyper- or hyporeflexia, or abnormal muscle tone activity, may be a sign of peripheral or central nervous system involvement. The differential diagnosis is based on the pathognomonic signs present in relation to other findings (e.g., hyper-reflexia associated with spasticity in hemiplegia of cortical origin) and is thoroughly discussed in the work of Brown (1982). Fine motor control typically is examined by having the child attempt to make rapid, repetitive finger-oscillatory movements between the index finger and thumb, fol-lowed by successive finger-tapping movements where each finger is touch-ed in succession by the thumb. By the age of 6, these movements should be mastered and executed with little difficulty (Herskowitz & Rosman, 1982). By itself, impaired performance on these fine motor tasks has no particular localizing significance other than indicating impaired motor system func-tioning. Finger-to-nose and heel-to-shin movements provide an index for assessing cerebellar integrity. Cerebellar tremor may be seen in conjunc-tion with cerebellar movement disorder, with the tremor present on inten-tion or a loss of rhythmicity and smoothness of movement during action.

Cranial Nerve Function

The cranial nerve exam historically has been the foundation of the neurological exam and has changed very little in the past century (Van Allen, 1969). For children, cranial nerves 1, 5, and 7 through 12 are tested essentially as in the adult. Optic nerve (second cranial nerve) function is a critical part of any neurological exam but represents some obstacles for the younger child. Simple visual acuity is usually measured first, fol-lowed by visual field testing, which may require some innovative meth-ods for younger children (see Touwen, 1979). Cranial nerves 3, 4, and 6 control ocular motility and are tested by observing eye movements. Younger children may have difficulty in following commands, and in such cases the examiner will have to depend on observation of spon-taneous performance.

Sensory-Perceptual Function

Simple touch usually is tested by the child's ability to report light touch. Two-point tactile discrimination is another test of simple tactile perception. By the time a child is 6 years of age, formal testing of stereog-nosis (tactile perception of a coin, paper clip, or key placed in the palm of the hand) also can be undertaken. By 8 years of age, formal graphesthesic perception can be tested using letters or numbers "written" on the palm or fingertips (Herskowitz & Rosman, 1982). These tests, along with the perception of double simultaneous tactile stimulation, constitute the assessment of higher parietal function. Abnormalities found on any of these assessment techniques typically imply impaired parietal lobe functioning contralateral to the side on which the tactile errors were made. Auditory screening is typically based on the child's ability to hear whisper speech by the examiner and the perception of double simultaneous auditory stimulation. Abnormalities within this aspect of the examination typically do not have clear pathognomonic significance but indicate the need for further investigation of the auditory system. Finally, double simultaneous visual stimulation is utilized to examine visual inattention/neglect in one hemifield or the other, and it is sometimes included in the cranial nerve evaluation when visual functioning is examined. Visual inattention/neglect/extinction in one visual field suggests contralateral occipital lobe involvement (and/or adjacent association cortical areas).

The Nature of Findings

The PNE is, at best, a screening exam and review of systems. It represents an overview of central nervous system (CNS) functioning from which some inferences can be made concerning the integrity or dysfunction of neurological systems. Pathological indicators on the standard PNE typically represent focal versus generalized dysfunction. For example, a child with a history of severe encephalitis may show generalized motor, sensory, and reflex abnormalities that point toward nonspecific cerebrocortical dysfunction, as opposed to the child who sustained a focal brain injury with resultant hemiplegia (a focal sign indicating contralateral frontal involvement) as the only neurological abnormality. Similarly, abnormalities found on the PNE typically imply some direct index or pathognomonic sign of underlying neurological deficit, the so-called hard neurological signs.

Anomalous Physical Development as Markers for CNS Pathology

Congenital physical anomalies may be indicators of abnormal brain development due to altered embryogenesis (genetic) or an insult (e.g., trauma, toxicity) early in pregnancy. The occurrence of CNS anomalies in relation to age of embryo or fetus is represented in Table 1. The presence of such physical anomalies is a direct indication of aberrant CNS organization and development (Williams & Caviness, 1984).

Table 2 presents the Yale Neuropsychoeducational Assessment Scales-Stigmata schedule, which overviews the potential physical stigmata that may be present. Although the presence of one of these anomalies is not necessarily clinically significant, numerous studies (see review by Shaywitz, 1982) have suggested that the presence of three or more of these minor anatomical defects may be associated with a variety of neu-

TABLE 1. Occurrence of CNS Anomalies in Relation to Age of Embryo or Fetus[a]

Days 18-19-20-21-22-23-24-25-26-27-28-29-30-31-32-33-34-35-36-37-38-39-40-41-42-43-44-45-46-47-48- Months 3-4-5- 6- 7-8- 9-10
49-50-51-52-53-54-55-56

Embryogenesis | Fetogenesis

Dysraphias ————————→ 27 days
(Anencephaly, spina bifida)
Holoprosencephalon ————————→ 29 days
A genesis of interhemispheric connections ————————

Abnormal cellular migration in the cerebral cortex ————————→ 6th month ————————→ 7th month
(Pachygyria, lissencephaly, heteropia of gray matter)

Porencephaly ————→ 9th month
Hydrencephaly ————→ 9th month

[a]The length of each arrow corresponds to the age of the embryo or fetus during which the causative (teratogenic) injury to the nervous system is believed to occur. For example, it is suggested that the insult to the brain that results in anencephaly occurs between day 18, which is the date of the appearance of the neural plate, and day 27, when the tubulation of the neural plate is terminated. The time indicators shown here for the production of anomalies are tentative; they are suggested on the basis of animal experiments and a few rare observations of embryos and fetuses presenting with a particular anomaly. (From Duckett, 1981.)

TABLE 2. Anomaly Grading Scale of the Yale
Neuropsychoeducational Assessment Scales

Hair:	Frontal bossing:
	Whorls: (1) (<1 or a line ≥ 1″ long)
	Electric hair: (Normal) (Fine; soon awry) (Very fine; will not comb)
	Coarse, brittle:
Eyes:	Strabismus:
	Ptosis:
	Crusting of lid:
	Epicanthus: (absent) (partial) (deep)
Ears:	Malformed
	Asymmetric:
	Pits or tags:
	Soft and pliable:
	Low set (above) (≤0.5 cm below) (>0.5 cm below) line through nosebridge and eye
	Lobe extension: (below attachment) (straight back) (toward crown)
Nose:	Antiverted nostrils:
	Hypoplastic tip:
	Hypoplastic philtrum:
Mouth:	Palate: (normal arch) (flat steeple ⌐⌐) (high steeple ⌒)
	Cleft palate—soft or hard:
	Tongue furrowed:
	Tongue with smooth-rough spots:
	Teeth—enamel hypoplasia; carious:
	Teeth small:
	Upper vermillion thin:
Jaw:	Prominent maxilla:
	Micrognathia:
	Prognathia:
	Midfacial hypoplasia:
Torso:	Webbed neck:
	Pectus excavatum:
	Pectus carinatum:
	Nipples widely spaced:
	Heart murmur:
	Vertebral defects:
	Hernia—umbilical, diaphragm, groin; diastasis recti
	Hypospadias:
Skin:	Thin skin—visible vascular pattern:
	Dry, coarse, rough:
	Café-au-lait:
	Hemangiomata:
	Nails—hypoplastic or dysplastic:
Hands:	Palm—coarse skin:
	Palm—single transverse crease:
	Small, broad hands:
	Thin, tapering hands:
	Joint limitation:
	Clinodactyly:
	Broad first toe or thumb:
Feet:	Gap between first and second toes:
	Partial syndactylia of 2nd and 3rd toes:
	Length of 2nd and third toes:
	(2nd > 3rd) (2nd = 3rd) (2nd < 3rd)

Note. From Shaywitz, 1982.

robehavioral syndromes, including mental retardation and associated intellectual deficits, learning disability, developmental delay, and attention deficit disorder. The presence of a minor congenital anomaly (MCA), although signifying the potential presence of some neurological irregularity, lacks specificity with respect to locus of neurological dysfunction. Whereas MCA findings appear to represent a "marker," with the presence of these findings being indicative of possible incomplete or irregular neuronal development, only limited clinical inferences can be made beyond this point. Such early factors may have a deleterious effect on subsequent development, as well as on the development of related systems (e.g., early dysfunction of perceptual systems may affect motor control, although no direct motor involvement is present). Thus, in children with MCAs, there is a greater likelihood of underlying aberrant neuronal development, which, in turn, may be associated with a greater likelihood of associated neurological abnormalities. However, the presence of MCAs should not be construed as pathognomonic indicators *per se.*

"Hard" versus "Soft" Neurological Findings

A standard PNE usually includes an examination of minor neurological dysfunction (Touwen, 1979). Whereas abnormalities of gait and station, reflex, motor strength, or primary sensation may indicate focal "hard" neurological signs, a variety of minor neurological abnormalities (the so-called soft neurological signs) may be elicited in some children whose neurological exam is otherwise normal. Minor neurological abnormalities also may coexist with more specific neurological abnormalities.

The most common minor neurological abnormalities include dysdiadochokinesia, associated movements (variously known as synkinetic movements, comovements, and mirror movements), and the so-called choreiform twitch. Associated movements are normally present in the infant and young child and decrease with age. In fact, the disappearance of the elicitation of associated movements is taken as a sign of functional maturation of the CNS (Herskowitz & Rosman, 1982). The presence of the "minor" neurological abnormalities beyond the age of 8 or 9, however, is felt to be suggestive of neuropathology, although the meaning of such signs in these older children remains in doubt. Numerous studies tend to indicate a higher incidence of cognitive dysfunction, learning difficulties, attention deficit disorder, and other psychiatric disturbance in children with neurological "soft signs" and MCAs (Kaufman, 1981; Rie & Rie, 1980; Shaffer et al., 1985; Shafer, Shaffer, O'Connor, & Stokman, 1983). But as Shaffer, O'Connor, Shafer, and Propis (1983) state, "the relationship of 'soft signs' to . . . specific syndromes is less certain."

Research to date suggests that the origin of minor neurological abnormalities is likely multifactorial. In some children, the presence of these characteristics may be a consequence of cerebral injury in the prenatal or perinatal period (see Table 1). For others, the presence of these irregularities is under genetic control and expression, representing developmental differences. In still others, there may be an interactive effect (e.g., motor maladroitness may interfere with critical time periods of motor development). Yet no research has demonstrated any direct relationship between the presence of such findings and specific neuropsychological impairments. Rather, these neurological "soft signs" appear to be "markers" suggestive of underlying neurological irregularity, and clinical correlation with presenting problem and other neurological findings is needed on an individual case basis.

Mental Status Characteristics of Neurologically Impaired Children

Behavioral observation and the evaluation of the child's interaction with the examiner are integral aspects of the PNE. First, the child's appearance should be noted with respect to appropriateness of dress, grooming, and hygiene. As children grow older, they tend to be more concerned about their appearance, but some children with neurological impairment may remain somewhat oblivious and uncaring about how they appear. An assessment of the child's general level of psychomotor activity is essential, particularly in terms of general activity level, degree of impulsivity, and attention. Some children with underlying neurological dysfunction tend to be more active, impulsive, and inattentive, characteristics also seen in attention deficit disorder.

There is some tendency in children with neurological impairment to be concrete in their interpretation of proverbs and to have difficulty with any mental task requiring verbal abstraction. This also serves as an informal assessment of the child's verbal intelligence. Likewise, speech content may provide further insight into the child's thought processes. Certain child psychiatric disorders, as with adults, will be manifested via distorted, illogical thinking. The mental status exam always should examine for delusions, hallucinations, tangentiality, or looseness of thinking as well as confusion (checking for orientation to time, place, and person). For the normal child, speech should be flowing, logical, and in direct relationship to questions asked. Further, it should contain spontaneous content rich in information concerning the child's interests, hobbies, and general sense of well-being. Insight and judgment are also elemental aspects of a mental status exam, and neurologically impaired children frequently will display some deficits in these realms. Shaffer et al. (1985), in a prospective study of children with minor neurological abnormalities first identified at age 7 and followed up 10 years later, found this group to be more anxious, withdrawn, and depressed.

Relationship between Pediatric Neurological Exam and Neuropsychological Assessment

The PNE constitutes a review of neurological systems, but by no means is it an exhaustive evaluation of them. Rather, the neurological exam is more of a screening procedure, the results of which direct the nature and type of further investigations. Much of the PNE is involved in assessing brain function that would be described as rudimentary and reflexive. Accordingly, a given patient may have a "normal" PNE but could have underlying cerebral damage/dysfunction. This is particularly true when cerebral involvement is in "silent" association cortical areas where no specific motor, sensory, or language deficit is present.

Neuropsychological assessment, on the other hand, provides a comprehensive evaluation of functions that are related to, or dependent on, higher cerebral processes. Neuropsychological assessment likewise provides an index of functional integrity of more basic cerebral processes. Accordingly, the two techniques overlap to a certain extent but for the most part are examining brain function at different levels and to different degrees.

The PNE, particularly when minor neurological abnormalities are found, may give only a hint that a neurological deficit may be present. In such cases, the neuropsychological evaluation may be the essential assessment tool in documenting the nature and type of impairment present. Also, a child that is experiencing learning problems, developmental delays, or change in conduct frequently will be taken first to the pediatrician to determine if there is some "medical" explanation for these behaviors (Dworkin, 1985; Schimschock, Milford-Cooley, & Cooley, 1984). In such cases, the PNE is the initial assessment tool, which in turn may lead to the more comprehensive neuropsychological assessment or other neurodiagnostic tests.

Several studies (see Touwen, 1979) have attempted to utilize PNE findings to predict neuropsychological outcome. These studies have been disappointing in that there appears to be little direct relationship between PNE findings and neuropsychological impairment. This should not be surprising, though, when one considers the complexity of human behavior, particularly cognitive processes, and the rather elementary nature of the PNE. These studies do support the role of the PNE as an initial assessment procedure that represents an overview of basic CNS integrity in which abnormal findings direct further studies.

NEURORADIOLOGICAL TESTS

Brain imaging via the methods of computerized axial tomography (CT) and magnetic resonance imaging (MRI) have revolutionized diag-

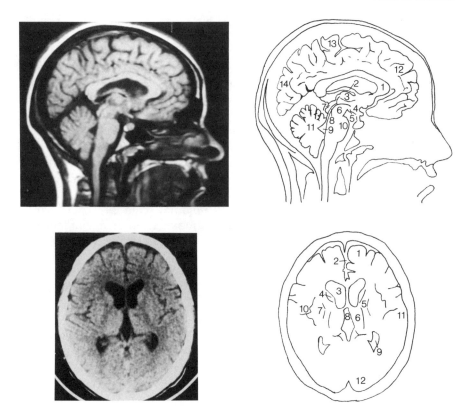

FIGURE 1. MRI and CT depictions of neuroanatomy. The MRI scan on top is taken in the sagittal plane and depicts normal brain anatomy. Major anatomic structures are labeled numerically (1-corpus callosum, 2-fornix, 3-thalamus, 4-hypothalamus, 5-mamillary bodies, 6-tegmentum, 7-tectum, 8-aqueduct of Sylvius, 9-fourth ventricle, 10-pons, 11-cerebellum, 12-frontal lobe, 13-parietal lobe, 14-occipital lobe, 15-temporal lobe). Note the clarity and resolution that can be obtained with MRI imaging. The CT scan on the bottom is in the horizontal plane. This patient was an 18-year-old male who had suffered a severe head injury 1 year prior to the CT. This scan was selected because it demonstrates frontal atrophy and ventricular enlargement, which permits better visualization of some of the major ana-tomic structures that are labeled numerically in the adjacent drawing (1-frontal lobe, 2-interhemispheric fissure, 3-anterior horn, lateral ventricle, 4-caudate nucleus, 5-internal capsule, 6-thalamus, 7-putamen/globus pallidus complex, 8-third ventricle, 9-posterior horn, lateral ventricle, 10-Sylvian fissure, 11-temporal lobe, 12-occipital lobe.

nostic neurology (Oldendorf, 1980). Current generation CT and MRI scan-ners can provide exceptional detail with respect to gross anatomy of the brain (see Figure 1). Both of the procedures are excellent in depicting major structural anomalies of the brain such as dysplasic errors in devel-opment (see Figure 2), hydrocephalus (see Figure 3), tumors (see Figure 4), degenerative effects due to infectious disorder (see Figure 5), con-

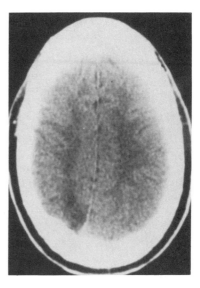

FIGURE 2. Cerebral dysplasia. Note the asymmetry between the two cerebral hemispheres and the density difference in the left occipital region. The decreased density in the left occipital region represents either a failure of neuronal development or early traumatic injury. This patient was dyslexic.

genital porencephaly (see Figure 6), and a host of other childhood disorders (see Bigler, 1984).

With the advent of these techniques, there was a period of great optimism concerning the advancement of "lesion-localization" work examining specific functions of specific brain regions (Kertesz, 1983). Prior

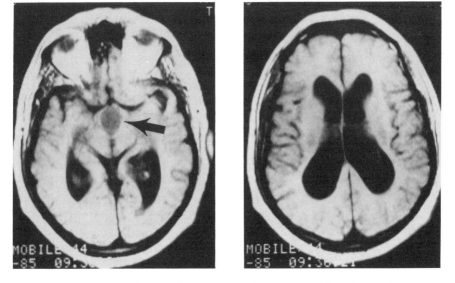

FIGURE 3. MRI scan depicting hydrocephalus in a patient with a pituitary tumor.

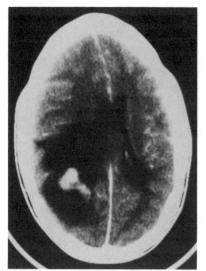

FIGURE 4. CT scan depicting tumor (astrocytoma) in a 16-year-old male patient who presented with a 10-year history of learning and behavioral problems.

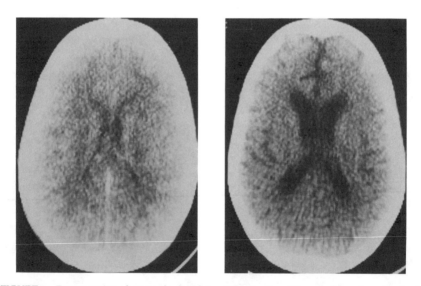

FIGURE 5. Degenerative changes depicted in a CT scan in a 13-year-old male patient who suffered from diffuse encephalitis. The CT on the left demonstrates compression of the ventricular system due to diffuse cerebral edema. As a consequence of the edema as well as the brain infection, diffuse neuronal degeneration evolved, as depicted in the CT on the right taken 3 months later. Premorbidly the patient's intellectual level was assumed to be in the normal range. Postinfection his WISC-R Full Scale IQ score was 64.

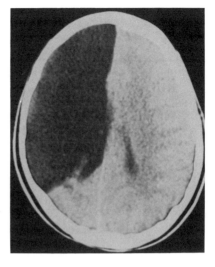

FIGURE 6. CT scan depicting porencephaly. Despite the absence of the left frontal and most of the left temporal and parietal lobes, this child had normal intellectual and language development (see Bigler & Naugle, 1984). Intellectual testing at age 4 demonstrated a Verbal IQ (VIQ) score of 102, a Performance IQ (PIQ) score of 100, and a Full Scale IQ (FSIQ) score of 101. Four years later, the results were almost identical (VIS = 98, PIQ = 98, FSIQ = 98). The child had no speech or language deficit, and achievement scores were at age- and grade-appropriate levels. This case clearly demonstrates cerebral plasticity in the immature nervous system.

to these imaging techniques, only invasive procedures were available for examining brain structure, or one had to wait for postmortem examination. Initially it was thought that CT analysis would provide the essential background for the lesion-localization work (Bigler, 1980). However, although there are some general relationships that have been demonstrated between neuropsychological outcome and CT and MRI findings, the relationships are certainly far from linear. For example, Bigler and colleagues (Bigler, Hubler, Cullum, & Turkheimer, 1985; Cullum & Bigler, 1986) have demonstrated only a modest relationship between overall neuropsychological performance and the degree of cerebral atrophy as a result of trauma or degenerative disease. A major confounding factor with child studies examining the relationship between anatomic irregularities and function is the cerebral plasticity issue. For example, Figure 7 depicts the CT results of a child who had major structural defects in posterior aspects of the cerebrum. Despit Despite having essentially no visual cortex or posterior parietal-temporal association cortical areas, the child was able to read at both age- and grade-appropriate levels, showed normal receptive language abilities, and had a Verbal IQ in the near superior range! None of these neuropsychological parameters would have been predicted from her grossly abnormal CT results.

In light of the various interpretive problems alluded to above, the best clinical approach to integrating CT and MRI data with neuropsychological outcome appears to be in the use of CT/MRI in the depiction of structural abnormalities and neuropsychological results for the depiction of abnormalities of function. It is tempting to imply functional abnormalities on the basis of CT/MRI information. Likewise, it is alluring to infer struc-

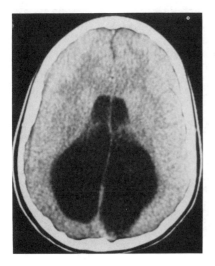

FIGURE 7. CT scan of a 12-year-old female patient with a history of a congenital occipital encephalocele, which was surgically removed at 4 years of age. Despite the marked structural abnormalities in the posterior aspect of both cerebral hemispheres and near complete absence of both occipital lobes, this child's Verbal IQ score was 119 on the Wechsler Intelligence Scale for Children-Revised. Despite being cortically blind for objects, she could read at age- and grade-appropriate levels [Wide Range Achievement Test-Revised Reading score was 8B (63%); Boder Test of Reading-Spelling Patterns Reading Quotient was 125, and on this measure she was reading at the 10th-grade level]. This case clearly demonstrates unexpectedly normal neuropsychological findings in a child with marked structural abnormalities.

tural abnormalities on the basis of neuropsychological test results. However, the clinician must remember that brain imaging with CT/MRI is not a measure of cognitive functioning, and that neuropsychological performance is not a direct measure of anatomic localization. The CT/MRI and neuropsychological results should be used to integrate information about a child's neurological status, both contributing to different aspects of neurological integrity.

In the future some of the problems associated with integrating structural data with functional information may be aided by such measures as regional cerebral blood flow (RCBF; Risberg, 1986) and positron emission tomography (PET) scanning (Heiss, Herholz, Pawlik, Wagner, & Wienhard, 1986). With these techniques it may be possible to determine the dynamic relationship between anatomical structure and function. Unfortunately, to date there have been few studies done with children, with the majority of the work being done with adults having some type of acquired neurological disorder.

ELECTRODIAGNOSTIC TESTS

The electroencephalogram (EEG) may be considered a measurement of the ambient electrical activity of the brain. Of clinical interest is the change or discontinuities that may occur within the four general EEG frequency bands—delta (0–4 Hz), theta (4–8 Hz), alpha (8–12 Hz), and beta (greater than 12 Hz). Pathology is frequently manifested when slow activity (delta, theta) is augmented or fast activity (alpha, beta) is diminished. For example, a focal abnormality may alter the EEG in such a fashion as to produce predominantly delta waves in that region, with other recording sites displaying relatively normal activity. This would be contrasted with diffuse slowing of the EEG, which would be seen in generalized disorders (see Figure 8; Kiloh, McComas, & Osselton, 1979).

The clinical parameters of pediatric EEG have been well established for over two decades (Kiloh *et al.* 1979). However, despite numerous studies examining the relationship between EEG variables and neuropsychological features, the results have generally lacked specificity (Brandeis & Lehmann, 1986; Capute, Niedermeyer, & Richardson, 1968; Hughes, 1971; Hughes & Denckla, 1978). Although there is a greater incidence of EEG abnormalities in children with learning disability, hyperactivity, psychiatric disorder, and developmental deficits (Golden, 1982), there are no distinctive EEG findings that are diagnostic of such conditions. The case illustrated in Figure 8 is representative of this problem.

Evoked potential (EP) testing may reveal the intactness of visual, auditory, and somatosensory pathways, and such findings may be useful in cerebral localization studies (Luders, Dinner, Lesser, & Morris, 1986).

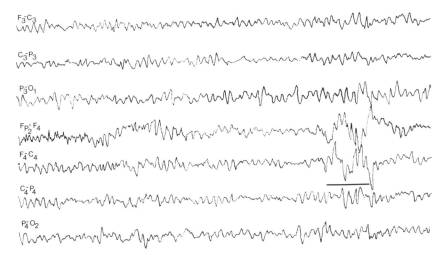

FIGURE 8. EEG in a 12-year-old right-handed male patient with a history of learning disorder. Asynchronous slow-wave (underlined) activity in the right parietal region is noted. This type of irregularity is seen with greater frequency in children with minor neurological abnormalities. It does not indicate any specific abnormality and is not epileptogenic. Such abnormalities frequently do not relate to any specific neurological or neuropsychological pattern. In this child his neuropsychological studies suggested language-based deficits that would implicate posterior left hemisphere dysfunction, but, as indicated, the EEG abnormality was in the right parietal region. Thus, such EEG abnormalities are a variant from normal but do not necessarily correlate with the *type* of neuropsychological impairment present, only with the presence of such impairment.

EP studies also have enjoyed great research popularity in a variety of psychiatric disorders, including attention deficit disorder (Klorman et al., 1983) and autism (Courschesne, Kilman, Galambos, & Lincoln, 1984). However, the clinical application of EP findings in relationship to cognitive processes and neuropsychological outcome remains specious at this time and under intense experimentation (Brandeis & Lehmann, 1986; Visser, Njiokiktjien, & De Rijke, 1982).

Traditional interpretation of EEG or EP studies is and has been accomplished by visual inspection. However, the advent of computer-assisted data analysis has permitted the development of a variety of innovative methods for analysis (John et al., 1977). To date, the procedure that appears to have the greatest promise is the Brain Electrical Activity Mapping (BEAM) technique pioneered by Duffy and colleagues (Duffy, Denckla, Bartels, & Sandini, 1980). The BEAM technique is illustrated in Figure 9. In a study examining BEAM findings in dyslexic boys and age-matched normal readers, Duffy and McAnulty (1985) demonstrated demarcated regional differences. The dyslexic children showed abnormalities in the medial frontal (supplementary motor area), the left anterolateral lobe (Broca's area), and the left posterior quandrant speech-associated areas (Wernicke's area, angular gyrus, posterior temporal lobe, and parietal lobe), with minor differences noted in the right parietal lobe. On the basis of these findings, Duffy and McAnulty have speculated that dyslexic individuals manifest some degree of dysfunction throughout cerebral regions involved in language-related functions.

Relationship between Electrodiagnostic Findings and Neuropsychological Assessment

In the era prior to brain imaging and computerized EEG (i.e., roughly pre-1970s), routine EEG studies were frequently used to establish the

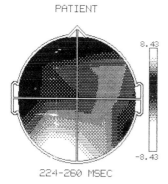

PATIENT

8.43

-8.43

224-260 MSEC

FIGURE 9. Representative BEAM study demonstrating an abnormality in the left occipital-parietal region. The patient had a history of cerebral trauma and subsequent cognitive deficit but had a normal routine EEG. Note how the BEAM technique aids in the localization/lateralization of EEG abnormalities.

locus of dysfunction according to lateralized electrophysiological abnormalities. Neuropsychological studies were then undertaken to explore lesion-localization and lateralization relationships. We now realize that this procedure was a rather primitive one at best, and although the focal EEG abnormality may be indiative of specific dysfunction in that area or region, it did not address the likelihood of secondary abnormalities and effects. This is exactly what the BEAM research has demonstrated—that the electrophysiological abnormalities in learning-disabled children and other children with minor neurological abnormalities may be more widespread than once considered. These findings are not at variance with anatomical studies (Galaburda, 1984; Kemper, 1984) that have demonstrated more delimited microanatomical lesions in critical language and association cortical regions in dyslexic subjects. It is likely that these "lesions" are strategically situated so as to interfere with neuronal interconnections, thereby producing effects distant from the locus of anatomic aberration. Alternately, there also may be multiple sites of dysfunction. Neuropsychological studies with learning-disabled children have frequently demonstrated that in addition to the specific learning deficit exhibited, they may perform less well than normal controls on a variety of neuropsychological measures unrelated to the primary deficit (Nussbaum & Bigler, 1986; Nussbaum, Bigler, & Koch, 1986; Rourke, Bakker, Fisk, & Strang, 1983). These neuropsychological findings support the BEAM research implicating multifocality and/or multiple system involvement in the neurological dysfunction associated with learning disorder.

Thus, neuropsychological findings and electrophysiological results may be expected to differ just as electrophysiological results do not directly correspond to underlying anatomic abnormalities (Kiloh et al., 1979). Accordingly, one should examine for consistencies in neuropsychological findings and electrophysiological results so as to identify unifying concepts of underlying neurological dysfunction. But where one deviates from the other, this does not necessarily imply a lack of consistency or superiority of one approach over the other. Neuropsychological findings will always be more descriptive of functional levels of performance (Gaddes, 1985), whereas electrophysiological techniques will remain a direct, objective measure of the electrical activity of the brain, with no particular reference as to function. For example, the current electrophysiological methods cannot be utilized to separate groups of children with average IQ from those with above-average IQ, but psychometric testing can. Similarly, whereas neuropsychological studies may be able, psychometrically and statistically, to differentiate between children with and without seizure disorder, such studies are poor at clinically differentiating seizure type, which is a rather straightforward task utilizing EEG parameters (e.g., 3 per second spike-and-wave activity is diagnostic of petit mal epilepsy; Kiloh et al., 1979; O'Donohoe, 1981).

PSYCHOLOGICAL ASSESSMENT

Traditional psychological evaluation of the child typically has included an assessment of intelligence, personality, academic performance, and emotional state (Krahn, 1985). The presence of "neurological" or "organic" signs sometimes has been an indirect objective of such evaluations. This is exemplified by the Draw-A-Person (DAP) test. Frequently, DAP results are rich in clinical information (Dileo, 1983), but such results also have been utilized as an index of intelligence and development (Harris, 1963). To a certain extent, the drawings also provide an index of maturation (Scott, 1981), and, because of this, irregularities in drawing may also indicate some form of perceptual-motor disturbance that is neurologically based (Carr, 1985). Hence, some of the paper-and-pencil tests such as the DAP have been viewed as demonstrating not only potential personality indicators but also neurological dysfunction.

Similarly, the development of the Bender Visual-Motor Gestalt test (BVMG) had its origin more in the realm of a maturational and personality measure rather than as a neurological measure (Bender, 1938). However, clinicians were quick to note that deficits in graphomotor ability occurred significantly more often in children with "organic" dysfunction, and hence the BVMG became *the* screening measure for organicity (Lacks, 1984). The era from 1930 to 1970 was a time period where the concept of "organicity" (Small, 1980) remained in vogue, but as neurodiagnostic sophistication increased, it became apparent that such screening measures as the BVMG (Bigler & Erfurth, 1981) and the concept of organicity, *per se*, were obsolete (Bigler, 1984).

The reason that some psychological tests have sensitivity to neurological processes is based on the direct relationship between developmental stages of psychological growth and physical neuromaturational growth (Rourke et al., 1983). This has been well demonstrated in an elegant study by Passler, Isaac, and Hynd (1985). They examined normal male and female children at four age levels between 6 and 12 years of age. They were particularly interested in examining the relationship between maturation and the mastery of tasks that had been shown to be sensitive to frontal lobe functioning. These tasks were selected because frontal lobe maturation is thought to be incomplete until adolescence (Nauta & Feirtag, 1986). The authors found that the greatest development occurred at the 6- and 8-year-old levels in terms of the child's performance on verbal and nonverbal tasks requiring proactive and retroactive inhibition, and tasks that elicited perseveration. By the age of 10, they found that the ability to inhibit attention to irrelevant stimuli and perseveratory responses was almost complete, with mastery present by age 12. If such a developmental model is used, failure to develop certain abilities by specified developmental stages may be a sign of neuromaturational deficit or specific neurological impairment (Whelihan & Lesher, 1985). Conversely, the expression of normal developmental staging probably represents normal neurological development. Thus, psychological measures that are sensitive to developmental stages may indirectly be associated with neuromaturational factors as well.

Based on extensive research and standardization over the past two decades, neuropsychological assessment has developed as an integrated and comprehensive approach to evaluating behavioral aspects of brain function (Bigler, 1984; Lezak, 1983). As a result, no single psychometric test is appropriate for assessing brain function. Rather, neuropsychological assessment encompasses a wide selection of standardized tests that carefully assess motor (including strength, dexterity, integrative control, and visuopraxic/graphomotor abilities), sensory (basic and complex aspects of visual, auditory, and tactile perception), language (both expressive and receptive abilities, as well as the psychoeducational aspects of reading, spelling, writing, and math abilities), memory (both verbal and nonverbal, as well as short- and long-term memory functions), and general cognition (including measures of reasoning, problem solving, and judgment, as well as standardized intellectual tests). Many tests that are now incorporated into comprehensive neuropsychological test batteries were originally designed for other purposes. This overlap between traditional psychological assessment and neuropsychological application can be exemplified by two tests, the Raven (1965) Coloured Progressive Matrices (CPM) and the Beery (1967) Developmental Test of Visual-Motor Integration (VMI). The CPM test was originally designed as a nonverbal, motor-free measure of intelligence. However, the CPM, from the neuropsychological standpoint, has found acceptance as a measure of visual-spatial reasoning that is more affected by posterior cerebral lesions than by anterior (Lezak, 1983). Similarly, the VMI test was originally designed as a "sensorimotor" test of visual-motor development, and an actual developmental index was established. Neuropsychologists have continued to use the developmental aspects of this measure, but they utilize it as a direct measure of constructional praxis as well.

In its infancy, clinical neuropsychology emerged from clinical psychology and neurology, and accordingly had to utilize the assessment methods employed at that time by those two disciplines. This is why there was so much early reliance on traditional psychometric tests for examining "brain function." Currently, clinical neuropsychology is in the process of carefully delineating those tests that are specific behavioral measures of brain function and creating novel measure that are based on current neuroscience theory. The field is beginning to move away from dependence on past psychometric measures that were developed for other purposes (Delis, Kramer, Kaplan, & Ober, 1986).

Intellectual Assessment versus Neuropsychological Assessment with Children: What's the Difference?

Test development in the measurement of intelligence predated the emergence of the field of human clinical neuropsychology. Nonetheless, because various measures of childhood intelligence are, in part, sensitive measures of development, and because cognitive functioning is related to brain function, these measures are also measures of cerebral integrity.

The prototype and standard of childhood intellectual testing is the Wechsler Intelligence Scale for Children-Revised (Wechsler, 1974). The development of the WISC-R—and its predecessor, the WISC (Wechsler, 1949)—took place in the embryonic stages of clinical neuropsychology. This was long before the specialization of hemispheric functioning was understood, and it is only fortuitous that Wechsler designed his test with verbal and performance test items. Thus, the WISC was developed as a measure of intelligence, not as a measure of neurological functioning. However, studies soon began to demonstrate its efficacy in distinguishing differential aspects of impaired ability in children with neurological disorders (Kaufman, Long, & O'Neal, 1986).

Kaufman *et al.* (1986) review the utilization of the WISC-R from a neurological standpoint. Factor-analytic studies have demonstrated three factors that have potential neuropsychological significance—a verbal comprehension factor, a perceptual organization factor, and a freedom from distractability factor. The first two loosely correspond to aspects of hemispheric specialization—namely, language versus manipulospatial abilities (i.e., left and right hemispheric functions). Despite this relationship, VIQ–PIQ differences on the WISC may not hold the same significance as that seen with adults (Boll & Barth, 1981). In part this is due to developmental and cerebral plasticity issues of the immature brain. Thus, whereas left hemisphere damage in the adult may affect VIQ more than PIQ, with the opposite holding true for right hemisphere damage, similar relationships may not be present with children (see Figure 6). For example, as reviewed by Boll and Barth (1981), children with congenital hemiplegic syndromes do not necessarily have VIQ–PIQ differences that correspond to the affected side (i.e., VIQ < PIQ in left-brain-damaged, right hemiplegic children). To examine this problem further, Riva and Cazzaniga (1986) studied children's performance on the WISC who had sustained unilateral cerebral lesions before and after 1 year of age. Their results indicated that left hemisphere lesions, regardless of whether they occurred before or after the first year of life, affected both verbal and performance scores, but with a greater negative impact when the lesion occurred early in life. Right hemisphere damage, irrespective of whether the lesion occurred prior to or after 1 year of age, affected only PIQ. Riva and Cazzaniga suggest that recovery from unilateral deficits in children is related to a hierarchy in cognitive development and that verbal skills are usually spared at the expense of nonverbal skills (see also Bigler & Naugle, 1984).

Accordingly, some neuropsychological inferences can and should be made from WISC-R results. However, the WISC-R is incomplete from the neuropsychological perspective because it does not provide a direct assessment of specific motor or sensory abilities, only incompletely assesses language, and provides no in-depth assessment of memory. Thus, although the WISC-R (like other measures of intelligence) is extremely valuable and worthwhile in the assessment of the child, it can be viewed only as an adjunct to a comprehensive neuropsychological test battery. Such a battery should assess cortical function in a thorough fashion, fully examining motor, sensory-perceptual, spatial-perceptual, memory (both verbal and nonverbal), graphomotor, language, and cognitive functions.

Recently, the Kaufman Assessment Battery for Children (K-ABC) was developed to overcome some of these problems (Kaufman & Kaufman, 1983). Instead of the Verbal-Performance schema, the K-ABC used the dichotomy of simultaneous versus sequential/successive processing. This differentiation is based, in part, on Luria's (1973) research that suggested sequential processing to be primarily a frontotemporal activity and simultaneous processing to be more related to parietoccipital functioning. However, in preliminary studies (Morris & Bigler, 1987) the results are equivocal at this point in terms of the advantages of this measure over the WISC-R in children with neurological disorders. Morris and Bigler found that the K-ABC Simultaneous Processing score demonstrated greater sensitivity for a variety of nonverbal, spatial-perceptual-motor deficits than did the PIQ measure from the WISC-R. However, this did not hold up for the Sequential score, with the WISC-R VIQ measures demonstrating a greater sensitivity for verbal-language deficits in neurologically impaired children.

Thus, traditional intellectual assessment methods yield only partial neuropsychological information. Accordingly, these methods should be considered as only a subset and not a substitute for the more complete neuropsychological assessment. This is certainly well demonstrated by the case illustrated in Figure 6. In this case, the child had shown average intellectual ability over a span of 4 years, with no significant VIQ–PIQ difference, despite the absence of two-thirds of her left cerebral hemisphere. However, she did have a moderate right-sided spastic hemiplegia and tactile sensory loss.

CONCLUSIONS

There was a time when neuropsychological testing was done in relative isolation with respect to other neurodiagnostic procedures. In fact, neuropsychological testing measures utilized prior to 1970 were as sensitive (or more sensitive) and less invasive than other techniques for assessing "organic" dysfunction (Small, 1980). However, with the diagnostic improvements in neuroradiology and electrophysiology, as well as the better understanding of minor neurological abnormalities in relation to a variety of neurobehavioral disorders, neuropsychology must continue to integrate its clinical findings in relation to these other areas. To that end, this chapter has attempted to integrate neuropsychological test findings in children with other assessment techniques. Despite certain limitations, particularly with respect to children, neuropsychological assessment techniques remain the best functional assessment tools for the evaluation of higher cortical functioning. They provide a crucial perspective that should be integrated with other neurodiagnostic and psychological procedures in gaining a comprehensive understanding of the neurologically impaired child.

REFERENCES

Beery, K. E. (1967). *Developmental Test of Visual-Motor Integration.* Chicago: Follett Educational Corporation.

Bender, L. A. (1938). A visual motor gestalt test and its clinical use (*Research Monographs,* 3). New York: American Orthopsychiatric Association.

Bigler, E. D. (1980). Neuropsychological assessment and brain scan results: A case study approach. *Clinical Neuropsychology, 2,* 13–24.

Bigler, E. D. (1984). *Diagnostic clinical neuropsychology.* Austin: University of Texas Press.

Bigler, E. D., & Ehrfurth, J. W. (1981). The continued inappropriate singular use of the Bender Visual Motor Gestalt Test. *Professional Psychology, 12,* 562–569.

Bigler, E. D., Hubler, D. W., Cullum, C. M., & Turkheimer, E. (1985). Intellectual and memory impairment in dementia: CT volume correlations. *Journal of Nervous and Mental Disease, 173.* 347–352.

Bigler, E. D., & Naugle, R. I. (1984). Case studies in cerebral plasticity. *International Journal of Clinical Neuropsychology, 7,* 12–23.

Boll, T., & Barth, J. T. (1981). Neuropsychology of brain damage in children. In S. B. Filskov & T. J. Boll (Eds.), *Handbook of clinical neuropsychology* (pp. 418–452). New York: Wiley.

Brandeis, D., & Lehmann, D. (1986). Event-related potentials of the brain and cognitive processes: Approaches and applications. *Neuropsychologia, 24,* 151–168.

Brown, S. B. (1982). Neurologic examination of the older child. In K. F. Swaiman & F. S. Wright (Eds.), *The practice of pediatric neurology* (pp. 110–129). St. Louis: C. V. Mosby.

Capute, A. J., Neidermeyer, E. F. L., & Richardson, F. (1968). The EEG in children with minimal cerebral dysfunction. *Pediatrics, 41,* 1104–1114.

Carr, A. C. (1985). Psychological testing of personality. In H. I. Kaplan & B. J. Sadock (Eds.), *Comprehensive textbook of psychiatry* (4th ed., pp. 514–535). New York: Williams & Wilkins.

Courchesne, E., Kilman, B. A., Galambos, R., & Lincoln, A. J. (1984). Autism: Processing of novel auditory information assessed by event-related potentials. *Electroencephalography and Clinical Neurophysiology: Evoked Potentials, 59,* 238–248.

Cullum, C. M., & Bigler, E. D. (1986). Ventricle size, cortical atrophy and the relationship with neuropsychological status in closed head injury: A quantitative analysis. *Journal of Clinical and Experimental Neuropsychology, 8,* 437–452.

Delis, D. C., Kramer, J. H., Kaplan, E., & Ober, B. A. (1986). *The California Verbal Learning Test*. Orlando, FL: Harcourt Brace Jovanovich.

Dileo, J. H. (1983). *Interpreting children's drawings*. New York: Brunner/Mazel.

Duckett, S. (1981). Neuropathological aspects: I. Congenital malformations. In P. Black (Ed.), *Brain dysfunction in children: Etiology, diagnosis and management* (pp. 17–46). New York: Raven Press.

Duffy, F. H., Denckla, M. B., Bartels, D. H., & Sandini, G. (1980). Dyslexia: Regional differences in brain electrical activity by topographic mapping. *Annals of Neurology, 7*, 412–420.

Duffy, F. H., & McAnulty, G. B. (1985). Brain electrical activity mapping (BEAM): The search for a physiological signature of dyslexia. In F. H. Duffy & N. Geschwind (Eds.), *Dyslexia: A neuroscientific approach to clinical evaluation* (pp. 105–122). Boston: Little, Brown.

Dworkin, P. H. (1985). *Learning and behavioral problems of schoolchildren*. Philadelphia: W. B. Saunders.

Gaddes, W. H. (1985). *Learning disabilities and brain function* (2nd ed.). New York: Springer-Verlag.

Galaburda, A. M. (1984). Anatomical asymmetries. In N. Geschwind & A. M. Galaburda (Eds.), *Cerebral dominance* (pp. 11–25). Cambridge, MA: Harvard University Press.

Golden, G. S. (1982). Neurobiological correlates of learning disabilities. *Annals of Neurology, 12*, 409–418.

Harris, D. B. (1963). *Children's drawings as a measure of intellect*. New York: Harcourt Brace & World.

Hartlage, P. L., & Krawiecki, N. S. (1984). The neurological assessment of children. In R. E. Tarter & G. Goldstein (Eds.), *Advances in clinical neuropsychology* (Vol. 2, pp. 63–77). New York: Plenum Press.

Heiss, W. D., Herholz, K., Pawlik, G., Wagner, R., & Wienhard, K. (1986). Positron emission tomography in neuropsychology. *Neuropsychologia, 24*, 141–149.

Herskowitz, J., & Rosman, N. P. (1982). *Pediatrics, neurology and psychiatry—Common ground*. New York: Macmillan.

Hughes, J. R. (1971). EEG and learning disabilities. In H. R. Myckleburst (Ed.), *Progress in learning disabilities* (Vol. 2, pp. 196–223). New York: Grune and Stratton.

Hughes, J. R., & Denckla, M. B. (1978). Outline of a pilot study of electroencephalographic correlates of dyslexia. In A. L. Benton & D. Pearl (Eds.), *Dyslexia: An appraisal of current knowledge* (pp. 217–245). New York: Oxford University Press.

John, E. R., Karmel, B. Z., Corning, W. D., Easton, P., Brown, D., Ahn, H., John, M., Harmony, T., Prichep, L., Toro, A., Garson, I., Bartlett, F., Thatcher, R.,Kaye, H., Valdes, P. & Schwartz, E. (1977). Neurometrics. *Science, 196*, 1393–1410.

Kaufman, A. S., & Kaufman, N. L. (1983). *Kaufman Assessment Battery for Children*. Circle Pines, MN: American Guidance Service.

Kaufman, A. S., Long, S. W., & O'Neal, M. R. (1986). Topical review of the WISC-R for pediatric neuroclinicians. *Journal of Child Neurology, 1*, 89–98.

Kaufman, D. M. (1981). *Clinical neurology for psychiatrists*. New York: Grune and Stratton.

Kemper, T. L. (1984). Asymmetrical lesions in dyslexia. In N. Geschwind & A. M. Galaburda (Eds.), *Cerebral dominance* (pp. 75–89). Cambridge, MA: Harvard University Press.

Kertesz, A. (1983). *Localization in neuropsychology*. New York: Academic Press.

Kiloh, L. G., McComas, A. J., & Osselton, J. W. (1979). *Clinical electroencephalography*. London: Butterworths.

Klorman, R., Salzman, L. F., Bauer, L. O., Coons, H. W., Borgstedt, A. D., & Halpern, W. I. (1983). Effects of two doses of methylphenidate on cross-situational and borderline hyperactive children's evoked potentials. *Electroencephalography and Clinical Neurophysiology, 56*, 169–185.

Krahn, G. L. (1985). The use of projective assessment techniques in pediatric settings. *Journal of Pediatric Psychology, 10*, 179–193.

Lacks, P. (1984). *Bender Gestalt screening for brain dysfunction.* New York: Wiley-Interscience.

Lezak, M. D. (1983). *Neuropsychological assessment.* New York: Oxford University Press.

Luders, H., Dinner, D. S., Lesser, R. P., & Morris, H. H. (1986). Evoked potentials in cortical localization. *Journal of Clinical Neurophysiology, 3,* 75–84.

Luria, A. R. (1973). *The working brain.* London: Penguin Press.

Morris, J. M., & Bigler, E. D. (1987). Hemispheric functioning and the K-ABC: Results in neurologically impaired children. *Developmental Neuropsychology, 3,* 67–79.

Nauta, W. J. H., & Feirtag, M. (1986). *Fundamental neuroanatomy.* New York: W. H. Freeman.

Nussbaum, N. L., & Bigler, E. D. (1986). Neuropsychological and behavioral profiles of empirically derived subgroups of learning disabled children. *International Journal of Clinical Neuropsychology, 7,* 82–89.

Nussbaum, N. L., Bigler, E. D., & Koch, W. (1986). Neuropsychologically derived subgroups of learning disabled children: Personality/behavioral dimensions. *Journal of Research and Development in Education, 19,* 57–67.

O'Donohoe, N. V. (1981). *Epilepsies of childhood.* London: Butterworths.

Oldendorf, W. H. (1980). *The quest for an image of brain.* New York: Raven Press.

Passler, M. A., Isaac, W., & Hynd, G. W. (1985). Neuropsychological development of behavior attributed to frontal lobe functioning in children. *Developmental Neuropsychology, 1,* 349–370.

Raven, J. C. (1965). *The Coloured Progressive Matrices Test.* London: H. K. Lewis.

Rie, H. E., & Rie, E. D. (1980). *Handbook of minimal brain dysfunction.* New York: Wiley.

Risberg, J. (1986). Regional cerebral blood flow in neuropsychology. *Neuropsychologia, 24,* 135–140.

Riva, D., & Cazzaniga, L. (1986). Late effects of unilateral brain lesions sustained before and after age one. *Neuropsychologia, 24,* 423–428.

Rourke, B. P., Bakker, D. J., Fisk, J. L., & Strang, J. D. (1983). *Child neuropsychology.* New York: Guilford Press.

Schimschock, J. R., Milford-Cooley, M., & Cooley, N. (1984). Practical management of children with apparent learning disabilities. *Neurologic clinics.* Philadelphia: W. B. Saunders.

Scott, L. H. (1981). Measuring intelligence with the Goodenough-Harris Test. *Psychological Bulletin, 89,* 483–505.

Shafer, S. Q., Shaffer, D., O'Connor, P. A., & Stokman, C. J. (1983). Hard thoughts on neurological "soft signs." In M. Rutter (Ed.), *Developmental neuropsychiatry* (pp. 133–143). New York: Guilford Press.

Shaffer, D., O'Connor, P. A., Shafer, S. Q., & Propis, S. (1983). Neurological "soft signs": Their origins and significance for behavior. In M. Rutter (Ed.), *Developmental neuropsychiatry* (pp. 144–163). New York: Guilford Press.

Shaffer, D., Schonfeld, I., O'Connor, P. A., Stokman, C., Trautman, P., Shafer, S., & Ng, S. (1985). Neurological soft signs, their relationship to psychiatric disorder and intelligence in childhood and adolescence. *Archives of General Psychiatry, 42,* 342–352.

Shaywitz, S. E. (1982). The Yale Neuropsychoeducational Assessment Scales. *Schizophrenia Bulletin, 8,* 360–424.

Small, L. (1980). *Neuropsychodiagnosis in psychotherapy* (2nd ed.). New York: Brunner/Mazel.

Touwen, B. C. L. (1979). *Examination of the child with minor neurological dysfunction* (2nd ed.). Philadelphia: J. B. Lippincott.

Van Allen, M. W. (1969). *Pictorial manual of neurologic tests.* Chicago: Year Book Medical Publishers.

Visser, S. L., Njiokiktjien, Ch. J., & De Rijke, W. (1982). Neurological condition at birth in relation to the electroencephalogram (EEG) and visual evoked potential (VEP) at the age of 5. *Electroencephalography and Clinical Neurophysiology, 54,* 458–468.

Wechsler, D. (1949). *Wechsler Intelligence Scale for Children.* New York: Psychological Corporation.

Wechsler, D. (1974). *Wechsler Intelligence Scale for Children-Revised.* New York: Psychological Corporation.

Whelihan, W. M., & Lesher, E. L. (1985). Neuropsychological changes in frontal functions with aging. *Developmental Neuropsychology, 1,* 371–380.

Williams, R., & Caviness, V. S. (1984). Normal and abnormal development of the brain. In R. E. Tartar & G. Goldstein (Eds.), *Advances in clinical neuropsychology* (Vol. 2, pp. 1–62). New York: Plenum Press.

Neuropsychological Diagnosis with Children
Actuarial and Clinical Models

W. GRANT WILLIS

Neuropsychological diagnosis with children is a highly specialized endeavor. It draws heavily from disciplines that encompass neuropsychology, functional psychodiagnosis, and pediatrics. It also departs from these established disciplines in some important ways. For example, unique issues in child neuropsychological diagnosis such as referral bias, assessment technique, and poor taxonomy distinguish it from functional psychodiagnosis, especially with adults. These issues, which serve to militate against high degrees of diagnostic accuracy, have been well articulated by Achenbach (1985), Fletcher and Taylor (1984), and Rapoport and Ismond (1984).

In terms of diagnostic accuracy, it is well established that actuarial (i.e., statistical) models are superior to clinical models (e.g., Goldberg & Werts, 1966; Meehl, 1973; Phelan, 1964; Wallach & Schoof, 1965). As nearly all practicing clinicians can attest, however, the solution is not so simple as to abandon clinical models in favor of actuarial ones. Rather, both models of diagnosis are not only necessary but also desirable. Thus, the focus in this chapter is to discuss the assets and liabilities of both of these models with special reference to the unique issues encountered in child neuropsychological diagnosis.

W. GRANT WILLIS • Department of Psychology, University of Rhode Island, Kingston, Rhode Island.

DIAGNOSTIC MODELS

The essential distinction between actuarial and clinical models of diagnosis is in terms of the ways that assessment data are combined in order to aid clinicians in arriving at some kind of decision (usually a diagnostic prediction). For actuarial models, multivariate statistical techniques are used to combine data; for clinical models, professional judgments are used for this task. A common misconception is that actuarial models require objective psychometric scores as data whereas clinical models allow for nonparametric clinical judgments. The kinds of assessment data that are collected and the methods that are used for data collection, however, are irrelevant to the distinction between actuarial and clinical models. Clinical interview data and nominal child characteristics are legitimate input for actuarial diagnostic rules, and standardized psychometric scores are easily (albeit sometimes inaccurately) incorporated into clinical judgments.

The relative superiority of one model over the other in terms of associated diagnostic accuracy has been studied and debated for many years (see Meehl, 1954). As already noted, the evidence at this point is clear: Actuarial models yield consistently higher probabilities of accurate diagnostic predictions than do clinical models, even when those predictions are made by highly experienced clinicians. The reason for this, however, cannot be due to the kinds of assessment data that are used in the two models; both models are operative with the same pool of information. Rather, the essential difference between these models centers on methods of integrating assessment data.

There are at least three important distinctions between actuarial and clinical models in terms of data integration. A thorough understanding of these distinctions can help to highlight some sources of inaccuracy commonly associated with clinical decision making.

Data–Diagnosis Contingency

In order to know how useful a particular source of assessment data is in terms of arriving at some diagnosis, clinicians must first understand the relationship (i.e., contingency) between those data and the diagnosis. For actuarial models, the contingency between assessment data and the diagnostic decision is estimated through statistical techniques. These techniques are typically multivariate in nature and may include, for example, discriminant analysis, multiple regression, and cluster analysis. Because data–diagnosis contingencies are established empirically, the probability of making an accurate diagnostic prediction can be determined and subsequently evaluated by the clinician. In contrast, for clinical models, the contingency between assessment data and the diagnostic decision is estimated by the clinician on the basis of factors such as experience and training. Because data–diagnosis contingencies are established subjectively, probabilities of diagnostic accuracy are assumed rather than determined and are not, therefore, subject to external evaluation.

In order to establish contingencies between assessment data and diagnoses, clinicians are forced to rely on their own judgment concerning the degree to which a particular combination of neuropsychological signs found on examination of the patient matches some neuropsychological syndrome or disorder. This is an arduous task because relying on professional experience and training (regardless of extent) is likely to bias judgment owing to selective retrievability of previous cases. Selective retrievability is associated with bias because it is affected by factors such as salience and familiarity, as opposed to more appropriate factors (in the sense of leading to more accurate diagnoses) such as the prevalence of a particular neuropsychological syndrome or disorder in some population of interest (cf. Tversky & Kahneman, 1973).

Consideration of Data

A second distinction between the models concerns the ways in which different sources of assessment data are considered. For actuarial models, data are considered simultaneously whereas in clinical models, data are typically considered independently. Because different sources of assessment data are usually interrelated (i.e., they are not truly independent), each source does not contribute entirely unique information to the diagnostic prediction. Thus, independent consideration of data frequently leads to diagnostic errors.

For example, if the degree of contingency between a particular neuropsychological sign (e.g., a test result) and a diagnosis is 0.7, then, in the absence of any other information about the patient, the clinician knows $0.7^2 \times 100\%$ or 49% of the total amount of information that is necessary in order to make a completely accurate diagnosis. It does not follow, however, that given another neuropsychological sign (e.g., age-inappropriate gait), for which the contingency with the diagnosis is say 0.4, that the clinician now knows $49\% + 0.4^2 \times 100\%$, or 65%, of the information required for certainty with respect to the diagnosis. Rather, the actual proportion of diagnostic information that the clinician has obtained is reduced by an amount that corresponds to the degree that the neuropsychological signs are themselves interrelated. These intercorrelations are accounted for when data integration is accomplished statistically. When data integration is accomplished clinically, however, the intercorrelations among neuropsychodiagnostic signs must be estimated. The difficulty of these estimations, of course, increases dramatically with the number of signs considered and is rarely undertaken in clinical practice.

An undesirable outcome of independent consideration of signs is that two highly correlated sources of assessment data may be weighted doubly in terms of their contributions to a diagnostic prediction. Moreover, when assessment data are highly congruent (i.e., correlated), clinicians often tend to express higher degrees of confidence in diagnoses than when such data are less dependent. It is much more sobering to view these situations in terms of redundancy as opposed to congruence. When they are viewed in the context of redundancy, it is clear why diagnoses that are based on simultaneously considered sources of assessment data are more likely to be accurate than sources that are overly weighted owing to independent consideration.

Relative Importance of Data

A final distinction between actuarial and clinical models concerns the relative importance (i.e., weights) attributed to particular assessment data across cases. For actuarial models, assessment data are weighted consistently across similar cases (where those weights are partially determined by the amount of diagnostic variance for which a datum accounts). In contrast, for clinical models, clinicians have the freedom to use assessment data differentially depending on factors that are unique to the case in point. For example, a result of an IQ test might be weighted relatively less in terms of its contribution to the diagnosis of a minority child than of an Anglo child; an assessed constructional apraxia might be weighted more in terms of its contribution to the diagnosis of a child with prior formal educational experience than to the diagnosis of a child without such experience.

This kind of differential weighting of signs is often couched in explanations regarding equality and nondiscriminatory assessment practices. The implicit assumption made when differential weights are assigned to individual sources of data contingent on the presence of putative moderator variables (e.g., race, educational experience), however, is that those sources of data are differentially predictive of the diagnosis depending on the moderator variable (Thorndike, 1982). In the absence of empirical verification of such differential predictability, assigning different weights to assessment data is more likely to introduce bias into the assessment rather than to eliminate it (Jensen, 1973; Mercer & Lewis, 1978; Mitchell, 1967; Scarr-Salapatek, 1971). This may be due, in part, to the phenomenon of illusory correlation that is common in situations where clinicians are required to perceive the covariation between assessment data and diagnoses without the benefit of empirical techniques (Chapman, 1967; Chapman & Chapman, 1967, 1969; Golding & Rorer, 1972; Kurtz & Garfield, 1978; Lueger & Petzel, 1979; Starr & Katkin, 1969).

ACTUARIAL MODELS

For actuarial models of diagnosis, rules (i.e., equations) are developed that specify how assessment data are to be combined. Applications of these rules result in empirically determined representations of diagnostic predictions or some other outcome for individual patients. Rules are typically multivariate (however, cf. Goldstein & Shelly, 1973). This means that several sources of assessment data can be considered concomitantly. Perhaps because of the relatively large amounts of assessment data that are typically collected for neuropsychological evaluations, many actuarial diagnostic models have been proposed, but mainly for adult populations. As the discipline of child neuropsychology continues to mature, it is reasonable to expect that diagnostic applications of the model to this population will also increase. Currently, the model is popular in the child psychopathology literature; however, most of the reports employing the model with child neuropsychological cases are exploratory rather than diagnostic at the present time.

Methods

There are numerous statistical methods that can be used to derive actuarial diagnostic rules, but three of the most popular methods are discriminant analysis, multiple regression, and cluster analysis (see Huberty, 1975, 1984; McDermott, 1982; Pedhazur, 1982; Tryon & Bailey, 1970). In all of these statistical methods, the variability among multiple sources of assessment data is analyzed.

In order to use discriminant analysis and multiple regression methods to derive an actuarial diagnostic rule, particular diagnostic outcomes must be specified prior to the analysis. For discriminant analysis methods, these outcomes are scaled in nominal units (e.g., diagnostic classifications), and the result of the analysis is an equation that indicates how the various sources of assessment data should be weighted and combined in order to discriminate maximally among the outcomes. Subsequently, clinicians can evaluate an empirically derived probability that suggests how closely a particular pattern of assessment data collected from a patient corresponds to similar data collected from some previously diagnosed group. For multiple regression methods, outcomes may be scaled in metric units; consequently, degrees of some criterion (e.g., level of impairment or prognostic information) can be predicted from the combined assessment data. The result of a multiple regression analysis is an equation that indicates how the various sources of assessment data should be weighted and combined in order to best predict the degree of some outcome of interest.

For cluster analysis methods, outcome variables such as diagnostic classification and prognostic information are not specified prior to the analysis. Instead, multiple sources of assessment data from each of a large number of patients are analyzed in order to determine if there are subgroups of patients that demonstrate similar patterns of assessment results. These subgroups are determined by successive comparisons in which patterns of patient assessment data are clustered such that, with reference to these data, the variability within subgroups is minimized whereas the variability among subgroups is maximized. Subsequently, similar to discriminant analysis, a clinician can evaluate how closely a particular pattern of assessment data collected from an individual patient corresponds to the pattern demonstrated by some natural subgroup. This method is essentially that which Achenbach (see Achenbach & Edelbrock, 1978) employed in order to establish empirical diagnostic categories in the field of child psychopathology. The method also has been readily embraced by researchers who are exploring potential relationships between specific learning disabilities in children and neuropsychological status (see Hooper & Willis, in press).

Given the relative assets of actuarial models of diagnostic decision making, it logically follows that diagnostic accuracy in child neuropsychology would improve as a function of the availability and application of actuarial rules. Responsible use of actuarial rules, however, demands critical evaluation. Clinicians should evaluate the technical aspects of actuarial rule derivation just as carefully as they would evaluate, for example, the psychometric properties of a test prior to its adoption in a case. In this respect, three important issues are (a) base rates in particular populations, (b) validity of criteria, and (c) stability of rules.

Base-Rate Considerations

When an actuarial diagnostic rule is published, the hit rate is usually presented as an index of that rule's accuracy. For example, Selz and Reitan (1979; see also Reitan, 1984) developed an actuarial rule to classify children aged 9 through 14 as normal, learning-disabled, or brain-damaged; their data are presented in Table 1. There were 25 children in each group who had been diagnosed independently according to the criteria for these categories. Using only the actuarial rule, 24 of the 25 normal children were correctly classified, 14 of the 25 learning-diasbled children were correctly classified, and 17 of the 25 brain-damaged children were correctly classified. Thus, from a total of 75 children, 24 + 14 + 17, or 55/75, were correctly classified; the hit rate in this case was 73.3%.

In order to evaluate a particular hit rate appropriately, it must be compared to a base rate. In the example, the base rates for each of the three diagnostic classifications were 25/75, or approximately 33.3%. This

TABLE 1. Classification Accuracy Table[a]

	Actual diagnosis		
Prediction	Normal	Learning-disabled	Brain-damaged
Normal	24	8	4
Learning-disabled	1	14	4
Brain-damaged	0	3	17

[a]From Selz and Reitan (1979). Copyright 1979 by the American Psychological Association. Adapted by permission.

means that if a clinician were to diagnose every patient in this population as, for example, brain-damaged, that diagnosis would be accurate for approximately 33.3% of the cases and inaccurate for approximately 66.7% of the cases. Because base rates establish some chance criterion of diagnostic accuracy, actuarial rules must, at the minimum, improve on those probabilities. Thus, the hit rate of 73.3% noted in the example would be compared with the base rate of 33.3% in order to determine improvement over chance.

In order to assess the significance of a difference between a hit rate and a base rate, clinicians can apply one of two criteria proposed by Huberty (1984). For one assessment, an overall hit rate is compared with the base rate for the largest diagnostic group. In the example taken from Selz and Reitan (1979), because the diagnostic groups are of equal size (i.e., 25 each), their associated base rates, of course, are also equal (i.e., 33.3% each); however, in many other instances base rates are not equal. In such instances, comparisons are made against the highest base rate. A standardized normal test statistic (i.e., z) for hit-rate–base-rate comparisons is

$$z = \frac{(o - e)\sqrt{N}}{\sqrt{e(N - e)}} \tag{1}$$

where o is the observed number of hits (cf. hit rate), e is the expected number of hits (i.e., the number of cases in the largest diagnostic group; cf. base rate), and N is the total number of cases in the sample. Substituting values in the example taken from Selz and Reitan for variables in Equation 1, $z = 7.35$ ($p < .001$). Thus, the hit rate obtained from using the actuarial rule significantly improved on the chance assignment of patients to diagnostic classifications.

Huberty (1984) also proposed a different kind of comparison that is useful when clinicians are interested in classification accuracy for a particular diagnostic group. For example, one might be interested in how

accurately a brain-damaged child might be identified by using the actuarial rule proposed by Selz and Reitan (1979). A standardized normal
statistic for this comparison is

$$z = \frac{(n_{gg} - e_g) \sqrt{n_g}}{\sqrt{e_g(n_g - e_g)}} \tag{2}$$

where n_{gg} is the number of correctly identified patients within the diagnostic group of interest (cf. o, hit rate), e_g is the number of patients within
that group expected to be diagnosed correctly by chance (calculated as
n_g^2/N; cf. e, base rate), and n_g is the number of patients within the diagnostic group of interest (cf. N). Substituting values from Selz and Reitan
for variables in Equation 2, $z = 3.69$ ($p < .001$). Thus, the accuracy associated with identifying brain-damaged children was significantly better
than chance.

Finally, Huberty (1984) further proposed an index that is useful in
determining the degree to which an actuarial rule can improve diagnostic
accuracy over chance levels. This index is

$$I = \frac{H_o - H_e}{1 - H_e} \tag{3}$$

where H_o is the observed hit rate, and H_e is the hit rate expected by chance
(i.e., base rate). This improvement-over-chance index (I) can be used in
the context of either Equation 1 or 2. For example, $Is = 0.60$ and 0.52, for
the overall and the brain-damaged classification comparisons, respectively. Thus, the use of the actuarial rule proposed by Selz and Reitan
(1979) improved diagnostic accuracy overall by 60% and within the brain-
damaged group by 52%.

Although comparisons between base rates and hit rates are relatively
straightforward and were, in fact, proposed by Meehl and Rosen (1955)
over three decades ago, they are frequently absent from current reports of
neuropsychological actuarial rules. For example, when evaluated in this
context, published neuropsychological actuarial rules often do not significantly improve on chance levels of diagnostic accuracy; worse yet, many
yield a level of diagnostic accuracy that is significantly poorer than
chance (see Willis, 1984). Thus, it is important for clinicians to evaluate
actuarial rules in terms of hit-rate to base-rate comparisons in order to
make informed decisions about the utility of those rules.

Validity of Diagnostic Criteria

Another methodological issue that must be considered concerns the
validity of the criteria (e.g., for diagnostic or prognostic outcomes) that

were used to establish the actuarial rule. The validity of any actuarial rule is necessarily limited by the validities of the criteria used to establish that rule. Moreover, the validities of those criteria are necessarily limited by their associated reliabilities. The problem is compounded in the case of children because of the often invasive nature of definitive diagnostic criteria for neuropsychological disorders, in addition to the limited data base describing the course and sequelae of particular disorders. Further, given the special circumstance that child (versus adult) psychological symptoms are usually pathological only in the context of developmental delays, diagnostic criteria used to establish actuarial rules for children should be referenced against particular age-level expectations.

The level of inference adopted by researchers who develop actuarial rules is another consideration of some importance with reference to validity. For example, particular subtypes of specific developmental disorders (SDD, cf. specific learning disabilities, SLD) are often assumed to be organically (neuropsychologically) based. This assumption may be at least partially predicated on the (perhaps erroneous) idea that if a particular form of observable neurological impairment can cause severe forms of a disorder such as epilepsy or cerebral palsy, then milder forms of such impairment may result in milder forms of disorders such as hyperactivity or SDD/SLD (Fletcher & Taylor, 1984; however, see Rosen, Sherman, & Galaburda, 1986). It is often the case that groups of children of varying ages are diagnosed as SDD/SLD according to DSM-III-R (American Psychiatric Association, 1987) or federal, state, and local educational agency criteria (primarily on the basis of psychoeducational assessment), and that such children are subsequently subtyped or differentiated from others on the basis of patterns of neuropsychological assessment data (Fisk & Rourke, 1979, 1983; Fletcher, Smidt, & Satz, 1979; Lyon, Stewart, & Freedman, 1982; Selz & Reitan, 1979). Two limitations inherent in these approaches are that (a) the validity of the external SDD/SLD diagnosis may be, in itself, questionable (see Shepard, Smith, & Vojir, 1983) and (b) because the diagnosis of these disorders is contingent on developmental comparisons, merging diagnosed children of greatly different chronological ages for the purpose of statistical analysis is probably inappropriate.

Stability and Generalizability of Actuarial Rules

Even when the criteria upon which actuarial rules are based are valid (and therefore also reliable), the actuarial rule can still lack validity. This is because the reliabilities of rules, *per se*, are relatively independent of criterion-related considerations. Thus, to the extent that actuarial rules lack reliability, they also lack validity. Actuarial rules are derived by analyzing the variability among multiple sources of assessment data via powerful multivariate methods. These methods, however, capitalize on all sources of variability present, even unspecified sources due to random factors (i.e., error). It is entirely possible, therefore, that, even when careful attention has been paid to issues concerning criterion validity, a particular actuarial rule could classify patients primarily on the basis of random variation among assessment data.

The problem is intensified in the clinical specialty of child neuropsychology because rules are developed typically with relatively large amounts of assessment data collected from each patient and relatively small numbers of patients in distinct diagnostic criterion groups. These circumstances potientiate the possibility that resulting actuarial rules can be largely determined on the basis of chance. For example, when the ratio of the number of patients to the number of assessment measures is low (i.e., approaches 1), application of the actuarial rule to new patients is associated with a higher probability of a diagnostic error than when that ratio is relatively higher (Fletcher, Rice, & Ray, 1978).

In order to address this problem properly, actuarial rules should be cross-validated. In the context of actuarial models of diagnosis, cross-validation is a procedure in which an actuarial rule, derived with one group of patients, is subsequently applied to a second (different) group of patients. The actuarial diagnostic or prognostic predictions from this second group of patients are then compared with independently determined diagnoses or prognoses. An index of relationship between the predicted and independent outcomes is then determined. This index is lower than that between the aggregate of assessment data and the predicted outcome in the initial analysis, and is a more stable, representative estimate of the true data–outcome contingency.

Many neuropsychological actuarial rules are not cross-validated; as such, the established hit rates are spuriously high owing to multivariate capitalization on random variation among assessment data. This methodological issue was well illustrated by Willson and Reynolds (1982), who conducted a secondary analysis of nine reports (a majority with child subjects) of actuarial rules for diagnosis. After estimates of cross-validation were made, only about half of the original 12 indexes of relationship remained statistically significant. Clearly, clinical applications of actuarial rules that have not been cross-validated are premature. In the absence of actual cross-validation, which often may be difficult to accomplish because of low numbers of patients in diagnostic groups, estimations can be made (see Cattin, 1980; Herzberg, 1969; Lachenbruch, 1967; Mosier, 1951).

CLINICAL JUDGMENT

There are at least three assumptions inherent in the responsible use of actuarial rules for child neuropsychological diagnosis. The first is that these rules are free from the methodological problems described. The second is that actuarial rules are readily available for clinical evaluation. The third is that when diagnostic errors are made (as they inevitably will be), the costs associated with different kinds of error are constant both across cases and for an individual patient (or at least match those estimated by the developer of the rule). In reality, certain kinds of error are much more costly (i.e., serious) than others in terms of a variety of criteria. Moreover, the current state of the field is such that, with children, the first two assumptions would often be violated as well.

In situations where these assumptions are violated, child neuro-psychologists cannot depend on actuarial rules to guide diagnostic decision making. Instead, assessment data must be aggregated clinically, and, as such, without thoughtful consideration of the cognitive processes involved, decisions are subject to a high degree of error. Moreover, even when methodologically sound actuarial rules are available, clinicians ideally will use these models of data integration as guides to help clarify the diagnostic or prognostic decision-making process, as opposed to an exclusive dependence on the application of rules per se. In the final analysis, of course, clinicians diagnose patients; rules and assessment data do not. The ultimate responsibility for accurate decisions lies with clinicians rather than with the tools they choose to help them think. As already noted, however, thoughtful clinical judgment demands systematically organized thinking. An examination of how interpretive strategies, debiasing techniques, assessment design, and decision rules can be useful in this respect follows.

Interpretive Strategies

Clinical decisions are often biased (and therefore erroneous) owing to the inconsistent use of particular strategies for interpreting assessment data (see also McDermott, 1981). Two major interpretive strategies are normative and ipsative. For normative strategies, each source of assessment data collected from a patient is compared with a reference group, and marked discrepancies from this normative distribution are considered as abnormal. In contrast, for ipsative strategies, the patient's own baseline (or average) level of functioning is taken as the reference point against which specific areas of functioning are compared. The latter interpretive strategy has become increasingly more widespread in recent years, especially in the pediatric literature (e.g., Kaufman & Kaufman, 1983; Reynolds, 1982; Reynolds & Clark, 1983; Reynolds & Gutkin, 1981; Reynolds & Kaufman, 1985).

These two interpretive strategies are well illustrated by Reitan's (e.g., Reitan & Davison, 1974) approach to neuropsychological test interpretation, which comprises four methods of inference (see also Selz, 1981).

Two of these methods are distinctly normative whereas the other two are ipsative. The two normative strategies concern level of performance and pathognomonic signs. Level-of-performance measures (e.g., numbers of errors on the Category Test) are compared against norms established for children of similar age levels in order to determine deficiencies in performance abilities. Although useful in that context, these measures are similarly limited, as are other kinds of normative data in child neuropsychological evaluations, because of difficulties in distinguishing developmental delays from deficits. Such distinctions are important in terms of diagnosis and prognosis as well as treatment planning. Additionally, premorbid levels of functioning are neglected sources of information when assessment data are considered primarily in a normative sense. Thus, an average level of performance may be interpreted mistakenly as asymptomatic in those cases where a premorbid level was actually superior. Pathognomonic signs (e.g., errors on Imperception Tests) are also normative sources of data in the sense that their presence is compared with that of some reference group. They are less susceptible to interpretive errors, however, because such signs can be (but are not always) symptomatic independent of developmental considerations. The two ipsative strategies concern pattern-of-performance measures (e.g., a particular configuration of test scores) and right–left differences (e.g., differences in finger-tapping rates between the hands). Both of these strategies involve intraindividual as opposed to normative group comparisons.

Most ipsative strategies are predicated on the assumption that each source of assessment data possesses an adequate degree of specificity for individual interpretation. In this context, specificity refers to that proportion of the variance of a particular source of assessment data that is reliable and unique (i.e., is independent of other sources). If a particular source of assessment data lacks specificity, then it should not ordinarily be interpreted in the typical ipsative sense as representing a unique function. Ipsative interpretations of most subtests from the Kaufman Assessment Battery for Children (Kaufman & Kaufman, 1983) and the Wechsler Intelligence Scale for Children-Revised (Wechsler, 1974), for example, are well established strategies because adequate degrees of subtest specificity, for the most part, have been documented (Kaufman & Kaufman, 1983; Reynolds & Kaufman, 1985).

When clinicians are consistent in applying interpretive strategies (whether normative, ipsative, or both) to assessment data, they are less likely to bias diagnostic and prognostic decisions. For example, an initial prejudicial choice of a particular approach (either for an individual patient or for a particular source of assessment data) can help to determine the outcome of a case. In these instances, diagnostic decisions may be inappropriately influenced by methodological rather than more important substantive issues.

Debiasing Techniques

Research investigating judgmental heuristics has delineated several cognitive biases associated with diagnostic inaccuracy as well as several possible debiasing techniques (Achenbach, 1985; Arkes, 1981). As noted previously, one common source of bias is an inappropriate conceptualization or assessment of symptom-diagnosis covariation. Table 2 is a prototypical contingency table of the relationship between a particular symptom (25-point discrepancy between the Verbal and Performance IQs on the WISC) and neurologic insult (presence vs. absence of brain damage). Entries in the table are estimated calculations based on data presented by Holroyd and Wright (1965), assuming a total of 100 cases and a liberal incidence estimate for childhood brain damage of 10%. These hypothetical data show that 30% of a sample of non brain-damaged children demonstrated a discrepancy of 25 or more points between Verbal and Performance IQ scores and 80% of a sample of brain-damaged children demonstrated this same symptom. Similar data (e.g., Black, 1976) are often misinterpreted as evidence that this size of discrepancy may be symptomatic of brain damage in children (e.g., Sattler, 1982, p. 460; however, cf. Sattler, 1988, pp. 705–706).

These kinds of interpretations of symptom–diagnosis contingencies are often made when some of the available data (e.g., the proportion of cases in which the symptom is absent but the diagnosis is present) are considered to be less important than others (e.g., the proportion of cases in which both the symptom and the diagnosis are present; see Arkes & Harkness, 1983; Nisbett & Ross, 1980). In fact, all data are equally important in determining the degree of relationship between the symptom and the diagnosis. An accurate assessment of this relationship for the data presented in Table 2 indicates that the interpretation noted is perhaps not as clear as it may seem.

Several pieces of information are required in order to determine the probability that the diagnosis of brain damage is correct or even if this symptom is likely to be from a brain-damaged child. This information includes (a) prior odds, (b) likelihood ratio, and (c) posterior odds (see Arkes, 1981). The ratio representing prior odds is simply the likelihood

TABLE 2. Symptom-Diagnosis Contingency Table

Symptom	Diagnosis	
	Brain-damaged	Non brain-damaged
≥25-point VIQ–PIQ discrepancy	8	27
<25-point VIQ–PIQ discrepancy	2	63

that the diagnosis is correct divided by the likelihood that the diagnosis is incorrect and is thus comparable to a base-rate index. Prior odds are subsequently modified when information concerning a symptom is obtained. Such information can be expressed as a likelihood ratio, which is the probability of obtaining that symptom if the diagnosis were correct divided by the probability of obtaining that symptom if the diagnosis were incorrect. Finally, the ratio representing posterior odds is the probability that the diagnosis is correct given the symptom and it is determined by the product of the prior odds and the likelihood ratio.

Substituting values from Table 2, the prior odds are $(8 + 2)/(27 + 63)$ or 10/90. The likelihood ratio is $(8/[8 + 2])/(27/[27 + 63])$ or 0.8/0.3. Consequently, the posterior odds are $(10/90)(0.8/0.3)$ or 8/27 (i.e.,0.3). Thus, the probability that a diagnosis of brain damage is correct when based on the 25-point VIQ–PIQ discrepancy is only 30%; the probability that a 25-point VIQ–PIQ discrepancy is from a brain-damaged child is only $8/(8 + 27)$ or 23%. Results fare even worse given more conservative incidence estimates for childhood brain damage. When all data in contingency tables are given proper consideration, symptom–diagnosis relationships can be perceived much more accurately.

In addition to this kind of Bayesian analysis of symptom–diagnosis covariation, clinicians should entertain alternative diagnostic or prognostic possibilities until all have been actively considered. This is because another source of error in clinical decision making is that, once a decision is made, the processing of subsequent assessment data may be biased. In this respect, clinicians should also endeavor to decrease the degree to which they rely on memory when assessment data are being aggregated. For example, biased decisions may result because unpresented symptoms that are consistent with a particular diagnosis tend to be remembered as having been presented, whereas symptoms that are actually presented, yet are inconsistent with the diagnosis, tend to be forgotten (Arkes & Harkness, 1980). Thus, it is not surprising that the most accurate clinicians are those who arrive at diagnostic decisions relatively later than less accurate clinicians (Elstein, Shulman, & Sprafka, 1978).

Assessment Design and Decision Rules

Careful consideration of how the neuropsychological assessment process is designed also can help to improve the accuracy of diagnostic and prognostic predictions. Data should be collected from a variety of settings, observers, and techniques in order to establish a comprehensive description of the neuropsychological status of the child. Additionally, clinicians should resist the temptation to evaluate only a particular domain of functioning because this may bias the ultimate decision from the outset. In this respect, the multiaxial system outlined in DSM-III-R (American Psychiatric Association, 1987) is useful for designing a comprehensive evaluation. It is the multiaxial process that is perhaps more useful (especially for childhood disorders) than the DSM-III-R diagnostic codes per se.

Consider the assessment situation that, from the point of view of accuracy, would be ideal: use of multiple techniques such as tests, observations, and interviews to collect information in each of the five DSM-III-R domains (i.e., clinical syndromes, developmental disorders, physical conditions, psychosocial stressors, global adaptive functioning). Further, a variety of assesssors would be used in the multiple settings in which the child interacts (e.g., home, school, clinic). This kind of design, in which technique, domain, assessor, and setting are crossed, would serve to minimize biased diagnostic and prognostic decisions by eliminating confounding influences inherent in more typical assessment situations. In a more typical situation, for example, a child suspected of being learning-disabled might be examined by a neuropsychologist in a clinic where the focus of that examination is primarily related to DSM-III-R Axis II domains. Information also might be solicited from the teacher at school via rating scales and work samples regarding academic performance, and from the mother via an interview regarding home-related and parental concerns. Here, potential differences among these three major sources of assessment information could be a function of technique, domain, assessor (or informant), setting, or some combination of factors. The confounding influences can only be reduced to the extent that multiple techniques, domains, assessors, and settings are used. Given a variety of constraints, idealized assessment designs are impractical, of course, but it is incumbent that clinicians be sensitive to the ways in which their diagnostic and prognostic decisions are influenced by deviations from such designs.

Finally, when child neuropsychologists are able to approach evaluations from a multidimensional perspective, they can expect that the large amount of assessment data collected often will be difficult to aggregate without the guidance of actuarial rules. Applying decision rules can be a useful strategy in such circumstances. Decision rules help to reduce bias by specifying a prescribed sequence of decisions that should be made, as well as the criteria (usually empirically derived) upon which those decisions should be based. McDermott and Watkins (1985) developed a comprehensive set of these rules for the diagnosis of childhood psychological disorders (see also Aaron, 1981; Spitzer, Skodol, Gibbon, & Williams, 1981). Similar to multivariate actuarial rules, however, decision rules should be carefully evaluated prior to their use because associated reliability and validity issues will limit the utility of the clinician's diagnostic prediction.

SUMMARY

There are a number of professional issues unique to the discipline of child neuropsychological diagnosis. Many of these issues can be addressed via a thorough consideration of the diagnostic models used by clinicians in order to aid decision making. For actuarial models, neuro-psychological assessment data are integrated statistically, whereas for clinical models, data are integrated more subjectively.

Actuarial models have been traditionally associated with higher de-grees of diagnostic accuracy than clinical models. In addition to meth-odological shortcomings of many actuarial rules for neuropsychological diagnosis, however, the general availability of those rules and relative costs of different kinds of associated errors are considerations that some-times limit utility. There are assets and liabilities associated with both diagnostic models. Indeed, the two models are complementary in many respects. An integrated diagnostic approach is necessary in order to achieve the highest possible degree of accuracy for the neuropsychologi-cal diagnosis of children.

REFERENCES

Aaron, P. G. (1981). Diagnosis and remediation of learning disabilities in children—A neuro-psychological key approach. In G. W. Hynd & J. E. Obrzut (Eds.), *Neuropsychological assessment and the school-age child* (pp. 303–333). New York: Grune and Stratton.

Achenbach, T. M. (1985). *Assessment and taxonomy of child and adolescent psycho-pathology.* Beverly Hills, CA: Sage.

Achenbach, T. M., & Edelbrock, C. S. (1978). The classification of child psychopathology: A review and analysis of empirical efforts. *Psychological Bulletin, 85,* 1275–1301.

American Psychiatric Association. (1987). *Diagnostic and statistical manual of mental dis-orders* (3rd ed., rev.). Washington, DC: Author.

Arkes, H. R. (1981). Impediments to accurate clinical judgment and possible ways to mini-mize their impact. *Journal of Consulting and Clinical Psychology, 49,* 323–330.

Arkes, H. R., & Harkness, A. R. (1980). The effect of making a diagnosis on subsequent recognition of symptoms. *Journal of Experimental Psychology: Human Learning and Memory, 6,* 568–575.

Arkes, H. R., & Harkness, A. R. (1983). Estimates of contingency between two dichotomous variables. *Journal of Experimental Psychology: General, 112,* 117–135.

Black, F. W. (1976). Cognitive, academic, and behavioral findings in children with suspected and documented neurological dysfunction. *Journal of Learning Disabilities, 9,* 182–187.

Cattin, P. (1980). Note on the estimation of the squared cross-validated multiple correlation of a regression model. *Psychological Bulletin, 87,* 63–65.

Chapman, L. (1967). Illusory correlation in observational report. *Journal of Verbal Learning and Verbal Behavior, 6,* 151–155.

Chapman, L., & Chapman, J. (1967). Genis of popular but erroneous psychodiagnostic obser-vations. *Journal of Abnormal Psychology, 72,* 193–204.

Chapman, L., & Chapman, J. (1969). Illusory correlation as an obstacle to the use of valid psychodiagnostic signs. *Journal of Abnormal Psychology, 74,* 271–280.

Elstein, A. S., Shulman, A. S., & Sprafka, S. A. (1978). *Medical problem solving: An analysis of clinical reasoning.* Cambridge, MA: Harvard University Press.

Fisk, J. L., & Rourke, B. P. (1979). Identification of subtypes of learning-disabled children at three age levels: A neuropsychological, multivariate approach. *Journal of Clinical Neu-ropsychology, 1,* 289–310.

Fisk, J. L., & Rourke, B. P. (1983). Neuropsychological subtyping of learning-disabled children: History, methods, implications. *Journal of Learning Disabilities, 16*, 529–531.

Fletcher, J. M., Rice, W. J., & Ray, R. M. (1978). Linear discriminant analysis in neuropsychological research: Some uses and abuses. *Cortex, 14*, 564–577.

Fletcher, J. M., Smidt, R. K., & Satz, P. (1979). Discriminant function strategies for the kindergarten prediction of reading achievement. *Journal of Clinical Neuropsychology, 1*, 151–166.

Fletcher, J. M., & Taylor, H. G. (1984). Neuropsychological approaches to children: Towards a developmental neuropsychology. *Journal of Clinical Neuropsychology, 6*, 39–56.

Goldberg, L. R., & Werts, C. E. (1966). The reliability of clinical judgments: A multitrait-multimethod approach. *Journal of Consulting Psychology, 30*, 199–206.

Golding, S. G., & Rorer, L. (1972). Illusory correlation and subjective judgment. *Journal of Abnormal Psychology, 80*, 249–260.

Goldstein, G., & Shelly, C. H. (1973). Univariate vs. multivariate analysis in neuropsychological test assessment of lateralized brain damage. *Cortex, 9*, 204–216.

Herzberg, P. A. (1969). The parameters of cross-validation. *Psychometrika, Monograph Supplement, No. 16.*

Holroyd, J., & Wright, F. (1965). Neurological implications of WISC verbal-performance discrepancies in a psychiatric setting. *Journal of Consulting Psychology, 29*, 206–212.

Hooper, S. R., & Willis, W. G. (in press). *Learning disability subtyping: Neuropsychological foundations, conceptual models, and issues in clinical differentiation.* New York: Plenum.

Huberty, C. J. (1975). Discriminant analysis. *Review of Educational Research, 45*, 543–598.

Huberty, C. J. (1984). Issues in the use and interpretation of discriminant analysis. *Psychological Bulletin, 95*, 156–171.

Jensen, A. (1973). *Education and group differences.* New York: Harper & Row.

Kaufman, A. S., & Kaufman, N. L. (1983). *Kaufman Assessment Battery for Children.* Circle Pines, MN: American Guidance Service.

Kurtz, R. M., & Garfield, S. L. (1978). Illusory correlation: A further exploration of Chapman's paradigm. *Journal of Consulting and Clinical Psychology, 46*, 1009–1015.

Lachenbruch, P. A. (1967). An almost unbiased method of obtaining confidence intervals for the probability of misclassification in discriminant analysis. *Biometrics, 23*, 639–645.

Lueger, R. J., & Petzel, T. P. (1979). Illusory correlation in clinical judgment: Effects of amount of information to be processed. *Journal of Consulting and Clinical Psychology, 47*, 1120–1121.

Lyon, R., Stewart, N., & Freedman, D. (1982). Neuropsychological characteristics of empirically derived subgroups of learning disabled readers. *Journal of Clinical Neuropsychology, 4*, 343–365.

McDermott, P. A. (1981). Sources of error in the psychoeducational diagnosis of children. *Journal of School Psychology, 19*, 31–44.

McDermott, P. A. (1982). Actuarial assessment for the grouping and classification of school children. In C. R. Reynolds & T. B. Gutkin (Eds.), *The handbook for school psychology* (pp. 243–272). New York: Wiley.

McDermott, P. A., & Watkins, M. W. (1985). *McDermott Multidimensional Assessment of Children.* Cleveland: OH: Psychological Corporation.

Meehl, P. E. (1954). *Clinical versus statistical prediction: A theoretical analysis and a review of the evidence.* Minneapolis: University of Minnesota Press.

Meehl, P. E. (1973). *Psychodiagnosis: Selected papers.* Minneapolis: University of Minnesota Press.

Meehl, P. E., & Rosen, A.(1955). Antecedent probability and the efficiency of psychometric signs, patterns, or cutting scores. *Psychological Bulletin, 52*, 194–216.

Mercer, J. R., & Lewis, J. F. (1978). *System of Multicultural Pluralistic Assessment.* New York: Psychological Corporation.

Mitchell, B. (1967). Predictive validity of the Metropolitan Readiness Test and the Murphy-Durrell Reading Readiness Analysis for white and negro pupils. *Educational and Psychological Measurement, 27*, 1047–1054.

Mosier, C. I. (1951). Problems and designs of cross-validation. *Educational and Psychological Measurement, 11*, 5–11.

Nisbett, R. E., & Ross, L. (1980). *Human inference: Strategies and shortcomings of social judgment.* Englewood Cliffs, NJ: Prentice-Hall.

Obrzut, J. E., Hynd, G. W., & Obrzut, A. (1983). Neuropsychological assessment of learning disabilities: A discriminant analysis. *Journal of Experimental Child Psychology, 35*, 46–55.

Pedhazur, E. J. (1982). *Multiple regression in behavioral research* (2nd ed.). New York: Holt, Rinehart & Winston.

Phelan, J. G. (1964). Rationale employed by clinical psychologists in diagnostic judgment. *Journal of Clinical Psychology, 20*, 454–458.

Rapoport, J. L., & Ismond, D. R. (1984). *DSM-III training guide for diagnosis of childhood disorders.* New York: Brunner/Mazel.

Reitan, R. M. (1984). An impairment index of brain functions in children. *Perceptual and Motor Skills, 58*, 875–881.

Reitan, R. M., & Davison, L. A. (Eds.). (1974). *Clinical neuropsychology: Current status and applications.* Washington, DC: V. H. Winston.

Reynolds, C. R. (1982). Determining statistically reliable strengths and weaknesses in the performance of single individuals on the Luria-Nebraska Neuropsychological Battery. *Journal of Consulting and Clinical Psychology, 50*, 525–529.

Reynolds, C. R., & Clark, J. H. (1983). Assessment of cognitive abilities. In K. D. Paget & B. Bracken (Eds.), *The psychoeducational assessment of preschool children* (pp. 163–189). New York: Grune and Stratton.

Reynolds, C. R., & Gutkin, T. B. (1981). Statistics for the interpretation of Bannatyne reorganization of WPPSI subtests. *Journal of Learning Disabilities, 14*, 446–467.

Reynolds, C. R., & Kaufman, A. S. (1985). Clinical assessment of children's intelligence with the Wechsler scales. In B. B. Wolman (Ed.), *Handbook of intelligence: Theories, measurements, and applications* (pp. 601–661). New York: Wiley.

Rosen, G. D., Sherman, G. F., & Galaburda, A. M. (1986). Biological interactions in dyslexia (pp. 155–173). In J. E. Obrzut & G. W. Hynd (Eds.), *Child neuropsychology: Vol. 1. Theory and research.* Orlando, FL: Academic Press.

Sattler, J. M. (1982). *Assessment of children's intelligence and special abilities* (2nd ed.). Boston: Allyn & Bacon.

Sattler, J. M. (1988). *Assessment of children* (3rd ed.). San Diego, CA: Jerome M. Sattler.

Scarr-Salapatek, S. (1971). Race, social class, and IQ. *Science, 174*, 1285–1295.

Selz, M. (1981). Halstead-Reitan neuropsychological test batteries for children. In G. W. Hynd & J. E. Obrzut (Eds.), *Neuropsychological assessment and the school-age child* (pp. 195–235). New York: Grune and Stratton.

Selz, M., & Reitan, R. M. (1979). Rules for neuropsychological diagnosis: Classification of brain function in older children. *Journal of Consulting and Clinical Psychology, 47*, 258–264.

Shepard, L. A., Smith, M. L., & Vojir, C. P. (1983). Characteristics of pupils identified as learning disabled. *American Educational Research Journal, 20*, 309–331.

Spitzer, R. L., Skodol, A. E., Gibbon, M., & Williams, J. B. W. (1981). *DSM-III case book.* Washington. DC: American Psychiatric Association.

Starr, J. G., & Katkin, E. (1969). The clinician as an aberrant actuary: Illusory correlation and the Incomplete Sentences Blank. *Journal of Abnormal Psychology, 74*, 670–675.

Thorndike, R. L. (1982). *Applied psychometrics.* Boston: Houghton Mifflin.

Tryon, R. C., & Bailey, D. E. (1970). *Cluster analysis.* New York: McGraw-Hill.

Tversky, A., & Kahneman, D. (1973). Availability: A heuristic for judging frequency and probability. *Cognitive Psychology, 5,* 207–232.

Wallach, M. S., & Schoof, K. (1965). Reliability of degree of disturbance rating. *Journal of Clinical Psychology, 21,* 273–275.

Wechsler, D. (1974). *Wechsler Intelligence Scale for Children-Revised.* New York: Psychological Corporation.

Willis, W. G. (1984). Reanalysis of an actuarial approach to neuropsychological diagnosis in consideration of base rates. *Journal of Consulting and Clinical Psychology, 52,* 567–569.

Willson, V. L., & Reynolds, C. R. (1982). Methodological and statistical problems in determining membership in clinical populations. *Clinical Neuropsychology, 4,* 134–138.

From Assessment to Treatment
Linkage to Interventions with Children

G. REID LYON, LOUISA MOATS, and JANE M. FLYNN

INTRODUCTION

Within the past decade, child clinical neuropsychologists have been called upon increasingly to make relevant and informed recommendations for the treatment of both documented (i.e., traumatic head injury) and putative (i.e., learning disabilities) neurologically based developmental disorders. This increase in requests for specific therapeutic recommendations reflects a change in how the role of the child clinical neuropsychologist is perceived and, in particular, how the data obtained from neuropsychological assessments are used.

Historically, neuropsychological assessment practices were applied primarily to identify the presence, nature, and possible site(s) of brain damage or dysfunction (Beaumont, 1983). However, the emphasis in clinical neuropsychology has shifted from assisting in the diagnosis of lesion type and location to the assessment of the functional capacities of the child in order to select and implement efficacious management, rehabilitation, and/or remediation programs.

There appear to be several reasons for this transition in the practice of clinical neuropsychology. For example, recent technical advances in specialized neurodiagnostic procedures for brain imaging gradually are replacing neuropsychological approaches to lesion classification (Stoddart

G. REID LYON • Departments of Neurology and Communication Science and Disorders, University of Vermont, Burlington, Vermont, Gundersen Medical Foundation, and Department of Special Education, St. Michael's College, Winooski, Vermont.   LOUISA MOATS • Associates in Counseling and Education, East Thetford, Vermont.   JANE M. FLYNN • Gundersen Medical Foundation, LaCrosse, Wisconsin.

& Knights, 1986). Less documentable, but equally influential, are the social, political, and educational trends that have created and fostered a
major role for neuropsychological treatment approaches in the fields of
learning disabilities and cognitive rehabilitation. Models for treatment
that claim to derive validity from biological science are appealing in the
field of learning disabilities (LD), in particular, where previously employed aptitude–treatment interaction models have failed to generate the
foundations of a clinical science (Lyon, 1987; Lyon & Moats, in press).
The heterogeneity of the LD population, although now recognized, continues to beg classification and validation (Lyon & Risucci, 1988). Thus,
treatment models that invoke biological explanations for intellectual and
behavioral differences are welcome in the void. A focus on intrinsic bio-
logic variables permits us to minimize the importance of educational,
cultural-familial, and societal causes for individual differences (Chall &
Mirsky, 1978) and, thus, to empower ourselves by defining treatment
problems in terms of simple, often dichotomous neurobehavioral constructs (e.g., right vs. left brain learners, sequential vs. simultaneous
processing).

   Taken at face value and for whatever reasons, the shift in emphasis
from neuropsychological assessment for classification purposes (i.e.,
presence or absence of brain damage) to assessment for prescriptive purposes (i.e., treatment) reflects a possibly productive transition toward
enhanced clinical relevance. Indeed, Alfano and Finlayson (1987) and
others (Lyon & Moats, in press; Newcomb, 1985) have pointed out recently that the power of the clinical contributions that evolve from neuropsychological practice ultimately depends upon the field's capacity to (1)
delineate neuropsychological strengths and weaknesses in a reliable and
valid fashion, (2) predict the extent to which these information-processing characteristics influence recovery of function and/or learning, and (3)
generate testable hypotheses concerned with remedial methodologies for
individuals who either lost or did not acquire information because of
known or suspected neural insult.

   Perusal of the current literature in both child and adult clinical neuropsychology reveals significant support for the concept of establishing
valid linkages between the information generated from neuropsychological assessment practices and the development of management, rehabilitation, and remediation programs (Rourke, Fisk, & Strang, 1986). However,
such support is generally given in the form of rhetorical and testimonial
presentation, case study information, or anecdotal reports. Although
these particular forums underscore the value of attempting to develop
valid neuropsychologically based treatment programs, we feel that popular views regarding the clinical benefits of such practices go beyond the
data. Given this observation, it should be made clear that our purpose in
this chapter is not to advocate dismissal of the concept of neuropsycho-

logical aptitude–treatment interaction as a useful clinical possibility. On the contrary, our goal is to clarify what actually is known about the relationships between neuropsychological assessment outcomes and treatment decisions and to make relevant recommendations regarding continued research and clinical practice.

Within this context, we first examine neuropsychological assessment principles frequently used with children with an eye toward delineating the purposes for which they were developed as well as their measurement and content characteristics. In doing so, we also attempt to point out how such characteristics relate or do not relate to the content of the clinical treatment process. Following this overview, we describe specific neuropsychological assessment models that have been reported to be useful in generating treatment programs for children with a range of neuropsychological deficiencies. Our purpose is to address the question of which models are most efficacious for the treatment of particular clinical populations (i.e., learning-disabled) and which ones hold the most promise for developing even more robust linkages between assessment outcome and instructional decision making. Finally, we present what we believe are the major limitations in clinical neuropsychological assessment practices that impede our ability to formulate relevant and powerful intervention programs for children with neurodevelopmental disorders. This discussion serves as the basis for what we hope are productive recommendations for enhancing the descriptive, predictive, and ecological validities of assessment practices as they relate to treatment methodologies.

NEUROPSYCHOLOGICAL ASSESSMENT: PURPOSES AND MEASUREMENT CHARACTERISTICS

In order to provide a context for conceptualizing how linkages can be forged between assessment and treatment, it is necessary to examine first the purposes (goals), psychometric properties, and task domains common to neuropsychological batteries and approaches. Given this information, one then can attempt to determine if the inferential process inherent in neuropsychological assessment can be related efficiently to specific treatment methodologies. The reader should note that concepts relevant to neuropsychological assessment have been covered in depth throughout this volume. Thus, what follows is a brief discussion of factors that guide the measurement of brain–behavior relationships.

One's purpose for conducting neuropsychological assessment obviously influences how brain–behavior relationships are measured and assessment results interpreted. As Boll (1981) pointed out, the primary purpose or goal of neuropsychology is to describe brain–behavior relationships in a reliable and valid manner. Boll also indicated that the ultimate, but yet to be realized goal is "the development of remediation and rehabilitation procedures based upon the empirically validated understanding of the behavioral consequences specific to the condition in question in each patient" (p. 582). Although it is noteworthy that Boll (1981) and others (Beaumont, 1983; Obrzut & Hynd, 1986; Rourke *et al.*, 1986) have emphasized the need for neuropsychology to establish valid relationships between assessment and treatment, it seems clear that the majority of batteries and allied procedures designed to infer brain function from behavior have been constructed by incorporating psychometric principles and task content primarily useful for descriptive purposes, not necessarily prescriptive purposes.

To clarify this point, consider the following. Prominent neuropsychological assessment batteries and diagnostic procedures have been developed and refined over the past 50 years by selecting or developing tasks and applying inferential interpretive methods to (1) understand the impact of brain damage or dysfunction on a range of human abilities, (2) differentiate reliably those individuals who present with brain damage and dysfunction from those who do not, and (3) discern the specific behavioral effects of different types of neuropathology (e.g., tumor vs. stroke vs. head injury).

It is reported frequently in the neuropsychology literature that these clinical outcomes are realized most effectively when (1) the assessment procedures consist of objective, standardized, and quantitative measures of an individual's neuropsychological ability structure (Alfano & Finlayson, 1987; Reitan, 1966; Reitan & Wolfson, 1985; Rourke, 1981; Rourke *et al.*, 1986); (2) the assessment procedures include measures that are scaled psychometrically to measure abilities on a continuous scale rather than on an interval scale (Golden, Hammeke, & Purisch, 1978); (3) the assessment tasks and measures are valid and reliable reflections of cerebral dysfunction and are not confounded by the effects of age and education (Finlayson, Johnson, & Reitan, 1977); and (4) the assessment tasks sample a broad range of abilities to include measures of general intellectual ability, the ability to retain verbal and nonverbal information, motor and psychomotor abilities, sensory-perceptual functions, receptive and expressive language skills, attentional skills, analytical reasoning and concept formation, and personality, behavioral, and emotional status (Alfano & Finlayson, 1987; Reitan & Wolfson, 1985).

A number of studies have shown that neuropsychological assessment batteries and allied procedures that have been developed according to these principles are valid for the purposes of identifying the presence of brain damage or dysfunction in both adults (Boll, 1981; Golden *et al.*, 1978; Reitan & Davison, 1974) and children (Hynd & Obrzut, 1986; Rourke, 1981; Rourke *et al.*, 1986; Teeter, 1986). Further, there are data indicating that widely used neuropsychological batteries (e.g., Halstead-

Reitan, Luria-Nebraska) are capable of describing the nature of the neural insult (e.g., type of lesion, site of lesion), particularly when applied to adult clinical populations and interpreted by skilled clinicians. There is also some evidence, albeit limited in scope, that the information derived from adult neuropsychological assessment batteries can be useful in constructing some remediation and rehabilitation programs (Diller & Gordon, 1981a, 1981b; Diller & Weinberg, 1977; Finlayson, Gowland, & Basmajian, 1986; Luria, 1966; Luria & Tzetkova, 1968; Rao & Bieliauskas, 1983).

Despite the success achieved by traditional neuropsychological assessment practices in the diagnosis and description of neuropathology in both adult and pediatric populations, the clinical utility and validity of such practices in designing treatment programs for children remains questionable. This appears to be the case for several reasons. First, a large portion of the assessment tasks that constitute the most widely used standardized neuropsychological batteries for children are downward extensions of batteries initially developed and validated on adult clinical populations. This is particularly true of the Halstead Neuropsychological Test Battery for Children (Reitan & Davison, 1974), the Reitan-Indiana Neuropsychological Test Battery (Reitan, 1969), and the Luria-Nebraska Battery-Children's Revision (Plaisted, Gustavson, Wilkening, & Golden, 1983). Likewise, the type of stimuli (content) used in tasks to assess specific brain–behavior relationships are downward extensions of stimulus items presented to adults.

These test development practices could compromise a battery's power in predicting which treatment methods are most efficacious for particular children because (1) the tasks employed and their content are based primarily on models of adult brain function and dysfunction that occur following a period of normal development; (2) many tasks are designed to assess the effects of focal neuropathology typically seen in adults (e.g., tumors, cerebral vascular accidents, penetrating head wounds) rather than the generalized neural disorders usually observed in children (e.g., closed head injury, anoxia, epilepsy, perinatal trauma); and (3) the neuropsychological task content may bear minimal relationship to the ecological demands that the child is facing in home and school environments. For example, even though many widely used children's batteries contain tasks assessing reading, mathematics, and writing skills, such tasks rarely possess adequate content validity. Consider that the Wide Range Achievement Test, a staple of many child neuropsychological batteries and procedures, assesses only the oral reading of single words, mathematics calculation, and spelling, leaving abilities in reading comprehension, math reasoning, and written language open to question.

Second, and related to the previous points, some neuropsychological assessment procedures employed with children use tasks that yield static measures of competence in neuropsychological ability structures. The data obtained from such measures reflect only a child's past and current declarative knowledge of perceptual, linguistic, cognitive, psychomotor, and academic skills, not how they use or do not use such abilities in their daily lives (Brown & Campione, 1986; Lyon & Moats, in press). A notable exception is the Category Test, known for its sensitivity to abstract concept formation, mental efficiency, and the ability to assess new learning (Boll, 1981).

Third, there is increasing concern that tasks making up neuropsychological assessment batteries for children primarily assess general cognitive ability, not distinct neuropsychological processes (Hynd & Obrzut, 1986; Seidenberg, Giordani, Berent, & Boll, 1983; Tramontana, Klee, & Boyd, 1984). Given this possibility, administering time-consuming batteries beyond administration of a Wechsler Intelligence Scale for Children-Revised (WlSC-R) may net redundant information. Further, the consistent finding that the WISC-R is not particularly useful for the development of instructional or remediation programs (Ysseldyke & Algozzine, 1982; Ysseldyke & Mirkin, 1981) does not bode favorably for the use of redundant neuropsychological batteries for the same purpose.

Fourth, issues related to development and brain maturation may obscure some possible benefits that accrue from administering standard neuropsychological batteries to children for the purposes of designing treatment programs. For instance, Hynd and Obrzut (1986) reported that a number of neuropsychological tasks simply are not age-appropriate, and no neuropsychological test battery has yet to establish adequate cross-sectioned norms. Further, these authors concluded that, without such norms, "it becomes nearly impossible to provide any accurate appraisal of the possible impairment of developing abilities" (p. 10).

Finally, as Lyon and Toomey (1985) have stressed, describing brain–behavior relationships through the application of assessment procedures does not ensure successful remediation of brain-based deficiencies. Whereas neuropsychological assessment may help to clarify the physiological correlates of dyslexia for example, altering the underlying neuropathology or identifying alternate intact processing routes via remediation may not be possible.

There is little doubt that attempts to use neuropsychological assessment data for the purposes of planning treatment programs reflect productive movement toward an exceedingly important clinical goal. However, forming clinically valid linkages between assessment and treatment methods may be hindered by the application of diagnostic procedures that were developed initially for descriptive rather than prescriptive purposes. Moreover, difficulties in identifying such linkages are exacerbated by inadequacies in the content, predictive, and ecological validities of standard neuropsychological tasks used with children, as well as limitations in understanding normative development. These points are elaborated in the following sections.

RELATING ASSESSMENT TO TREATMENT: MODELS AND STUDIES

In general, neuropsychological models of developmental disorders conceptualize a child's learning strengths and weaknesses as manifestations of efficient or inefficient brain regions and/or systems (Gaddes, 1980; Hartlage & Telzrow, 1983; Obrzut & Hynd, 1986; Rourke, Bakker, Fiske, & Strang, 1983). A variety of standard neuropsychological batteries as well as selected neuropsychological assessment procedures have been employed to elucidate such patterns of strengths and weaknesses.

Despite the meager data base, it may be useful to examine specific findings that have been obtained from both clinical and empirical study of the assessment–treatment interface for no other reason than to explicate current clinical trends and future research possibilities. For clarity, we have organized our review of the extant literature in this area first to address treatment approaches and models that are linked to data obtained from standard neuropsychological assessment batteries. This review is followed by a review of intervention studies associated with the use of selected batteries. Treatment approaches will be examined with respect to their orientation (e.g., remediating strengths, weaknesses, or both) as well as to their demonstrated efficacy.

STANDARDIZED ASSESSMENT BATTERIES: IMPLICATIONS FOR TREATMENT

A number of recent papers have discussed the application of standardized neuropsychological assessment methods in formulating treatment programs for children (Alfano & Finlayson, 1987; Gunnison, 1984; Teeter, 1986). These efforts typically involve the use of assessment data obtained from the Halstead-Reitan Neuropsychological Test Batteries and Allied Procedures (Reitan, 1980), the Luria-Nebraska Battery-Children's Revision (Plaisted et al., 1983), and the Kaufman Assessment Battery for Children (K-ABC; Kaufman & Kaufman, 1983). A discussion of these particular assessment methods and their relationship to treatment follows.

The Halstead-Reitan: Linkages to Treatment

The Halstead-Reitan assessment procedures (Boll, 1981; Hartlage & Hartlage, 1977; Teeter, 1986) are a mainstay of clinical neuropsychological practice with children. The Halstead-Reitan procedures have been reported to be sensitive to brain dysfunction in a number of developmental disorders, including asthma (Dunleavy & Beade, 1980), autism (Dawson, 1983), Gilles de la Tourette's syndrome (Bornstein, King, & Carroll, 1983), juvenile delinquency (Yendall, Fromm-Auch, & Davies, 1982), and epilepsy (Herman, 1982). An abundance of data show that the Halstead-Reitan batteries are valid for the differential diagnosis of brain damage in children (Boll & Reitan, 1972; Reed, Reitan, & Klove, 1965; Reitan, 1979). Further, the batteries have been found useful for the neuropsychological classification of minimal brain dysfunction in young children (ages 5–8) (Reitan & Boll, 1973) and learning disabilities in older children (ages 9–14) (Reitan, 1980: Selz & Reitan, 1979).

In 1980, Reitan initiated formal attempts to relate neuropsychological assessment data explicitly to treatment through the development of a program titled Reitan Evaluation of Hemispheric Abilities and Brain Improvement Training (REHABIT). According to Reitan (1979, 1980), the efficacy of REHABIT for the purposes of remediation is dependent upon (1) a comprehensive neuropsychological evaluation (using the Halstead-Reitan procedures) that clearly identifies areas of brain-related strengths and weaknesses and, (2) a determination from the assessment data as to whether the particular neuropsychological deficits reflect neural-cognitive deficiencies or generalized cognitive problems affecting several functional systems.

According to Reitan (1980), direct linkages between assessment and treatment are forged by the training concepts inherent in the REHABIT model. For example, REHABIT proposes treating the general area of neuropsychological deficit directly by using alternate forms of neuropsychological tests as training items. According to Alfano and Finlayson (1987), such an approach seems reasonable because challenging the areas measured by neuropsychological tasks could provide direct stimulation of the wide range of neural functions that they assess. (For an alternate point of view, refer to Mann, 1979; Mann & Sabatino, 1985.) Following this general form of deficit training, remediation in five specific areas (tracts) is carried out using previously developed educational materials and tasks. The tracts include (1) Tract A, materials for the development of expressive and receptive language and verbal skills; (2) Tract B, materials to develop abstract language functions to include verbal reasoning, verbal concept formation, and verbal organization; (3) Tract C, materials designed to enhance general reasoning capabilities; (4) Tract D, materials for developing abstract visual-spatial and temporal-sequential concepts; and (5) Tract E, materials designed to promote understanding of basic visual-spatial and manipulation skills. Thus, Tracts A and B are generally linked to left hemisphere functions, Tracts D and E to right hemisphere functions, and Tract C to general logical analysis and reasoning functions subserved by all functional systems.

Data to support the REHABIT rehabilitation and remediation concepts are difficult to find. Reitan (1979, 1980) does report a few case studies, but the information provided in them cannot be construed as empirical validation for the REHABIT model In fact, reviews of similar neuropsychological process remediation models (Lyon & Moats, in press; Mann, 1979) have indicated that such practices suffer from a lack of both construct and ecological validity, particularly with respect to their application with children who display academic achievement deficits without demonstrable brain injury. In the absence of empirical validation for the REHABIT model, the clinician is ultimately responsible for judging whether the time spent in assessment and training activities is in the best interests of the child.

Rourke and his colleagues (Rourke et al., 1983, 1986) have argued convincingly that the aims, content, and style of neuropsychological assessments are improved significantly when a comprehensive battery of neuropsychological tasks are administered to children and the data interpreted according to several frames of reference (level of performance, pathognomonic signs, differential [pattern] score approach, comparisons of performance on two sides of the body, pre- and postlesion comparisons). Rourke's (1975, 1981) orientation to assessment practices and how assessment data relate to treatment is influenced significantly by his use of Reitan's neuropsychological measurement concepts and modes of clinical interpretation (Rourke, 1981). As such, Rourke's concepts of how brain-related deficiencies in children should be assessed and related to remediation are presented in this section.

Rourke et al. (1986) propose that linkages are best formed between assessment and remediation when a developmental neuropsychological model is employed. Within the context of such a model, specific information related to the child's neuropsychological ability structure is collected and interpreted in relation to (1) the immediate demands in the environment (e.g., school and social demands); (2) hypothesized long-range demands (e.g , occupational and social functioning); (3) specific short- and long-term behavioral outcomes that best characterize the child with respect to developmental status, information-processing strengths and weaknesses, and neuropsychological status; (4) an ideal remediation program for the child given the above information; and (5) the development of a realistic remediation program given the child's characteristics and the actual availability of remedial sources for family, school, and child.

Rourke's developmental neuropsychological remediation/habilitation model appears to have potential for linking assessment data to treatment because it stresses a comprehensive analysis of how child variables interact systematically with environmental factors and the pragmatics of clinical service delivery. However, as with other models incorporating the use of Halstead-Reitan tasks and modes of clinical interpretation (i.e., REHABIT), there simply are not the empirical data to support the validity and clinical efficacy of Rourke's (Rourke et al., 1983, 1986) model. Clearly, however, the model does offer well-reasoned and comprehensive guidelines for intervention that can serve as clinical frames of reference.

The Luria-Nebraska: Linkages to Treatment

A. R. Luria's (1973, 1980) seminal conceptualization of the human brain as being composed of functional units has led to the development of a standardized neuropsychological assessment battery for use with both adults and children. The Luria-Nebraska Battery-Children's Revision (Plaisted et al., 1983) has been found to be sensitive in detecting demonstrable neuroencephalopathy in children (Teeter, 1986). Some recent studies also have shown that the battery can discriminate between learning-disabled children and normally achieving students (Geary & Gilger, 1984; Nolan, Hammeke, & Barkley, 1983).

To date, no formal attempts have been made to relate assessment data obtained from the Luria-Nebraska to structured remediation programs for children. However, Luria's (1973) concepts of brain–behavior relationships can be clinically useful if applied to intervention practices in an informed manner. This conclusion may be a reasonable one for at least two reasons. First, Luria's model incorporates concepts related to both brain systems and their development. As such, a dynamic theoretical basis exists from which to make predictions about outcome and potential for remediation. Second, Luria's model argues that disturbances in complex cognitive functions can be related to a wide variety of brain-related deficiencies. For example, failure to learn to write could be attributable to deficits in any of several brain systems. Thus, children who display written language deficits may not respond equally well to the same remediation procedure.

One additional point is in order. Luria (1963, 1973, 1980) advocated the use of dynamic, nonstandardized assessment methods that could vary across patients depending upon the nature of the clinical question. He supported the use of these procedures with substantial clinical case-study data. Further, Luria (1963, 1980) presented a rationale for applying assessment procedures directly to the treatment and rehabilitation process and reported case-history data to substantiate his point of view. It is possible that attempts to standardize Luria's dynamic assessment methods could reduce their power in relating assessment findings to treatment program planning. The reader should keep in mind that this possibility remains an open question.

The K-ABC: Linkages to Treatment

Another standardized assessment tool that relies on neuropsychological constructs is the Kaufman Assessment Battery for Children (K-ABC;

Kaufman & Kaufman, 1983). Emphasizing a dual-processing model of cognition, the K-ABC Test purports to measure simultaneous and successive information-processing strengths and weaknesses in children up to 12 years of age. In addition to scores on the Simultaneous and Successive scales, a third Achievement test cluster is used to measure acquired knowledge and verbal learning ability. The test user then is encouraged to formulate hypotheses regarding remediation of academic deficiencies that emphasize the preferred processing mode of the subject. Unique to the K-ABC remediation framework (Gunnison, 1984) is the specificity of these recommendations to academic domains—reading, arithmetic reasoning, and written language—and the well-elaborated models of intervention that attempt to code both learner behavior and task demands along the simultaneous–sequential dichotomy.

Unfortunately, the usefulness of the K-ABC even for descriptive and classification purposes has not been accepted uniformly. For example, Sternberg (1984) argued that the test lacks construct validity, a problem that may be related to the authors' misrepresentation or misreading of the evidence supporting a simultaneous–successive processing dichotomy. Further, in equating processing style with scores on selected tasks, the test fails to assess constructs that pertain to dynamic problem solving. Selecting and conducting remediation on the basis of K-ABC results thereby would constitute a tenuous practice.

Empirical support for remediation based on the K-ABC, as with other neuropsychological approaches reviewed in this chapter, is sparse. Although Gunnison and her colleagues (research in press), cited in Gunnison, 1984) have shown meaningful gains in reading for children taught with methods described as simultaneous or sequential in emphasis, both the assumptions underlying the aptitude–treatment linkages and the data base supporting them are weak (Ayres & Cooley, 1986; Salvia & Hritchko, 1984). Where the logical–intuitive classification of child responses and teaching strategies appears to have most value is in the provision of a conceptual framework for diagnostic teaching. The concept of dual-processing modes may simply encourage the clinician to behave in a flexible manner when alternative representations of concepts are needed by the learner.

SELECTED ASSESSMENT BATTERIES: LINKAGES TO TREATMENT

The majority of studies that have attempted to identify empirically the linkages between assessment data and treatment options have measured children's neuropsychological characteristics with tasks that are not standardized in battery form. Generally, the tasks are selected on the basis of their relevance to a particular theoretical test of a research question. Because the tasks included in selected assessment batteries lack a common standardization sample from which to derive scores, control groups matched on relevant variables generally are assessed along with the clinical group of interest.

In the main, studies employing this type of assessment approach are conducted for the purpose of establishing a classification scheme for children who are included in heterogeneous clinical populations (i.e., learning disabilities). Within this classification context, children are assigned to different subtypes on the basis of their performance on the selected neuro-psychological tasks. Once a classification solution is obtained, it must be validated internally and externally. Internal validation is achieved by ensuring that the subtypes identified are reliable, replicable, and robust enough to include most members of the clinical population of interest. External validity is examined by determining whether the classification solution is useful for description, prediction, and clinical practice. One specific way to address external validity is to determine whether subtypes differ from one another in response to treatment (Lyon & Risucci, 1988). It is this area of classification research that is relevant to this chapter.

To date, a number of research programs have reported preliminary data that suggest that subtypes respond differently to various forms of remediation. Although all of the published investigations have been carried out with learning-disabled readers (dyslexics), the studies differ with respect to theoretical orientation, assessment tasks used to form subtypes, and classification methodology. For example, Lyon and his colleagues have identified several subtypes by applying empirical multivariate quantitative clustering methods to information-processing task scores obtained by large samples of LD readers. External validity studies have then involved attempts to teach the disabled learners and to determine subtype–teaching method interactions. In contrast, Bakker (1983) has classified dyslexics into two major subtypes according to clinical criteria, the most important of which is left/right ear asymmetrics in dichotic listening tasks. External validation consisted of hemisphere-specific stimulation via presentation of words to right and left visual fields and identifying whether subtypes responded differently to both the site of presentation and the type of stimulus used. Flynn and her associates (Flynn, 1987) have concentrated on clinically identifying dyslexic subtypes on the basis of their reading and spelling error patterns. She has presented compelling pilot data showing that children with particular patterns respond well to specific methods of reading instruction. Each of these research programs is reviewed in more detail in this section. Emphasis is placed on describing the theoretical orientation that drives the selection of assessment tasks used in the various research programs, the types of remediation procedures employed, and the clinical relationship between tasks and interventions.

Empirical Subtype Intervention Studies: The Lyon Research Program

Lyon and his associates (Lyon, 1983, 1985a, 1985b; Lyon, Stewart, & Freedman, 1982; Lyon & Watson, 1981) have questioned the appropriateness of a single-deficit classification model for reading disability and hypothesized that LD readers (dyslexics) constitute a population that is composed of a number of subtypes, each of which is defined by its own particular array of linguistic, perceptual, and reading characteristics. The theoretical background underlying Lyon's research can be viewed as a logical extension of Luria's (1966, 1973) clinical neuropsychological theory and Benson and Geschwind's (1975) multiple syndrome model of alexia. For example, Lyon (1983) proposed that reading development is a complex process that requires the concerted participation of cognitive, linguistic, and perceptual subskills. As such, deficiencies in any one subskill can limit the acquisition of fluent decoding and/or comprehension abilities.

Within this theoretical context, an initial series of studies was conducted (Lyon, Rietta, Watson, Porch, & Rhodes, 1981; Lyon & Watson, 1981) in which a battery of tasks designed to assess linguistic and perceptual skills related to reading development was administered to 100 LD readers and 50 normal readers matched for age (11–12 years) and IQ ($M = 104$). The data were submitted to a series of cluster analyses to test the hypothesis that subtypes could be identified. Six distinct subtypes were delineated and characterized by significantly different patterns of linguistic and perceptual deficits. The six-subtype solution remained stable across internal validation studies employing different variable subsets and clustering algorithms. Further, 94% of subjects were recovered into similar subtypes in a cross-validation study using a new subject sample (Lyon, 1983). A brief description of each of the subtypes' information-processing characteristics is provided here, followed by an overview of the intervention program. Readers are referred to cited references for specific details.

Children who were assigned empirically to subtype 1 ($n = 10$) exhibited significant deficits in language comprehension, the ability to blend phonemes, visual-motor integration, visual-spatial skills, and visual memory skills, with strengths in naming and auditory discrimination skills. Analysis of the reading and spelling errors made by members of subtype 1 indicated significant deficits in the development of both a sight word vocabulary and word attack skills.

Children in subtype 2 ($n = 12$) also exhibited a pattern of mixed deficits but in a milder form than observed in subtype 1. Specifically, significant problems in language comprehension, auditory memory, and visual-motor integration were observed and may have been related to the reading problems of these subjects. No deficits were seen in these young-sters' performance on naming, auditory discrimination, sound blending, visual-spatial, and visual memory tasks. Subtype 2 members produced mixed visual and phonetic errors when reading but to a much milder degree than did subtype 1 children.

Members of subtype 3 (n = 12) manifested selective deficits in lan-guage comprehension and sound blending, with corresponding strengths in all other linguistic and visual-perceptual skills measured. The oral reading errors made by subtype 3 youngsters were primarily phonetic in nature, as would be expected from their diagnostic profile.

Children in subtype 4 (n = 32) displayed significant deficiencies on visual-motor integration tasks and average performance on all other mea-sures. These youngsters displayed an assorted sample of oral reading errors, though most errors were made when attempting to read phonet-ically irregular words.

Subtype 5 (n = 12) members displayed significant deficits in lan-guage comprehension, auditory memory, and sound blending, with corre-sponding strengths in all measured visual-perceptual and visual-motor skills. These characteristics appeared related to the severity of their oral reading and written spelling errors. The major academic characteristic that distinguished subtype 5 youngsters from the other children was their consistently poor application of word attack (phonetic) skills to the read-ing and spelling process.

The pattern of scores obtained by members of subtype 6 (n = 16) indicated a normal diagnostic profile. These results were unexpected. It is quite possible that these children were reading poorly for reasons that were not detected by the assessment battery.

Following this subtype identification study, an external validation investigation (Lyon, 1983) was carried out to determine whether subtypes would respond differently to reading instruction. However, because of the relatively small sample size, a standard aptitude-by-treatment study could not be designed appropriately. Therefore, it was decided to explore the possibility that the six subtypes might respond differently to one teaching condition. Since the children for this exploratory study had to be matched for preintervention achievement levels and other relevant vari-ables (age, IQ, sex, socioeconomic status), the initial subject pool available from the subtype identification study was reduced to 30. Thus, random assignment of children from each of the six subtypes to several teaching conditions was not feasible.

In light of these logistical difficulties, five subjects were selected from each of the six subtypes. They were matched on their ability to read single words, age, IQ, race, and sex. All 30 subjects were white males ranging in age from 12.3 years to 12.7 years and in Full Scale IQ from 103.5 to 105. Preintervention grade equivalents on the Reading Recognition subtest of the Peabody Individual Achievement Test (PIAT) ranged from 3.0 to 3.3, with percentile ranks ranging from 4 to 8. It was not possible to control for the amount and type of previous reading instruction experienced by the children, their present curriculum, and the amount of time spent in class-rooms for learning-disabled youngsters. Thus, the results obtained from this study must be evaluated in light of these confounding features.

The teaching method selected for the study was a synthetic phonics program (Traub & Bloom, 1975). This program was chosen because of its sequenced format, its coverage of major phonics concepts, and its famil-iarity to the teachers in training who were providing the instruction. All subjects were provided 1 hour of reading instruction per week (in addi-tion to their special and regular classroom instruction) for 26 weeks.

Following the 26 hours of phonics instruction, the 30 children were posttested with the PIAT Reading Recognition subtest, and gain scores employing percentile ranks and grade equivalents were computed. A one-way analysis of variance indicated significant differences among the six subtypes for both types of gain scores achieved from preintervention to posttesting. An analysis of subtype gain scores and subsequent pairwise comparisons indicated that members of subtype 6 made the most progress (mean percentile rank gain = 18.0), followed by members of subtype 4 (mean percentile rank gain = 8.2). On the other hand, subtypes 1, 2, 3, and 5 made minimal gains in percentile ranks and were not significantly dif-ferent from one another in terms of gains achieved. Subtypes 6 and 4 were both significantly different from one another and from all other subtypes with respect to their improvement in the oral reading of single words.

The data obtained in this subtype remediation study indicate that, for some subtypes, a synthetic phonics teaching intervention appeared to enhance significantly the ability to read single words accurately. Clearly, members of subtypes 6 and 4 demonstrated robust improvements in their decoding capabilities. Whether or not the absence of auditory-verbal defi-cits in these two subtypes was associated with their good response to instruction cannot be answered clearly at this time, but one could hypoth-esize that this might be the case. This hypothesis is made more tenable by the observation that those subtypes with the most severe auditory recep-tive and auditory expressive language deficits made either minimal gains (e.g., subtypes 2 and 3) or no gains (e.g., subtypes 1 and 5) in the ability to pronounce single words accurately and efficiently.

In a related program of research carried out with younger disabled readers (Lyon, 1985a; Lyon et al., 1982), five LD subtypes were identifed and validated internally and externally by using different variable sub-tests, clustering algorithms, and subtype–teaching method interaction studies. Again, a brief description of each of the subtypes' information-processing characteristics is provided, followed by an overview of the external validation intervention program.

Children assigned to subtype 1 (n = 18) manifested significant deficits in visual perception, visual-spatial analysis and reasoning, and visual-motor integration. Visual memory was also below average but not significantly so. All measured auditory receptive and auditory expressive skills were within the average range. The reading errors made by members of subtype 1 appeared to be related to their diagnostic deficit profile. Frequent mispronunciations due to confusion of visually similar words were noted, as were reading errors involving medial vowels and vowel combinations.

Children in subtype 2 (n = 10) displayed selective deficits in morphosyntactic skills, sound blending, language comprehension, auditory memory, auditory discrimination, and naming ability, with corresponding strengths in all measured visual-perceptual skills. These deficits across auditory receptive and auditory expressive language domains appeared to seriously impede their ability to decode single words and to apply decoding principles to the pronunciation of nonsense words.

Members of subtype 3 (n = 12) scored in the normal range on all diagnostic measures and, thus, can be compared with youngsters in the subtype identified by Lyon and Watson (1981) that scored significantly below normal on reading tasks without concomitant low performance on diagnostic test batteries. It is possible that members of subtype 3 read inefficiently for social or affective reasons rather than because of inherent oral language or perceptual deficiencies. It is also quite possible that the diagnostic battery employed did not assess effectively all skills relevant to the developmental reading process. As was the case with Lyon and Watson's (1981) subtype 6 (normal diagnostic profile), members of subtype 3 scored higher than all other subgroups on the reading measures. These youngsters did have relatively more difficulties in comprehending reading passages than in the other measured reading skills. No systematic patterns of errors could be identified from analysis of their performance on word recognition and word attack measures.

Children in subtype 4 (n = 15) displayed significant deficiencies in sound blending, language comprehension, auditory memory, naming ability, and some aspects of visual perception. The difficulties manifested by subtype 4 members in remembering, analyzing, synthesizing, and correctly sequencing verbal and visual information appeared to have a significant effect on their ability to decode phonetically regular real and nonsense words. For example, in measures of oral reading and word attack skills, a large proportion of subtype 4 youngsters could not approximate the correct pronunciation of many words.

Members of subtype 5 (n = 9) manifested significant mixed deficits in morphosyntactic skill, sound blending, visual perception, visual-motor integration, visual-spatial analysis, and visual memory. These youngsters committed primarily "visual" errors when reading single words (both real and nonsense), apparently reflecting their deficiencies in visual analysis and memory.

Following the subtype identification phase with younger disabled readers, Lyon (1985a) carried out a pilot remediation study. Similar to the Lyon (1983) subtype remediation study, a relatively low sample size and other logistical difficulties (funding, sample migration) prohibited any attempts to assign members randomly from each of the five identified subtypes to a variety of teaching approaches. However, rather than teaching all subtype members with the same general methods and materials, as was done in the first intervention study, one subtype (subtype 2) was split, with half of the members receiving reading instruction via a synthetic phonics approach and the other half receiving instruction through a combined whole-word and analytic phonics methodology.

Although this approach represents a significant departure from the experimental design necessary for an aptitude (subtype)-treatment (teaching method) interaction study, Lyon attempted to gain preliminary information about how children who are very similar to one another diagnostically would respond to different teaching methods. Subtype 2 (n = 10) was chosen as the target subtype for this pilot study because all of its members displayed both significant receptive language deficits (auditory discrimination), auditory comprehension, auditory memory) and auditory expressive deficits (retrieval, syntax, sequencing) within the context of robust visual perceptual-motor-memory strengths. Because all of the subtype 2 members also manifested significant difficulties reading single words and connected language, the opportunity existed to determine how two different reading approaches affected these skills in the presence of a number of linguistic subskill impairments.

For this pilot study, five children were randomly assigned to a synthetic phonics approach (Traub & Bloom, 1975), whereas the remaining five were placed randomly in a combined sight word, contextual analysis, structural analysis, and analytic phonics group. Preintervention assessment using the Woodcock Reading Mastery Word Identification subtest indicated that the five children in each remediation group were reading between the 8th and 10th percentile ranks for age. The mean percentile ranks for the two groups were not significantly different (Mann-Whitney $Z > .05$) prior to the initiation of the remediation programs.

Both remediation groups received approximately 30 hours of individualized instruction (3 hours a week for 10 weeks). Unfortunately, it was not possible to control for the type of previous exposure to reading instruction or for the type of ongoing regular and special class instruction the children were receiving in their typical school day. Thus, as in the Lyon (1983) study, any conclusions drawn from the results of this study must be interpreted in light of these confounding factors.

The synthetic phonics remediation group was taught via the scope and sequence presented in the Traub and Bloom (1975) reading program. A brief description of the instructional format for this approach was presented earlier. The combined remediation group learned to label whole words (three nouns, three verbs) rapidly by first pairing the word with pictures, then recognizing the names of the words (by a pointing response), and then finally reading the words in isolation. Following the development of rapid reading ability for these six words, function words (the, is, was, are) were introduced and taught. Following stable reading of these words, short sentences using combinations of the sight and function words were constructed and read in order to introduce the concept of contextual analysis and to develop metalinguistic awareness of reading as a meaningful language skill. Following contextual reading drills, the combined group received instruction in structural analysis and the reading and comprehension of the morphosyntactical markers -ed, -s, and -ing. These morphemes were written on anagrams and introduced into context so that the children could readily grasp their effect on syntax and meaning. Finally, analytic phonics drills were initiated to develop letter–sound correspondences with the context of whole words. Specifically, phonetically regular words that could be read rapidly by sight were presented, and children were first asked to recognize a particular letter-sound correspondence ("Point to the letter that makes the /a/ sound") and then to give a recall response ("What sound(s) does this letter make?"). As children became more adept at recalling grapheme–phoneme relations, drills in auditory analysis and blending were initiated.

Following the 30 hours of remediation, children in both groups were posttested with an alternate form of the Woodcock Reading Mastery Word Identification subtest. Significant differences were found between the two remediation groups with respect to postintervention reading percentile rank scores (Mann-Whitney $Z < .0003$). Children within the combined remediation group gained, on the average, 11 percentile rank points, whereas members of the synthetic phonics group gained approximately 1 percentile rank point.

There is little doubt that subtype 2 members responded significantly differently to two forms of reading instruction. Apparently, the auditory receptive and auditory expressive language deficits that characterized each member of the subtype 2 impeded their response to a reading instructional method that required learning letter–sound correspondences in isolation followed by blending and contextual reading components. A tentative hypothesis might be that subtype 2 children did not have the auditory language subskills necessary for success with this approach but could deploy their relatively robust visual-perceptual and memory skills more effectively with whole words, as seen within the combined remediation. A more tenable hypothesis is that whole-word reading placed far less linguistic demands on these readers than alphabetic approaches that require a phonological awareness of sound structure and acoustic boundaries and the relationship of these units to letter sequences. Thus, whereas subtype 2 members learned to read whole words in structured, isolated context, their ability to generalize phonological and orthographic concepts to read new words is most likely to remain limited.

In general, the data derived from this series of subtype identification and remediation studies support a model of dyslexia that presumes that a number of diverse information-processing deficits can have specific reading disability as a common correlate. Although the results from these basic research endeavors are interesting, the findings have limited clinical utility for a number of reasons. First, the kinds of subtypes identified and their descriptions are limited by the range and quality of the tests that provide the data for cluster analysis. For example, the tasks selected for use in Lyon's assessment batteries did not provide adequate coverage of some linguistic factors (particularly phonology) implicated in the developmental reading process. Second, the specific nature of the relationship between subtype assessment characteristics and response to reading instruction is difficult to determine because the assessment tasks are indirect measures of associated symptomatology. Third, it is not well understood if the correlated information-processing deficits constitute necessary and/or sufficient conditions for reading disability. Fourth, methodological limitations in sample size and the number and type of dependent reading measures preclude adequate interpretations and confident generalization of the subtype–teaching method interaction studies. Finally, even though particular teaching (treatment) approaches had differential effects for some subtypes, it is difficult to determine if the effects should be attributed to subtype characteristics, the instructional program, the interaction between the two, the teacher, time spent in remediation, or previous or concomitant educational experiences.

Clinical Subtype Intervention Studies: The Bakker Research Program

Bakker and his colleagues (Bakker, 1983; Bakker, Moerland, & Goe-koop-Hoefkens, 1981; Bakker & Vinke, 1985) have developed a classification model of reading disability that stresses the importance of balance in the functional development of the two hemispheres of the brain. He hypothesized that each of two dyslexic subgroups represents functional overdevelopment of one hemisphere for reading behavior. Thus, L-type dyslexics, who are hypothesized to be overreliant on a left hemisphere strategy for reading, are fast and inaccurate decoders of text, whereas P-types are believed to be overreliant on a right hemisphere strategy reflected in slow, relatively accurate reading. The groups are classified independently through dichotic listening tasks, with L-types showing a right ear advantage and P-types showing a left ear advantage.

Although a subtyping system that uses dichotic listening tasks as a key variable for classification might be constrained by unreliability (Lyon & Risucci, 1988), Bakker's theoretical constructs have been validated externally by intervention studies (Bakker & Vinke, 1985). In these studies, structured presentation of reading stimuli produced changes in both event-related potentials and reading behaviors in the direction predicted by the balance model. The intervention paradigm assessed the effects of both direct hemisphere stimulation through right or left visual-field presentation of words, and indirect stimulation through the presentation of modified text formats. Thus, L-types were forced to attend to the graphic features of text with mixed and altered typefaces, whereas P-types were required to attend to the alphabetic code by having pictures and titles removed from the text, as well as having to rhyme and perform temporal order tasks. Significant changes in both event-related potentials and reading improvement in experimental groups followed stimulation of the underused hemisphere of the given subtype.

Although Bakker's work is promising in its demonstration of theoretically predicted changes in reading behavior as a consequence of clearly conceived treatment methodologies, the work needs to be interpreted with caution. Subject description and identification continue to be problematic; for example, in the Bakker and Vinke (1985) study, subjects were selected with IQs of 70 and above, and the mean IQ was a low average of 85. There were no group differences reported with respect to discrepancies between ability and achievement. This becomes important only because the results may not generalize to dyslexic samples chosen by commonly used sample marker variables. Further, the sample was teacher-selected, remediation sessions occurred only once per week for 22 sessions, and no control for concurrent reading instruction of the subjects in their classrooms was reported. The L-type and P-type dyslexics were not well differentiated according to reading behaviors. Without further internal validation, it will be difficult to evaluate the similarities between Bakker's classification system and others, as well as to apply Bakker's model more generally in clinical treatment.

Direct Assessment Intervention Studies: The Flynn Research Program

The work of one of the authors (Flynn, 1987) suggests that direct assessment of reading and spelling behaviors within a neuropsychological framework provides useful linkages to treatment. Assessment tasks in Flynn's studies were chosen on the basis of a conceptualization of reading as an interactive process composed of lower-level processes (phonology, memory, perception, attention) and higher-level processes (syntax, semantics, experiential knowledge, executive monitoring) that operate simultaneously and synergistically to produce fluent reading. Ecological assessment of intact, deficient, and compensatory reading strategies included multiple oral reading samples using the reading model to classify errors and the Boder Test of Reading-Spelling patterns (BTRSP; Boder & Jarrico, 1982). Thus, test content was directly related to the tasks that children face on a daily basis.

The BTRSP was chosen as a direct measurement of word-recognition skills involving phonology, memory, and perception. Dyslexic children were classified as dysphonetic (deficient in sequential auditory processes), dyseidetic (deficient in visual-spatial skills), or mixed (deficient in both processes), according to an adaptation of the Boder procedures (Boder & Jarriso, 1982). The initial thrust of this research was to investigate the construct validity of the BTRSP through external validation studies involving quantitative neurophysiology and subtype–treatment remediation programs. As the reader will note, results of the studies indicate that a reconceptualization of the dyslexic subtypes originally proposed by Boder may offer greater explanatory power and lead more directly to testable reading remediation hypotheses.

With this direct assessment model, subtypes of children who demonstrated distinct profiles of reading behaviors were identified. One subtype, described as deficient in phonetic development, demonstrated difficulty with syntactical and alphabetic skills. Generally, semantics and sight word recognition skills were areas of strength. Oral reading was characterized by global substitutions, difficulty with sound–symbol relationships, and semantic substitutions. Often, comprehension was relatively intact despite numerous reading inaccuracies. Conversely, children with presumed deficits in whole word recognition skills displayed excellent phonetic analysis skills. Characteristically slow but accurate readers, they often failed to understand the meaning of a passage.

The question of whether these clinical description of reading profiles represent reliable, replicable subtypes that have ecological and predictive validity (i.e., lead to testable remediation hypotheses and prognoses) was investigated through external validation studies, including quantitative neurophysiology studies and a subtype–treatment remediation project. In the first neurophysiology study (Flynn & Deering, 1987), 44 children (ages 7–10) were assessed using direct measures of reading and spelling behaviors, a neurological evaluation, and spectral analysis of theta and alpha brain waves during cognitive tasks. The results suggested that distinct subtypes of reading-disabled children could be formed using direct measures of word recognition skills. The data also suggested that reading disability in the subtype of children identified variously as dyseidetic (Boder, 1971, 1973), L-type dyslexics (Bakker & Vinke, 1985), visual or visual-spatial (Johnson & Myklebust, 1967; Mattis, French, & Rapin, 1975; Pirozzolo, 1981) may be attributable to overutilization of early-developing linguistic skills (phonological decoding) rather than deficient visual perceptual processes.

Although this study clearly differentiated the dyseidetic dyslexics from other groups on three of the six cognitive tasks, the direction and location of neurophysiologic difference was initially quite surprising given previous reports of this subtype's characteristics. For example, dyseidetic children's reading disabilities have been attributed to deficient visual-spatial abilities referable to atypical, right hemisphere development with concomitant strength in phonetic skills (Boder, 1971, 1973; Boder & Jarrico, 1982). In the Flynn and Deering (1987) investigation, however, dyseidetic children demonstrated significant increases from resting baseline in left temporal-parietal theta compared with the other groups. That this difference occurred in the area of the angular gyrus, presumed to be important in phonetic decoding (Hynd & Hynd, 1984), suggested that the reportedly normal phonetic skills of dyseidetic children may, in fact, indicate overutilization of a processing strategy that results in, or is caused by, relative inefficiency of right hemisphere visual gestalt abilities.

A second study of 64 children (ages 8–9), subtyped according to modified Boder procedures (Boder & Jarrico, 1982) and oral reading patterns, provided replicated evidence of increased left theta activity in dyseidetic children during task engagement (Flynn & Deering, 1987). Further external validation studies investigated the efficacy of the classification system for prescribing remediation (Flynn, 1987). Using the neuropsychological principle of teaching to intact or compensatory processes, a subtype–treatment research program was initiated. The study involved 22 first-, second-, and third-graders classified as dysphonetic or dyseidetic. Children were randomly assigned to a treatment group and received a full year of remediation, three sessions per week. The reading approaches included (1) a language experience, analytic phonetic approach using the Initial Teaching Alphabet; (2) Distar, a synthetic phonics approach; and (3) a multisensory, analytic phonetic approach using regular orthography.

Data derived from the reading remediation project provided additional validation of ecologically based assessment procedures for subtyping dyslexic children (Flynn, 1987). However, the data also demonstrated the inadequacy of a design that implies a simple match between reading subtype and remediation system. Specifically, within each treatment condition, there were some children who benefited whereas others with the same reading profile made less than average gains.

Data from the neurophysiology and remediation studies suggest that not all children fail to develop fluent reading behaviors for the same reason, that distinct subtypes of dyslexic children can be identified on the basis of direct measurements of reading and spelling behaviors, and that, to some degree, responses of subtyped children to specific reading approaches can be predicted. The data also suggest that more dynamic, interactive models of the teaching–learning situation must be developed in order to describe and predict adequately how the child's processing deficits covary with instructional variables (e.g., the reading system and the learning context).

SOME FINAL THOUGHTS, CONCLUSIONS, AND DIRECTIONS

There is little doubt that establishing clinically valid linkages between neuropsychological assessment and the development of treatment options for children in need of rehabilitation and remediation is a laudable goal. Ecologically valid assessment data could provide a framework for the systematic development of hypotheses to determine which specific treatment methods and materials have the highest probability of success for a particular child with a particular array of neuropsychological characteristics. However, our review of efforts to achieve this goal indicates that a substantial distance remains to be traveled before one can conclude that the time spent in carrying out neuropsychological assessment contributes significantly to the treatment process. The first step in closing this distance is actually twofold. First, shortcomings inherent in neuropsychological assessment for treatment purposes must be recognized, and, second, a productive course and set of refinements to help correct our clinical weaknesses must be suggested.

Throughout this chapter, we have noted that linkages between assessment and treatment are weakened by factors associated with the limited construct, content, and ecological validities of the test batteries employed. We also have pointed out that a number of persistent difficulties in relating assessment to treatment stem from our use of assessment tasks that were not designed initially to predict and guide treatment options. In addition, specific issues associated with clinical training, developmental appropriateness of assessment tasks used with children, and the problem of static versus dynamic assessment also need to be addressed if clinical progress is to be made regarding the assessment–treatment interface. Our intent in the remainder of this chapter is to provide some meaningful direction with respect to these issues.

Professional Preparation and Experience

A majority of clinical neuropsychologists feel unprepared to undertake the task of recommending treatment or intervention options on the basis of assessment data. This may be expected, as Craig (1979) and others (Hynd & Obrzut, 1986) have pointed out, because clinical neuropsychologists spend significantly greater clinical time in assessment activities than practicing in an intervention context. Although this lack of experience with treatment issues is problematic, a more fundamental reason for clinical naivete in treatment situations is limited preparation. As

Hynd and Obrzut (1986) have reported, clinical neuropsychologists receive little or no formal training in intervention practices, particularly educational practices. Training programs typically emphasize assessment, diagnosis, and consultation with only general exposure to treatment methodologies. Moreover, when neuropsychologists are exposed to intervention and treatment approaches, such experiences usually take place in settings somewhat removed from the populations and problems that ultimately will demand expert clinical treatment services. More specifically, the types of intervention and treatment strategies applied with adults in hospital settings often are not generalizable to the school-related difficulties seen in pediatric populations.

If, in fact, clinical neuropsychology is to undertake a responsible role in applied settings where treatment is not only a logical but necessary outcome of assessment, then substantial improvements in formal clinical training must occur. Supervised practica and internships under the tutelage of master teachers and clinicians, preceded by relevant coursework in applied academic content areas, would seem helpful in this regard.

Developmental Issues in Assessment

In addition to improvements in professional preparation, advances in establishing clinically meaningful linkages between assessment and treatment could be fostered by emphasizing an understanding of developmental factors in child clinical practice. Test design, interpretation of data, and the application of instructional methodologies must be informed by a developmental perspective. A prime example of a neuropsychologically based assessment tool that could benefit from a reexamination of its developmental appropriateness is the Boder Test of Reading-Spelling Patterns (BTRSP; Boder & Jarrico, 1982). This instrument, which is used in some studies to assign dyslexics to dysphonetic, dyseidetic, and mixed-deficit subtypes, is a clinical-inferential tool yielding a classification based on direct assessment of reading and spelling behavior. It also is employed in clinical practice as a basis for remedial prescriptions. Although the test is designed ostensibly for all school-aged children, the methods for error analysis and classification of children to subtypes do not change with age. There is insufficient consideration given to the manner in which spelling strategies shift with normal development. Thus, a diagnostic term such as *dysphonetic* may capture the essence of the problem at one beginning stage of reading and spelling but mask the essence of the difficulty at more advanced developmental stages. Indeed, spelling strategies do shift in dyslexics over time (Cook, 1981), both in response to instruction and as a function of intelligence (Moats, 1983). This is but one example of how assessment data can be confounded by the lack of an informed developmental perspective.

No doubt, the majority of neuropsychological batteries that are down-ward extensions of adult batteries and which do not have adequate cross-sectional norms suffer from the same developmental inadequacies. Cer-tainly, it would be erroneous to prescribe remedial treatment techniques on the basis of these types of assessment data until external validation studies are conducted to evaluate the relationships among assessment strategies, clinical subtypes, developmental level, and response to instruction.

The Need for Dynamic Assessment

As mentioned throughout this chapter, most neuropsychological tests are static measures of competence designed to allow standardized com-parisons of a child with other children in specified populations. Such comparisons yield only indirect and nonspecific information regarding the nature of the child's problem as it is manifested in his learning con-text. The test data do not address motivational factors and their impact on learning, nor do they inform the teacher or clinician about the child's spontaneous use of strategies or procedural knowledge in learning.

One notable exception is the Halstead Category Test, one of the most sensitive measures of brain dysfunction, which does assess the child's ability to learn from corrective feedback on one kind of nonverbal prob-lem-solving task. Its potential as a dynamic assessment tool is great, but it usually is used merely as a normative measure to add to the evidence for or against the presence of brain dysfunction. In fact, the power of the Category Test lies in its ability to sample the domains of impairment most commonly associated with brain dysfunction, such as adaptation, gener-alization, memory for recent experience, conceptual organization, con-sistency of response capability, and ability to reason abstractly. As a test, it successfully departs from truncated, structured, single ability measures that do not sample adequately the cognitive characteristics most relevant to academic performance and adaptation in general. More tools of this kind are needed in our assessment batteries if neuropsychology is going to provide evaluations relevant for the individualization of therapy or teaching.

At the present time, one of the more promising examples of dynamic neuropsychological assessment is the work of Ylvisaker and his col-leagues (Szekeres, Ylvisaker, & Cohen, 1987) in closed head injury re-habilitation. Their delineation of variables to consider in the selection and training of compensatory strategies (Haasbauer-Krupa, Henry, Szekeres, & Ylvisaker, 1985) acknowledges the complex interaction of cognitive, motivational, and personality factors in recovery from head injury. Their approach to rehabilitation involves dynamic observations of patient response to real-life situations and meaningful activities in natural settings. Ylvisaker and associates also systematically evaluate patients' performances according to (1) the efficiency or rate of performance, (2) the level of conceptualization or mastery that the patient can comprehend, (3) the scope or variety of contexts in which performance can be maintained, and (4) the manner of performance (impulsive–reflective, flexible–rigid, active–passive, dependent–independent). Functional integrative performance is the appropriate target of therapy, rather than the direct rehabilitation of basic cognitive processes such as attention and memory, which may result in improvements on neuropsychological tests but which may not generalize to everyday life.

Given the arguments against static measurement (failure of tests to predict real-life adaptation, to identify satisfactorily the impact of specific cognitive impairments on complex adaptive behavior, and to predict responses to specific interventions), one might ask if child neuropsychological test batteries, as currently designed, have any purpose or relevance in the treatment of documented or putative developmental disorders. Should we delete their use in rehabilitation settings? Should we bypass neuropsychological testing of learning-disabled students, for example, in favor of curriculum-based assessment or analysis of the learner's characteristics during instruction in a given context? We do not believe so. A number of advances have been made in the development of neuropsychological assessment batteries that consist of tasks that are ecologically valid and direct measurements of processes crucial to the development of reading and spelling behavior (Flynn, this chapter; Hynd, 1986). There is also an increased awareness that establishing valid linkages between assessment data and treatment options will require tasks and modes of clinical interpretation that are as dynamic and flexible as the learning process itself (Lyon & Moats, in press).

The Need for Continued Classification Research

In order to relate assessment findings ultimately to treatment options and predicted outcomes, the phenotypic or behavioral expression of different developmental disorders must be clearly defined, characterized, and categorized. To this end, subtype research must capitalize on what we know about theoretically driven dynamic assessment procedures, the developmental nature of both brain function and human learning, and the methodological requirements for taxonomic research (Lyon & Risucci, 1988). Some subtyping efforts (e.g., Bakker, 1983; Flynn, 1987; Flynn & Deering, 1987; Hynd, 1986; Lyon, 1985b; Lyon & Risucci, 1988) are making some advances in these directions with an eye toward treatment relevance for children. Significant work remains to be done, however, before any classification scheme has precise descriptive, communicative, and predictive power. An informed understanding of some of the issues raised in this chapter may help clinicians fill the therapeutic breech until systematic and reliable linkages between assessment and treatment are forged.

REFERENCES

Alfano, D. P., & Finlayson, M. A. J. (1987). Clinical neuropsychology in rehabilitation. *Clinical Neuropsychologist, 1,* 105–123.

Ayres, R. R., & Cooley, E. J. (1986). Sequential versus simultaneous processing on the K-ABC: Validity in predicting learning success. *Journal of Psychoeducational Assessment, 4,* 211–220.

Bakker, D. (1983). Hemispheric specialization and specific reading retardation. In M. Rutter (Ed.), *Developmental neuropsychiatry* (pp. 203–232). New York: Guilford Press.

Bakker, D., & Vinke, J. (1985). Effects of hemisphere specific stimulation on brain activity and reading in dyslexics. *Journal of Clinical and Experimental Neuropsychology, 7,* 505–525.

Bakker, D. J., Moerland, R., GoeKoop-Hoefkens, M. (1981). Affects of hemisphere-specific stimulation on the reading performance of dyslexic boys: A pilot study. *Journal of Clinical Neuropsychology 3,* 155–159.

Beaumont, J. G. (1983). *Introduction to neuropsychology.* New York: Guilford Press.

Benson, D. F., & Geschwind, N. (1975). The alexias. In D. J. Vinkis & G. W. Bruyn (Eds.), *Handbook of clinical neurology* (Vol. 4). New York: American Elsevier.

Boder, E. (1971). Developmental dyslexia: Prevailing diagnostic concepts and a new diagnostic approach. In H. Mykelbust (Ed.), *Progress in learning disabilities* (Vol. 2). New York: Grune and Stratton.

Boder, E. (1973). Developmental dyslexia: A diagnostic approach based on three atypical reading-spelling patterns. *Developmental Medicine and Child Neurology, 15,* 663–687.

Boder, E. D., & Jarrico, S. (1982). *The Boder Test of Reading-Spelling Patterns. A diagnostic screening test for subtypes of reading disability.* Orlando, FL: Grune and Stratton.

Boll, T. J. (1981). The Halstead-Reitan Neuropsychological Test Battery. In S. B. Filskov & T. J. Boll (Eds.), *Handbook of clinical neuropsychology* (pp. 577–607). New York: Wiley.

Boll, T. J., & Reitan, R. M. (1972). Comparative ability interrelationships in normal and brain-damaged children. *Journal of Clinical Psychology, 28,* 152–156.

Bornstein, R. A., King, G., & Carroll, A. (1983). Neuropsychological abnormalities in Gilles de la Tourette's syndrome. *Journal of Nervous and Mental Disease, 171,* 497–502.

Brown, A. L., & Campione, J. C. (1986). Psychological theory and the study of learning disabilities. *American Psychologist, 14,* 1059–1068.

Chall, J. S., & Mirsky, A. F. (1978). The implications for education. In J. S. Chall & A. F. Mirsky (Eds.), *Education and the brain: The seventy-seventh yearbook of the National Society for the Study of Education.* Chicago: University of Chicago Press.

Cook, L. (1981). Misspelling analysis in dyslexia. Observation of developmental strategy shifts. *Bulletin of the Orton Society, 31,* 123–134.

Craig, D. L. (1979). Neuropsychological assessment in public psychiatric hospitals: The current state of practice. *Clinical Neuropsychology, 1,* 1–7.

Dawson, G. (1983). Lateralized brain dysfunction in autism: Evidence from the Halstead-Reitan Neuropsychological Battery. *Journal of Autism and Developmental Disorders, 13,* 269–286.

Diller, L., & Gordon, W. A. (1981a). Intervention for cognitive deficits in brain-injured adults. *Journal of Consulting and Clinical Psychology, 49,* 822–839.

Diller, L., & Gordon, W. A. (1981b). Rehabilitation and clinical neuropsychology. In S. B. Filskov & T. J. Boll (Eds.), *Handbook of clinical neuropsychology* (pp. 702–7330). New York: Wiley.

Diller, L., & Weinberg, J. (1977). Hemi-inattention in rehabilitation: The evolution of a rational remediation program. In E. A. Weinstein & R. P. Friedland (Eds.), *Advances in neurology* (Vol 18, pp. 62–82). New York: Raven Press.

Dunleavy, R. A., & Baade, L. A. (1980). Neuropsychological correlates of severe asthma in children 9–14 years old. *Journal of Consulting and Clinical Psychology, 48,* 564–577.

Finlayson, M. A. J., Gowland, C., & Basmajian, J. V. (1986). Neuropsychological predictors of treatment response following stroke. *Journal of Clinical and Experimental Neuropsychology, 7,* 647. (Abstract)

Finlayson, M. A. J., Johnson, K. A., & Reitan, R. M. (1977). Relationship of level of education to neuropsychological measures in brain-damaged and non brain-damaged adults. *Journal of Consulting and Clinical Psychology, 45,* 536–542.

Flynn, J. (1987). *Neurophysiologic characteristics of dyslexic subtypes and response to remediation.* Grant awarded by the Initial Teaching Alphabet Foundation, Roslyn, New York.

Flynn, J. & Deering, W. (1987). *Subtypes of dyslexia: Investigation of Boder's system for identification and classification of dyslexic children using quantitative neurophysiology.* Manuscript submitted for publication.

Gaddes, W. H. (1980). *Learning disabilities and brain function: A neuropsychological approach.* New York: Springer-Verlag.

Geary, D. C., & Gilger, J. W. (1984). The Luria-Nebraska Neuropsychological Battery-Children's Revision: Comparison of learning disabled and normal children matched on Full Scale IQ. *Perceptual and Motor Skills, 58,* 115–118.

Golden, C. J., Hammeke, T., & Purisch, H. (1978). Diagnostic validity of a standardized neuropsychological battery derived from Luria's neuropsychological tests. *Journal of Consulting and Clinical Psychology, 46,* 1258–1265.

Gunnison, J. A. (1984). Developing educational intervention from assessments involving the K-ABC. *Journal of Special Education, 18,* 325–344.

Haasbauer-Krupa, J., Henry, K., Szekeres, S. & Ylvisaker, M. (1985). Cognitive rehabilitation therapy, late stages of recovery. In M. Ylvisaker (Ed.), *Head injury rehabilitation: Children and adolescents.* San Diego: College Hill Press.

Hartlage, L. C., & Hartlage, P. L. (1977). Application of neuropsychological principles in the diagnosis of learning disabilities. In L. Tarnapol & M. Tarnapol (Eds.), *Brain function and reading disabilities.* Baltimore: University Park Press.

Hartlage, L. C., & Telzrow, K. F. (1983). The neuropsychological basis of educational intervention. *Journal of Learning Disabilities, 16,* 521–526.

Herman, B. P. (1982). Neuropsychological function and psychopathology in children with epilepsy. *Epilepsia, 23,* 545–554.

Hynd, C. R. (1986). Educational intervention in children with developmental learning disorders. In J. E. Obrzut & G. W. Hynd (Eds.), *Child neuropsychology* (Vol. 2, pp. 265–297). Orlando, FL: Academic Press.

Hynd, G., & Hynd, C. (1984). Dyslexia: Neuroanatomical/neurolinguistic perspectives. *Reading Research Quarterly, 29,* 482–498.

Hynd, G. W., & Obrzut, J. E. (1986). Clinical child neuropsychology: Issues and perspectives. In J. E. Obrzut & G. W. Hynd (Eds.), *Child neuropsychology* (Vol. 2, pp. 3–14). Orlando, FL: Academic Press.

Johnson, D. J., & Mykelbust, H. R. (1967). *Learning disabilities: Educational principles and practices.* New York: Grune and Stratton.

Kaufman, A. S., & Kaufman, N. L. (1983). *Kaufman Assessment Battery for Children: Interpretive manual.* Circle Pines, MN: American Guidance Service.

Luria, A. R. (1963). *Restoration of function after brain injury.* New York: Macmillan.

Luria, A. R. (1966). *Higher cortical functions in man.* New York: Basic Books.

Luria, A. R. (1973). *The working brain: An introduction to neuropsychology.* New York: Basic Books.

Luria, A. R. (1980). *Higher cortical functions in man,* (2nd ed). New York: Basic Books.

Luria, A. R., & Tzetkova, L. S. (1968). The re-education of brain-damaged patients and its psychopedagogical application. In J. Hellmuth (Ed.), *Learning disorders* (pp. 139–154). Seattle: Special Child Publications.

Lyon, G. R. (1983). Subgroups of learning disabled readers: Clinical and empirical identification. In H. R. Mykelbust (Ed.), *Progress in learning disabilities* (Vol. 5, pp. 103–134). New York: Grune and Stratton.

Lyon, G. R. (1985a). Educational validation of learning disability subtypes: In B. P. Rourke (Ed.), *Neuropsychology of learning disabilities: Essentials of subtype analysis* (pp. 228–256). New York: Guilford Press.

Lyon, G. R. (1985b). Identification and remediation of learning disability subtypes: Preliminary findings. *Learning Disabilities Focus, 1*, 21–35.

Lyon, G. R. (1987). Learning disabilities research: False starts and broken promises. In S. Vaughn & C. Bos (Eds.), *Research in learning disabilities: Issues and future directions* (pp. 69–85). San Diego: College Hill Press.

Lyon, G. R., & Moats, L. C. (in press). Critical issues in the instruction of the learning disabled. *Journal of Consulting and Clinical Psychology.*

Lyon, G. R., Rietta, S., Watson, B., Porch, B., & Rhodes, J. (1981). Selected linguistic and perceptual abilities of empirically derived subgroups of learning disabled readers. *Journal of School Psychology, 19*, 152–166.

Lyon, G. R., & Risucci, D. (1988). Classification issues in learning disabilities. In K. A. Kavale (Ed.), *Learning disabilities: State of the art and practice.* San Diego: College Hill Press.

Lyon, G. R., Stewart, N., & Freedman, D. (1982). Neuropsychological characteristics of empirically derived subgroups of learning disabled readers. *Journal of Clinical Neuropsychology, 4*, 343–365.

Lyon, G. R., & Toomey, F. (1985). Neurological, neuropsychological, and cognitive-developmental approaches to learning disabilities. *Topics in Learning Disabilities, 2*, 1–15.

Lyon, G. R., & Watson, B. (1981). Empirically derived subgroups of learning disabled readers: Diagnostic characteristics. *Journal of Learning Disabilities, 14*, 256–261.

Mann, L. (1979). *On the trail of process.* New York: Grune and Stratton.

Mann, L., & Sabatino, D. A. (1985). *Foundations of cognitive process in remedial and special education.* Rockville, MD: Aspen.

Mattis, S., French, J., & Rapin, I. (1975). Dyslexia in children and young adults. Three independent neuropsychological syndromes. *Developmental Medicine and Child Neurology, 17*, 150–163.

Moats, L. (1983). A comparison of the spelling errors of older dyslexic and normal second grade children. *Annals of Dyslexia, 33*, 121–140.

Newcomb, F. (1985). Neuropsychological qua interface. *Journal of Clinical and Experimental Neuropsychology, 7*, 663–681.

Nolan, D. R., Hammeke, T. A., & Barkley, R. A. (1983). A comparison of the neuropsychological performance in two groups of learning disabled children. *Journal of Clinical Child Psychology, 12*, 13–21.

Obrzut, J. E., & Hynd, G. W. (1986). *Child neuropsychology* (Vol. 2). Orlando, FL: Academic Press.

Pirozzolo, F. (1981). Language and brain: Neuropsychological aspects of developmental reading disability. *School Psychology Review, 10*, 350–355.

Plaisted, J. R., Gustavson, J. L., Wilkening, G. N., & Golden, C. J. (1983). The Luria-Nebraska Neuropsychological Battery-Children's Revision: Theory and current research findings. *Journal of Clinical Child Psychology, 12*, 13–21.

Rao, S. M., & Bieliauskas, L. A. (1983). Cognitive rehabilitation two and one-half years post right temporal lobectomy. *Journal of Clinical Neuropsychology, 5*, 313–320.

Reed, H. B. C., Reitan, R. M., & Klove, H. (1965). Influence of cerebral lesions in psychological test performance of older children. *Journal of Consulting Psychology, 29*, 247–251.

Reitan, R. M. (1966). A research program on the psychological effects of brain lesions in human beings. In R. M. Ellis (Ed.), *International review of research in mental retardation* (pp. 153–218). New York: Academic Press.

Reitan, R. M. (1969). *Manual for administration of neuropsychological test batteries for adults and children.* Indianapolis: Author.

Reitan, R. M. (1979). *Neuropsychology and rehabilitation.* Tucson: Author.

Reitan, R. M. (1980). *REHABIT—Reitan evaluation of hemispheric abilities and brain improvement training.* Tucson: Reitan Neuropsychological Laboratory and University of Arizona.

Reitan, R. M., & Boll, T. J. (1973). Neuropsychological correlates of minimal brain dysfunction. *Annals of the New York Academy of Sciences, 205,* 65–88.

Reitan, R. M., & Davison, L. A. (1974). *Clinical neuropsychology: Current status and applications.* Washington, DC: V. H. Winston.

Reitan, R. M., & Wolfson, D. (1985). *The Halstead-Reitan Neuropsychological Test Battery: Theory and clinical interpretation.* Tucson: Neuropsychology Press.

Rourke, B. P. (1975). Brain–behavior relationships in children with learning disabilities: A research program. *American Psychologist, 30,* 911–920.

Rourke, B. P. (1981). Neuropsychological assessment of children with learning disabilities. In S. B. Filskov & T. J. Boll (Eds.), *Handbook of clinical neuropsychology* (pp. 453–478). New York: Wiley.

Rourke, B. P., Bakker, D., Fiske, J. L., & Strang, J. D. (1983). *Child neuropsychology: An introduction to theory, research, and clinical practice.* New York: Guilford Press.

Rourke, B. P., Fiske, J. L., & Strang, J. D. (1986). *The neuropsychological assessment of children: A treatment-oriented approach.* New York: Guilford Press.

Salvia, J., & Hritcko, T. (1984. The K–ABC and ability training. *The Journal of Special Education, 18,* 345–356.

Seidenberg, M., Giordani, B., Berent, S., & Boll, T. J. (1983). IQ level and performance on the Halstead-Reitan Neuropsychological Test Battery for Older Children. *Journal of Consulting and Clinical Psychology, 51,* 406–413.

Selz, M. J., & Reitan, R. M. (1979). Rules for neuropsychological diagnosis: Classification of brain function in older children. *Journal of Consulting and Clinical Psychology, 47,* 258–264.

Sternberg, R. J. (1984). An information processing analysis and critique. *Journal of Special Education, 18,* 269–279.

Stoddart, C., & Knights, R. M. (1986). Neuropsychological assessment of children: Alternative approaches. In J. E. Obrzut & G. W. Hynd (Eds.), *Child neuropsychology* (Vol. 2, pp. 229–244). Orlando, FL: Academic Press.

Szekeres, S., Ylvisaker, M., & Cohen, S. (1987). A framework for cognitive rehabilitation therapy. In M. Ylvisaker & E. M. R. Gobble (Eds.), *Community re-entry for head-injured adults.* Boston: Little, Brown.

Teeter, P. A. (1986). Standard neuropsychological test batteries for children. In J. E. Obrzut & G. W. Hynd (Eds.), *Child neuropsychology* (Vol. 2, pp. 187–227). Orlando, FL: Academic Press.

Tramontana, M. G., Klee, S. N., & Boyd, T. A. (1984). WISC-R interrelationships with the Halstead-Reitan and Children's Luria Neuropsychological Batteries. *Clinical Neuropsychology, 6,* 1–8.

Traub, N., & Bloom, C. (1975). *Recipe for reading.* Cambridge, MA: Educators Publishing Service.

Yendall, L. T., Fromm-Auch, D., & Davies, P. (1982). Neuropsychological improvement of persistent delinquency. *Journal of Nervous and Mental Disease, 170,* 257–265.

Ysseldyke, J. E., & Algozzine, B. (1982). *Critical issues in special and remediation education.* Boston: Houghton Mifflin.

Ysseldyke, J. E., & Mirkin, P. K. (1981). The use of assessment information to plan instructional interventions: A review of the research. In C. Reynolds & T. Gutkin (Eds.), *A handbook for school psychology* (pp. 113–132). New York: Wiley.

III

Special Topics in Assessment

Attention

RUSSELL A. BARKLEY

INTRODUCTION

Attention is a multidimensional construct referring to a variety of relationships between environmental stimuli or tasks and behavioral responses. Although it has enjoyed widespread investigation in both humans and animals, this was not always so. Much of our understanding of this complicated psychological construct comes from investigations and reviews of the literature published since 1960, although it received some consideration by earlier prominent psychologists such as James (1890) and Titchener (1924).

Attempts at defining a global construct of attention have proven difficult because of its involvement with so many different activities or behaviors across a diversity of tasks and contexts. Instead, more recent investigators (see Egeth & Bevan, 1973; Hale & Lewis, 1979) have subdivided it into more specific components, such as selective or sustained attention, distractibility, orientation, search, and alertness. Even these components, however, are not easily operationalized and one typically must examine the nature of the task used to assess the construct or component before fully appreciating what actually is being measured. Moreover, these components overlap with other mental or neuropsychological constructs, such as memory and its aspects, motor planning and execution, arousal, impulsivity, and the regulation of behavior by rules, to name but a few. This often has led to confusion in efforts to infer the nature of attention and its deficits in individuals with neuropsychological impairment in whom other related brain functions also may be deficient.

Given this theoretical and experimental guagmire, it is easy to see

RUSSELL A. BARKLEY • Department of Psychiatry, University of Massachusetts Medical Center, Worcester, Massachusetts.

why relatively simple measures of attention typically have not been in-cluded in the test batteries frequently given by either clinical child psy-chologists (Rosenberg & Beck, 1986) or child neuropsychologists (Plai-sted, Gustavson, Wilkening, & Golden, 1983; Rourke, 1981). What types of attention should be assessed and how to do so conveniently in routine clinical practice remain unresolved issues in clinical child neuropsychol-ogy. Yet much of the research literature on attention has been conducted with children, and a considerable amount of this with children having a quasi-neuropsychological disorder known as attention deficit disorder (ADD), with or without hyperactivity (American Psychiatric Association, 1980). In fact, ADD is probably the most well studied of childhood psy-chological disorders (Barkley, 1988; Ross & Ross, 1982; Weiss & Hechtman, 1979).

It is the purpose of this chapter to draw upon this wealth of research to provide (1) an appreciation for the importance of attention in child neuropsychological assessment, (2) an understanding of its components, (3) a brief survey of currently available methods of clinical assessment, and (4) awareness of some of the critical issues that remain to be ad-dressed in each of these domains. Psychophysiological measures or corre-lates of attention will not be reviewed in this chapter owing to their rare inclusion in neuropsychological assessments of children and their indi-rectness as indices of attention as a cognitive or behavioral construct. Instead, the focus of this chapter is upon behavioral measures of attention and its components.

Importance of Attention in Child Neuropsychology

To understand the importance of attentional deficits and their assess-ment, one need only examine the prevalence of these deficits within those populations likely to be seen by child psychologists and neuropsycholo-gists.

Prevalence of Attention Deficits

Epidemiological surveys suggest that as many as 49% of boys and 27% of girls are described as inattentive by their teachers (Lapouse & Monk, 1958; Werry & Quay, 1971). Clearly, being inattentive is a relatively common occurrence in normal children. Serious deficits in attention (e.g., greater than 1.5 to 2 standard deviations from the mean) appear to occur in at least 3 to 10% of the school-age population of children, making them among the most prevalent of all childhood neuropsychological disorders (Barkley, 1981; Ross & Ross, 1982). Most of these children are diagnosed as having an attention deficit disorder—a disorder characterized by de-velopmentally inappropriate levels of inattention, impulsivity, and, in many cases, overactivity.

Attentional deficits are also commonly associated with other child psychiatric and developmental disorders, such as autism, pervasive developmental disorders, such as autism, pervasive developmental disorder, depression, conduct disorders, and learning disabilities (Mash & Terdal, 1988). Further, childhood neurological disorders often have attention deficits among their sequelae. Children experiencing closed head injury (Boll, 1983), leukemia and its treatments (Brouwers, Riccardi, Poplack, & Fedio, 1984), epilepsy and its treatments (Holdsworth & Whitmore, 1974; Wolf & Forsythe, 1978), anoxia/hypoxia (O'Dougherty, Nuechterlein, & Drew, 1984), tic disorders and Gilles de la Tourette's syndrome (Barkley, 1988b), lead and other toxin poisonings (Needleman *et al.*, 1979), or exposure to biological hazards during the perinatal period (Nichols, 1980) all have an increased incidence of attentional deficits—some as high as 70% (e.g., Tourette's syndrome). Child neuropsychologists are therefore likely to encounter a large case load of children with some type and degree of deficiency in attention and must be knowledgeable of its assessment.

Interaction of Attention with Other Neuropsychological Functions

The necessity for an understanding and assessment of attention in child neuropsychology is further underscored by the almost ubiquitous influence of attention on other cognitive or neuropsychological abilities and their assessment. It virtually goes without saying that few standard psychological or neuropsychological tests can be administered without a modicum of selective and sustained attention by the child. Attention plays a key role not only in the evaluation of other neuropsychological functions but also in the proficiency of these functions. Deficits in some types of short-term memory problem-solving strategies, effectiveness of both perceptual and memory search strategies, and motor planning, coordination, and execution are commonly seen in children with attention deficits (Douglas, 1983). These attentional deficits may have negative effects on the child's social interactions with parents, peers, and teachers (Barkley, 1985; Whalen, Henker, & Dotemoto, 1980). Given these findings, it is clear that deficits in attention can have wide-ranging effects on the child's cognitive, academic, and social functioning. Surely such an influential variable as attention deserves greater emphasis in our evaluation of children.

Use of Attentional Measures in Clinical Practice

Regrettably, the use of standardized or systematic measures of attention in clinical practice has not been commonplace. Recent surveys of clinical child psychologists have shown that the vast majority rely on parent interviews, informal observations of behavior in the office, intelligence measures, or drawing-and-copying tests to assess attentional deficits (Rosenberg & Beck, 1986). As will be shown later, each of these sources of information is highly flawed as a method of evaluating attentional deficits. Standard practice in child neuropsychology is not much better in that descriptions of neuropsychological assessment batteries (Boll, 1981; Plaisted et al., 1983) do not typically include systematic or standardized assessments of attention and its components. In general, current clinical practices for evaluating attention either are highly impressionistic or rely on poorly validated measures.

Components of Attention

Numerous attempts have been made to define attention, many of which are lacking in precision and operational terms (Gibson & Rader, 1979). Early philosophers viewed attention as a mental faculty dispensed by organisms from a limited pool or capacity. In such conceptualizations, attention is "paid" or deployed by the organism as if it were withdrawn from a limited cognitive bank account or staging area that could be depleted (Mackworth, 1976). Other theorists speculate that there is not just a limited reservoir of attention but also a limited range of stimuli or activities to which an organism can optimally attend simultaneously. What determines these limits is not clear in these formulations.

Current conceptualizations as well as experimental research with children suggest that attention may be best understood as a multidimensional construct having numerous components (Piontrowski & Calfee, 1979). There exists at least some consensus for the following dimensions: Alertness or arousal appears to refer to the degree of general sensitivity of the child to the environment. Alertness seems to mean a generalized wakefulness or state of responsivity, but to nothing in particular. Selective or focused attention most commonly refers to the child's ability to focus on critical stimuli, or those essential to the task, while ignoring unessential elements. Deficits in this component may be thought of as inattention. It is closely linked to distractibility, which refers to the extent to which a child responds to the unessential or irrelevant aspects of a task. Although it is not typically considered a component of attention, extensive research of ADD children (Douglas & Peters, 1979; Milich & Kramer, 1984) suggests that impulsivity closely overlaps with these aspects of attention. It often means the speed and accuracy with which a child reacts to an event or task. Rapid, inaccurate responding is defined as impulsivity (Milich & Kramer, 1984). Sustained attention means the duration of a child's responding to a task or stimulus and is sometimes referred to as vigilance. It seems more accurate, however, to view vigilance as an aspect of sustained attention in which the child persists in directing his sensory perception to a task so as to detect and respond to the sporadic occurence of a target stimulus. *Span of apprehension* has been used to refer to the number of stimuli or amount of information to which a child can effectively attend simultaneously. The term *search* denotes the strategies or rules that a child may employ in interacting with or attending to a stimulus.

Hemi-inattention, or neglect, is a neuropsychological term referring to a rare disorder of selective attention involving failure to respond to target stimuli occurring in a particular sensory half-field or quadrant while responding to the same target stimulus in the opposing half-field or remaining quadrants (see Heilman & Valenstein, 1985). In such cases, it must be clear that the individual retains sensory perception in the particular sensory field in question (e.g., is not blind or does not have a visual field cut) but fails to respond to certain stimuli placed within that field. It is more often evident in adults than in children after lesions to the right posterior cerebral hemisphere, has most often been reported in vision as compared with other sensory modalities, and is more commonly found in left versus right sensory fields. When asked to copy a cross on a page, patients with hemi-inattention ignore the left half of the cross, drawing only its right side. Such male patients may shave only the right side of the face or dress only the right side of the body. When seen in children, neglect is usually an acute symptom noted immediately following a lesion. It resolves rapidly, usually within a matter of hours. Although, in its most dramatic form, neglect is a rare condition, little research has been conducted on whether lesser degrees of hemi-inattention exist in adults or children with a history of posterior lesions of the right hemisphere or impairment in functions subserved by this cortical region. Such a deficit might appear as a slight decrease in the probability of detecting stimuli in one hemifield versus another over numerous trials on a task.

These components of attention do not appear to be independent. Deficits in one component of attention, such as vigilance, are often associated with deficits in others, such as impulsivity, selective attention, and distractibility (Bremer & Stern, 1976; Klee & Garfinkel, 1983). The relationships, although statistically significant, are of a low to moderate degree. Whereas overlap exists across the components of attention, they are not identical and deserve recognition as separate, semi-independent components.

Most standard approaches to psychological or neuropsychological assessment rarely assess all of the components of attention. This is not to say that every aspect of attention should be evaluated in every child referred for assessment. Nevertheless, both clinician and researcher need to be sensitive to the existence of these components, assessing selective components more objectively where history, current concerns, or clinical impressions suggest potential deficits.

Developmental Considerations

Because children's mental and physical abilities seem almost in a constant state of change and maturation, attention and its components should be found to vary considerably with development. Ample research documents an increase in the specificity of perception or focus of attention with increasing age (Gibson & Rader, 1979). This progressive differentiation of selective attention with experience and maturation results in greater economy of effort as children learn to distinguish "signal" from "noise" more efficiently, or relevance from irrelevance in stimulus displays. Also with maturation comes a lengthening of children's attention span, such that more time is spent looking at, exploring, manipulating, and generally interacting with an object than occurred in prior stages of development (Milich, 1984). Children demonstrate increased vigilance or duration of sustained perception to a signal detection task as well as a commensurate decrease in impulsivity with increased maturation (Gordon, McClure, & Post, 1983; Salkind & Nelson, 1980). After age 12 years, response time remains relatively unchanged whereas accuracy continues to improve, implying an ongoing development in efficiency of attentional search strategies at these later ages.

Seemingly at odds with the progressive specificity of attention with age, children also display greater breadth of attention or span of apprehension with development. In other words, they are able to attend to a far larger array of stimuli simultaneously as they mature (Gibson & Rader, 1979). This should not be surprising, however, given that greater specificity or sharpness of attention may permit older children to monitor and respond simultaneously to larger and more complex stimulus arrays with heightened efficiency. Along with these changes appears to come a decline in their proneness to distraction by task-irrelevant stimuli (Woodcock, 1976). Condry, McMahon, and Levy (1979) have shown that older children also seem better able to effectively utilize warning stimuli, or information preceding a task or activity, than do younger children. This suggests a greater preparedness to attend with increasing age in children (Gibson & Rader, 1979). Perhaps related to this, children acquire and utilize progressively more efficient, complex, and effective search strategies over time so as to expend attention more economically during problem-solving activities (Salkind & Nelson. 1980).

With these changes in attention, particularly those related to greater sustained attention, the duration of children's compliance with parental commands and requests increases (Barkley, Karlsson, & Pollard, 1985). This is accompanied by a corresponding decline in the amount of direction, commands, and control exerted by caregivers over the children's play and task performance activities. Such findings underscore the importance of attention in social functioning. Deficits in the components of

attention emanate into social exchanges with others, resulting in re-
ciprocal changes in the manner in which such children are treated by
others (Whalen & Henker, 1980).

A Behavioral Conceptualization of Attention

In a functional analysis, attention is not viewed as a behavior, cognitive ability, or mental construct. It refers to a *relationship* between
stimuli (e.g., tasks or events) and behavioral responses. As such, it describes a correlation, or a lack of one, between the environment and children's activities. Labeling a lack of or weak correlation between two variables as a "deficit" or "disorder" in the child, as in attention deficit
disorder, is ludicrous, for we have simply blamed a low-order correlation
as the basis for the children's problems. It would seem more useful to
study the variables that may account for these relationships because these
variables will shed greater light on what may be neuropsychologically
impaired in inattentive children (Barkley, in press).

Attention refers to the probability that a particular behavior will occur in the presence of a given stimulus. This is referred to as stimulus
control, but stimuli do not actually control the behavior in any physical
sense. They merely set the occasion for a change in response probabilities
(Skinner, 1953, 1969). Different components of attention refer to different
aspects of stimulus control. When children fail to respond to a task or to
sustain or inhibit their responding (inattention and impulsivity, respectively), this simply indicates that the instructions given to the children
and or the task itself exert little stimulus control over the children's behavior. It does not tell us why this relationship has failed to occur or to be
maintained over time by some children when it has occurred or been
maintained successfully by others.

Whether or not stimulus control exists is dependent upon a number
of factors (e.g., the integrity and maturation of the nervous system, the
physical properties of the stimulus). However, one of the greatest determinants is the learning history of the children. Behaviors that have been
reinforced or punished in the presence of a stimulus will subsequently
occur with greater or lesser probability, respectively, when that stimulus
is presented again. Such children are said to be developing selective attention, in the former case, or impulse control, in the latter. The sustained
performance or inhibition of those behaviors in the continued presence of
that stimulus is chiefly a function of the types and schedules of consequences occurring in that situation. Where strong or potent reinforcers or
punishers are provided in a frequent schedule for that behavior, its performance will be sustained or inhibited for longer durations than when weak
or infrequent consequences occur. This suggests that some types of inat-

tention to certain tasks may arise from an inadequate reinforcement history surrounding that task (i.e., the child simply has not had an adequate opportunity to learn the task).

However, when children provided with an adequate learning history fail to develop adequate attention to certain tasks, it is possible that disturbances in certain neurological substrates are involved. Neurological insults that disrupt previously established stimulus–response relations or preclude their adequate development will appear as inattention, impulsivity, or poor sustained attention. A behavioral analysis suggests that some types of inattention may result from disruption of neural substrates for certain sensory analyzers, whereas others arise from impairments in the substrates mediating reinforcement and punishment and their connections with the somatosensory or motor cortex or their association areas. The type of deficit in attention may eventually prove to have some localizing significance in neuropsychological assessment. Similarly, the manner in which certain drugs affect different components of attention may shed light on which functional parameters (e.g., detection, reinforcement, schedules) and neurological substrates mediate these drug effects.

Unfortunately, previous neuropsychological research on attention has seriously neglected the role of response consequences and their schedules in the development and maintenance of attention. As a result, the neurological substrates that mediate different aspects or components of attention are not well understood. Present research on neurological centers related to memory and reinforcement and drug effects on reinforcement centers, however, may offer promising developments in our understanding of attention in child neuropsychology (Gray, 1972, 1982).

Implications for Assessment

This functional analysis of attention suggests that current methods of assessment may be focusing exclusively upon the controlling effects of various stimuli or task parameters (e.g., color, shape, complexity) on behavior without assessing the role of response consequences in attention to tasks. Recent research (Douglas, 1983; Draeger, Prior, & Samson, 1986) clearly shows that performance on such well-respected measures of attention as the continuous performance task are greatly affected by the motivational factors in the setting. Attention deficits may be seen to appear or disappear as response consequences are manipulated. Moreover, recent research on stimulant drugs suggests that they affect attention by enhancing the reinforcement value of stimuli (Stein, 1985). Measures must therefore be developed that systematically evaluate the role of such consequences and their schedules in the functional relations we call "attention" if a more complete assessment of this construct is to occur.

Methods must also be developed that attempt to discriminate more

accurately among the components of attention if the localizing significance of the components is to be realized. For instance, poor sustained
attention may have more to do with problems with rapid extinction to the
reinforcing properties of tasks, whereas impulsivity may reflect underreac-
tivity in the substrates mediating punishment. Behavioral reward and
punishment systems appear to be mediated by different neurological substrates. If measures of sustained attention can be divorced from the effects
of impulsivity, they may yield greater neuropsychological utility than has
heretofore been the case with such commonly used measures as vigilance
tasks. Similarly, poor selective attention may actually be a function of the
parameters of the task stimuli themselves, such as sequential versus spatial arrangement, symbolic versus concrete content, sensory modality,
color, etc. This implies that there may be many subtypes or patterns of
poor selective attention having differing neuropsychological significance.

ASSESSMENT OF ATTENTION

Many methods exist for assessing different aspects of attention in
children. Most are only in their early stages of development, lacking adequate research on their psychometric properties or norms. This section
will discuss some of the more commonly used measures of attention since
a complete description of the numerous methods used in research is beyond the scope and intent of this chapter. Like measures of other constructs, measures of attention can be valuable for establishing the degree
of statistical deviance of children's attention from some norm and perhaps can serve as a criterion for a particular diagnosis, as in attention
deficit disorders. They also can be used to select subjects for research on
attentional deficits, formulate treatment planning, assess changes as a
function of treatment or recovery after injury, and further study qualitative and quantitative changes in attention throughout development. These
measures can be categorized into behavior rating scales, psychometric
tests and laboratory measures, and direct observational systems, all having their own benefits and limitations.

Behavior Rating Scales

Behavior rating scales and checklists have become quite popular methods for assessing certain dimensions of child behavior in research and
clinical practice. Over 70% of clinical child psychologists and 60% of
school psychologists now employ rating scales as routine measures in their
assessment of children with attention deficit disorders (Rosenberg & Beck,
1986). Child neuropsychologists would be wise to do the same. Such
questionnaires have numerous advantages (see Barkley, 1987). They are

able to (1) evaluate a variety of different types of behavior in a very short time (usually minutes), (2) collapse observations of children's attention over lengthy time intervals (weeks to months) that would not be possible with other tests or measures, (3) collect information about the child's attentional characteristics in the natural environment without the need for cumbersome and expensive direct observations, (4) assess the views of important caregivers in the child's daily life concerning the nature of the child's attention to various activities, (5) establish the statistical diviance of the child's attention from peer-referenced normative data available for most rating scales, (6) be repeated frequently over time to assess treatment effects and recovery of function, and (7) provide quantification of qualitative properties of children's attention through the use of Likert scaling of such qualitative items.

Nevertheless, like other types of measures, rating scales have their own inherent limitations. These include such things as bias or confounding of ratings by characteristics of the rater, the loss of information on the functional parameters (i.e., contexts, consequences) surrounding attention by rating only the behaviors involved, the ambiguity of the meaning of items and their scaling reference points, and other disadvantages (see Barkley, 1987). Such drawbacks often can be overcome by employing several different types of measures (tests and observations) along with rating scales. Those scales assessing some aspect of attention are shown in Table 1 and are briefly described below.

Conners Rating Scales

The most widely used rating scales of attention in children have been the Conners scales for parents and teachers (Conners, 1969, 1970; Goyette, Conners, & Ulrich, 1978). The original Conners Parent Rating Scale (Conners, 1970) consists of items of various behavior problems in children, such as aggression, restlessness, fears, enuresis, learning problems, and psychosomatic complaints. The Revised Parent Rating Scale (Goyette et al., 1978) was reduced in length. Each item on either scale is scored on a 4-point dimension of severity (not at all, just a little, pretty much, and very much). Several of the items on each scale pertain to inattention, distractibility, and impulsivity. These can be examined for their degree of rated occurrence as well as combined to constitute a separate subscale of attention. However, factor analyses of the parent scales have not revealed a separate factor of inattention apart from hyperactivity and impulsivity (Conners, 1970; Goyette et al., 1978). This suggests that parents view these behaviors as falling along a homogeneous dimension of disruptive behavior labeled impulsive-hyperactive rather than distinguishing inattention as a separate problem. Normative data are available for the original (C. K.

TABLE 1. Rating Scales for Assessing Attention in Children

Rating scale[a]	Rater	N of items	Norms	Ages (years)	Relevant scales
CPRS	Parent	73	Yes	3–17	Hyperactive
CPRS-R	Parent	48	Yes	3–17	Hyperactive
CTRS	Teacher	39	Yes	5–17	Inattentive
CTRS-R	Teacher	28	Yes	5–17	Inattentive
CBCL	Parent	118	Yes	4–16	Hyperactive
CBCL-TRF	Teacher	118	Yes	6–16	Inattentive
CAP	Teacher	12	Yes	6–16	Inattentive
RBPC	Parent and teacher	89	Yes	5–16	Attention
PBQ	Teacher	30	Yes	3–5	Hyperactive-distractible
ACTeRS	Teacher	24	Yes	5–11	Attention

[a]CPRS = Conners Parent Rating Scale, CPRS-R = Conners Parent Rating Scale-Revised, CTRS = Conners Teacher Rating Scale, CTRS-R = Conners Teacher Rating Scale-Revised, CBCL = Child Behavior Checklist, CBCL-TRF = Child Behavior Checklist-Techer Report Form, CAP = Child Assessment Profile, RBPC = Revised Behavior Problem Profile, PBQ = Preschool Behavior Questionnaire, ACTeRS = Add-H Comprehensive Teacher Rating Scale.

Conners, Department of Psychiatry, Children's Hospital National Medical Center, 111 Michigan Avenue NW, Washington, D.C.) and revised versions (Goyette et al., 1978).

The Conners Teacher Rating Scale (Conners, 1969) contains items constituting a variety of behavioral and learning problems. Its more recent shortened revision (Goyette et al., 1978), like the original scale, is scored along a 4-point dimension of frequency/severity identical to the parent scales (see Barkley, 1981). Three of the items appear to assess attentional deficits. Unlike the parent scales, these items, along with five others, do load on a single dimension that has been labeled Inattentive-Passive. Normative data are available for the original Teachers Rating Scale (Trites, Blouin, & LaPrade, 1982) and the revised scale (Goyette et al., 1978). Users should keep in mind that the Inattentive-Passive factor also comprises items that do not necessarily reflect attention deficits, and so this scale would not constitute a pure or homogeneous rating of attentional problems.

Both the parent and teacher scales have satisfactory reliability and validity, correlate well with other rating scales of similar behaviors, and have been shown to discriminate children with attention deficit disorders (ADD) from non-ADD clinic-referred children and normal children (see Barkley, 1987). They also have been demonstrated repeatedly to be sensitive to stimulant drug effects on ADD children (Cantwell & Carlson, 1978).

Child Behavior Checklist (CBCL)

Achenbach and Edelbrock (1983) have developed a global rating scale of child psychopathology having both parent and teacher report forms. The parent rating scale items are scored on a 3-point scale (0, 1, 2). They yield information concerning the child's social competence as well as psychopathology. One of these scales has been labeled Hyperactive and comprises items assessing inattention, impulsivity, and overactivity. Like the Conners parent scales, research on this scale shows that parent ratings result in a single dimension comprising these three symptoms rather than separate factors for each. Reliability and validity are well established (Achenbach & Edelbrock, 1983; Barkley, 1987), and normative data are available. The scale is useful for assessing ADD in children but is limited for evaluating more pure deficits in the components of attention discussed above.

The teacher report form of this scale also yields information on different dimensions of psychopathology. One of these scales has been labeled Inattention and another Nervous-Overactive. The Inattention scale appears to be quite useful for assessing attentional deficits in children and, along with the Nervous-Overactive scale, is extremely helpful in establishing diagnoses of ADD (with or without hyperactivity) in children. Normative data are available (Edelbrock & Achenbach, 1984). Reliability and validity of the scales appear satisfactory (see Barkley, 1987). As with the Conners teacher scales, however, the Inattention factor on this scale is partially confounded with items assessing behaviors other than inattention. Again, the scale seems more useful in assessing ADD in children as compared with the more selective deficits in the components of attention.

Edelbrock Child Assessment Profile (CAP)

Edelbrock (personal communication) has extracted seven items from the Inattention scale and five from the Overactive scale of the CBCL teacher form that have the highest loadings on these factors, respectively. These have been cast into a separate rating scale shown in Figure 1. Normative data for 1100 children ages 6 through 16 years by sex are provided in Table 2. Scores of 11 or higher on the Inattention subscale would place the child above the 98th percentile relative to normal children. This rating scale seems useful for assessing ADD and its subtypes (with and without hyperactivity). But, unlike other rating scales, the inattention subscale also is helpful in evaluating a more pure construct of attention unconfounded by items concerning other behavioral problems, such as immaturity or affective symptoms.

Child's Name:	:	FOR OFFICE USE ONLY
Today's Date:	:	
Filled Out By:	:	

Below is a list of items that describes pupils. For each item that describes the pupil *now* or *within the past week*, check whether the item is Not True, Somewhat or Sometimes True, or Very or Often True. Please check all items as well as you can, even if some do not seem to apply to this pupil.

	Not True	Somewhat or Sometimes True	Very or Often True
1. Fails to finish things he/she starts	[ ]	[ ]	[ ]
2. Can't concentrate, can't pay attention for long ..	[ ]	[ ]	[ ]
3. Can't sit still, restless, or hyperactive	[ ]	[ ]	[ ]
4. Fidgets	[ ]	[ ]	[ ]
5. Daydreams or gets lost in his/her thoughts	[ ]	[ ]	[ ]
6. Impulsive or acts without thinking	[ ]	[ ]	[ ]
7. Difficulty following directions	[ ]	[ ]	[ ]
8. Talks out of turn	[ ]	[ ]	[ ]
9. Messy work	[ ]	[ ]	[ ]
10. Inattentive, easily distracted	[ ]	[ ]	[ ]
11. Talks too much	[ ]	[ ]	[ ]
12. Fails to carry out assigned tasks	[ ]	[ ]	[ ]

Please feel free to write any comments about the pupil's work or behavior in the last week.

FIGURE 1. CAP rating scale. (c) Copyright 1986 Craig Edelbrock, Psychiatry, UMMS, Worcester, MA 01605.

Revised Behavior Problem Checklist (RBPC)

This is a recent revision of one of the more widely used rating scales in research on childhood behavioral disorders (the Behavior Problem Checklist). The RBPC uses a 3-point scale (0, 1, and 2) for each item, and scoring is based on item placement within empirically derived factors. The RPBC now has a subscale for assessing attention problems/immaturity separate from a motor excess scale. Normative data are available for grades K through 12, using teachers as raters, and for 248 children, ages 5 to 16 years, using mothers' ratings (Quay & Peterson, 1983). The scale seems to have satisfactory reliability and validity (Barkley, 1987). Like those scales reviewed above, this one seems most helpful for evaluating the major symptoms of ADD in children as opposed to assessing more specific deficits in various components of attention.

TABLE 2. Normative Cutoff Points for the
Inattention, Overactivity, and Total Scores
for the Edelbrock CAP Scale

Cutoff points	Total (1100)[a]	Boys (550)	Girls (550)
	Inattention[b]		
Median	1	2	0
69th percentile	3	4	2
84th percentile	6	7	5
93rd percentile	8	9	7
98th percentile	11	12	10
	Overactivity		
Median	0	1	0
69th percentile	1	2	1
84th percentile	4	4	2
93rd percentile	6	6	5
98th percentile	8	8	7
	Total score		
Median	2	4	1
69th percentile	6	7	4
84th percentile	10	11	8
93rd percentile	14	15	11
98th percentile	19	20	16

[a]Numbers in parentheses are sample sizes.
[b]Inattention score is the sum of items 1, 2, 5, 7, 9, 10, and 12.
The Overactivity score is the sum of items 3, 4, 6, 8, and 11.
Table entries are raw scores that fall at or below the designated percentile range. The 93rd percentile is the recommended upper limit of the normal range. Scores exceeding
this cutoff are in the clinical range. All scores are based on
teacher reports.

Preschool Behavior Questionnaire (PBQ)

The PBQ was designed for teachers' use with preschool-age children
as a screening measure for those who might be at risk for later adjustment
problems and psychopathology in school. It consists of 30 items and is
completed by teachers or their aides. A 3-point scale (0, 1, 2) is used to
rate each item, many of which deal with aggressiveness, anxiety, conduct
problems, hyperactivity, and distractibility. As with many other scales,
factor analysis of the items has yielded a hyperactivity-distractibility factor that can be scored separately. Normative data are based on a sample of
496 children (Behar & Stringfield, 1974). Reliability and validity appear to
be satisfactory (Barkley, 1987). Like the Conners scales, the PBQ has little
utility in delineating subtypes of attentional deficits since the hyperac-

tivity scale is confounded with items pertaining to restlessness and immature conduct.

ADD-H Comprehensive Teacher Rating Scale (ACTeRS)

This scale was developed to provide more refined ratings of the major
symptoms of ADD in children: attention, hyperactivity, social problems,
and oppositional behavior (Ullman, Sleator, & Sprague, 1984). Items were
chosen that loaded on only one factor to avoid contamination of the scales
with items also correlating with the other behavior scales. This scale
relies on teachers reports and uses a 5-point scale for rating each item.
Normative data are provided with the manual for 1347 children. Only
recently developed, the scale has some preliminary findings on its various
reliabilities that appear to be satisfactory. Further studies of its validity
and utility are awaited. Like the Edelbrock CAP Scale, this scale is useful
not only for assessing subtypes of ADD in elementary-age children but
also for evaluating a more pure construct of attention using the Attention
Subscale.

Psychometric Tests and Laboratory Measures

A plethora of laboratory measures and tests have been devised to
evaluate various aspects of attention, seemingly limited only by the
creativity of the investigator and the technology available. In fact, because
practically every test or laboratory task requires the subject's attention
and cooperation before conclusions can be drawn about performance,
virtually every test serves in some fashion as a measure of attention.
However, as already noted, to the extent that the measure requires other
neuropsychological functions to perform it satisfactorily, the more cautious must be the conclusions about attentional deficits from poor performance on it. Not surprisingly, then, tests of attention usually involve
quite simple instructions, stimuli, and motor responses so as to minimize
confounding by other cognitive deficits. A few of the more widely used or
promising laboratory tasks and tests are reviewed below. The reader interested in a review of other measures should consult the excellent reviews by Douglas (1983; Douglas & Peters, 1979) dealing with attentional
deficits in learning-disabled and ADD children.

Compared with rating scales, psychometric tests and lab measures
have the ability to conduct a finer analysis of the components of attention
and the effects of manipulating various task parameters upon them.
Where adequate normative data are available, these measures can assist in
providing an objective index of the children's deviance from normal attentional processes and are less affected by potential rater bias that can

easily influence behavior rating scales. Many of the measures reviewed below are brief, can be easily administered, and have a number of research articles dealing with their reliability and validity. Most are hampered, however, by some confounding with other cognitive abilities necessary to conduct the task. This can be partially overcome by using a battery of tests that sample a variety of the major neuropsychological functions with some redundancy across tests in the functions that they evaluate. Performance on these other tests may then provide clues as to the basis for the poor performance on the attentional measure(s).

Another limitation of many of these tests is their low to moderate relationship with other measures of attention taken in the children's natural environment, such as direct observations in the classroom or parent ratings. There is a tendency among newly trained neuropsychologists to attribute greater credibility to the findings from a test than from those derived from parent or teacher reports or direct observations, perhaps because the former seem somehow to be more objective. It is worth recalling that tests often utilize very brief samples of behavior taken in settings, such as offices, that are not especially representative of the children's more natural habitats. In such cases, where test results conflict with other sources of information about attention, further investigation of the discrepancy is clearly required. In some of these instances, it may be the "objective" test results that should be disregarded. As noted earlier, the use of multiple measures of attention derived from multiple sources can overcome many of these limitations.

Reaction Time (RT) Tasks

Probably one of the oldest measures of assessing vigilance or attention span is the reaction time task. These tasks can be configured into a variety of formats, some of which simply involve pressing or releasing a button as soon as a signal appears. Others utilize multiple signals and multiple response keys corresponding with the signals. Some may include a warning stimulus to the subject with a fixed or variable time interval prior to the onset of the signal. In all of these, the primary dependent measure is typically the speed with which the subject presses/releases the button after the signal appears. Often measured in hundredths of seconds, the subject's RT may be elicited over multiple trials, with the average reaction time across trials serving as the score. Other investigators also have calculated the standard deviation of scores around this mean to evaluate variability of performance. Monitoring the number of times the subject presses the button before the signal or at the incorrect signal also can serve as a measure of poor inhibition or impulse control (often referred to as errors of commission). These tasks require the maintenance of vigilance to simple stimuli or the inhibition of responses to competing stimuli over prolonged periods of time.

Studies often find children with ADD to have greater mean reaction times, greater variability of reaction times, and more errors of commission than matched normal children (Douglas, 1983; Douglas & Peters, 1979). Other studies have found impaired reaction times in long-term survivors of childhood leukemia (Brouwers *et al.*, 1984) and as sequelae of closed head injury in children (Levin, Benton, & Grossman, 1982). In studies using a warning stimulus prior to signal onset, ADD, brain-damaged, and mentally retarded children have all been noted to profit less from this warning than normal children, resulting in slower reaction times within these groups (Czudner & Rourke, 1972; Gosling & Jenness, 1974). Many studies have shown both stimulant drugs and various reinforcement contingencies to improve, if not normalize, these reaction time deficits in children (Barkley, 1977a, 1977b; Douglas, 1983).

To the casual observer, reaction time tasks may seem as simple and pure a measure of vigilance as one is likely to find. Although this may be true, the interpretation of reaction time scores as reflecting attentional deficits must be done with some caution. It is possible that deficits in sensory perception, motor programming and execution, language comprehension, and rule-governed behavior (e.g., following experimental instructions) may impair reaction time performance. However, where such deficits do not exist, then problems with vigilance may be concluded from poor performances on these tasks.

Continuous Performance Tasks (CPT)

The CPT is similar to an RT task except that many different stimuli may be used and the subject is required to respond to only one type while inhibiting responses to others (Rosvold, Mirsky, Sarason, Bransome, & Beck, 1956). For instance, flashing letters of the alphabet on a screen and instructing the child to respond only to the letter X after it follows an A may serve as a simple CPT. Most of the tasks available last from 8 to 15 minutes.

Measures often derived from these tasks are total correct responses, errors of commission (false hits), and errors of omission (missed hits) (Douglas, 1983). Commission errors are believed to reflect impulsivity whereas omission errors reflect inattention. Reaction time may or may not be taken in these tasks. Others (Buchsbaum & Sostek, 1980) have applied signal detection theory to analysis of the results of the CPT, calculating two additional dependent measures. Sensitivity, or d', refers to the attentiveness component of vigilance and is calculated as Z (hit rate) − Z (false alarm rate). Hit rate is total hits/total signals, whereas false alarm rate is false hits/(total of target signals − total of all signals). Response bias, or Beta, refers to a subject's tendency to respond when a signal has occurred instead of responding when one has not occurred. It is believed to reflect impulsivity and motivational factors, and it is calculated as Y (hit rate)/Y (false alarm rate).

Some investigators (Buchsbaum & Sostek, 1980) have developed a CPT in which the interval between stimulus presentations varies as a function of the prior success or failure in detecting the last signal presented. If the subject gets a correct hit, the speed of presentation of the stimuli increases, whereas an incorrect hit results in a decrease in the rate of presentation. This permits calculation of an additional dependent measure known as the interstimulus interval (ISI). ISI is the average interval between stimuli over the trials of the task.

Besides RT tasks, CPTs have been demonstrated to be some of the most discriminating measures between ADD and normal children and to be quite sensitive to medication effects (Barkley, 1977a; Douglas, 1983; Swanson & Kinsbourne, 1979). They also correlate to modest but significant degrees with other tests of attention and impulsivity, teacher ratings of hyperactivity in the classroom, and clinic playroom observations of on-task behavior (Klee & Garfinkel, 1983; Prinz, Tarnowski, & May, 1984).

With developments in microcomputer technology, it has become quite feasible to create software capable of running CPTs on personal computers. V. Berman (personal communication, July 18, 1985; University of Nebraska-Lincoln, Department of Special Education, 301 Barkley Memorial Center, Lincoln, NE 68583−0783) has developed a CPT for the Apple IIe that utilizes geometric shapes rather than letters as the stimuli. The target stimulus is an airplane. As in the Buchsbaum and Sostek (1980) CPT, the interval between stimulus presentations varies as a function of prior success at detecting signals. This task also incorporates distracting stimuli that flash to the left or right of the target stimulus display area, permitting a measure of vigilance during distracting and nondistracting conditions. Within the distraction trials, scores can be tabulated for distractions to the left and right visual fields separately. This task would seem to have some promise in assessing hemiinattention in addition to vigilance. Normative data for the ISI measure are available based only on a sample of 230 children in grades K through 9. Others (Klee & Garfinkel, 1983; Prinz et al., 1984) have also developed computerized CPT programs, but these do not yet have normative data available.

Gordon et al. (1983) has provided the first commercially marketed CPT for use in the assessment and diagnosis of ADD children. The device is a portable CPT housed in a metal child-proof box containing a microprocessor. Numbers are flashed on a display screen, and the subject is to respond by pushing a button only when the number 1 (ages 3 to 5 years) or the numbers 1 then 9 (ages 6 to 16 years) appear. The device computes the measures of number correct, number of commissions, and number of omissions. Normative data are available for more than 1400 children between 3 and 16 years of age. A recent modification of the task now permits it to flash distracting numbers to the left and right of the target display area for assessment of vigilance with and without distractors. The advantages of Gordon's CPT task, besides its construction, are the availability of normative data on a large sample of children over a wide age range, its satisfactory discrimination of ADD from non-ADD children (Gordon et al., 1983), its sensitivity to stimulant drug effects (Barkley, Fischer, Newby, & Breen, 1988). and its significant correlation with teacher ratings of inattentive and hyperactive behavior (Gordon, 1983).

In general, CPT tasks appear to be a convenient way of assessing vigilance and impulsivity in children. The availability of software programs for personal computers and normative data on some versions permits the use of these tasks for clinical and research purposes.

Cancellation Tasks

Several paper-and-pencil versions of CPT tasks have been used as methods of assessing attention, primarily vigilance and impulsivity. These tasks typically involve having the subject scan a series of symbols (i.e., letters, numbers, shapes) in rows on paper. The subject is typically required to draw a line through or under the target stimulus using a pencil. One such task is the Children's Checking Task (CCT), developed by Margolis (1971). The task consists of a series of 15 numerals per row printed in 16 rows on a page. There are seven pages to the task. A tape recorder reads off the numbers in each row, and the child is required to draw a line through each number as it is read. Discrepancies between the tape and the printed page are to be circled. There are seven discrepancies between the tape and the printed pages. The task takes about 30 minutes. Scores are derived for errors of omission (missed discrepancies) and errors of commission (numbers circled when no discrepancy exists). The task discriminates educationally handicapped from normally achieving students (Keough & Margolis, 1976) and ADD from reading-disabled children (Brown & Wynne, 1982). It also appears to correlate to a modest but significant degree with other measures of attention (Keough & Margolis, 1976).

Another cancellation task is the Underlining Test developed by Doehring and used extensively in neuropsychological studies by Rourke and his colleagues (Rourke & Gates, 1980; Rourke & Orr, 1977). The task consists of 14 subtests. Each subtest varies as to whether it involves numbers, geometric shapes, letters or letter combinations, or words. In each subscale, the child is required to scan rows of these symbols on a page and to underline a particular one that matches a sample provided at the top of the page. The child's speed and accuracy in performing the task are recorded. The subtests range in degree of difficulty, with subtests 1 and 13 being identical to assess practice effects, and another subtest (14) involving stimuli (rectangles) that are all identical, and all of which the child must underline. This is designed to control for motor speed. Normative data are available (Rourke & Gates, 1980), and impairments on the tests have some relationship to reading and spelling deficits in children (Rourke & Orr, 1977). The test would seem to require adequate visual perception, spatial discrimination, number and letter facility, and adequate motor speed and coordination. Where these are intact but performance on the task is impaired, deficits in selective attention may be hypothesized.

Children's Embedded Figures Test (CEFT)

A commonly used test of selective attention and visual discrimination has been the CEFT (Witkin, Oltman, Raskin, & Karp, 1971). Some have interpreted the test as a measure of "coming to attention" (Keough & Margolis, 1976), field dependence-independence and global versus analytic perception (Schain, Ward, & Guthrie, 1977). The test involves 27 pictures of figures within which a simple figure (tent or house) is embedded. The scores are the mean time to respond and the number of correct responses. Normative data are available for ages 5 to 12 years, and reliability of the test is quite satisfactory (Schain et al., 1977). The test has been used to assess selective attention in studies of hyperactive, hypoxic, educationally handicapped, and epileptic children (Brown & Wynne, 1982; Keough & Margolis, 1976; Schain et al., 1977). It appears to correlate significantly and moderately with the Children's Checking Test, described above, and Kagan's Matching Familiar Figures Test (see below). Hence, it would appear that the task assesses impulsivity and vigilance as well as selective attention.

Mazes

Maze performance has frequently been used in child neuropsychological research as a measure of motor planning, speed, and execution, as well as impulsivity and sustained attention (Reitan & Davison, 1974; Rourke, Bakker, Fisk, & Strang, 1983). Poor maze performances have been noted in ADD children (Milich & Kramer, 1984), children surviving closed head injury (Klonoff, Low, & Clark, 1977), and epileptic children undergoing treatments with anticonvulsants (Schain et al., 1977). Such tests also have proven sensitive to stimulant drug effects in ADD children (Barkley, 1977a, 1977b).

Probably the most commonly used maze test is the Porteus Mazes (1965). Although originally intended as a measure of intelligence, the test has been most typically used to assess impulsivity, sustained attention, and the motor parameters noted above. In this paper-and-pencil task, the printed mazes progress across a range of increasingly difficult configurations. A year level, test quotient, and Q score are obtained, the latter believed to assess impulsivity. Another paper-and-pencil maze test is an optional subtest of the Wechsler Intelligence Scale for Children-Revised (1974), for which normative data are available. A maze test often used in neuropsychological evaluations is part of the Wisconsin version of the Halstead-Reitan Neuropsychological Test Battery (Matthews & Klove, 1965). It involves the child's using a metal stylus to traverse a raised metal maze. The child's speed of performance, number of contacts with the sides of the maze, and time in contact with the sides is recorded.

Matching Familiar Figures Test (MFFT)

The most widely employed measure of impulsivity is undoubtedly Kagan's MFFT (Kagan, Rosman, Day, Albert, & Phillips, 1964). The test involves presenting the child with a sample figure (i.e., a house) and simultaneously displaying six very similar figures, one of which is identical to the sample figure. The child is to point to the figure that matches the sample. The time to the first response and the number of errors are recorded. Scores are then derived for mean time to response and total errors across the 12 trials. Normative data are available for ages 5 through 12 years for a sample of over 2800 children (Salkind & Nelson, 1980). Impairments in test performance have been reported for ADD children (Douglas & Peters, 1979; Milich & Kramer, 1984), impulsive educationally handicapped children (Keough & Margolis, 1976), behavior-disordered children (Brown & Quay, 1977), and epileptic children receiving anticonvulsants (Schain et al., 1977). The test scores correlate to a low, but significant, degree with continuous performance tests, Arithmetic and Coding subtests from the WISC-R, the Children's Checking Test, and the Children's Embedded Figures Test (Keough & Margolis, 1976; Klee & Garfinkel, 1983). Numerous studies have shown the test to be sensitive to stimulant drug effects in ADD children (Barkley, 1977b; Cantwell & Carlson, 1978).

Direct Reinforcement of Latency (DRL) Tasks

A relatively recent attempt has been made by Gordon (1979; Gordon et al., 1983) to utilize a DRL paradigm to assess impulse control in children. The task requires a child to sit before a metal box containing a microprocessor that administers and scores the test. The child is required to press a button, wait a while, and press it again. If the child has waited long enough, a point is earned. Cumulative points are recorded on a display screen. The child is not informed of the delay interval (6 seconds) but is reinforced with points on each trial that exceeds the standard interval. The test is brief (8 minutes), and normative data are available for more than 1400 children. The test discriminates ADD from non-ADD clinic-referred children, and it correlates moderately and significantly with the MFFT, the Conners parent and teacher rating scales, and the Child Behavior Checklist Teacher Report Form (Gordon et al., 1983). Although promising, the task has not proven sensitive to stimulant drug effects with ADD children (Barkley et al., 1988).

Span of Apprehension Test

The concept of span of apprehension has been used to refer to the amount of information a child is able to attend to simultaneously. The child is shown matrices on a display screen. Some of the 16 cells contain a T, an F, or noise letters. The number of noise or nonsignal letters is varied across trials (2, 4, or 8 noise letters), as is the location of one of the signal or target letters (T, F). Matrices are presented via a tachistoscope for 100-msec exposures while the child focuses upon a fixation point. The number of letters scanned by the child is the span of apprehension (A) and is calculated as $A = D (2 Pc - 1)$, where D is the number of letters in the display, and Pc the percent correct of recognition of target stimuli. Studies have shown the task to discriminate ADD from normal children (Denton & McIntyre, 1978) and to correlate with direct observations of attention during a clinic playroom task (Prinz et al., 1984). However, normative data for the task are lacking, and the necessity of using a tachistoscope for presentation makes the task unwieldy for young children and inconvenient for clinical practice.

Goldman-Fristoe-Woodcock (GFW) Selective Attention Test

One of the few tests of auditory, as opposed to visual, selective attention is the GFW (Woodcock, 1976). This test has been used occasionally in studies of learning-disabled, ADD, and normal children (Foch & Plomin, 1980; Plomin & Foch, 1981). The test requires the child to wear earphones and listen to words presented on a tape recording. The child is to point to printed pictures of the words provided on the tape. Part of the test involves no background noise on the tape during word presentation, whereas other parts have increasing background noise (white noise and cafeteria sounds). So constructed, the test appears to be more a measure of distractibility to extraneous sounds while reading than one of selective attention.

Freedom From Distractibility (FFD) Factor of the WISC-R

Factor analysis of the WISC-R by Kaufman (1975) demonstrated a three-factor solution now widely accepted as the predominant cognitive constructs assessed by this intellectual test. One of these three factors comprised the Arithmetic, Digit Span, and Coding subtests and was named Freedom From Distractibility (FFD). It was so named in part out of tradition because a comparable factor emerged in analyses of other Wechsler batteries and "because of research with hyperactive children showing that drug therapy leads to decreased distractibility and improved memory and arithmetic skills in these youngsters" (Kaufman, 1980, p. 179).

Since its introduction over a decade ago, clinicians and researchers alike have interpreted deficits on this factor as reflecting distractibility or poor attention. The subtests constituting the factor do show low, but significant, correlations with other measures of attention, such as vigilance and impulsivity (Klee & Garfinkel, 1983). Evidence is conflicting, however, as to whether deficits on these subtests discriminate ADD from non-ADD or reading-disabled children (Brown & Wynne, 1982; Milich & Loney, 1974). Deficits in these subtests have been found in long-term survivors of acute lymphoblastic leukemia (Goff, Anderson, & Cooper, 1980). However, where deficits in FFD subtests are found, it is not clear that they necessarily reflect deficiencies in attention (e.g., distractibility). These subtests also appear to require adequate short-term memory, numerical facility (Arithmetic and Digit Span), arithmetic calculation, and visuospatial constructional skills as well as visual-motor speed (Coding subtest). As a result, a number of investigators (Kaufman, 1980; Ownby & Matthews, 1985; Stewart & Moely, 1983) have urged caution in interpreting these subtests as measures of distractibility, believing its label to be an oversimplification and misleading (Ownby & Matthews, 1985). Complex cognitive processes appear to be involved in these tests, precluding any straightforward interpretation of performance deficits in them as reflecting inattention.

Direct Observational Measures

Although often not included in standard neuropsychological test batteries with children, systematic direct observational recordings of behavior during various situations readily reveal deficits in attention and impulse control. They have most often been used in studying ADD children, especially during task performances (Abikoff, Gittelman-Klein, & Klein, 1977; Ross & Ross, 1982). Direct observations of behavior systematically recorded alleviate many of the limitations of other assessment methods, such as unrepresentativeness or rater bias. Such observational systems are exquisitely sensitive to stimulant drug treatments and behavior modification interventions (Barkley, 1977b; Barkley et al., 1988; Mash & Dalby, 1979). They are more ecologically representative of the children's actual attentional deficits when taken in natural settings than are laboratory measures or psychometric tests. Moreover, they permit close analysis of the environmental variables of which the inattentiveness may be a function. For instance, deficits in sustained attention in ADD children may not always be apparent in free-play settings, but they are commonly noted when the children are assigned tasks to perform by others (Routh & Schroeder, 1976). These attentional deficits may be readily improved by the addition of frequent reinforcement or punishment (Pfiffner, Rosen, & O'Leary, 1985), or by altering the salience of the stimuli to which the children must attend (Ross & Ross, 1982).

Probably the most commonly used behavioral observation measure of attention is the direct recording of "on-task" or "off-task" behavior, either in the child's regular classroom (Abikoff et al., 1977; Pfiffner et al., 1985) or in clinic analogue situations using one-way observation mirrors (Barkley, 1977a; Barkley et al., 1988). Coding may involve simply using a stopwatch to time the duration of the child's visual focusing on the task (Barkley, 1977a; Prinz et al., 1984). or recording whether or not on-task or off-task behavior was noted during a series of brief time intervals, say 15 seconds (Barkley et al., 1988). In the latter case, the dependent measure is expressed as the percentage of the total observation intervals in which the child demonstrated these behaviors.

Such observational systems correlate well with observer ratings when taken in the same classroom (Kazdin, Esvelt-Dawson, & Loar, 1983), and with laboratory measures of vigilance, impulsivity, and span of apprehension when taken in clinic playroom settings (Prinz et al., 1984). Clinic playroom observations during task performance also have shown surprisingly high stability over a 2-year interval (Milich, 1984) and appear to be as sensitive to dose effects of stimulant medication as those taken in classroom settings (Barkley et al., 1988; Rapport, Stoner, DuPaul, Birmingham, & Tucker, 1985). In these analogue situations, measures also are taken of the children's work productivity as a behavioral by-product of the children's on-task activities (Prinz et al., 1984).

Other investigators have recorded the number of toy changes or the mean duration of play with each toy during free-play situations in clinic playrooms as reflections of sustained attention (Barkley, 1977a; Routh & Schroeder, 1976). These tend to have poor test-retest reliability (Plomin & Foch, 1981). In some cases, the number of times a child looked at a particular stimulus, such as a television monitor, served as the measure of attention (Prinz et al., 1984).

Direct observational measures seem to be convenient to employ, especially if clinic analogue settings are used. They also are particularly sensitive to treatment manipulations. However, their main drawback at present remains the lack of normative data for use in establishing deviance of attention during initial clinic evaluations. This is less of an issue in child neuropsychological research, but it is a major problem for clinical practice. Nevertheless, such recordings may still prove useful in measuring within-subject changes in behavior due to stimulant medication or other interventions in clinical practice.

DISCUSSION

This brief review of assessment techniques suggests that many measures are flawed in their evaluation of attention, often because of confounding of attentional components with each other or with other neuropsychological constructs. Most rating scales do not evaluate pure components of attention and are hampered by possible sources of rater bias. Although convenient, they lack the precision desired in a finer-grain analysis of attentional components within neuropsychological research. Still, as crude initial screening measures to detect attentional deficits in large populations of children, they would seem quite valuable. They also offer the advantage of identifying those natural settings in which the attentional deficits are creating the greatest difficulties in adjustment and performance. This suggests that the inclusion of such rating scales in research and practice would be prudent but that more objective. systematic, and specific laboratory measures of attentional components also must be included.

Among the psychometric and laboratory measures, reaction time and vigilance tasks appear to have the greatest sensitivity in detecting attention deficits, particularly in sustained attention and impulsivity. Measures of selective attention and distractibility are not as well developed or investigated, and those of span of apprehension and attentional search have received minimal research in the neuropsychological literature. Just as measures of memory and its components must be more refined and standardized (see Chapter 7, this volume), those of attention must be more narrow or specialized in the type of attention assessed. Differences in the components of attention within each sensory modality, between spatial and sequentially presented material, and between symbolic and concrete contents probably exist yet are unappreciated by the crude methods now employed. The application of signal detection theory to measures of vigilance has proven helpful in this regard, separating inattention from impulsivity in the analysis of performance scores. Similar approaches to other components of attention might prove fruitful.

Of even greater promise would appear to be a functional analysis of attention as a term describing numerous contingent relations between stimuli and responses that are a function of not only stimulus parameters and task instructions but also the consequences for responding and their schedules. This implies that a full appreciation of attention and its components will come only when the manner in which variations in response consequences affect behavior are systematically assessed. Although this is evaluated to a limited degree on tasks such as the Wisconsin Card Sort Test and the Halstead-Reitan Categories task, the way in which response consequences affect subsequent responding is not controlled in a sufficiently systematic or standardized way across subjects to assess this aspect of attention. More promising would seem to be the use of very simple behavioral paradigms, such as vigilance tasks, in which response consequences are systematically manipulated to evaluate different rates of behavioral extinction (poor sustained attention) or disinhibition (impulsivity) under differing schedules of consequences.

The acceptance of attention as multidimensional implies that the separate components of attention could be used to construct profiles of performance for each child. A taxonomy of more homogeneous subtypes of children having disorders of attention could then be created from these typologies. Present research suggests that children with deficits in selective attention may constitute a different subtype from those with poor sustained attention, who in turn may differ from those with deficits in impulse control. Each may stem from different etiologies, be mediated by different neurological subtrates, have differing developmental courses, and respond differently to various treatments. As research on reading disorders has unfolded to reveal more homogeneous subtypes (see Chapter 11, this volume), each having different developmental courses and treatment implications, so too will this likely be seen in the field of attention if as much effort and research interest can be brought to bear on the problem.

SUMMARY

Attention is a multidimensional construct that refers to a variety of functional relationships between environmental stimuli or tasks and children's behaviors. Deficits in attention are quite prevalent within normal, psychiatric, and neurological populations of children, yet they are often ignored in the systematic assessment of such children. Even when they are evaluated, the methods for doing so are often highly impressionistic or of questionable validity. More appropriate measures are available in the recent research literature but have yet to be adopted to any widespread degree in clinical practice. Such adoption is strongly encouraged.

The major components of attention appear to be arousal and alertness, selective or focused attention, distractibility, sustained attention, impulsivity, span of apprehension, and search. Developmental research indicates increasing economy, efficiency, and effectiveness in these components with maturation well into the adolescent years.

A functional analysis of these components suggests that they are under different aspects of stimulus control. Stimulus control occurs as a function of the type of stimulus or task, its inherent reinforcement properties, the nature of rules given with the task, the type and schedule of consequences for responding to the task, and the integrity of the developing nervous system. Disturbances in any or all of these may disrupt "attention." As such, deficits in the components of attention may result from improper task construction, inadequate learning histories, or neurological impairments in the sensory association cortex, in the reinforcement or punishment centers, in the feedback loops between these centers and the sensory-motor association areas, or in the prefrontal zones (executive cortex).

Numerous methods of assessing attention were reviewed. These are categorized into behavior rating scales, laboratory measures, psychometric tests, and direct observational methods. Although each type offers unique strengths and limitations, the former can be capitalized upon and the latter overcome by the inclusion of at least one measure of each type in the clinical assessment of children. It may eventually prove important to assess each component of attention within specific sensory modalities, once adequate measures of such are developed and studied for their significance. What is now required is a concerted effort of increased research, such as that seen with the learning disabilities. Such an effort should incorporate the views of behavioral analysis to advance our understanding of this perplexing construct and to better serve the large segment of the childhood population afflicted with deficits in the components of attention.

REFERENCES

Abikoff, H., Gittelman-Klein, R., & Klein, D. (1977). Validation of a classroom observation code for hyperactive children. *Journal of Consulting and Clinical Psychology, 45,* 772–783.

Achenbach, T. M., & Edelbrock, C. (1983). *Manual for the Child Behavior Checklist and Revised Child Behavior Profile.* Burlington, VT: Thomas Achenbach.

American Psychiatric Association. (1980). *Diagnostic and statistical manual of mental disorders* (3rd ed.). Washington, D.C.

Barkley, R. (1977a). A review of stimulant drug research with hyperactive children. *Journal of Child Psychology and Psychiatry, 18,* 137–165.

Barkley, R. (1977b). The effects of methylphenidate on various measures of activity level and attention in hyperkinetic children. *Journal of Abnormal Child Psychology, 5,* 351–369.

Barkley, R. A. (1981). *Hyperactive children: A handbook for diagnosis and treatment.* New York: Guilford Press.

Barkley, R. A. (1985). Family interaction patterns in hyperactive children: Precursors to aggressive behavior? In M. Wolraich & D. Routh (Eds.), *Advances in behavioral pediatrics* (pp. 117–150). Greenwich, CT: JAI Press.

Barkley, R. A. (1987). A review of child behavior checklists and rating scales for research in child psychopathology. In M. Rutter, A. H. Tuma, & I. S. Lann (Eds.), *Assessment and diagnosis in child psychopathology.* New York: Guilford Press.

Barkley, R. A. (1988a). Attention deficit disorders. In E. Mash & L. Terdal (Eds.), *Behavioral assessment of childhood disorders* (2nd ed.). New York: Guilford Press.

Barkley, R. A. (1988b). Tic disorders and Tourette's syndrome. In E. Mash & L. Terdal (Eds.), *Behavioral assessment of childhood disorders* (2nd ed.). New York: Guilford Press.

Barkley, R. A. (in press). The problem of stimulus control and rule-governed behavior in attention deficit disorder with hyperactivity. In L. Bloomingdale & J. Swanson (Eds.), *Attention deficit disorders* (vol. 3). New York: Pergamon.

Barkley, R., Fischer, M., Newby, R. F., & Breen, M. J. (1988). Development of a multi-method clinical protocol for assessing stimulant drug responding in ADD children. *Journal of Clinical Child Psychology, 17,* 14–24.

Barkley, R., Karlsson, J., & Pollard, S. (1985). Effects of age on the mother–child interactions of hyperactive boys. *Journal of Abnormal Child Psychology, 13,* 631–637.

Behar, L., & Stringfield, S. (1974). A behavior rating scale for the preschool child. *Developmental Psychology, 10,* 601–610.

Boll, T. J. (1981). The Halstead-Reitan Neuropsychological Test Battery. In S. Filskov & T. Boll (Eds.), *Handbook of clinical neuropsychology* (Vol. 1, pp. 577–607). New York: Wiley.

Boll, T. J. (1983). Minor head injury in children—Out of sight but not out of mind. *Journal of Clinical Child Psychology, 12,* 74–80.

Bremer, D. A., & Stern, J. A. (1976). Attention and distractibility during reading in hyperactive boys. *Journal of Abnormal Child Psychology, 4,* 381–387.

Brouwers, P., Riccardi, R., Poplack, D., & Fedio, P. (1984). Attentional deficits in long term survivors of childhood acute lymphoblastic leukemia (ALL). *Journal of Clinical Neuropsychology, 6,* 325–336.

Brown, R. T., & Quay, L. C. (1977). Reflection-impulsivity in normal and behavior-disordered children. *Journal of Abnormal Child Psychology, 5,* 457–462.

Brown, R. T., & Wynne, M. E. (1982). Correlates of teacher ratings, sustained attention, and impulsivity in hyperactive and normal boys. *Journal of Clinical Child Psychology, 11,* 262–267.

Buchsbaum, M. S. & Sostek, A. J. (1980). An adaptive continuous performance test: Vigilance characteristics and reliability for 400 male students. *Perceptual and Motor Skills, 51,* 707–713.

Cantwell, D. P., & Carlson, G. (1978). Stimulants. In J. Werry (Ed.), *Pediatric psychopharmacology* (pp. 171–207). New York: Brunner/Mazel.

Condry, S., McMahon, M., & Levy, A. (1979). A developmental investigation of selective attention to graphic, phonetic, and semantic information in words. *Perception and Psychophysics, 25,* 88–94.

Conners, C. K. (1969). A teacher rating scale for use in drug studies with children. *American Journal of Psychiatry, 126,* 884.

Conners, C. K. (1970). Symptom patterns in hyperkinetic, neurotic, and normal children. *Child Development, 41,* 667–682.

Czudner, G., & Rourke, B. P. (1972). Age differences in visual reaction time of "brain-damaged" and normal children under regular and irregular preparatory interval conditions. *Journal of Experimental Child Psychology, 13,* 516–526.

Denton, C. L., & McIntyre, C. W. (1978). Span of apprehension in hyperactive boys. *Journal of Abnormal Child Psychology, 6*, 19–24.

Douglas, V. I. (1983). Attention and cognitive problems. In M. Rutter (Ed.), *Developmental neuropsychiatry* (pp. 280–329). New York: Guilford Press.

Douglas, V. I., & Peters, K. G. (1979). Toward a clearer definition of the attentional deficit of hyperactive children. In G. A. Hale & M. Lewis (Eds.), *Attention and cognitive development* (pp. 173–248). New York: Plenum.

Draeger, S., Prior, M., & Sanson, A. (1986). Visual and auditory attention performance in hyperactive children: Competence or compliance *Journal of Abnormal Child Psychology, 14*, 411–424.

Edelbrock, C., & Achenbach, T. A. (1984). The Teacher Version of the Child Behavior Profile: I. Boys aged 6–11. *Journal of Consulting and Clinical Psychology, 52*, 207–217.

Egeth, H., & Bevan, W. (1973). Attention. In B. B. Wolman (Ed.), *Handbook of general psychology*. Englewood Cliffs, NJ: Prentice-Hall.

Foch, T. T., & Plomin. R. (1980). Specific cognitive abilities in 5- to 11-year-old twins. *Behavior Genetics, 10*, 507–520.

Gibson, E., & Rader, N. (1979). Attention: Perceiver as performer. In G. Hale & M. Lewis (Eds.), *Attention and cognitive development* (pp. 1–22). New York: Plenum.

Goff, J. R., Anderson, H. R., & Cooper, P. F. (1980). Distractibility and memory deficits in long-term survivors of acute lymphoblastic leukemia. *Developmental and Behavioral Pediatrics, 1*, 158–163.

Gordon, M. (1979). The assessment of impulsivity and mediating behaviors in hyperactive and nonhyperactive children. *Journal of Abnormal Child Psychology, 7*, 317–326.

Gordon, M., McClure, F. D., & Post, E. M. (1983). *Interpretive guide to the Gordon Diagnostic System*. DeWitt, NY: Gordon Systems.

Gosling, H., & Jenness, D. (1974). Temporal variables in simple reaction times of mentally retarded boys. *American Journal of Mental Deficiency, 79*, 214–224.

Goyette, C. H., Conners, C. K., & Ulrich, R. F. (1978). Normative data for Revised Conners Parent and Teacher Rating Scales. *Journal of Abnormal Child Psychology, 6*, 221–236.

Gray, J. A. (1972). Learning theory, the conceptual nervous system, and personality. In V. D. Neblitsin & J. A. Gray (Eds.), *Biological bases of individual behavior* (pp. 370–398). New York: Academic Press.

Gray, J. A. (1982). *The neuropsychology of anxiety: An enquiry into the functions of the septo-hippocampal system*. New York: Oxford University Press.

Hale, G., & Lewis, M. (1979). *Attention and cognitive development*. New York: Plenum.

Heilman, K., & Valenstein, F. (1985) *Clinical neuropsychology* (2nd ed.). New York: Oxford University Press.

Holdsworth, L., & Whitmore, K. (1974). A study of children with epilepsy attending ordinary schools. I: Their seizure patterns, progress, and behaviour in school. *Developmental and Child Neurology, 16*, 746–758.

James, W. (1890). *The principles of psychology*. New York: Holt.

Kagan, J., Rosman, B., Day, D., Albert, J., & Phillips, W. (1964). Information processing in the child: Significance of analytic and reflective attitudes. *Psychological Monographs, 78*,(1, Whole No. 578).

Kaufman, A. S. (1975). Factor analysis of the WISC-R at eleven age levels between 6½ and 16½ years. *Journal of Consulting and Clinical Psychology, 43*, 135–147.

Kaufman, A. S. (1980). Issues in psychological assessment: Interpreting the WISC-R intelligently. In B. Lahey & A. Kazdin (Eds.), *Advances in clinical child psychology* (Vol. 3, pp. 177–214). New York: Plenum.

Kazdin, A. E., Esveldt-Dawson, K. & Loar, L. L. (1983). Correspondence of teacher ratings and direct observations of classroom behavior of psychiatric inpatient children. *Journal of Abnormal Child Psychology, 11*, 549–564.

Keough, B. K., & Margolis, J. S. (1976). A component analysis of attentional problems of educationally handicapped boys. *Journal of Abnormal Child Psychology, 4*, 349–359.

Klee, S. H., & Garfinkel, B. D. (1983). The computerized continuous performance task: A new measure of inattention. *Journal of Abnormal Child Psychology, 11*, 487–496.

Klonoff, H., Low, M., & Clark, C. (1977). Head injuries in children: A prospective five year follow-up. *Journal of Neurology, Neurosurgery, and Psychiatry, 40*, 1211–1219.

Lapouse, R., & Monk, M. (1958). An epidemiological study of behavior characteristics in children. *American Journal of Public Health, 48*, 1134–1144.

Levin, H. S., Benton, A. L., & Grossman, R. G. (1982). *Neurobehavioral consequences of closed head injury.* New York: Oxford University Press.

Mackworth, J. (1976). Development of attention. In V. Hamilton & M. D. Vernon (Eds.), *The development of cognitive processes.* New York: Academic Press.

Margolis, J. S. (1971). *Academic correlates of sustained attention.* Unpublished doctoral dissertation, University of California, Los Angeles.

Mash, E. J., & Dalby, J. T. (1979). Behavioral interventions for hyperactivity. In R. Trites (Ed.), *Hyperactivity in children: etiology, measurement, and treatment implications* (pp. 161–216). Baltimore University Park Press.

Mash, E., & Terdal, L. (1987). *Behavioral assessment of childhood disorders* (2nd ed.). New York: Guilford Press.

Matthews, C. G., & Klove, H. (1965). *Manual for the Wisconsin adaptation of the Halstead-Reitan Neuropsychological Test Battery.* Madison: University of Wisconsin Hospitals.

Milich, R. (1984). Cross-sectional and logitudinal observations of activity level and sustained attention in a normative sample. *Journal of Abnormal Child Psychology, 12*, 261–276.

Milich, R., & Kramer, J. (1984). Reflections on impulsivity: An empirical investigation of impulsivity as a construct. In K. Gadow & I. Bialer (Eds.), *Advances in learning and behavioral disabilities* (Vol. 3, pp. 57–94). Greenwich, CT: JAI Press.

Milich, R., & Loney, J. (1974). The factor composition of the WISC for hyperkinetic/MBD males. *Journal of Learning Disabilities, 12*, 67–71.

Needleman, H. L., Gunnoe, C., Leviton, A., Reed, R., Peresie, H., Maher, C., & Barrett, P. (1979). Deficits in psychologic and classroom performance of children with elevated dentine lead levels. *New England Journal of Medicine, 300*, 689–695.

Nichols, P. (1980). Early antecedents of hyperactivity. *Neurology, 30*, 439.

O'Dougherty, M., Nuechterlein, K. H., & Drew, B. (1984). Hyperactive and hypoxic children: Signal detection, sustained attention, and behavior. *Journal of Abnormal Psychology, 93*, 178–191.

Ownby, R. L., & Matthews, C. G. (1985). On the meaning of the WISC-R third factor: Relations to selected neuropsychological measures. *Journal of Consulting and Clinical Psychology, 53*, 531–534.

Pfiffner, L. J., Rosen, L. A., & O'Leary, S. G. (1985). The efficacy of an all-positive approach to classroom management. *Journal of Applied Behavior Analysis, 18*, 257–262.

Piontrowski, D., & Calfee, R. (1979). Attention in the classroom. In G. Hale & M. Lewis (Eds.), *Attention and cognitive development* (pp. 297–330). New York: Plenum.

Plaisted, J. R., Gustavson, J. L., Wilkening, G. N., & Golden, C. J. (1983). The Luria-Nebraska Neuropsychological Battery-Children's Revision: Theory and current research findings. *Journal of Clinical Child Psychology, 12*, 13–21.

Plomin, R., & Foch, T. T. (1981). Hyperactivity and pediatrician diagnoses, parental ratings, specific cognitive abilities, and laboratory measures. *Journal of Abnormal Child Psychology, 9*, 55–64.

Porteus, S. (1965). *Porteus Maze Tests: Fifty years' application.* Palo Alto, CA: Pacific Books.

Prinz, R. J., Tarnowski, K. J., & Nay, S. M. (1984). Assessment of sustained attention and distraction in children using a classroom analogue task. *Journal of Clinical Child Psychology, 13*, 250–256.

Quay, H. C., & Peterson, D. R. (1983). *Interim manual for the Revised Behavior Problem Checklist*. Unpublished manuscript, University of Miami.

Rapport, M. D., Stoner, G., DuPaul, G. J., Birmingham, B. K., & Tucker, S. (1985). Methylphenidate in hyperactive children: Differential effects of dose on academic learning, and social behavior. *Journal of Abnormal Child Psychology, 13,* 227–244.

Reitan, R. & Davison, L. (1974). *Clinical Neuropsychology:* current status and applications. New York: Wiley.

Rosenbert, R. P., & Beck, S. (1986). Preferred assessment methods and treatment modalities for hyperactive children among clinical child and school psychologists. *Journal of Clinical Child Psychology, 15,* 142–147.

Ross, D. M., & Ross, S. A. (1982). *Hyperactivity: Current issues, research, and theory* (2nd ed.). New York: Wiley.

Rosvold, H. E., Mirsky, A. F., Sarason, I., Bransome, E. D., & Beck, L. H. (1956). A continuous performance test of brain damage. *Journal of Consulting Psychology, 20,* 343–350.

Rourke, B. P. (1981). Neuropsychological assessment of children with learning disabilities. In S. Filskov & T. Boll (Eds.), *Handbook of clinical neuropsychology* (Vol. 1, pp. 453–480). New York: Wiley.

Rourke, B. P., Bakker D. J., Fisk, J. L., & Strang, J. D. (1983). *Child neuropsychology.* New York: Guilford Press.

Rourke, B. P., & Gates, R. D. (1980). *Underlining test: Preliminary norms.* Windsor, Ontario: Authors.

Rourke, B. P., & Orr, R. R. (1977). Prediction of the reading and spelling performances of normal and retarded readers: Four-year follow-up. *Journal of Abnormal Child Psychology, 5,* 9–20.

Routh, D. K., & Schroeder, C. S. (1976). Standardized playroom measures as indices of hyperactivity. *Journal of Abnormal Child Psychology, 4,* 199–207.

Salkind, N. J., & Nelson, C. F. (1980). A note on the developmental nature of reflection-impulsivity. *Developmental Psychology, 16,* 237–238.

Schain, R. J., Ward, J. W., & Guthrie, D. (1977). Carbamazine as an anticonvulsant in children. *Neurology, 27,* 476–480.

Skinner, B. F. (1953). *Science and human behavior.* New York: Macmillan.

Skinner, B. F. (1969). *Contingencies of reinforcement: A theoretical analysis.* New York: Appleton-Century-Crofts.

Stein, L. (1985, October). *Methylphenidate and the effects of reinforcement.* Paper presented at the Hogg Foundation Conference on Attention Deficit Disorders, San Antonio, TX.

Stewart, K. J., & Moely, B. E. (1983). The WISC-R third factor: What does it mean? *Journal of Consulting and Clinical Psychology, 51,* 940–941.

Swanson, J., & Kinsbourne, M. (1979). The cognitive effects of stimulant drugs on hyperactive children. In G. Hale & M. Lewis (Eds.), *Attention and cognitive development* (pp. 249–274). New York: Plenum.

Titchener, E. B. (1924). *A textbook of psychology.* New York: Macmillan.

Trites, R. L., Blouin, A. G. A., & LaPrade, K. (1982). Factor analysis of the Conners Teacher Rating Scale based on a large normative sample. *Journal of Consulting and Clinical Psychology, 50,* 615–623.

Ullmann, R. K., Sleator, E. K., & Sprague, R. L. (1984). A new rating scale for diagnosis and monitoring of ADD children. *Psychopharmacology Bulletin, 20,* 160–164.

Wechsler, D. (1974). *The Wechsler Intelligence Scale for Children-Revised.* New York: Psychological Corp.

Weiss, G., & Hechtman, L. (1979). The hyperactive child syndrome. *Science, 205,* 1348–1354.

Werry, J., & Quay, H. (1971). The prevalence of behavior symptoms in younger elementary school children. *American Journal of Orthopsychiatry, 41,* 136–143.

Whalen, C., & Henker, B. (1980). *Hyperactive children: The social ecology of identification and treatment.* New York: Academic Press.

Whalen, C., Henker, B., & Dotemoto, S. (1980). Methylphenidate and hyperactivity: Effects on teacher behaviors. *Science, 208,* 1280–1282.

Witkin, H. A., Oltman, P., Raskin, E., & Karp, S. (1971). *Manual for the Children's Embedded Figures Test.* Palo Alto, CA: Consulting Psychologists Press.

Wolf, S. M., & Forsythe, A. (1978). Behavior disturbance, phenobarbital, and febrile seizures. *Pediatrics, 61,* 728–731.

Woodcock, R. W. (1976). *Goldman-Fristoe-Woodcock Auditory Skills Test Battery Technical Manual.* Circle Pines, MN: American Guidance Service.

Clinical Assessment of Memory in Children

A Developmental Framework for Practice

THOMAS A. BOYD

INTRODUCTION

An assessment of memory functions has long been considered an essential component of the neuropsychiatric mental status exam, as well as the more comprehensive, standardized neuropsychological evaluation. The vast proliferation of literature on the experimental investigation of human learning and memory (Craik, 1979; Horton & Mills, 1984) amply attests to the interest and importance attached to understanding and measuring this realm of cognitive activity. Russell (1981) has pointed out that this rich heritage of research provides a sound practical and theoretical foundation for the construction of clinical memory tests but has not led to parallel advances in their actual construction. Not even such clinically derived theories as Luria's (1973, 1976, 1980) on the neuropsychological mechanisms underlying memory and its disorders have led to the construction of a comprehensive and valid psychometric assessment of memory.

The lack of a sound psychometric tool for assessing memory functions is a well-recognized deficiency in the field of adult neuropsychology (Erickson & Scott, 1977; Russell, 1981). Lezak's (1983) authoritative review of memory functions and associated adult assessment procedures amply illustrates the lack of theoretically derived, well-validated, and extensively normed instruments available to clinical practitioners. The woeful state of current practice is, perhaps, best illustrated by clinicians'

THOMAS A. BOYD • Cleveland Metropolitan General Hospital, and Case Western Reserve University School of Medicine, Cleveland, Ohio.

continued reliance on the Wechsler Memory Scale (WMS; Stone & Wechsler, 1945; Wechsler, 1945) despite its numerous clinical and psychometric limitations (Prigitano, 1977, 1978). It is difficult to understand the efforts to salvage this instrument since it seems highly unlikely that repeated efforts to revise (Russell, 1975; Stones, 1979), restandardize (Hulicka, 1966; Ivison, 1977; Klonoff & Kennedy, 1966), or revamp the WMS will do much to advance the efforts of clinical practice to keep pace with theoretical and technical developments.

When one considers the singular importance of learning and memory to the developmental tasks of the school-age child, the dearth of appropriate instruments for assessing the memory performance of children represents an even larger gap between current knowledge and clinical practice. The topic of memory in childhood has become one of the most active areas of research in cognitive development since the late 1960s (Kail & Hagen, 1982), and an increasing number of reviews have appeared in the literature that provide an overview and synthesis of advances in the field (cf. Brown, 1975, 1979; Brown, Bransford, Ferrara, & Campione, 1983; Hagen, Jongeward, & Kail, 1975; Kail & Hagen, 1982; Pressley & Brainerd, 1985). Concurrently, though unrelated, child neuropsychology has emerged as a subspecialty within clinical neuropsychology with its own growing body of literature. Yet not a single text devoted to the discipline of child neuropsychology has specifically addressed the topic of either memory development or memory assessment (e.g., Gaddes, 1980; Hynd & Obrzut, 1981; Obrzut & Hynd, 1986; Rourke, Bakker, Fisk, & Strang, 1983; Spreen, Tupper, Risser, Tuokko, & Edgell, 1984; Tarter & Goldstein, 1984).

Ironically, then, it seems that memory assessment has been a forgotten area in clinical neuropsychology, particularly in the subspecialty devoted to children. Present trends in clinical neuropsychology are actively promoting movement away from merely descriptive diagnostic endeavors toward prescriptive, treatment-oriented assessments that bridge the gap between functional neuropsychological diagnosis and rehabilitation (e.g., Rourke, Fisk, & Strang, 1986; Wedding, Horton, & Webster, 1986). This is a propitious time, then, for taking the steps necessary for developing effective memory assessment techniques that incorporate mainline trends in clinical neuropsychology.

This chapter is intended as a preliminary step in the process necessary for the construction of a developmentally based, prescriptive assessment of memory functions in children. Beginning with a critical review of currently available clinical assessment instruments, this chapter will proceed with a selected review of research models on the development of memory in childhood. This will provide a heuristic framework for understanding the cognitive-developmental changes and situational variables that influence mnemonic performance. Implicit to these models is a set of guidelines or principles that can be used profitably in the selection and construction of memory tasks sensitive to developmental changes in memory performance. The chapter will conclude with a description of clinically relevant tasks and procedures recommended for inclusion in a children's memory battery.

CURRENT STATUS OF MEMORY ASSESSMENT WITH CHILDREN

Table 1 presents a selected listing of published tests and procedures available for assessing memory abilities in children. Inclusion in the list was based primarily on popularity and high frequency of use in general clinical child and psychoeducational practice and, secondarily, on a test's representativeness of a genre of procedures commonly employed in practice.

Because memory abilities exhibit a clear and reliable developmental progression over a wide age span (Hagen et al., 1975), tests of memory have been included in standardized intelligence batteries since their introduction (Anastasi, 1982). This fact is recognized in each of the four major intelligence tests currently in use, particularly the McCarthy Scales and the newly revised Stanford-Binet, each of which permits the computation of a short-term memory score that can be compared with other broad areas of a child's functioning. Cooper (1982) has developed a qualitative appraisal of memory based on asking the child to recall various portions of the Wechsler Intelligence Scale for Children-Revised (WISC-R) following its administration. It is surprising to note that, except for the WISC-R, each of the listed intelligence tests devotes proportionally more attention to the assessment of memory abilities than either of the two major standardized neuropsychological batteries listed in Table 1. Memory assessment appears to be a rather incidental component to the Halstead-Reitan procedures, whereas the memory scale of the Luria-Nebraska and its children's revision possess limited item pools and potentially serious psychometric weaknesses that severly limit their interpretive value (Lezak, 1983).

Diagnostic psychoeducational batteries frequently contain subtests or procedures that tap children's memory abilities, such as the Detroit Tests of Learning Aptitude (DTLA; Baker & Leland, 1967). The DLTA has been revised recently (DTLA-2; Hammill, 1985) and deserves mention here because of the battery's inclusion of complementary verbal and nonverbal measures of short-term memory. Although the revision represents an improvement, the DTLA-2 shares a number of problems with its predecessor. These include poor design and limited reliability for some subtests, particularly some of the memory subtests, and unsupported claims for validity (Radencich, 1986).

TABLE 1. Selected Listing of Published and Procedures for Assessing Children's Memory

Assessment instrument subtest	Task description	Stimulus input	Response output	Age range (years-months)	Comment
Wechsler Intelligence Scale for Children-Revised (Wechsler, 1974)				6-0 to 16-11	Based on Guilford's (1967) Structure of Intellect Model. Vocabulary also may be a measure of long-term verbal memory. Digit Span can be adapted to pointing (Smith, 1975). Cooper (1982) has developed a Post-Wechsler Memory Scale.
Information	Long-term verbal recall of general information	Verbal	Verbal		
Digit Span	Short-term memory span for digits	Verbal	Verbal/ pointing		
Arithmetic	Numerical reasoning, long-term memory	Verbal	Verbal		
Stanford-Binet Intelligence Scale (Thorndike, Hagen, & Sattler, 1986)				2-0 to 18	Short-term memory comprises one of three broadband factors in the tests' hierarchical model of cognitive abilities. A standard Age Score is derived for short-term memory. Overcomes limitations of the 1960 Stanford-Binet (Herman & Merrill, 1960/1973) owing to discontinuous presentation of memory tasks across age levels.
Bead Memory	Replication of bead sequences from memory	Visual	Motor		
Memory for Sentences	Sentence repetition	Verbal	Verbal		
Memory for Digits	Short-term memory span for digits	Verbal	Verbal		
Memory for Objects	Sequential pointing to objects previously displayed	Visual	Motor		

Test / Subtest	Description	Input	Output	Age range	Comments
McCarthy Scales of Children's Abilities (McCarthy, 1972)					
Pictorial Memory	Short-term memory for objects	Visual/verbal	Verbal	2-6 to 8-6	Difficult to make comparisons between subtest scores.
Tapping Sequence	Short-term nonverbal sequential memory	Visual/auditory	Motor		
Verbal Memory I and II	Word and sentence repetition; short-term story recall	Verbal	Verbal		
Numerical Memory I and II	Short-term memory span for digits	Verbal	Verbal		
Kaufman Assessment Battery for Children (Kaufman & Kaufman, 1983a, 1983b)					
Face Recognition	Short-term memory for faces	Visual	Motor	2-6 to 4-11	All of the achievement subtests are considered to involve long-term memory (Kaufman & Kaufman, 1983b).
Hand Movements	Short-term recall of sequential hand movements	Visual	Motor	2-6 to 12-5	
Number Recall	Short-term recall of sequential hand movements	Verbal	Verbal	2-6 to 12-5	
Word Order	Short-term memory span for digits	Verbal	Verbal/motor	4-0 to 12-5	
Spatial Memory	Sequential touching of previously named objects; Recall locations of pictures arranged randomly on a page	Visual	Motor	5-0 to 12-5	
Detroit Tests of Learning Aptitude (2nd ed.) DTLA-2 (Hammill, 1985)					
Sentence Imitation	Sentence repetition	Verbal	Verbal	6-0 to 17-11	Revision of the DTLA (Baker & Leland, 1967). Poor subtest reliability (Ra-
Oral Directions	Perform orally directed series of actions	Verbal	Motor		

(continued)

TABLE 1. (Continued)

Assessment instrument subtest	Task description	Stimulus input	Response output	Age range (years-months)	Comment
Word Sequences	Repeat string of unrelated words	Verbal	Verbal		dencich, 1986).
Design Reproduction	Draw geometric form from memory	Visual	Motor		
Object Sentences	Written recall of series of pictured objects	Visual	Motor/verbal		
Letter Sequences	Written recall of sequence of letters	Visual	Motor/verbal		
Halstead-Reitan Neuropsychological Batteries (Reitan & Davison, 1974)					No specific measures of verbal memory appear in the battery other than those associated with WISC-R.
Target Test	Reproduction of visual-spatial configurations	Visual	Visual-motor	5 to 8	
Tactual Performance Test	Draw shapes and location of stimulus blocks from memory	Tactile	Visual-motor	5 to 14	
Category Test	Recall of previously learned decision principles	Visual	Motor/nonverbal	9 to 14	
Luria-Nebraska Neuropsychological Battery (Golden, Hammeke, & Purisch, 1980)					
Memory Scale	Eleven memory tasks (13 test items) assessing short-term verbal and nonverbal memory with and without interference	Verbal	Verbal	13 to adult	Test is normed on an adult sample but frequently applied to adolescents.
Luria-Nebraska Neuropsychological Battery Chil-		Visual	Verbal/motor		

dren's Revision (Golden, 1981)

Test	Description	Modality	Modality	Age	Comments
Memory Scale	Eight memory tasks (8 items) assessing short-term verbal and nonverbal memory with and without interference	Verbal / Visual	Verbal	8 to 12	Test items are based on adult version of the LNNB.
Denman Neuropsychological Memory Scale (Denman, 1984)	11 subtests measuring immediate recall, short-term memory, and memory for remotely stored information across verbal (6 subtests) and nonverbal (5 subtests) domains	Verbal / Visual-motor / Auditory	Verbal/motor / Verbal / Visual-motor / Verbal	10 to adult	Format of battery highly similar to Wechsler Intelligence Scales. Major weaknesses apparent in test construction. Poor norms and validity.
Benton Revised Visual Retention Test (Benton, 1974)					
Administration A	10-second exposure to geometric shapes with immediate recall reproduction	Visual	Motor	8 to adult	Norms for age 8 to 14 for Administration A and C only.
Administration B	5-second exposure with immediate recall			15 to adult	Norms take into account age and intelligence level. No norms for Administration D.
Administration C	Copy shapes; no recall				3 alternate forms.
Administration D	10-second exposure with recall after 15-second delay				
Memory for Designs Test (Graham & Kendall, 1960)	15 geometric designs, exposed one at a time for 5 seconds followed by immediate recall/reproduction	Visual	Motor	8-6 to 60	Corrections for age and intelligence are recommended for children. Scoring system of questionable reliability.
Auditory-Verbal Learning Test (Rey, 1964)	Immediate recall of 15-word list with repeated trials	Verbal	Verbal	5 to 15 Adults	Limited norms available.

The Benton Visual Retention Test (Benton, 1974), the Memory for Designs Test (Graham & Kendall, 1960), the Auditory Verbal Learning Test (Rey, 1964), and other similar single-task procedures represent the mainstay of specific memory assessment in clinical practice. Beyond restrictions in their task composition and complexity, most of these procedures possess distinct psychometric weaknesses, such as poor reliability, as well as inadequacies in their standardization and limitations in age-based norms. Further, systematic comparison across these various measures is invalidated by the differences in their standardization and psychometric properties.

The Denman Neuropsychology Memory Scale (DNMS; Denman, 1984), to date, does not appear to be a frequently employed test in clinical practice. Nevertheless, it has been included in Table 1 because it represents a contemporary effort to address some of the deficiencies cited in the preceding paragraph regarding single-task procedures. The DNMS comprises six Verbal subtests and five Nonverbal subtests packaged in a format similar to the Wechsler intelligence scales. Scores are derived for each subtest ($M = 10$, $SD = 3$) and for Verbal, Nonverbal, and Full Scale Memory Quotients ($M = 100$, $SD = 15$). The subtests of the DNMS have been based on existing assessment methods drawn from clinical tradition, and their combined standardization within a single battery ostensibly permits valid systematic comparisons across the various subtests and between broad domains of memory (i.e., Verbal and Nonverbal). Unfortunately, the DNMS is a seriously flawed psychometric instrument that, even upon casual review, is severely limited in its clinical utility (Hooper & Boyd, 1987). The subtests of the DNMS provide solely a quantitative assessment of memory functions to the exclusion of important qualitative factors (e.g., there are no cross-modal pairings of stimulus materials). The normative base for the battery is extraordinarily weak at present and not representative of the general population. In general, it does not appear that appropriate standards for test construction (i.e., the establishment of reliability and validity) were followed. Aslo, it represents a rather ambitious attempt to assess memory functions across nearly a 60-year age span (age 10 and older) without recourse to a theoretical model of memory development.

Although the DNMS is not by any means unique in the kind and seriousness of its deficiencies, it amply illustrates the fallacy inherent to any modern effort to develop a battery of memory tests simply by collecting new norms for a set of unimodal traditional methods. Memory processes are not simple, and measurement tools consisting of a variety of separate unimodal measures, no matter how venerated, will only continue the tradition of piecemeal assessment and will not adequately evaluate the complexities of memory performance and its dysfunctions.

The foregoing caveats regarding memory tests and their construction are pertinent to both child- and adult-oriented instruments. A further caution is necessary, though, when considering the composition of a children's memory battery. Here, perhaps even more than in other areas of child assessment, one must be strongly cautioned against the simple adoption of scaled-down adult procedures. Whereas clinical models of memory functions may be appropriate to the assessment of acquired disorders of memory in adults (e.g., Luria, 1976), these models ignore the important developmental influences operative in the growing child. The central nervous system of the child is undergoing rapid change, and both quantitative and qualitative differences in the organization and pathology of higher cognitive functions should be expected from those found in adults (Hooper & Boyd, 1986). Accordingly, appropriate assessment instruments must employ a cognitive-developmental framework that takes into consideration the profound quantitative and qualitative changes in mnemonic performance across the age span. Assessment approaches that ignore these important issues may lack any meaningful diagnostic and prescriptive relevance.

MODELS OF MEMORY DEVELOPMENT IN CHILDHOOD

In this section, a selected review of models of memory that contain developmental implications will be presented. The intent is not to be exhaustive but, rather, to highlight trends within the literature that have both developmental and clinical relevance. Following a brief introduction, this section will discuss the information-processing models of memory proposed by Atkinson and Shiffrin (1968) and Craik and Lockhart (1972), the tetrahedral model of memory proposed by Jenkins (1979), and, finally, a developmentally sensitive model of memory performance proposed by Brown (1975).

One dominant theme is evident throughout the literature: The developmental changes that mark the progression toward mnemonic competence are attributable to the child's growing proficiency in the use of strategies to aid the encoding and retrieval of information. As summarized by Kail and Hagen (1982), the attainment of mnemonic competence follows an invariant developmental pattern: (1) infrequent use of strategies in children aged 6 and younger, (2) a transitional phase from 7 to 10 years of age when strategies begin to emerge, are implemented with increasing consistency, and become gradually refined, and (3) the beginning of mature strategy use with further gradual refinement in the effectiveness and flexibility with which they are implemented.

In fact, Kail and Hagen (1982) argued that the developmental progression in strategic competence is what accounts for the nature of individual differences in children's memory, rather than the concept of a "general memory ability." For example, Stevenson, Parker, and Wilkinson (1975) administered 11 memory tasks to 255 5-year-olds and found a median correlation of only .14, with less than half of the correlations reaching statistical significance. Similarly, Kail (1975) found a median correlation of only .18 among eight memory tasks administered to a sample of 8- and 9-year-olds. Of course, cross-validation of these results and replication of the findings with other measures of memory and with different samples will be necessary before firm conclusions can be drawn. However, the findings do suggest that the concept of a "general memory ability" does not adequately account for individual differences in children's memory performance.

From a different perspective, Kail (1979) tested the hypothesis that children of the same age may vary in the accuracy of their memory performance depending on whether or not they are efficient and consistent in the execution of mnemonic strategies. He tested 8- and 11-year old children on a battery of memory tasks that included measures for which strategies were appropriate, as well as measures presumed to be relatively free of strategic influence. The data were then factor-analyzed. Consistent with the hypothesis, the three strategy measures loaded on a single factor for the 11-year-old sample, but on three separate factors for the 8-year-olds. Thus, strategic competence appeared to emerge as a source of individual differences with increasing age.

Information-Processing Models

Although no universally accepted model of memory development has appeared to date, information-processing models of memory are extant. These embrace the concept of memory as a dynamic phenomenon that undergoes predictable changes with development. To be discussed are the multistore model of memory proposed by Atkinson and Shiffrin (1968) and the levels-of-processing model proposed by Craik and Lockhart (1972).

The Multistore Model of Memory

The multistore model of memory accommodates developmental changes in two ways. A distinction is made between *structural features* of memory (i.e., the physical system and built-in processes of memory that impose the biological limitations of memory abilities) and *control processes*, such as mnemonic strategies. which are under the direction and control of the individual. The structural features are composed of three components: (1) a sensory register that provides a literal copy of information but is subject to rapid decay, (2) a short-term store that functions as the individual's working memory and, although greatly limited in capacity, can maintain information by rehearsal, and (3) a long-term store with unlimited capacity. Changes in memory ability that occur during infancy and early childhood are usually attributed to changes in the child's structural features that possibly reflect developments in neural structure (Kail & Hagen, 1982). Age-related improvements in school-age children are attributed to increasing sophistication in the child's available control processes. These self-directed processes control the flow of information among the three structural components and are described as "transient phenomena under the control of the subject; their appearance depends on such factors as instructional set, the experimental task, and the past history of the subject" (Atkinson & Shiffrin, 1968, p. 106). This latter point has important clinical significance because it anticipates the model proposed by Jenkins (1979), which will be discussed later in this section.

The Levels-of-Processing Model of Memory

Craik and Lockhart (1972) have proposed a second information-processing model of memory that is also quite compatible with the strategic-developmental hypothesis. This model abandons the multistore structural components of the Atkinson and Shiffrin model in favor of a depth or levels-of-processing approach, which places greater emphasis on the role of subject-controlled processing in memory. Accordingly, a memory trace is the product of perceptual analyses of incoming stimuli that proceed through a number of levels. The persistence of a memory trace is dependent on the level of processing. Highly transient traces result from initial levels when only physical or sensory features of a stimulus are processed. More durable and resistant traces result from deeper levels of processing which are concerned with pattern recognition and the extraction of meaning, and which are more cognitive and more semantic in nature. The individual memorizer plays an active role in directing the amount and type of processing employed in response to the particular material and the nature of the task demands. Developmentally, the model is consistent with the hypothesis that with increasing maturity an individual attains greater control and flexibility over the activation of deeper levels of processing (i.e., strategy use).

Both of the information-processing models discussed were proposed to explain adult memory behavior, and they predate much of the important research on memory development in children. However, the relative emphasis placed on conscious and strategic mnemonic activity, particularly in the levels-of-processing model, render both theories highly compatible with observed developmental memory phenomena. Nevertheless, few direct links have been drawn in the literature between general memory theory and developmental research (Kail & Hagen, 1982). Although various authors (e.g., Brown, 1975; Brown et al., 1983; Hagen et al., 1975;

Kail, 1979; Ornstein, 1978; Paris & Lindauer, 1982) have used these and other general models of memory as frameworks for organizing the developmental literature on memory, the models possess few specific developmental implications and do not furnish any particular insights to the task of constructing a clinically relevant battery of memory tests.

Interactionist Models of Memory

In what follows, two additional models will be described that can provide a more specific heuristic framework for classifying developmental memory phenomena. Implicit to these models are principles that can be used to guide the construction of a clinical memory battery for children. These include the Tetrahedral Model (Jenkins, 1979) and Brown's (1975) Developmentally Sensitive Memory Model.

The Tetrahedral Model of Memory

The first of these is a general model proposed by Jenkins (1979) that has been adapted specifically by Brown and her colleagues (1983) to organize the developmental literature on memory. The tetrahedral model is illustrated in Figure 1 as a pyramid in which each of the four vertices represents a major factor that should be considered in the construction of a learning or memory task. The four factors are (1) the nature of the materials to be learned, (2) the criterial task, (3) the learner's activities, and (4) the characteristics of the learner. The first two of these factors define the assessment paradigm, whereas the latter two define the mnemonic activities and competencies of the child being assessed. The tetrahedral model accounts for the complexity of memory operations, and consequently their assessment, by recognizing that each of the four vertices interacts with all others in determining the outcome of a memory task. This interdependence of factors was anticipated by the information-processing models of Atkinson and Shiffrin (1968) and Craik and Lockhart (1972). Each of the four factors will be discussed briefly below, with a special focus on highlighting interactions that elicit developmental differences in memory performance.

Stimulus Materials. The first point of the pyramid concerns the nature of the materials that must be remembered. Materials may vary according to a variety of dimensions such as the modality of presentation, the physical and psychological structure, degree of conceptual difficulty, sequence of presentation, and even the number of stimuli presented. Variations along any of these dimensions interact with the other factors in important ways. For example, the degree of prior familiarity with the type

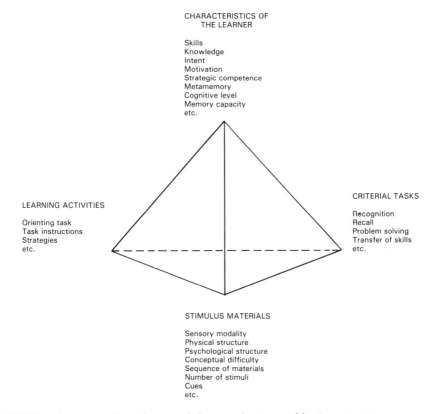

FIGURE 1. An organizational framework for considering variables important to memory assessment. (Adapted from Jenkins, 1979, and Brown, Bransford, Ferrara, & Campione, 1983.)

of stimulus material (learner variable) may affect the child's selection and the relative success of particular strategic approaches (activity variable).

Also, although recognition memory is generally assumed to be less difficult than verbatim recall (task variables), the difference may depend considerably on whether the material is familiar (e.g., words) or not (e.g., nonsense syllables) (Jenkins, 1979). Likewise, changing the structure of the material while holding the type of material constant can alter a child's success on a memory task (Moley, 1977; Ornstein & Corsale, 1980; Perlmutter & Myers, 1979). Accordingly, the speed of identifying the second word of a pair is greater if the words are drawn from the same categories (e.g., dog-lion) as opposed to different ones (e.g., dog-piano) (Sperber, McCauley, Ragin, & Weil, 1979). Further, compared with younger and/or impaired learners, older and/or efficient learners show a preference for taxonomic (e.g., horse-cow) groupings over thematic (e.g., horse-saddle) groupings of materials that enhance both their learning rate (Smiley & Brown, 1979) and memory performance (Overcast, Murphy, Smiley, & Brown, 1975).

Criterial Tasks. The second point of the pyramid, the criterial task, is the dependent measure in memory investigations. As noted above, whether the criterial task requires recognition or recall may impact significantly on a child's relative success. The interaction between the criterial task and the learner's activities is at the heart of the levels-of-processing paradigm in memory research (Jenkins, 1979). If the learner's activities are focused toward deeper, semantic levels of processing, then superior recall will be expected. However, it is possible to construct memory tasks in a manner that precludes particular strategies, such as using materials that are not semantically related or introducing activities that intervene between learning and recall as a means of circumventing rehearsal strategies. The degree of mastery over the material to be learned also can be assessed by using criterial tasks that require inferential problem solving, or transferring acquired knowledge to new contexts.

Learning Activities. The third point of the tetrahedral model, the activities of the learner, represents a major source of variance in any developmental model of memory. As stated previously, developmental changes in memory performance are attributable in large part to the child's growing competency in strategic mnemonic activity. To the extent that the examiner's selection of either materials or criterial tasks minimizes opportunities for employing strategies, developmental differences in memory performance will *not* be observed; that is, older children will produce levels and patterns of performance similar to those of younger children and slower learners (Brown *et al.*, 1983).

Even an understanding that there is *a need to remember* appears to follow a developmental progression. Appel *et al.* (1972) found that in response to different task instructions such as "to look at" or "to remember," younger children did not necessarily modify their cognitive activity in relation to the stimuli. Their level of performance was nearly identical on the two tasks. In contrast, older children recognized the distinct cognitive implications of the "to remember" condition and engaged in a variety of mnemonic strategies that enhanced their performance.

However, Istomina (1975) dramatically demonstrated that the purpose of a memory task can effectively alter the younger child's success on it. Children were able to recall nearly twice as many items from a five-word list under a "naturalistic" play situation where the words represented items to be bought at a grocery store than was the case when the items were presented solely for the purpose of learning and remembering them. That is, the younger child was more likely to remember when learning was an incidental by-product of an intrinsically interesting activity, rather than when learning was presented as an end in itself.

Characteristics of the Learner. The fourth point in the pyramid, characteristics of the learner, purposely has been left for last. As a heuristic model, one could classify a memory experiment by noting the interactions among the four factors of the tetrahedron. This process could begin by entering the pyramid from any point because there is no hierarchical ranking of factorial interactions, nor is there any fixed direction to the path of interactions. However, when we move from the realm of classifying research experiments to the task of constructing a battery of memory tasks that are differentially sensitive to developmental phenomena, we necessarily impose a certain hierarchy and direction to the factorial interactions of interest in the model. When we engage in clinical assessment, we are in pursuit of information about only one factor in the pyramid, namely, the characteristics of the learner. This information is unknown at the start, and by systematically varying and controlling interactions involving the stimulus materials, the criterial task, and the learner's activities, our intent is to determine the mnemonic characteristics intrinsic to the learner.

That this is possible to accomplish is evident in the nomothetic endeavors of developmental memory research. It follows logically that this should be no less possible in the idiographic task of assessing individuals clinically. Through the use of a battery of memory tests that systematically vary levels across the first three factors described above, it is practicable to determine clinically the relative mnemonic competence of a given individual.

With the possible exception of motivation, which may be more subject to situational variation, each of the learner characteristics listed in Figure 1 changes over the course of development. The mature learner should differ from the immature learner by possessing more skills and by having a greater fund of knowledge and experience, a greater clarity of intent in learning situations, and a more advanced level of cognitive development. The issue of whether memory capacity, also referred to as working memory or attentional capacity, undergoes a developmental increase remains controversial in the literature. Although it is well recognized that manifest performance on memory-span tasks such as digit span increases with age (Wechsler, 1974), what has been disputed is whether this enhanced performance reflects an increase in the short-term store capacity of the child or whether it is related to other age-dependent changes in cognitive operations.

Pascual-Leone (1970) hypothesized that increased memory span corresponded with the growth in capacity of a central computing space that he termed M-space, and some investigators have provided supportive evidence for his theory (Burtis, 1982). Case, Kurland and Goldberg (1982), however, have proposed that the total processing space required for short-term memory operations remains constant throughout development. The increments in functional memory capacity result from reductions in the space required for executing memory operations. This is made possible by the growing speed, efficiency, and automaticity of these basic processes. Chi (1976) suggested that restrictions in the young child's knowledge base, which may limit the richness of associations of various memory chunks in the system, may underlie these basic processing inefficiencies.

Brown et al. (1983) consider the capacity-development issue as moot and conclude that there is insufficient evidence to support the contention that total processing capacity increases with age. Rather, they propose that the interaction of developmental changes in the child's knowledge base, efficiency of basic processes, and the use of strategies accounts for the observed increments in memory span. These, in turn, are dependent on the factorial interactions of the tetrahedral model.

The importance of strategic competence to developmental models of memory has been stressed throughout this section and will not be further elaborated here. However, one final characteristic of the learner listed in Figure 1 remains to be discussed. The concept of metamemory (Flavell, 1970; Flavell & Wellman, 1977; Kreutzer, Leonard, & Flavell, 1975)—that is, knowing about knowing—is an important developmental variable influencing interactions involving all factors of the tetrahedral model. The model serves to remind clinical and experimental investigators that knowledge of interactions within the tetrahedron are essential to an effective understanding of memory abilities. Similarly, the maturing child also needs to know something about his or her own characteristics as a learner, the significance of various learning activities, the demand characteristics of various tasks, and the inherent nature of various materials in order to become an effective learner, or to "learn how to learn" (Brown et al., 1983).

The multifactorial nature of the tetrahedral model cannot be over-emphasized in its importance, although the sheer number of possible interactions places a cumbersome burden on the practical limitations of time and needs for efficiency in clinical practice. In addition to six 2-factor interactions, the model allows for three 3-factor interactions and one 4-factor interaction; each of these would be subject to systematic variation across the several characteristics of each factor in order to exhaust all the possibilities permitted by the model. A set of guidelines is required that would assist the clinician in selecting which permutations of the tetrahedral interactions are likely to be most sensitive to developmental changes in memory, or in discriminating competent from incompetent memory abilities. Fortunately, a second model, to be described below, provides just such a set of guidelines.

A Developmentally Sensitive Model of Memory

Ann Brown (1975) has proposed a model of developmental changes in memory that takes into account important themes in the developmental literature on memory. As shown in Figure 2, these themes are expressed as dichotomies, although they more realistically should be thought of as continua. Each theme influences the degree to which a particular task is developmentally sensitive.

The first theme is the *strategy versus no strategy* distinction. As previously noted, to the extent that a given memory task requires the efficient use of strategic operations for success, it will discriminate immature and inefficient learners from mature and efficient learners. A second dichotomy pertains to the difference between *mediation and production* deficiencies (Flavell, 1970). A mediation deficiency is implicated when a child is unable to employ a potential mediator or strategy spontaneously for a given task, and cannot be induced to do so by the examiner even when given specific instructions or demonstrations. A production deficiency refers to the situation where a child can be induced through training or instruction to use a strategy despite previous failure to employ that strategy spontaneously.

The third dichotomy involves the distinction between *episodic and semantic* memory systems. Episodic memory refers to memory for directly experienced instances of discrete perceptual cues that are relatively meaningless and cannot be deduced inferentially or generalized, and the criterial task is a reproduction of the actual stimulus (in other words, the prototypical laboratory memory task). In contrast, semantic memory is concerned with meaningful holistic units experienced in context that can be retrieved through imaginative reconstruction of the ideas fundamental to the stimulus information. One can even retrieve knowledge not directly experienced but inferred or generalized from the semantic information presented. Recall for categorical lists or paragraphs are examples of the semantic memory system.

In particular, tasks constructed according to the factorial combinations of strategic–nonstrategic and episodic–semantic distinctions should possess differential sensitivity to developmental effects. Analogous to an analysis of variance model, two major types of developmental effects can be seen. Level differences, reflecting improved performance (e.g., more items recalled, more accurate recall) with age, would be akin to a main effect for a developmental stage. Pattern differences refer to interactions between a developmental stage and task variables, such as is illustrated by the growing preference for taxonomic over thematic categorization by older children (Overcast et al., 1975).

Examination of the four types of tasks permitted by the model yields a set of general predictions about their relative degree of developmental

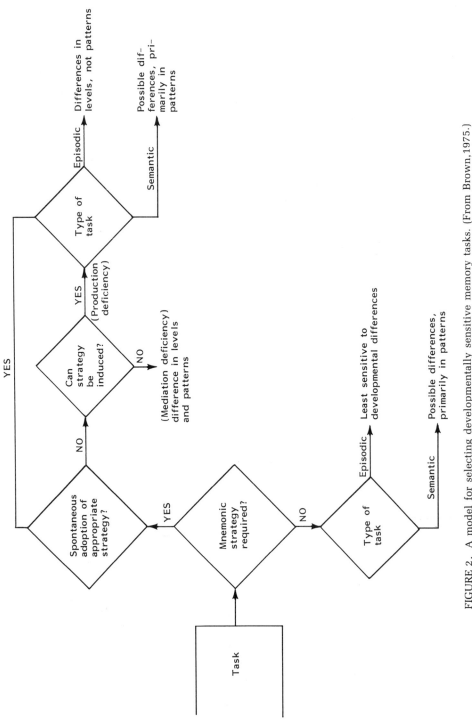

FIGURE 2. A model for selecting developmentally sensitive memory tasks. (From Brown, 1975.)

sensitivity (Brown, 1975). The nonstrategic-episodic combination will include tasks that minimize demands for active retrieval or acquisition strategies, and are not dependent on the semantic memory system for success. Tasks of this type should be the least sensitive to developmental trends and, therefore, should not discriminate between younger and older children or unsophisticated and sophisticated learners. The strategic-episodic pairing should elicit differences in the sheer level of performance (i.e., more items recalled, more accurate recall), but not in the pattern of performance (e.g., the order of stimulus presentation is varied across trials so as to disrupt primacy vs. recency effects for older children). Nonstrategic-semantic tasks should be sensitive primarily to pattern differences that reflect the congruence or incongruence between the material to be learned and the child's level of cognitive development. If the child can assimilate the material, then effective learning should occur. The strategic-semantic variation should disclose differences in both performance levels and patterns.

SUGGESTIONS FOR A CHILDREN'S MEMORY BATTERY: GENERAL FORMAT

As noted earlier, implicit to the memory models devised by Jenkins (1979) and Brown (1975) are a set of principles that can be used to guide the construction of a developmentally based clinical battery of memory tests. Before embarking on a description of the types of tasks that might be nominated for inclusion in such a battery, we should consider several points about the general format of such a battery.

First, because the hallmark of strategy use is improved performance over trials, it is essential that tasks incorporate multiple trials in order to elicit evidence of this important source of developmental differences (Murphy, Puff, & Campione, 1977). An interesting variation of the traditional multiple trial learning task is the selective reminding procedure developed by Buschke (1973, 1974) for verbal word recall, and recently modified by Gilliam, Fletcher, and Levin (1986) for use with nonverbal material. The technique permits simultaneous analysis of a child's storage, retention, and retrieval abilities, and it could be adapted easily to incorporate the strategic–nonstrategic and episodic–semantic dimensions proposed by Brown (1975). Such a procedure may be highly sensitive to differences between normal and disabled learners (Howe, Brainerd, & Kingman, 1985).

Another format issue relates to prescriptive planning and the need to build in test mechanisms that provide clues for remediation. For example, pairwise combinations of visually and auditorally presented materials can be arranged in ways that either minimize or facilitate strategy use, thus permitting a continuum of developmental sensitivity. Relative differences in performance on paired recall and unimodal recall could also provide a potentially important clue for prescriptive planning.

However, perhaps the most important source of information relevant to planning prescriptive interventions may come from an assessment of the child's metamemory status. The child's awareness of various mnemonic phenomena and their interrelations may impact significantly on his or her level and pattern of performance. When the level of a child's metamemory status is below that expected for his or her chronological age, immature levels and patterns of performance also can be expected. Increasing a child's awareness of metamemory variables may help improve memory abilities (Brown, 1978; Meichenbaum & Asarnow, 1978). Accordingly, a metamemory interview, such as that developed by Kreutzer et al. (1975), should constitute the initial portion of the memory assessment. For example, does the child understand that a longer interval between learning and recall increases task difficulty, or that verbatim recall is more difficult than paraphrased recall? This should be supplemented by requests for predictive, concurrent, and retrospective verbalizations occurring, respectively, before, during, and after task performance (Brown et al., 1983).

A third format issue relates to the importance of attentional abilities for successful performance on all psychometric tests (see Chapter 6, this volume), and perhaps memory tests in particular. Disturbances in attention can interfere significantly with a child's demonstration of memory skills (Cecci & Tishman, 1984), and thus an assessment of attention should precede the administration of memory tasks.

SUGGESTIONS FOR A CHILDREN'S MEMORY BATTERY: TYPES OF TASKS

Turning now to the four ideal tasks outlined by Brown (1975), attention must be paid to the sequence of their presentation so as to minimize the potential contamination effects between tasks. In general, for reasons elaborated below, the sequence of presentation should proceed through a continuum from nonstrategic to strategic tasks, first with semantic materials followed by an examination of episodic memory abilities.

Nonstrategic-semantic tasks should reflect learning that arises as the automatic results of meaningful activity. Essentially, these tasks assess incidental memory, and because the orienting instructions would not direct the child toward intentional learning, these tasks must precede those that would induce specific learning sets. If the material of these tasks matches the child's level of cognitive development, then memory for the substance of the material will be involuntary (Brown, 1975, 1979; Brown et al., 1983).

Relatively little of the research literature has examined this type of learning, although several task paradigms seem appropriate. Basically, the child is asked to interact with a set of stimulus materials that permit semantic encoding for a purpose that is not ostensibly for memorizing, and recall of the material then is assessed. For example, the child could be asked to categorize a series of pictured objects, or to evaluate a list of words semantically (e.g., pleasant–unpleasant). Coding tasks also could be employed, where the child's recall for the association between coded pairs would be assessed following completion of a clerical coding task (e.g., numbers and shapes). A task similar to the WISC-R Picture Arrangement subtest also could be adapted. Following a child's successful sequencing of pictorial stories, a verbal recall of the stories would be obtained. Finally, a visual-motor task similar to the Bender Visual-Motor Gestalt Test could be used to assess incidental recall for designs. However, to comply with the semantic requirements of this category, the shapes to be copied should be compatible with simple verbal labels. The designs also should be very simple in order to minimize the graphomotor skills required.

The selection of tasks for the strategic-semantic category is complicated by the fact that semantic memory appears to occur as the automatic result of comprehension (Brown, 1975). Wickens's (1972; Esrov, Hall, & LaFaver, 1974) "release from interference" paradigm is one useful technique for determining the salience of various levels of semantic relatedness to the encoding abilities of the child. A series of "release" tasks that utilize a range of semantic categories could be employed for this purpose. "False recognition procedures" (Bach & Underwood, 1970) that contain a variety of distractors (e.g., acoustic, thematic, taxonomic) also can be used to assess the relative dominance of semantic encoding strategies of the child. Of course, the use of sentences and paragraphs provides a rich domain of semantic material that can be adapted in a variety of ways to assess the child's strategic competence (cf., Brown, 1975; Brown et al., 1983; Hagen et al., 1975; Kail & Hagen, 1982).

The nonstrategic-episodic category of tasks should not demand any obvious strategies for efficient performance and should not include stimuli that can be semantically encoded. These tasks would be relatively insensitive to developmental differences. Nevertheless, these types of tasks should be included because they would provide the best measure of basic memory capacity against which performance on developmentally sensitive tasks can be compared. Three types of tasks are particularly suited to the nonstrategic-episodic criteria.

In a recognition memory task, the child is shown a lengthy series of unrelated pictures sequentially, several of which will appear a second time in the series. The child is asked to identify whether a picture has been seen previously or not. The procedure could also be modified for use with an orally presented list of unrelated words. Although such a procedure suffers from a possible ceiling effect, the additional use of a judgment-of-recency task overcomes this difficulty, since even adults would not show a ceiling effect. Here, the child again is shown a lengthy series of pictures (or list of words). Later, pairs of pictures (or words) from the list are presented to the child, who is asked to judge which member of the pair was presented more recently in the list. To minimize developmental effects predicated on mnemonic strategies such as rehearsal, the series should contain 20 or more items (Kail & Hagen, 1982). The third type of task appropriate to the nonstrategic-episodic category involves memory search rates (Naus & Ornstein, 1977). The child is presented a target stimulus consisting of a set of digits, letters, pictures, or shapes, and then is asked to search from memory for the target stimulus among an array of similar configurations.

The strategic-episodic combination of tasks are constructed in a manner such that the use of strategies appropriate to the task should enhance a child's performance. However, consideration should be given to minimizing the potential for semantic encoding. Five task types are considered here. The first two represent modifications of the judgment-of-recency task described above. With shorter lists, perhaps 7 to 12 pictures, rehearsal strategies become a useful mnemonic and enhance performance in older, more efficient learners. Similarly, the provision of cues, such as color-coding early, middle, and later members of the stimulus series (Brown, Campione, & Gilliard, 1974), also can aid the judgment of strategic learners.

The third task nominated for inclusion in this category is a modification of the memory search paradigm discussed earlier. When the target stimuli consist of mixed sets of letters and numbers, older children are able to conduct their search approximately 25% more rapidly than when the set contains only letters or numbers (Naus & Ornstein, 1977). The fourth strategic-episodic task consists of recall for serial position (Hagen & Kingsley, 1968), where the child is shown briefly a series of eight cards, one at a time, which are placed face down in front of the child in the same sequence as presented. Then a cue card is shown by the examiner, and the child is asked to point to the face-down card that matches the cue card. Multiple trials are employed, but the order of the cards is varied across trials, and the child is tested for each of the eight serial positions. Results on this task can be contrasted with a similar task that requires verbal labeling of the pictures as they are presented. Developmental interactions between labeling and no-labeling conditions and recall of serial position (primacy vs. regency) can provide useful information on the influence of strategy use on performance. A fifth type of task consists of traditional memory-span tasks, such as digit span, or variations of traditional multiple trial learning tasks using series of related words.

The foregoing list of representative tasks is not intended to be exhaustive. Creative application of the principles illustrated in the developmental models of memory potentially could generate a wide array of valid memory tasks exhibiting differential sensitivity to developmental factors.

CLINICAL RELEVANCE OF THE MODELS

The memory models reviewed in this chapter and the corresponding tasks selected to illustrate their application were derived on the basis of developmental considerations. The models predict that use of the four types of ideal tasks will permit an assessment of memory functions that discriminates older from younger, or sophisticated from unsophisticated, learners. However, the implications of these models for assessing pathological conditions of memory are less direct, although several hypotheses can be made. First, children with impaired mnestic functions should more closely resemble younger children than same-age peers in both the level and, increasingly with age, the pattern of their performance. Second, impairment on developmentally insensitive memory tasks, such as those comprising the combination of nonstrategic and episodic features, might herald deficits in basic-level encoding processes symptomatic of problems in attention/concentration or of damage to subcortical memory areas. A corollary to this would be that developmentally sensitive tasks (i.e., strategic-episodic, nonstrategic-semantic, strategic-semantic), in the absence of these more basic deficits in encoding, likely would be more sensitive to disturbances in areas of higher cortical functioning.

Prediction of the usual effects on memory performance relative to right versus left hemisphere damage would form the basis of a third hypothesis. That is, one would expect that recall of stimulus materials that can be semantically organized would be generally poorer in children with left hemisphere injuries, whereas performance with nonsemantic materials would be relatively unaffected. Conversely, right hemisphere injuries would be expected to impair differentially the recall of nonverbal (i.e., cannot be coded linguistically) materials.

A fourth hypothesis pertains to the strategic–nonstrategic dichotomy. Tasks that incorporate strategic dimensions and, therefore, involve the planning, implementation, and evaluation of mnemonic activities, may be particularly sensitive to anterior brain injuries or perhaps frontal lobe immaturity. In contrast, nonstrategic tasks may emphasize the more perceptually based mnemonic activities of posterior cerebral regions. Exploration of production and mediation deficiencies also may prove helpful in making diagnostic and prescriptive discriminations. For example, a production deficiency may not be indicative of brain pathology, per se, and has obvious implications for remedial interventions (e.g., the child could be tutored in the use of mnemonic strategies). Mediation deficiencies, on the other hand, would require further analyses to determine the nature and cause of the disturbance and, by implication, would warrant a variety of perhaps quite different remedial interventions depending on the particular findings.

The formation of more specific hypotheses must await the actual construction of a battery of memory tasks for children. Whereas the guidelines presented here can be profitably applied to such a task, many decisions about the particular content and format of such a battery will have to be made empirically.

CONCLUSIONS

This chapter has presented a critique of contemporary approaches to clinical memory assessment, particularly in the domain of clinical child neuropsychology. Current practice is viewed as seriously flawed and in need of a complete overhaul. As a preliminary step in this endeavor, an approach that takes advantage of the rich heritage of developmental research on memory has been proposed. Recommendations have been made for the types of tasks which will best sample a clinically relevant range of developmental memory phenomena, and which should be considered for inclusion in a children's memory battery. Several hypotheses also are offered regarding the potential clinical relevance of such a battery in assessing memory disturbances in children.

REFERENCES

Anastasi, A. (1982). Psychological testing. New York: Macmillan.

Appel, L., Cooper, R., McCarrell, N., Sims-Knight, J., Yussen, S., & Flavell, J. (1972). The development of the distinction between perceiving and memorizing. Child Development, 43, 1365–1381.

Atkinson, R., & Shiffrin, R. (1968). Human memory: A proposed system and its control processes. In K. W. Spence & J. T. Spence (Eds.), The psychology of learning and motivation (Vol. 2). New York: Academic Press.

Bach, M., & Underwood, B. (1970). Developmental changes in memory attributes. Journal of Educational Psychology, 61, 292–296.

Baker, H., & Leland, B. (1967). Detroit Tests of Learning Aptitude. Indianapolis: Bobbs-Merrill.

Benton, A. L. (1974). Revised Visual Retention Test: Clinical and experimental applications (4th ed.). New York: Psychological Corporation.

Bransford, J. D. (1979). *Human cognition: Learning, understanding, and remembering.* Belmont, CA: Wadsworth.

Brown, A. (1975). The development of memory: Knowing, knowing about knowing, and knowing how to know. In H. W. Reese (Ed.), *Advances in child development and behavior* (Vol. 10, pp. 103–152). New York: Academic Press.

Brown, A. (1978). Knowing when, where and how to remember: A problem in metacognition. In R. Glaser (Ed.), *Advances in instructional psychology.* Hillsdale, NJ: Erlbaum.

Brown, A. (1979). Theories of memory and the problems of development: Activity, growth, and knowledge. In L. S. Cermak & F. I. M. Craik (Eds.), *Levels of processing in human memory* (pp. 225–258). Hillsdale, NJ: Erlbaum.

Brown, A., Bransford, J., Ferrara, R., & Campione, J. (1983). Learning, remembering, and understanding. In P. Mussen, J. Flavell, & E. Markman (Eds.), *Handbook of child psychology* (Vol. 3, pp. 77–166). New York: Wiley.

Brown, A., Campione, J., & Gilliard, D. (1974). Recency judgments in children: A production deficiency in the use of redundant background cues. *Developmental Psychology, 10,* 303.

Burtis, P. (1982). Capacity increase and chunking in the development of short-term memory. *Journal of Experimental Child Psychology, 34,* 387–413.

Buschke, H. (1973). Selective reminding for analysis of memory and learning. *Journal of Verbal Learning and Verbal Behavior, 12,* 543–550.

Buschke, H. (1974). Components of verbal learning in children: Analysis by selective reminding. *Journal of Experimental Child Psychology, 18,* 488–496.

Case, R., Kurland, D., & Goldberg, J. (1982). Operational efficiency and the growth of short-term memory span. *Journal of Experimental Child Psychology 33,* 386–404.

Cecci, S., & Tishman, J. (1984). Hyperactivity and incidential memory: Evidence for attentional diffusion. *Child Development, 55,* 2192–2203.

Chi, M. (1976). Short-term memory limitations in children: Capacity on processing deficits? *Memory and Cognition, 4,* 559–572.

Cooper, S. (1982). The Post-Wechsler Memory Scale. *Journal of Clinical Psychology, 38,* 380–387.

Craik, F. I. M. (1979). Human memory. *Annual Review of Psychology, 30,* 63–102.

Craik, F., & Lockhart, R. (1972). Levels of processing: A framework for memory research. *Journal of Verbal Learning and Verbal Behavior, 11,* 671–684.

Denman, S. B. (1984). *Denman Neuropsychology Memory Scale.* Charleston, SC: Sidney B. Denman.

Erickson, R. C., & Scott, M. L. (1977). Clinical memory testing: A review. *Psychological Bulletin, 34,* 1130–1149.

Esrov, L., Hall, J., & LaFaver, D. (1974). Preschoolers conceptual and acoustic encoding as evidenced by release from PI. *Bulletin of the Psychonomic Society, 4,* 89–90.

Flavell, J. (1970). Developmental studies of mediated memory. In H. W. Reese & L. P. Lipsitt (Eds.), *Advances in child development and behavior* (Vol. 5, pp. 181–211). New York: Academic Press.

Flavell, J., & Wellman, H. (1977). Metamemory. In R. V. Kail & J. W. Hagen (Eds.), *Perspectives on the development of memory and cognition.* Hillsdale, NJ: Erlbaum.

Gaddes, W. H. (1980). *Learning disabilities and brain function: A neuropsychological approach.* New York: Springer-Verlag.

Gilliam, D., Fletcher, J., & Levin, H. (1986, February). *Development of verbal, nonverbal and recognition memory in children.* Paper presented at the Annual Meeting of the International Neuropsychological Society, Denver, CO.

Golden, C. (1981). The Luria-Nebraska Children's Battery: Theory and formulation. In G. Hynd & J. Obrzut (Eds.), *Neuropsychological assessment and the school-age child* (pp. 277–302). New York: Grune and Stratton.

Golden, C., Hammeke, T., & Purisch, A. (1980). *The Luria-Nebraska Neuropsychological Battery manual*. Los Angeles: Western Psychological Services.

Graham, F., & Kendall, B. (1960). Memory for Designs Test: Revised general manual. *Perceptual and Motor Skills, Monograph Supplement No. 2—VIII, 11*, 147–188.

Guilford, J. P. (1967). *The nature of human intelligence*. New York: McGraw-Hill.

Hagen, J., Jongeward, R., & Kail, R. (1975). Cognitive perspectives on the development of memory. In H. W. Reese (Ed.), *Advances in child development and behavior* (Vol. 10, pp. 57–101). New York: Academic Press.

Hagen, J., & Kingsley, P. (1968). Labeling efforts in short-term memory. *Child Development, 39*, 113–121.

Hammill, D. (1985). *Detroit Tests of Learning Aptitude-DTLA-2*. Austin, TX: PRO-ED.

Hooper, S. R., & Boyd, T. A. (1986). Neurodevelopmental learning disorders. In J. E. Obrzut & G. W. Hynd (Eds.), *Child neuropsychology, Volume 2: Clinical Practice*. New York: Academic Press.

Hooper, S., & Boyd, T. (1987). Test review: The Denman Neuropsychology Memory Scale. *International Journal of Clinical Neuropsychology, 9*, 141–144.

Horton, D. L., & Mills, C. B. (1984). Human learning and memory. *Annual Review of Psychology, 35*, 361–394.

Howe, M., Brainerd, C., & Kingman, J. (1985). Storage-retrieval processes of normal and learning-disabled children: A stages-of-learning analysis of picture-word effects. *Child Development, 56*, 1120–1133.

Hulicka, I. M. (1966). Age differences in Wechsler Memory Scale scores. *Journal of Genetic Psychology, 109*, 135–145.

Hynd, G. W., & Obrzut, J. E. (Eds.). (1981). *Neuropsychological assessment and the school-age child: Issues and procedures*. New York: Grune and Stratton.

Istomina, Z. (1975). The development of voluntary memory in preschool-age children. *Soviet Psychology, 13*, 5–64.

Ivison, D. J. (1977). The Wechsler Memory Scale: Preliminary findings toward an Australian standardization. *Australian Psychologist, 12*, 303–312.

Jenkins, J. J. (1979). Four points to remember: A tetrahedral model of memory experiments. In L. S. Cermak & F. I. M. Craik (Eds.), *Levels of processing in human memory* (pp. 429–446). Hillsdale, NJ: Erlbaum.

Kagan, J., Klein, R., Finley, G., Rogoff, B., & Nolan, E. (1979). A cross-cultural study of cognitive development. *Monographs of the Society for Research in Child Development, 44*(5, Serial No. 180).

Kail, R. (1975). *Interrelations in children's use of mnemonic strategies*. Unpublished doctoral dissertation, University of Michigan.

Kail, R. (1979). Use of strategies and individual differences in children's memory. *Developmental Psychology, 15*, 251–255.

Kail, R., & Hagen, J. W. (1982). Memory in childhood. In B. Wolman, G. Stricker, S. Ellman, P. Keith-Spiegel, & D. Palermo (Eds.), *Handbook of developmental psychology* (pp. 350–366). Englewood Cliffs, NJ: Prentice-Hall.

Kaufman, A. & Kaufman, N. (1983a). *Administration and scoring manual for the Kaufman Assessment Battery for Children*. Circle Pines, MN: American Guidance Service.

Kaufman, A., & Kaufman, N. (1983b). *Interpretive manual for the Kaufman Assessment Battery for Children*. Circle Pines, MN: American Guidance Service.

Klonoff, H., & Kennedy, M. A. (1966). A comparative study of cognitive functioning in old age. *Journal of Gerontology, 21*, 239–243.

Kreutzer, M., Leonard, C., & Flavell, J. (1975). An interview study of children's knowledge about memory. *Monographs of the Society for Research in Child Development, 40*,(1, Whole No. 159).

Lezak, M. D. (1983). *Neuropsychological assessment* (2nd ed.). New York: Oxford University Press.

Luria, A. R. (1973). *The working brain.* New York: Basic Books.

Luria, A. R. (1976). *The neuropsychology of memory.* New York: Wiley.

Luria. A. R. (1980). *Higher cortical functions in man* (2nd ed.). New York: Basic Books.

McCarthy, D. (1972). *Manual for the McCarthy Scales of Children's Abilities.* New York: Psychological Corporation.

Meichenbaum, D., & Asarnow, J. (1978). Cognitive behavior modification and metacognitive development: Implications for the classroom. In P. Kendall & S. Hollon (Eds.), *Cognitive-behavioral interventions: Theory, research, and procedures.* New York: Academic Press.

Moley, B. E. (1977). Organizational factors in the development of memory. In R. V. Kail & J. W. Hagen (Eds.), *Perspectives on the development of memory and cognition.* Hillsdale, NJ: Erlbaum.

Murphy, M. D., Puff, C. R., & Campione, J. C. (1977). *Clustering measures and organization.* Paper presented at the meeting of the Society for Research on Child Development, New Orleans.

Naus, M. J., & Ornstein, P. (1977). Developmental differences in the memory search of categorized lists. *Developmental Psychology, 13,* 60–68.

Obrzut, J. E., & Hynd, G. W. (Eds.). (1986). *Child Neuropsychology. Volume I: Theory and research. Volume II: Clinical practice.* New York: Academic Press.

Ornstein, P. A. (Ed.). (1978). *Memory development in children.* Hillsdale, NJ: Erlbaum.

Ornstein, P., & Corsale, K. (1980). Organizational factors in children's memory. In C. R. Puff (Ed.), *Memory organization and structure.* New York: Academic Press.

Overcast, T., Murphy, M., Smiley, S., & Brown, A. (1975). The effects of instruction on recall and recognition of categorized lists in the elderly. *Bulletin of the Psychonomic Society, 5,* 339–341.

Paris, S., & Lindauer, B. (1982). The development of cognitive skills during childhood. In B. Wolman, G. Stricker, S. Ellman, P. Keith-Spiegal, & D. Palermo (Eds.), *Handbook of developmental psychology.* Englewood Cliffs, NJ: Prentice-Hall.

Pascual-Leone, J. (1970). A mathematical model for the transition rule in Piaget's developmental stages. *Acta Psychologica, 32,* 301–345.

Perlmutter, M., & Myers, N. (1979). Development of recall in 2- to 4-year-old children. *Developmental Psychology, 15,* 73–83.

Pressley, M., & Brainerd, C. (Eds.). (1985). *Cognitive learning and memory in children.* New York: Springer-Verlag.

Prigatano, G. P. (1977). The Wechsler Memory Scale is a poor screening test for brain dysfunction. *Journal of Clinical Psychology, 33,* 772–777.

Prigatano, G. P. (1978). Wechsler Memory Scale: A selective review of the literature. *Journal of Clinical Psychology, 34,* 816–832.

Radencich, M. C. (1986). Test review: Detroit Tests of Learning Aptitude (DTLA-2). *Journal of Psychoeducational Assessment, 4,* 173–181.

Reitan, R. M., & Davison, L. A. (1974). *Clinical neuropsychology: Current status and applications.* New York: Wiley.

Rey, A. (1964). *L'examen clinique en psychologie.* Paris: Presses Universitaires de France.

Rourke, B. P., Bakker, D. J., Fisk, J. L., & Strang, J. D. (1983). *Child neuropsychology: An introduction to theory, research and clinical practice.* New York: Guilford Press.

Rourke, B., Fisk, J., & Strang, J. (1986). *Neuropsychological assessment of children: A treatment-oriented approach.* New York: Guilford Press.

Russell, E. W. (1975). A multiple scoring method for the assessment of complex memory functions. *Journal of Consulting and Clinical Psychology, 43,* 800–809.

Russell, E. W. (1981). The pathology and clinical examination of memory. In S. B. Filskov & T. J. Boll (Eds.), *Handbook of clinical neuropsychology* (pp. 287–319). New York: Wiley.

Rutter, M. (Ed.). (1983). *Developmental neuropsychiatry.* New York: Guilford Press.

Smiley, S. S., & Brown, A. L. (1979). Conceptual preference for thematic and taxonomic relations: A nonmonotonic age trend from preschool to old age. *Journal of Experimental Child Psychology, 28,* 249–257

Smith, A. (1975). Neuropsychological testing in neurological disorders. In W. J. Friedlander (Ed.), *Advances in neurology* (Vol. 7). New York: Raven Press.

Sperber, R. D., McCauley, C., Ragin, R., & Weil, C. (1979). Semantic priming effects on picture and word processing. *Memory and Cognition, 7,* 339–345.

Spreen, O., Tupper, D., Risser, A., Tuokko, H., & Edgell, D. (1984). *Human developmental neuropsychology.* New York: Oxford University Press.

Stevenson, H., Parker, T., & Wilkinson, A. (1975). *Ratings and measures of memory processes in young children.* Unpublished manuscript, University of Michigan.

Stone, C. P., & Wechsler, D. A. (1945). *Wechsler Memory Scale Form II.* New York: Psychological Corporation.

Stones, M. J. (1979). Rekitting the Wechsler paired-associate task: The Waterford Index. *Journal of Clinical Psychology, 35,* 626–630.

Tarter. R. E., & Goldstein, G. (1984). *Advances in clinical neuropsychology* (Vol. 2). New York: Plenum Press.

Terman, L., & Merrill, M. (1973). *Stanford-Binet Intelligence Scale.* Boston: Houghton Mifflin. (Original work published 1960)

Thorndike, R., Hagen, E., & Sattler, J. (1986). *Guide for administering and scoring the Stanford-Binet Intelligence Scale: Fourth Edition.* Chicago: Riverside.

Wechsler, D. A. (1945). A standardized memory scale for clinical use. *Journal of Psychology, 19,* 87–95.

Wechsler, D. A. (1974). *Manual for the Wechsler Intelligence Scale for Children-Revised.* New York: Psychological Corporation.

Wedding, D., Horton, A. M., & Webster, J. (Eds.). (1986). *The neuropsychology handbook: Behavioral and clinical perspectives.* New York: Springer.

Wickens, D. (1972). Characteristics of word encoding. In A. W. Melton & E. Martin (Eds.), *Coding processes in human memory.* Washington, D.C.: D. H. Winston.

Assessing Functional Laterality

JEFFREY W. GRAY and RAYMOND S. DEAN

INTRODUCTION

A considerable amount of research evidence suggests that the cerebral hemispheres of the human brain serve independent cognitive functions. Neuropsychological assessments rely upon this concept in making inferences concerning the integrity of the brain. Because individual differences exist in the degree to which functions are lateralized to one hemisphere or the other, most neuropsychological approaches include some measure of laterality. Although this is a rather complex matter with adults, developmental factors complicate the procedure further with children.

A number of investigators have suggested that microanatonomical and psychophysiological differences in the hemispheres of the brain are present as early as the 30th week of gestation (Molfese, Freeman, & Palermo, 1975; Wada, Clarke, & Hamm, 1975). However, whereas elementary lateralization appears to be present in newborns, more complex patterns of hemispheric specialization continue to develop throughout childhood (e.g., Satz, Bakker, Teunissen, Goebel, & van der Vlught, 1975). Investigators also have suggested that the failure to establish consistent functional lateralization may well predict a number of behavioral anomalies.

As early as the 19th century, researchers examined the complex link between psychological functions and their localization within the brain. On the basis of clinical observations of brain-injured patients, Jackson (1874/1932) proposed that two different, yet coexisting, modes of cognitive processing exist and follow hemispheric lines. Congruent with Broca's (1864/1960) earlier observations, Jackson (1874/1932) argued that

JEFFREY W. GRAY • Neuropsychology Laboratory, Ball State University, Muncie, Indiana.   RAYMOND S. DEAN • Neuropsychology Laboratory, Ball State University, Muncie, Indiana, and University of Indiana School of Medicine.

language/verbal processing was served by the left cerebral hemisphere. Further support for this notion came with investigations of patients who had undergone surgery that partially severed the major nerve connections between the hemispheres (corpus callosum; Gazzaniga, 1970; Gazzaniga & Sperry, 1962; Sperry, Gazzaniga, & Bogen, 1969). Specifically, results of such investigations suggested that in most right-handed and many left-handed individuals, linguistic functions are served primarily by the left hemisphere of the brain (Gazzaniga, 1970), whereas visual-spatial abilities are mediated primarily by the right hemisphere (Sperry, et al., 1969).

Investigations with normal subjects confirmed that although there is considerable interhemispheric communication, the two cerebral hemispheres of the brain serve specialized functions (e.g., Milner, 1971; Witelson, 1976). From this point of view, the left hemisphere in most individuals is seen to be better prepared to process information in a more analytical, temporal, logical, or sequential fashion than is necessary for the production and decoding of language (Gruber & Segalowitz, 1977). Conversely, the right hemisphere would seem more able to process information in a holistic, simultaneous, or concrete fashion, and thus it is better able to deal with information of a spatial, manipulative nature (e.g., Bogen & Gazzaniga, 1965).

In this chapter, important aspects of laterality assessment with children will be discussed. A number of methods of laterality assessment will be reviewed with a focus on their clinical utility. In addition, clinical guidelines for assessing cerebral laterality in children will be examined, with an emphasis on both administration and interpretation. Finally, a review and integration of the literature as it applies to the clinical significance of inconsistent hemispheric lateralization for language disorders will be presented.

METHODS OF LATERALITY ASSESSMENT

Clearly, the most predominant difficulty in assessing cerebral laterality is the inaccessibility of the brain. For this reason, the majority of our information regarding hemispheric specialization is based on inferential methods. The measures utilized have ranged from intracarotid sodium amytal injections (Milner, Branch, & Rasmussen, 1964) to an assessment of children's right or left turning hair whorl (Tjossem, Hansen, & Ripley, 1961). A number of behavioral methods are currently used to assess cerebral laterality. The most commonly used and clinically useful methods of laterality assessment include perceptual asymmetry techniques, electrophysiological procedures, self-report methods, and measure of unimanual performance on various types of motor tasks.

Perceptual Asymmetry Techniques

As is the case with most measures of cerebral laterality, perceptual asymmetry techniques infer a cerebral difference in organization based on a lateral difference in performance. The two most commonly used perceptual asymmetry procedures include dichotic listening and split visual half-field techniques.

Dichotic Listening

Considered to be one of the most widely used methods of investigating cerebral laterality, the dichotic listening technique was originally introduced by Broadbent in 1954 and subsequently refined by Kimura (1961a, 1961b, 1963). This technique involves presenting two different auditory stimuli to each ear simultaneously. Because contralateral auditory pathways have a greater number of ear-to-hemisphere nerve fibers than do the ipsilateral connections (Majkowski, Bochenck, Bochenck, Knapik-Fijalkowska, & Kopec, 1971), and the contralateral input "blocks" or occludes information passing along the ipsilateral path (Gruber & Segalowitz, 1977), the dominant hemisphere for a particular stimulus should produce more correct recall for input to the contralateral ear. Thus, information from the right ear would reach the left hemisphere more quickly than it would the right hemisphere, whereas the opposite would be true for a left ear input. This being the case, if a subject is consistently faster and more accurate in identifying information presented to a particular ear, it is concluded that the cerebral hemisphere opposite the more proficient ear has a specialized function with regard to that type of stimulus.

The dichotic listening task has proven to be a reliable clinical procedure in assessing cerebral laterality in children (e.g., Hynd & Obrzut, 1977). Easily administered, this method simply involves presenting the child with pairs of auditory stimuli (e.g., digits, nonsense words, sentences, consonant-vowel-consonant syllables) to each ear simultaneously, and asking the subject to recall or recognize the stimulus perceived. Stimuli are presented by means of a dual-channel tape recorder equipped with stereophonic headphones. Thus, the dichotic listening task may be administered in most clinical settings. However, portability may be problematic.

As may be expected, early research in the area of dichotic listening was conducted with brain-damaged subjects (Kimura, 1961a). Along these lines, Kimura (1961a) found that patients who had undergone temporal lobe excision showed a depressed performance on the ear contralateral to the damaged area. More important, she also found that patients with documented left hemispheric speech lateralization (from sodium amytal tests) showed a right ear advantage (REA). However, those subjects with right hemisphere specialization for language were found to have a left ear superiority, regardless of their hand preference. Similarily, Kimura (1961b) examined the dichotic listening performances of normal right-handed subjects and again found a significant right ear superiority. On the basis of these findings, she concluded that the ear contralateral to the hemisphere specialized for language was more efficient at processing verbal stimuli.

In support of Kimura's (1961a, 1961b) earlier findings, more recent evidence from dichotic listening studies has indicated that normal adults (e.g., Dean & Hua, 1982) and children (e.g., Hynd & Obrzut, 1977) show an REA for verbal material. Among the most robust and replicated findings in contemporary experimental psychology, these data are often used to support the inference of left hemisphere specialization for language. Indeed, numerous authors have argued that the dichotic listening paradigm is the most valid noninvasive method of inferring hemisperic lateralization for language (Witelson, 1977). At the same time, however, this procedure is not without methodological problems (Satz, 1976). Factors such as attentional bias, perceptual set, and memory (Bryden, 1982), acoustic variables (i.e., signal intensity, signal-to-noise ratio; Berlin & Cullen, 1977), and response distortions (e.g., Birkett, 1977) all have been implicated as contributing to major methodological deficiencies.

In response to such methodological problems, a number of procedural improvements have been suggested (e.g., Studdert-Kennedy & Shankweiler, 1970). One such alteration involves the presentation of single pairs of consonant-vowel-consonant (CVC) nonsense syllables rather than whole stimulus lists. The use of single pairs is seen as "reducing the memory load on the subject . . . and eliminating many of the response organization factors that complicate the interpretation of list data" (Bryden, 1982, pp. 46–47). In a different approach, Geffen, Traub, and Stierman (1978) introduced large word-pair lists in which a target word was randomly presented to one ear or the other. The subject was instructed to respond via a button-press upon perception of the predetermined target word. Under these conditions, the collection of both accuracy and latency data was possible. Importantly, normal subjects have been shown to have a right ear advantage with regard to both accuracy and speed of responding.

Perhaps the most important methodological refinement, the attentional monitoring procedure differs from those previously discussed in that subjects are required to attend and respond to dichotic stimuli only in one prespecified ear. This directed dichotic task eliminates the possibility of order effects because stimulus items are presented in counterbalanced fashion. It has been argued that when used in conjunction with single-pair stimulus material, this procedure may overcome the majority of the most frequently cited methodological problems (Bryden, 1982). Thus, this may be the most clinically useful dichotic listening procedure. More recently, high-technological tapes also have been developed to control for a number of these acoustic variables (e.g., Auditech).

Visual Half-Field Procedures

Similar to the dichotic listening paradigm in terms of its neurological assumptions, the visual half-field (VHF) procedure involves either bilaterally or unilaterally presenting stimuli to the visual half-fields. Because of the physiological structure of the human visual system, stimuli presented to one VHF are received first by the contralateral cerebral hemisphere. Thus, stimuli presented to the right VHF are transmitted directly to the left visual cortex, whereas material presented to the left VHF is initially transmitted to the right visual cortex.

Although analogous to the dichotic listening procedure, the VHF technique has not proven to be as clinically useful. Indeed, a number of methodological difficulties make the interpretation of data obtained from such procedures somewhat ambiguous. Importantly, the possibility of eye movement may jeopardize the validity of this paradigm. In this regard, a number of modifications have been suggested. One early approach involved the fixation of the stimulus on the retina, thus assuming a valid VHF projection. To this end, a number of investigators have used contact lenses (Pritchard, Heron, & Hebb, 1960) or prolonged afterimage paradigms (MacKinnon, Forde, & Piggens, 1969).

In a more common approach, stimuli are presented tachistoscopically to both VHFs simultaneously. It has been fairly well established that very brief exposure durations (i.e., less than 200 msec) reduce the possibility of eye movement during presentations (e.g., Marcel & Rajan, 1975). However, it is important to note that the validity of this procedure is dependent upon the subject's cooperation in initially fixating on a central point (see Kimura & Durnford, 1974). Methodological deficiencies notwithstanding, a left VHF (right hemisphere) advantage has typically been found for nonverbal visual-spatial tasks whereas a right VHF (left hemisphere) superiority has been shown for more verbally oriented stimuli (e.g., Witelson, 1977).

Following the lead of Heron (1957), much of the early research involving this paradigm used a unilateral presentation of material (see Kershner, 1977). However, more recent investigations have emphasized the methodological problems of this approach and stressed a bilateral method of stimulus presentation (see Dean, 1981). Although this method partially controls for fixation effects, the possibility of directional scanning of visually encoded material cannot be ruled out. Consequently, it is possible that verbal stimuli such as words or letters may evoke postexposure attentional scanning (Kershner, 1977). For this reason, clinical inferences regarding hemisphere specialization made on the basis of a subject's VHF performance may be tentative at best.

Electrophysiological Measures

As a result of the inherent methodological difficulties in perceptual asymmetry paradigms, a number of researchers and clinicians have opted to use more direct measures of hemispheric lateralization. For various reasons, most have relied upon measures of the electrical activity in the brain. Two of the most common indices include the ongoing electroencephalogram (EEG) and the average evoked potential (AEP). Both procedures involve the examination of electrical activity in a general area of the cerebral cortex as measured from EEG leads. An alpha wave pattern (8–13 Hz) has most often been associated with a relaxed, resting state and is seen as reflecting a decrease in electrical activity in a particular area of the brain. Beta waves (greater than 13 Hz), on the other hand, are found with an alert or aroused state (e.g., attending to a stimulus). Given these assumptions, one would expect differential alpha activity in the two cerebral hemispheres depending upon the task at hand.

Whereas early research involving these procedures focused on lateral differences in electrical activity when the subject was at rest, recent emphasis has been upon the examination of brain wave activity of subjects performing various tasks (Bryden, 1982). These investigations have shown less activity (i.e., a predominance of alpha) in postcentral areas of the right hemisphere when normal right-handed subjects are involved in verbal analytic tasks (Doyle, Ornstein, & Galin, 1974; Galin & Ornstein, 1972; Morgan, McDonald, & McDonald, 1971). In contrast, a predominance of alpha waves has been found in the left hemisphere of normal individuals when they are required to perform more spatially oriented tasks (Doyle et al., 1974; Galin & Ornstein, 1972; Morgan et al., 1971). The combined results of these investigations support the existence of a verbal-analytic versus spatial-holistic processing difference between the two hemispheres. However, in an investigation that examined subjects' block design performance, Galin, Johnstone, and Herron (1978) found increased beta activity in the left hemisphere concomitant with increased task complexity. Interestingly, it appeared that as this predominantly right hemispheric task became more difficult, the analytical, sequential mode of processing most often attributed to the left hemisphere was activated. It is important to note that this also may apply to dichotic listening and visual half-field paradigms. Thus, the clinician must pay close attention to the particular stimuli and task demands used with such techniques, and should interpret the data with caution.

Consistent with EEG findings, the majority of investigations using the evoked potential paradigm have shown a significantly larger AEP in the left hemisphere for verbal stimuli and an increased right hemisphere AEP for nonverbal musical stimuli (e.g., Shucard, Shucard, & Thomas, 1977). Of particular interest, Molfese and his colleagues (Molfese & Hess, 1978;

Molfese & Molfese, 1979a, 1979b) have shown a similar hemispheric asymmetry in preschool children and newborns.

Although these seemingly more direct physiological measures of laterality have appeal, they are not without methodological difficulties. Indeed, such extraneous variables as skull thickness and electrode placement may affect electrophysiological asymmetry (Galin & Ornstein, 1972) and, consequently, reliability. Thus, increased alpha activity may be associated as much with procedural components as it is with hemispheric lateralization of functions. In this regard, a number of investigations have suggested that the use of EEG procedures in conjunction with behavioral techniques of laterality assessment may offset many of these methodological problems (e.g., Davidson & Schwartz, 1977). At the present time, however, little data exist that support the valid use of EEG measures of laterality on a large-scale clinical basis. Moreover, problems with availability and portability make the routine clinical use of these highly technical procedures impractical.

Lateral Preference Measures

Because the performance on unimanual motor activities has been shown to be controlled primarily by the contralateral cerebral hemisphere, it has been suggested that the consistency in lateral preference may be a behavioral expression of hemispheric dominance. Probably related in part to its deceptive ease in assessment, hand preference may be the most clinically utilized index of cerebral laterality (Dean, 1981, 1984). Indeed, most clinical examinations and neuropsychological batteries incorporate some method of assessing handedness. Related to this clinical preoccupation with handedness is the long-held notion that mixed-hand preference may be a predictor of mixed or confused hemispheric lateralization of language (e.g., Orton, 1937).

Estimates of handedness based on large samples suggest that about 90% of normally functioning individuals are right-hand-dominant for unimanual activities. The remaining 10% consist of individuals who are considered as either consistently left-handed or mixed-dominant (Oldfield, 1971). However, a number of investigators have argued that more recent liberal societal views on left-handedness may well be associated with an increase in the prevalence of left-handedness (Bryden, 1982).

Hand preference is most often assessed by means of a structured self-report format, and a number of inventories for assessing handedness are available (Annett, 1970; Crovitz & Zener, 1962; Oldfield, 1971; Reitan, 1969). Generally speaking, these query the subject's hand preference for a number of everyday activities. Moreover, the subject often is asked to perform each task physically.

Perhaps the most commonly used measure, the Edinburgh Handedness Inventory (EHI) was developed by Oldfield (1971). In the initial phase of construction, 20 items that asked about the subject's hand use for simple unimanual activities were selected from an existing measure of handedness (Humphrey, 1951). From the original pool of 20 items, 10 were selected on the basis of their ability to discriminate between left- and right-handed subjects. In its present form, subjects are asked to respond by indicating their left–right preference for 10 commonly performed tasks.

A "laterality quotient" (LQ) is then calculated by summing across each hand, subtracting the total of the left hand from that of the right hand, dividing this difference by the total of the two hands, and multiplying by 100 (see Oldfield, 1971). Because the EHI is so simple to administer and score, it is not surprising to find that it is the most commonly used group measure of hand preference.

Although handedness inventories like the EHI appear to have some clinical utility, they are not without their methodological difficulties. Generally speaking, these inventories have failed to demonstrate clinically acceptable estimates of item stability and concurrent validity. Using items from the three most commonly used inventories (i.e., Annett, 1970; Crovitz & Zener, 1962; Oldfield, 1971), Raczkowski, Kalat, and Nebes (1974) found that only 74% of their subjects responded reliably between two administrations. Moreover, only 78% of the subjects' actual performances were consistent with their initial self-report of hand preference for the various tasks. Somewhat surprisingly, only 1 of the 23 items produced perfect correlations between subjects' initial response and both the actual performance and second response to the item. It may be that a number of the items on these inventories represent activities that are not performed routinely, making it difficult for the subjects to anticipate their responses (Raczkowski et al., 1974).

More important to the focus of this chapter, it has become obvious that simple handedness does not relate directly to the lateralization of higher mental functions (Dean, 1982; Kinsbourne & Hiscock, 1977). Indeed, a review of the recent literature leads to the conclusion that the relationship between handedness and hemispheric specialization is weak. In fact, the clinician is more likely to be correct if he or she simply assumes that language is served by the left hemisphere in all subjects regardless of their hand preference (Dean, 1984). In support of this, Lake and Bryden (1976) showed that a large proportion of both right- and left-handed individuals are left-hemisphere-dominant for language. More specifically, Milner (1974) reported that in as many as 95% of all right-handed, and 70% of left-handed individuals, language is served by the left cerebral hemisphere. In contrast to early notions of a right hemispheric language dominance for all left-handed individuals, Milner (1974) showed that only 30% of all left-handed individuals have right hemisphere or inconsistent hemispheric specialization for language.

Consistent with Milner's (1974) findings, Satz (1972, 1976) has suggested that differences between left-handed persons in language lateralization may be attributed to the differences in the etiology of the left-hand preference. He has argued in favor of both a genetically or environmentally predisposed left-handedness and a form of left-handedness that arises out of early brain damage and/or a developmental anomaly in the left hemisphere. In light of more recent findings (see Satz, 1976), the early hypotheses (e.g., Orton, 1937) that offered handedness as a definitive indicator of language lateralization now seem rather simplistic.

With this in mind, it is not surprising to find that investigations examining the relationship between left/mixed handedness and children's learning problems have produced inconsistent results. Indeed, such findings have led a number of authors to conclude that the relationship between hand preference and language or scholastic achievement is minimal at best (Beaumont & Rugg, 1978; Benton, 1975; Hardyck, Petrinovich, & Goldman, 1977). Supporting this argument, Dunlop, Dunlop, and Fenelon (1973) found that simple hand preference accounted for little of the total variance associated with language lateralization as measured by dichotic listening. In contrast, these authors showed a clear relationship between eye/hand use and chronic learning problems.

Although measures of lateral preference (e.g., handedness) have been used most often to classify subjects in a nominal fashion (left, right, mixed), it has been argued that lateral preference data may be more clinically useful if they are treated in a continuous manner (see Dean, 1978, 1981, 1982, 1984; Shankweiler & Studdert-Kennedy, 1975). Similarly, it seems reasonable that whereas simple handedness may not reliably reflect cerebral organization, *coherently lateralized cerebral systems* (e.g., visually guided fine motor performance) may offer more clinical utility in the examination of cerebral lateralization (Dean, 1982). Indeed, a number of investigations have shown preference for visually guided motor tasks (e.g., picking up a penny) to be most sensitive to other measures of neuropsychological impairment (Dean, Schwartz, & Smith, 1981; Gray, Dean, & Seretny, in press). This point of view tends to support Luria's (1966) position that lateral dominance of the hemispheres varies as a function of the cerebral system under investigation. Thus, lateral preference patterns differ not only between individuals but within individuals as a function of the task variable under investigation.

Dean (1978) developed a multifactorial measure of lateral preference that treats lateral preference in a continuous fashion (Laterality Preference Schedule; LPS). This 49-item self-report measure requires respondents to indicate their lateral preference for unimanual tasks on a 5-point Likert scale. All items produced both stability and predictive validity estimates of at least 0.80. An individual's score for each item is computed using weights for each response category (i.e., right always = 1, right mostly = 2, right and left equally often = 3, left mostly = 4, left always = 5). Scores for each of the six-factor analytically derived subscales are obtained by multiplying the total number of responses for a given category by the appropriate weight and then summing across the categories (Dean, 1982). The six factors were identified as general laterality, visually guided motor activities, eye preference, ear use, strength, and foot preference. Preference scores for the general index (across all six subscales) range from 49 (right always on each item) to 245 (left always on each item).

In contrast to measures of simple hand preference, the summary scores on the LPS allow the placement of a subject on a left–right continuum. From a practical point of view, the LPS can be administered on either a group or an individual basis. Moreover, there are reasonably good normative data on children available to compare an individual's scores.

Although the LPS may be limited by its inventory format, it seems to offer a cost-effective and psychometrically sound method of assessing laterality. The LPS subscales have been shown to have a differential relationship with a number of cognitive (Dean et al., 1981) and personality (Dean, Schwartz, & Hua, in press) variables, and to correlate significantly with dichotic listening results (Dean & Hua, 1982). Nonetheless, clinicians should interpret the results for individual patients with caution. The validity and reliability of the LPS are jeopardized when it is used with severely reading-disabled or very young children. However, it is important to note that if the instructions are read to the child, these potential problems may be at least partially remedied. Even so, the LPS is perhaps not appropriate for clinical use with children under 9 years of age.

Unimanual Performance Measures

A number of authors have argued that unimanual performance on psychomotor/motor tasks may provide the most accurate assessment of laterality (Reynolds, Hartlage, & Haak, 1981). Such procedures simply involve the observation and comparison of the actual performance of the two sides of the body on various tasks. Performance measures have ranged from ratchet-twirling speed to dart-throwing accuracy (Provins & Cunliffe, 1972). However, the most frequently utilized performance measures include tasks of relative hand strength (e.g., Woo & Pearson, 1927) and motor speed (Annett, 1970, 1976; Peters & Durding, 1978). For the clinical setting, it is often recommended that multiple performance measures be used (e.g., motor speed and manual dexterity).

Many test batteries of neuropsychological functioning include tasks that lend themselves to comparison of right side versus left side performance. For example, the Halstead-Reitan Neuropsychological Battery (Reitan, 1969) contains several tasks that allow comparisons between performance on the left and right sides of the body. The Finger Oscillation Test is a measure of overall motor speed and manual dexterity. As such, it lends itself to a comparison of the tapping speed of the dominant and nondominant hands, thus allowing the assessment of lateral differences. The dynamometer, a measure of grip strength, also allows comparison of the preferred and nonpreferred hands.

Although performance measures appear to be clinically useful, they present a number of methodological problems. As was the case with measures of simple handedness, many performance measures may lack the reliability that is necessary for clinical use. In an attempt to delineate this issue, Sappington (1980) examined the test-retest stability of three popular performance measures (i.e., dowel balancing, peg placement, and grip strength). He found stability estimates ranging from only 0.29 to 0.62. Although two of the three coefficients were statistically significant, they were too low to be of practical value. In a related investigation, Provins and Cunliffe (1972) found stability estimates ranging from 0.15 to 0.94. However, only handwriting speed and manual dexterity produced significantly consistent performances. An examination of the literature in this area leads to the conclusion that measures of manual dexterity (e.g., finger tapping) may hold the most clinical utility (Peters & Durding, 1978; Provins & Cunliffe, 1972). Moreover, a number of investigators have recommended the combined use of performance measures and other measures of lateral preference (Bryden, 1982; Dean, 1984). The rationale for this is based on data showing low concordance (i.e., < 0.50) between laterality measures when different methodologies are utilized. Such results question the view of laterality as a unitary factor and suggest that lateralization may be viewed better as system-specific (Dean, 1982). Thus, the use of multiple measures of laterality permits more specific statements to be made with respect to the individual's particular pattern of lateral dominance.

APPLICATIONS WITH LEARNING-DISABLED/LANGUAGE-IMPAIRED CHILDREN

The assessment of cerebral laterality is an integral component of most neuropsychological evaluations. Although measures of laterality may serve a number of purposes, they are utilized most often to infer the lateralization of language. Because unimanual activities are served primarily by the contralateral cerebral hemisphere, inconsistent performance in such activities historically has been seen to reflect confused (incomplete) lateralization of cortical functions (Annett, 1976; Orton,

1937; Zangwill, 1962). Moreover, a number of investigators have offered data suggesting a strong relationship between language disorders and bilateral representation of language functions in the brain (e.g., Zangwill, 1960, 1962). Thus, the clinical preoccupation with lateralization of language has a rich historical base.

Indeed, as early as the 19th century researchers were interested in the relationship between children's learning problems and neurological abnormalities (Jackson, 1874/1932). Most notably. Orton (1937) attributed a number of language difficulties in children to a failure to establish cerebral dominance. On the basis of his clinical observation of a higher incidence of dyslexia in children with inconsistent handedness, Orton (1937) hypothesized a similar confusion at the cerebral level. He argued that the failure of one of the cerebral hemispheres to achieve functional superiority may well be related to these children's inability to process information adequately. Although Orton's early notions may have been somewhat simplistic (Critchley, 1970), the relationship between inconsistent lateralization and learning disorders in children remains one of the most researched and controversial issues in education and neuropsychology. Moreover, because evidence has shown that the failure to attain a clear hemispheric dominance may be related to numerous maladjusted behaviors (Dean et al., 1981; Walker & Birch. 1970; Zangwill, 1962), most child neuropsychologists include some form of laterality measure in their assessment battery.

In light of Orton's (1937) original hypothesis of inconsistent cerebral lateralization in children with learning problems, it would be expected that children with reading and language difficulties would fail to show the consistent REA for speech stimuli found in normals. Contrary to this notion, the majority of studies in this area actually have found REA for dyslexic (Sparrow & Satz, 1970; Witelson, 1977) and learning-disabled children (Hynd, Obrzut, Weed, & Hynd, 1979). Taken together with previous findings with normals, such results suggest that the left cerebral hemisphere is specialized for linguistic functions in both learning-disordered and normally functioning children.

Although a number of investigations have failed to show REA for speech in children with learning disorders (i.e., incomplete left hemisphere dominance), it is important to note that the vast majority of these results may be attributed to factors other than inconsistent cerebral laterality (Summers & Taylor, 1972; Witelson & Rabinovitch, 1972; Zurif & Carson, 1970). For instance, Zurif and Carson (1970) interpreted their findings as suggesting inconsistent cerebral laterality for poor readers. Clearly, this conclusion was questionable, given that normal subjects in this study also failed to show an REA. In the same manner, Witelson and Rabinovitch (1972) speculated that their results were indicative of incomplete cerebral dominance in a group of reading-disabled children.

However, like Zurif and Carson (1970), they failed to find an REA for good readers.

As a result of the popular conceptualization that linguistically disabled children may suffer delayed cerebral lateralization (e.g., Critchley, 1970), numerous investigations have attempted to examine the developmental implications of ear asymmetry for a number of clinical populations when compared with normal controls (Bakker, 1973; Hynd et al., 1979; Satz, 1976; Satz, Rardin, & Ross, 1971; Sparrow & Satz, 1970). Overall, few studies have reported the expected ear-by-age interaction for groups. Thus, it appears that there is little evidence to support the developmental lag hypothesis of cerebral lateralization in children with learning disorders.

In contrast, the majority of investigations have shown a less pronounced right VHF dominance for linguistic material in language-disabled children when compared with normal controls (Kershner, 1977; Marcel, Katz, & Smith, 1974; Marcel & Rajan, 1975; McKeever & Van Deventer, 1975). Using both a bilateral and a unilateral presentation, McKeever and Van Deventer (1975) compared the VHF performance of dyslexic and normal controls. As a control for eye movements, subjects in this investigation were required to focus on and subsequently identify a "fixation number" prior to their reporting any experimental stimuli. Although both groups showed an overall right visual half-field advantage under the unilateral presentation, dyslexic subjects performed much more poorly on the word recognition task than did the normal controls. Of particular interest, dyslexic subjects differed more from their normal cohorts on RVF than on LVF presentations. Under the bilateral presentation, however, dyslexic children showed a normal right VHF advantage. Although McKeever and Van Deventer acknowledged the inconsistency of these findings, they interpreted the results as indicating an impaired "left hemisphere functioning" for dyslexic subjects in this study. Clearly, whereas this interpretation was consistent with the unilateral presentation, it was not supported by the results under the bilateral condition. These findings suggest that the use of bilateral versus unilateral presentation can make a difference in measurement.

In a second experiment, these investigators presented subjects with verbal stimuli via a visual half-field procedure as well as a dichotic listening paradigm. Interestingly, their dyslexic subjects showed a normal left hemispheric superiority for the auditory presentation (REA) but a reduction in asymmetry for stimuli presented visually. Moreover, there was little correspondence between the ear advantage and VHF performance of the dyslexic subjects. In a related investigation, Tomlinson-Keasey and Kelly (1979) found a significant relationship between right hemispheric specialization for words and linguistic disabilities in third-grade children. Conversely, as a left VHF advantage (right hemisphere) for pictures increased, a concomitant increase in mathematical skill occurred. Thus, in general, VHF research indicates less of a left hemispheric specialization for children with learning problems when linguistic material is presented visually.

Using a multifactor measure of lateral preference, Dean et al. (1981) found a clear association between inconsistent lateralization of visually guided motor performance and learning disabilities. In contrast, however, they found little difference between learning-disabled children and normal controls when lateral preference patterns were summed across factors. Thus, as previously mentioned, it is important to consider not only individual differences but also the individual tasks utilized to infer cerebral laterality. Dean (1979) also showed that children with stronger verbal than nonverbal abilities presented a more anomalous pattern in their cerebral lateralization than children with either similar verbal–nonverbal abilities or verbal skills less than nonverbal functioning. Taken together, these findings provided partial support for Hines and Satz's (1974) argument suggesting a functional disassociation in visual-verbal systems that covaries with the degree of lateral symmetry.

CLINICAL IMPLICATIONS

Although inconsistent cerebral lateralization of language may be related to some learning disorders, the relationship is not as simple as was once thought (Dean, 1981). Indeed, it appears that although evidence of normal language lateralization exists when measured in auditory fashion (i.e., dichotic listening), many language-disabled children show less clear language lateralization when assessed visually (i.e., VHF). Beaumont and Rugg (1978) have attempted to reconcile these seemingly contradictory findings. Expanding upon Pizzamiglio's (1976) and Geschwind's (1974) hypotheses, Beaumont and Rugg have argued that learning problems associated with confused lateralization have a basis in a functional disassociation in visual and verbal systems that covaries with the degree of lateral symmetry. Thus, for learning-disabled children, the ability to move comfortably between verbal and nonverbal strategies may be impaired. In this regard, Dean (1979), Levy (1969), and Hines and Satz (1977) have shown a difficulty in the integration of visual and verbal strategies that varies with the individual lateral preference patterns.

The assessment of cerebral laterality will continue to be an important component of neuropsychological assessment. However, clinicians need to be aware of the many practical assessment and complex theoretical issues when using these data in clinical settings. As discussed in this chapter, a number of methods of laterality assessment exist. One of the most well known, the dichotic listening paradigm, appears to have considerable clinical appeal. However, this procedure may not offer the portability necessary for some clinical settings. Similarly, the visual half-field procedure is both bulky and costly. Although seen as a more direct measure of laterality, EEG techniques lack the data necessary for large-scale clinical use. Measures of handedness may be the most widely used index of laterality; however, in light of the interaction between hand preference and both social learning and environmental effects, the relationship between simple handedness and cerebral lateralization is equivocal. Problems with inventory techniques notwithstanding, multifactorial inventories of laterality may offer the single most economical and psychometrically sound method of evaluating lateral preference patterns in most clinical settings. However, as noted before, these may not be appropriate for use with reading-disabled or younger children. Regardless of the procedure used, it is important to interpret the data obtained from such measures in light of other clinical and psychometric findings. Perhaps the most reliable method of laterality assessment involves the use of multiple measures. With the agreement of multiple measures comes the clinical assurance that generalizations concerning the patient's functional lateralization are warranted. Conversely, important implications may be drawn on the basis of the *pattern* of findings and how they vary according to the procedure, mode of input, and type of task used.

REFERENCES

Annett, M. (1970). A classification of hand preference by association analysis. *British Journal of Psychology, 61,* 303–321.

Annett, M. (1976). A coordination of hand preference and skill replicated. *British Journal of Psychology, 67,* 587–592.

Bakker, D. J. (1973). Hemispheric specialization and stages in the learning-to-read process. *Bulletin of the Orton Society, 23,* 15–27.

Beaumont, J. G., & Rugg, M. D. (1978). Neuropsychological laterality of function and dyslexia: A new hypothesis. *Dyslexia Review, 1,* 18–21.

Benton, A. L. (1975). Developmental dyslexia: Neurological aspects. In W. J. Friedlander (Ed.), *Advances in neurology* (Vol. 7, pp. 195–230). New York: Raven Press.

Berlin, C. I., & Cullen, J. K. (1977). Acoustic problems in dichotic listening tasks. In S. J. Segalowitz & F. A. Gruber (Eds.), *Language development and neurological theory* (pp. 75–88). New York: Academic Press.

Birkett, P. (1977). Measures of laterality and theories of hemispheric process. *Neuropsychologia, 15,* 693–696.

Bogen, J. E., & Gazzaniga, M. S. (1965). Cerebral commissurotoma in man: Minor hemisphere dominance for certain visuo-spatial functions. *Journal of Neurosurgery, 23,* 394–399.

Broadbent, P. E. (1954). The role of auditory localization in attention and memory span. *Journal of Experimental Psychology, 47,* 191–196.

Broca, P. (1960). Remarks on the seat of the faculty of articulate language, followed by an observation of aphemia. In G. Von Bonln (Ed). *Some papers on the cerebral cortex.* Springfield, IL: Thomas. (Original work published 1865)

Bryden, M. P. (1982). *Laterality: Functional asymmetry in the intact brain.* New York: Academic Press.

Critchley, M. (1970). *The dyslexic child* (2nd ed.). London: Heinemann.

Crovitz, H. F., & Zener, K. (1962). A group-test for assessing hand and eye dominance. *American Journal of Psychology, 75,* 271–276.

Davidson, R. J., & Schwartz, G. (1977). The influence of musical training on patterns of EEG asymmetry during musical and non-musical self-generalization tasks. *Psychophysiology, 14,* 58–63.

Dean, R. S. (1978). Cerebral laterality and reading comprehension. *Neuropsychologia, 16,* 633–636.

Dean, R. S. (1979). Cerebral laterality and verbal-performance discrepancies in intelligence. *Journal of School Psychology, 17,* 145–150.

Dean, R. S. (1981). Cerebral dominance and childhood learning disorders: Theoretical perspectives. *School Psychology Review, 10,* 373–378.

Dean, R. S. (1982). Assessing patterns of lateral preference. *Journal of Clinical Neuropsychology, 4,* 124–128.

Dean, R. S. (1984). Functional lateralization of the brain. *Journal of Special Education, 18,* 240–256.

Dean, R. S., & Hua, M. S. (1982). Laterality effects in cued auditory asymmetries. *Neuropsychologia, 20.* 685–690.

Dean, R. S., Schwartz, N. H., & Hua, M. (in press). Lateral preference patterns in schizophrenia and affective disorders, *Journal of Abnormal Psychology.*

Dean, R. S., Schwartz, N. H., & Smith, L. S. (1981). Lateral reference patterns as a discriminator of learning disabilities. *Journal of Consulting and Clinical Psychology, 49,* 227–235.

Doyle, J. C., Ornstein, R., & Galin, D. (1974). Lateral specialization of cognitive mode: II. EEG frequency analysis. *Psychophysiology, 11,* 567–578.

Dunlop, D. B., Dunlop, P., & Fenelon, B. (1973). Vision laterality analysis in children with reading disability: The results of new techniques of examination. *Cortex, 9,* 227–236.

Galin, D., Johnstone, J., & Herron, J. (1978). Effects of task difficulty on EEG measures of cerebral engagement. *Neuropsychologia, 16,* 461–472.

Galin, D., & Ornstein, R. (1972). Lateral specialization of cognitive mode: An EEG study. *Psychophysiology, 9,* 412–418.

Gazzaniga, M. S. (1970). *The bisected brain.* New York: Appleton-Century-Crofts.

Geffen, G., Traub, E., & Stierman, I. (1978). Language laterality assessed by unilateral ECT and dichotic monitoring. *Journal of Neurology, Neurosurgery, and Psychiatry, 41,* 354–360.

Geschwind, N. (1974). *Selected papers on language and the brain.* The Netherlands: D. Reidal.

Gray, J. W., Dean, R. S., & Seretny M. L. (1986). Lateral preference as a predictor of cognitive rigidity, *Journal of Clinical Psychology, 42,* 956–960.

Gruber, F. A., & Segalowitz, S. J. (1977). Some issues and methods in the neuropsychology of language. In S. J. Segalowitz & F. A. Gruber (Eds.), *Language development and neurological theory* (pp. 3–19). New York: Academic Press.

Hardyck, C., Petrinovich, L. F., & Goldman, R. D. (1977). Left-handedness and cognitive deficit. *Cortex, 17,* 266–279.

Heron, W. (1957). Perception as a function of retinal locus and attention. *American Journal of Psychology, 70,* 38–48.

Hines, D., & Satz, P. (1977). Cross-model asymmetries in perception related to asymmetry in cerebral function. *Neuropsychologia, 12,* 239–247.

Humphrey, M. (1951). *Handedness and cerebral dominance.* Bachelor of Science thesis, Oxford University.

Hynd, G. W., & Obrzut, J. E. (1977). Effects of grade level and sex on the magnitude of the dichotic ear advantage. *Neuropsychologia, 15,* 689–692.

Hynd, G. W., Obrzut, J. E., Weed, W., & Hynd, C. R. (1979). Development of cerebral dominance: Dichotic lstening asymmetry in normal and learning-disabled children. *Journal of Experimental Child Psychology, 28,* 445–454.

Jackson, J. H. (1874). On the duality of the brain. *Medical Press, 1,* 19. Reprinted in J. Taylor (Ed.), *Selected writings of John Hughlings Jackson* (Vol. 2). London: Hodder and Stoughton, 1932.

Kershner, J. B. (1977). Cerebral dominance in disabled readers, good readers, and gifted children: Search for a valid model. *Child Development, 48,* 61–67.

Kimura, D. (1961a). Cerebral dominance and the perception of verbal stimuli. *Canadian Journal of Psychology, 15,* 166–171.

Kimura, D. (1961b). Some effects of temporal lobe damage on auditory perception. *Canadian Journal of Psychology, 15,* 156–165.

Kimura, D. (1963). Right temporal lobe damage. *Archives of Neurology, 8,* 264–271.

Kimura, D., & Durnford, M. (1974). Normal studies on the function of the right hemisphere in vision. In S. J. Dimond & J. G. Beaumont (Eds.), *Hemisphere functions in the human brain* (pp. 159–175). London: Elek Scientific Books.

Kinsbourne, M., & Hiscock, M. (1977). Does cerebral dominance develop? In S. J. Segalowitz & F. A. Gruber (Eds.), *Language development and neurological theory* (pp. 171–191). New York: Academic Press.

Lake, D., & Bryden, M. (1976). Handedness and sex differences in hemispheric asymmetry. *Brain and Language. 3,* 266–282.

Levy, J. (1969). Possible basis for the evaluation of lateral specialization of the human brain. *Nature, 224,* 614–615.

Luria, A. R. (1966). *Human brain and psychological processes.* New York: Harper & Row.

MacKinnon, G. E., Forde, J., & Piggens, D. J. (1969). Stabilized images, steadily fixated figures, and prolonged after images. *Canadian Journal of Psychology, 23,* 184–195.

Majkowski, J., Bochenck, Z., Bochenck, W., Knapik-Fijalkowska, D., & Kopec, J. (1971). Latency of average evoked potentials to contralateral and ipsalateral auditory stimulation in normal subjects. *Brain Research, 25,* 416–419.

Marcel, T., Katz, L., & Smith, M. (1974). Laterality and reading proficiency. *Neuropsychologia, 12,* 131–139.

Marcel, T., & Rajan, P. (1975). Lateral specialization for recognition of words and faces in good and poor readers. *Neuropsychologia, 13,* 489–497.

McKeever, W F., & Van Deventer, A. D. (1975). Dyslexic adolescents: Evidence of impaired visual and auditory language processing associated with normal lateralization and visual responsivity. *Cortex, 11,* 361–378.

Milner, B. (1971). Interhemispheric differences and psychological processes. *British Medical Bulletin, 27,* 272–277.

Milner, B. (1974). Hemispheric specialization: Scope and limits. In F. O. Schmitt & F. G. Warden (Eds.), *The neurosciences: Third study programme* (pp. 75–89). Cambridge, MA: M.I.T. Press.

Milner, B., Branch, C., & Rasmussen, T. (1964). Observations on cerebral dominance. In A. V. S. DeRenck & M. O'Connor (Eds.), *Disorders of language (CIBA Foundation Symposium)* (pp. 200–241). London: Churchill.

Molfese, D. L., Freeman, R. B., & Palermo, D. (1975). The ontogeny of brain lateralization for speech and nonspeech stimuli. *Brain and Language, 2,* 356–368.

Molfese, D. L., & Hess, T. M. (1978). Hemispheric specialization for VOT perception in the preschool child. *Journal of Experimental Child Psychology, 26,* 71–84.

Molfese, D. L., & Molfese, V. J. (1979a). Hemisphere and stimulus differences as reflected in the cortical responses of newborn infants to speech stimuli. *Developmental Psychology, 15,* 505–511.

Molfese, D. L., & Molfese, V. J. (1979b). VOT distinctions in infants: Learned or innate. In H. A. Whitaker & H. Whitaker (Eds.), *Studies in neurolinguistics* (Vol. 4, pp. 21–35). New York: Academic Press.

Morgan, A., McDonald, P. J., & McDonald, H. (1971). Differences in bilateral alpha activity as a function of experimental tasks, with a note on lateral eye movements and hypnotizability. *Neuropsychologia, 9,* 459–469.

Oldfield, R. C. (1971). The assessment and analysis of handedness: The Edinburgh inventory. *Neuropsychologia, 9,* 94–113.

Orton, S. T. (1937). Specific reading disability—strephosymbolia. *Journal of the American Medical Association, 90,* 1095–1099.

Peters, M., & Durding, B. (1978). Handedness as continuous variable. *Canadian Journal of Psychology, 32,* 257–261.

Pizzamiglio, L. (1976). Cognitive approach to hemispheric dominance. In R. M. Knights & D. Bakker (Eds.), *The neuropsychology of learning disorders* (pp. 265–272). Baltimore: University Park Press.

Pritchard, R. M., Heron, W., & Hebb, D. O. (1960). Visual perception approached by the method of stabilized images. *Canadian Journal of Psychology, 14,* 66–77.

Provins, K. A., & Cunliffe, P. (1972). Motor performance tests of handedness and motivation. *Perceptual and Motor Skills, 35,* 143–150.

Raczkowski, D., Kalat, J. W., & Nebes, R. (1974). Reliability and validity of some handedness questionnaire items. *Neuropsychologia, 12,* 43–47.

Reitan, R. M. (1969). *Manual for administration of neuropsychological test batteries for adults and children.* Indianapolis: Author.

Reynolds, C. R., Hartlage, L. C., & Haak, R. (1981). The relationship between lateral preference, as determined by neuropsychological test performance, and aptitude–achievement discrepancies. *Clinical Neuropsychology, 3,* 19–21.

Sappington, J. T. (1980). Measures of lateral dominance: Interrelationships and temporal stability. *Perceptual and Motor Skills, 50,* 783–790.

Satz, P. (1972). Pathological left-handedness: An explanatory model. *Cortex, 8,* 121–135.

Satz, P. (1976). Cerebral dominance and reading disability: An old problem revisited. In R. M. Knights & D. Bakker (Eds.), *The neuropsychology of learning disorders* (pp. 273–294). Baltimore: University Park Press.

Satz, P., Bakker, D. J., Teunissen, J., Goebel, R., & van der Vlugt, H. (1975). Developmental parameters of the ear asymmetry. A multivariate approach. *Brain and Language, 2,* 71–85.

Satz, P., Rardin, D., & Ross, J. (1971). An evaluation of a theory of specific developmental dyslexia. *Child Development, 42,* 2009–2021.

Shankweiler, D., & Studdert-Kennedy, M. (1975). A continuum of lateralization for speech perception. *Brain and Language, 2,* 212–225.

Shucard, D. W., Shucard, J. L., & Thomas, D. G. (1977). Auditory evoked potentials as probes of hemispheric differences in cognitive processing. *Science, 197,* 1295–1297.

Sparrow, S., & Satz, P. (1970). Dyslexia, laterality, and neuropsychological development. In D. J. Bakker & P. Satz (Eds.). *Specific reading disability: Advances in theory and method* (pp. 41–60). Rotterdam: Rotterdam University Press.

Sperry, R. W., Gazzaniga, M. S., & Bogen, J. H. (1969). Interhemispheric relationships: The neocortical commissures: Syndromes of hemispheric disconnection. In P. Vinken & G. W. Bruyn (Eds.), *Handbook of clinical neurology* (Vol. 4, pp. 273–290). New York: Wiley.

Studdert-Kennedy, M., & Shankweiler, D. (1970). Hemispheric specialization for speech perception. *Journal of the Acoustical Society of America, 48,* 579–594.

Summers, R. K., & Taylor, M. L. (1972). Cerebral speech dominance in language-disordered and normal children. *Cortex, 8,* 224–232.

Tjossem, T. D., Hansen, T. J., & Ripley, H. S. (1961). *An investigation of reading difficulty in young children.* Paper presented at the 117th annual meeting of the American Psychological Association, Chicago.

Tomlinson-Keasey, C., & Kelly, R. R. (1979). Is hemispheric specialization important to scholastic achievement? *Cortex, 15,* 97–107.

Wada, J., Clark, R., & Hamm, A. (1975). Cerebral hemispheric asymmetry in humans. *Archives of Neurology. 32,* 239–246.

Walker, H. A., & Birch, H. G. (1970). Lateral preference and right-left awareness in schizophrenic children. *Journal of Nervous and Mental Disease, 15,* 341–351.

Witelson, S. F. (1976). Early hemispheric specialization and interhemisphere plasticity: An empirical and theoretical review. In S. Segalowitz & F. Gruber (Eds.), *Language and development and neurologic theory* (pp. 213–286). New York: Academic Press.

Witelson, S. F. (1977). Developmental dyslexia: Two right hemispheres and none left. *Science, 195,* 309–311.

Witelson, S. F., & Rabinovitch, M. S. (1972). Children's recall strategies in dichotic listening. *Journal of Experimental Child Psychology, 12,* 106–113.

Woo, T. L., & Pearson, K. (1927). Dextrality and sinistrality. *Biometrika, 19,* 192–198.

Zangwill, O. C. (1960). *Cerebral dominance and its relationship to psychological function.* London: Oliver & Boyd.

Zangwill, O. C. (1962). Dyslexia in relation to cerebral dominance. In J. Money (Ed.), *Reading disability* (pp. 103–113). Baltimore: Johns Hopkins.

Zurif, E. F., & Carson, G. (1970). Dyslexia in relation to cerebral dominance and temporal analysis. *Neuropsychologia, 8,* 351–361.

Infant and Early Childhood Assessment

GLEN P. AYLWARD

THE STATUS OF NEUROPSYCHOLOGICAL ASSESSMENT IN INFANCY AND EARLY CHILDHOOD

Neuropsychological assessment of infants and young children is a fledgling area. This type of evaluation was previously accomplished by means of a neurological examination performed by a pediatric neurologist or a developmental examination administered by a developmental psychologist. There has not been complete concordance between the two assessments since underlying neural function or maturation is not necessarily reflected in developmental acquisitions. Because the aims of these assessments and the information derived from each can overlap and differ, boundaries have not been clearly defined and the area has been essentially relegated to a "no-man's-land" status. Recently, general interest in neuropsychological assessment has grown rapidly, so it is logical that this interest should also extend to children 4 years of age and below. However, despite the obvious need for theoretical frameworks and acceptable techniques, few exist currently.

Many terms are used to describe infant and early childhood assessment. These include *neurological, psychological, developmental, neuromotor, neurodevelopmental, psychomotor, sensorimotor, neurobehavioral,* and *neuropsychological.* The last term, however, is used rarely. The reason for this lack of use may be related to the definitions of neuropsychology that predominate. For example, neuropsychology is defined as

---

GLEN P. AYLWARD • Division of Developmental and Behavioral Pediatrics, Departments of Pediatrics and Psychiatry, Southern Illinois University School of Medicine, Springfield, Illinois.

the "behavioral expression of brain dysfunction" (Lezak, 1983), or "the investigation of the role of individual brain systems in complex forms of mental activity" (Luria, 1973). For various reasons, such definitions are not appropriate in the case of the infant or young child.

Assessment of the infant and the young child is generally undertaken to measure achievement in different functional areas; development is considered to reflect an increase in the number of abilities (Touwen, 1973). Early in life, particularly in the neonatal period and early infancy, the limited behavioral repertoire and the more direct, less complex relationship between neural function and overt behavior make it extremely difficult to separate developmental (psychological) from neurological functions. However, with increased age there is more divergence between the two. It is likely that divergence is influenced by both maturation (changes in underlying physical (neural) structure) and environmental influences. Development is the result of the interaction between maturation and environmental influences, although the infant's nervous system must reach a critical level of maturation prior to effective utilization of environmental input.

Neuropsychology of infancy and early childhood could best be defined as the assessment of brain–behavior relationships in the context of developmental change and maturation. Assessment of early neuropsychological functions occurs against a backdrop of qualitative cognitive, behavioral, and structural change; the functions that are assessed are more variable and become increasingly more complex. Because the nervous system of the infant and the young child (particularly the former) develops rapidly, examinations must be age-specific. Interpretation of findings may be influenced by either a functional delay in development, neural dysfunction, or both. Further, the frequently used actuarial approach may not be as appropriate as more qualitative approaches, owing to the central nervous system dynamics that occur during development. For these reasons, early neuropsychological assessment differs markedly from assessment of older individuals.

There are several uses for early neuropsychological assessment: immediate diagnosis, change in status, prognosis, and research into early brain–behavior relationships. The utility of immediate diagnosis for treatment purposes is straightforward. Repeat assessments provide information related to improvement or decline in an infant's status by provision of baseline and subsequent data. Prognostic issues are particularly important for parents, physicians, and educators. Finally, early assessment enables investigators to gain knowledge about the developing nervous system and to apply this knowledge in clinical situations.

The need for early neuropsychological assessment is increasing in direct response to advances in neonatology and pediatrics. Early assessment is particularly important in populations "at risk," from which many children who will later manifest neuropsychological dysfunction are derived (Kalverboer, Touwen, & Prechtl, 1973). Tjossem (1976) identified three categories of risk: established, environmental, and biological. Established risk involves medical disorders of a known etiology in which compromised developmental outcome is well documented (e.g., Down's syndrome). Environmental risk includes the quality of the mother–infant interaction, opportunities for stimulation, and health care. The biological risk category consists of infants and young children who have been exposed to potentially noxious prenatal, perinatal, or postnatal events (i.e., those babies who are typically involved in follow-up studies).

Neuropsychological assessment over the first 4 years is particularly important for this last category since progress in perinatal medicine has resulted in a decrease in severe central nervous system damage in neonates (e.g., Vohr & Hack, 1982). However, mild or moderate impairment is now more frequent. This degree of dysfunction is often subtle but can nonetheless prevent realization of a child's full potential. These high-prevalence/low-severity disabilities are often precursors of subsequent learning disabilities (Levine, 1983). The need for early neuropsychological assessment is underscored further by the fact that these subtle difficulties could easily be overlooked in a general neurological examination or in developmental indices. Early neuropsychological evaluation also could be applied to degenerative disorders, inborn errors of metabolism, pervasive developmental disorders, acute trauma, oncology, and other handicapping conditions in pediatric populations.

Finally, Public Law 94-142 (The Education for All Handicapped Children Act, 1975), also has contributed to the increased need for detailed, early neuropsychological assessment. Under this law, evaluation of children with a broad range of developmental disabilities (emotional disorders, mental retardation, physical disabilities, and sensory impairments) is required. Early evaluation enables the placement of children in early childhood education programs and also may help to specify areas needing emphasis in birth-to-3 stimulation programs that have been legislated in many states.

CONCEPTUAL ISSUES IN EARLY NEUROPSYCHOLOGICAL ASSESSMENT

Differences in Assessing School-Age versus Younger Children

Assessment procedures developed to test school-age children or adults are not applicable at younger ages (Bayley, 1969; Ulrey & Schnell, 1982). Reasons for this lack of applicability include behavioral state, temperament, limitations of the test instruments, the need to consider both qualitative and quantitative data, and the issue of noncompliance.

Behavioral State

The behavioral state of the neonate is defined as the level of nervous system arousal (Prechtl, 1977). States, originally developed by correlating observed behavior with measures of physiological function, are generally classified as quiet sleep, rapid eye movement sleep, quiet wakefulness, active wakefulness, and crying. Behavioral states are critical because the quality of elicited reflexes often varies as a function of state (Lenard, von Bernuth, & Prechtl, 1968; Prechtl, Vlach, Lenard, & Grant, 1967). State also influences habituation to external stimuli, muscle tone, and deep tendon reflexes. Many neurobehavioral items are best administered in specific behavioral states. States also afford insight into an infant's reactivity and therefore can aid in assessment. Prechtl has included states in the criteria for the diagnosis of several abnormal syndromes (Prechtl, 1977; Prechtl & Beintema, 1964). A predominance of certain states (e.g., crying) has been associated with subtle central nervous system dysfunction (Parmelee & Michaelis, 1971).

The influence of these behavioral states on assessment becomes less important with increasing age. However, problems in physical discomfort such as hunger, thirst, sleepiness, crying, and bowel and bladder distention continue to be important (Ulrey, 1982). Therefore, more flexibility in neuropsychological testing is needed at these younger ages.

Temperament

Temperament is analogous to behavioral style, a biologically based behavioral predisposition in spontaneous and reactive behavior (Chess & Thomas, 1983). There are three major classifications of temperament. The *difficult child*, estimated to comprise 10% of the general population, is characterized by irregularity in biological function, negative withdrawal responses to new situations, negative mood and intensity, and nonadaptability or slow adaptability to change. The *slow-to-warm-up infant* (15%) typically displays negative responses of a mild intensity to new stimuli and slow adaptability after repeated contact. In contrast, the *easy child*, (40% of the population) adopts a positive response to new stimuli, adapts quickly and easily to change, and has a predominantly positive mood. These behavioral styles persist and can affect test scores of infants and young children in various ways (see Hertzig, 1983).

Test Limitations/Qualitative and Quantitative Information

Reference norms, derived from apparently normal populations of infants and children are typically used in the neuropsychological assessment of handicapped and at-risk babies (Yang, 1979). As a result, it is common for young, severely handicapped babies to be deemed untestable. This is especially true among infants with severe motor impairment because our current infant assessment instruments rely heavily on motor responses. In neuropsychological assessment of young infants, the presence or absence of a behavior, and the qualitative manner in which a task is carried out should be evaluated, with emphasis on the inclusion of incidental observations. Many have argued that systematic assessment of test-taking behavior should be included in the general evaluation of infants and young children. This is evident in the development of the Bayley (1969) Infant Behavior Record, which is used in addition to the Mental and Psychomotor Developmental Indices.

There are other limitations as well. Hanson, Smith, and Hume (1984), using the Griffiths Scales of Mental Development, question the reliability of maternal report, the administration of certain items, and scoring criteria. Discrepancies in scoring were found to be greatest at younger ages. Disagreement in the scoring of what is observed may not be the issue; the potential problem is in deciding whether to accept a behavior as the child's optimum performance. The examiner's judgment of response quality (i.e., whether the response is the best of which the infant is capable) is difficult to quantify, and traditional reliability measures do not take this into account.

Noncompliance

This problem is reflected in the "nontestable" classification on the Denver Developmental Screening Test (Frankenburg & Dodds, 1967). Ounsted, Cockburn, and Moar (1983) reported lower global developmental scores in infants who were not cooperative, and noncompliant behavior in 18% of their 4-year-olds precluded computation of a developmental score. Many infants refused gross motor tasks, whereas those who were minimally cooperative (enough for completion of a score) frequently displayed compromised visual-motor function. These investigators also report an increased probability of subsequent problems in the noncooperative infants. It is possible that an unwillingness to attempt certain tasks reflects an inability to perform these tasks, and this needs to be differentiated in early neuropsychological assessment. There also is evidence that abnormal infants behave differently on tests (Oski & Honig, 1978), and behavior that is poorly adaptive and observed infrequently may indicate abnormality and thus have diagnostic utility (Wolf & Lozoff, 1985).

Consistency of Dysfunction

Prediction

Early neurobehavioral diagnosis in severely impaired infants is fairly straightforward (Davies, 1984). Prediction, however, is less certain. Prediction rates may account for as much as 49% of the variance between early and later measures in *significantly damaged infants,* usually those with developmental quotients less than 80 (Aylward & Kenny, 1979). Similar predictive accuracy is reported in newborn infants who manifest Prechtl's (1977) neurological syndromes (hyperexcitability, apathy, hemi-syndrome). However, these prediction rates are for groups, not individuals, and there is much individual variability in cognitive, motor, and neurological diagnoses over the first 3 years (Aylward, Gustafson, Verhulst, & Colliver, 1987).

Diagnosis and longitudinal prediction are difficult in those infants who are not overtly abnormal at an early age but whose performance is suspect. Coolman et al. (1985) found a 50% incidence of mild neuromotor dysfunction in their high-risk nursery population, 75% of whom were normal by age 2. Seven percent of the babies displayed moderate dysfunction, and half of these were normal by 2. In another investigation (Aylward et al., 1987), using approximately 275 infants followed to age 3, function was divided into cognitive, motor, and neurological spheres. Seventy-one percent of the babies who were cognitively suspect at 40 weeks were normal by 3 years of age, 88% of the babies suspected to have motor defects improved by age 3 whereas 93% of the infants defined as neurologically suspect at 40 weeks had improved. Certain neurobehavioral conditions, such as hypotonia or head lag, are less persistent over time than other neurological conditions (Bierman-van Eendenburg, Jurgens-van der Zee, Olinga, Huisjes, & Touwen, 1981; Dubowitz et al., 1984; Hack, Caron, Rivers, & Fanaroff, 1983).

Central Nervous System Change

These data suggest that central nervous system dysfunction at birth is not permanent since the majority of babies apparently recover (Touwen, 1978). Although there is a high false positive rate, these actually may be "pseudo-false positives," which reflect reversible dysfunctions influenced by maturation and development. The concept of developmental discontinuity holds that structure to function relationships change. Neural development is not a linear progression in the number of elements and interconnections; rather, there also is a retrogressive process. Prechtl (1984) has identified the second month after birth as an age characterized by major transitions in neural and sensory functions, whereas Amiel-Tison (1982) suggests that major changes occur in the first 6 months. Although there is much evidence to support the concept of plasticity of the nervous system, there also is evidence that early injury causes permanent qualitative change in neural organization and interconnections. This may explain the so-called silent period (Amiel-Tison, 1982; Prechtl, 1977), in which dysfunction observed in the first few days of life often disappears, only to reappear later.

Psychometric Concerns

Several methodological problems that may affect the reliability of early neuropsychological assessment have been delineated (Aylward & Kenny, 1979): the criterion measure used, the age at which testing is administered (i.e., the key age or the age of acquisition of new behaviors), maturity, and strongly canalized sensory-motor development. Correction for prematurity (Hunt, 1981; Siegel, 1983) may obscure subtle neuropsychological findings by overcorrecting for gestational age. Any of these factors could significantly affect neuropsychological status and therefore must be considered.

Role of the Environment

Sameroff (1975) emphasizes a biological–environmental interaction in his transactional model of development. This model was expanded in the risk-route concept (Aylward & Kenny, 1979), in which outcome is thought to be affected by three spheres of influence: medical/biological, environmental/psychosocial, and behavioral/developmental. This model has been applied in the assessment of consistency in cognitive, motor, and neurological dysfunction (Aylward et al., 1987). Infants who were *cognitively* normal at either 40 weeks or 9 months (corrected age) had a 20% chance of becoming cognitively abnormal by 36 months, yet those who were *motorically* or *neurologically* normal had a 90% chance of remaining so. When the influence of various background variables on diagnostic consistency was assessed, consistency in cognitive function from 9 to 36 months was influenced by environmental variables (center, race, and a composite index of socioeconomic status). In contrast, motor function from 9 to 36 months (which was most consistent) was influenced only by the infant's gender. Consistency in neurological diagnosis was influenced by a mix of several environmental and biological factors. Thus, it appears that early assessments are adequate for diagnosis of motor and neurological function, but that longer follow-up is necessary for cognitive assessment, owing to the stronger environmental effects on this function.

Classification of Early Neuropsychological Findings

From the previous sections it is apparent that early neuropsychological assessment is a hybrid, but yet unique, process that incorporates techniques from neurological, clinical, and developmental approaches. Therefore, it helps to list the various functions that may be measured or observed in early assessment. Test instruments that are available to measure these functions are outlined in a subsequent section.

A proposed classification schema for early neuropsychological assessment is found in Table 1. This schema is a synthesis of several classi-

TABLE 1. Classification Schema for Early Neuropsychological Assessment

I. Basic neurological functions (intactness)	
Reflexes	Left/right discrepancies
Asymmetries	Motor inhibition
Stereotyped/lateralized postures	Protective reflexes
Muscle tone	Auditory orientation
Visual tracking/intactness	
II. Receptive functions	
Visual perception	Spatial relations
Auditory/language	Tactile processing
III. Expressive functions	
A. Fine motor/oral motor	B. Gross motor
Visual–motor integration	Motility
Language/speech	Coordination
Fine motor-constructional	
Visual-spatial orientation	
Articulation	
IV. Processing	
A. Memory and learning	Anticipatory behaviors
Temporal-sequential organization (auditory)	Visual sequencing
Visual memory	
Word retrieval	
B. Thinking/reasoning	
Cognitive-adaptive (problem solving)	Number Concepts
Abstracting (verbal, nonverbal)	Imitation
Seriation/classification	Judgment
V. Mental activity	
A. Attentional activities/level of consciousness	
Conceptual tracking/concentration	Alertness
Perseveration	Distractibility
Behavioral states	
B. Activity	
Arousal	
Cognitive	
Motor	

fications (e.g., Levine, 1983; Lezak, 1983) with applicability extended to the neonatal period and early childhood. Since neuropsychological assessment must be age-specific, all functions are not tested at each age. Some functions (e.g., reflexes, muscle tone) are predominant during the neonatal period, when behavior is less complex and more neurologically oriented. Other functions, such as temporal-sequential organization or verbal abstract abilities, are not testable until later, coinciding with increased cortical development. There is much overlap between functions and between classes of functions.

Basic Neurological Functions

This classification encompasses measurement of general functional intactness. Early reflexes (Moro, Babinski, palmar grasp), asymmetries in movement or muscle control (upper vs. lower extremities), and lateralized or stereotyped postures (asymmetric tonic neck reflex, fisted hands) are included. In addition, left–right discrepancies such as impaired midline behaviors, hemiplegias, prematurely established handedness, muscle tone (hypo- or hypertonia, head control), motor inhibition (mirroring, reflex overflow), and visual and auditory intactness (conjugate gaze, nystagmus, tracking skills, response to sounds) are involved. This classification also includes protective reactions in response to change in the infant's body orientation in space (e.g., parachute reactions). Keen observation skills are critical because some functions can be evaluated in a present/absent manner, whereas others are based on more qualitative, subjective judgment.

Receptive Functions

Receptive functions involve the entry of information into the central processing system, utilizing sensation and perception. This class of function becomes more complex with age. Visual, auditory, and tactile abilities are involved, but owing to testing instruments, visual and auditory functions are emphasized more than tactile processes in early assessment. Tactile function is assessed in the first several months of life in the form of proprioceptive reflexes, grasping, and mouthing objects. Auditory discrimination and verbal receptive skills also are involved in this functional grouping.

Expressive Functions

Expressive functions refer to behaviors produced by the child and observed by the examiner. The repertoire of behavior reflecting expressive functions increases with age. Fine motor abilities include eye–hand coordination, manipulating with the fingers, constructional abilities, and psychomotor speed. Oral motor and language functions consist of what is said and how it is articulated. Gross motor function involves motility, coordination, ambulation, and gait. Deficits in this area are often defined as apraxias, dysphasias, anomias, or dyskinesias.

Processing

Processing includes two components: memory/learning and thinking/reasoning. Memory/learning involves visual and auditory short-term memory (registration and immediate memory) and long-term memory.

Early functions include habituation, object permanency, stranger anxiety, and recognition of self in a mirror. Time sequence relationships, such as digit span and recall of objects presented visually, and word retrieval (naming pictures or objects), are later memory/learning functions in the young child.

Thinking/reasoning is often called higher-order processing, in which the infant or child synthesizes information. These complex processes are thought to provide better prognostic indicators of an infant's true potential, particularly in motorically impaired infants. In such cases, if spikes of age-appropriate function in these areas are observed against a backdrop of lower levels of motor and neurologic function, long-term mental deficiencies may not be as likely. Problem solving, imitation, conceptual grouping, body image concepts, counting and sorting, and performance on form boards are later abilities that fall in this subcategory.

Mental Activity

This class of function consists of two components: attentional activities/level of consciousness, and activity. Attentional activities are heavily dependent upon developmental age since such skills are poorly developed in younger infants and children. These functions can therefore be diagnostically useful when attentional behavior is compared with what is expected at a specific age. Many of these functions also determine how an infant approaches test taking. Behavioral states are important early; later, alertness becomes more crucial. Activity, whether characterized as hypo- or hyperactivity, will affect test-taking behavior, but it is also of diagnostic utility because diffuse neuropsychological dysfunction can be reflected in either excessively high or low activity levels.

In summary, it is important to emphasize that the classes of function in Table 1 are interrelated, and that the divisions are provided to form a conceptual framework. For example, when an infant follows commands, receptive functions (temporal-sequential) as well as expressive abilities are involved. Similarly, on form boards, receptive functions (visual perceptual), processing (thinking/reasoning), and mental activities (attention and concentration) are employed. Nonetheless, careful analysis of data obtained in early neuropsychological assessment enables the progressive discrimination of areas of adequate function and those of deficit.

ASSESSMENT INSTRUMENTS

There are few, if any, tests that are designed specifically to provide neuropsychological data for infants and young children. However, many tests yield neuropsychological information but simply have not been identified as doing so previously. Early neuropsychological assessment of infants and young children can therefore be accomplished by drawing on tests from neurology and developmental psychology.

Many of these tests are discussed subsequently. The listing found in Table 2 is selective and not exhaustive. The test instruments that are included are those that are used frequently by examiners of infants and young children, and are specifically useful in children under the age of 4. Other lists of developmental and cognitive tests are available (Frankenburg, 1983; Ulrey, 1981).

In Table 2, five test instruments for neonates, five assessments for infants, and four tests applicable to the assessment of young children are listed. A brief description of the test, the information that is derived, and comments about the strengths (+) and weaknesses (−) of each instrument are provided.

Assessment instruments, and the functions assessed by each are found in Table 3, which is a synthesis of Tables 1 and 2. The assessment instruments are classified as newborn/neonatal, infancy, and toddler/early childhood.

Newborn/Neonatal

Neuropsychological functions measured by assessment instruments in this age range cluster in the neurological function/intactness, expressive (gross motor), and mental activity groupings (level of consciousness, activity). All examinations are adequate to assess intactness, although the examiner's additional observations are necessary in some.

Infancy

At this age, assessments cluster in the receptive, expressive, and processing groupings. Sensorimotor skills are generally emphasized; these include visual/motor integrative, fine motor-constructive, and gross motor functions. Visual/perceptual abilities are also heavily weighted. Inclusion of more neurological function items in assessment at this age is necessary. The other major deficiency is found in the mental activity grouping. In both cases, additional items and observations could be included. Reflexes are evaluated only with the Milani-Comparetti exam at this age; this suggests the advisability of incorporating this assessment instrument with other more developmentally oriented techniques.

Early Childhood

As in the infancy age range, little emphasis is placed on the neurological function and mental activity groupings. Gross motor skills are

TABLE 2. Assessment Instruments Used in Early Neuropsychological Testing

Assessment instrument	Description	Information	Comment
Age: Newborn			
Brazelton Neonatal Behavioral Assessment Scale (Brazelton, 1973)	27 behavioral items (9-point scale), 20 elicited responses (3-point scale)	How infant responds to caretakers and environment; states, habituation, orientation (visual, auditory), muscle tone, activity; "best performance"	(+) Clinical instrument, provides good research information, recovery from stress; (−) some problems with data interpretation and scaling, poor long-range prediction
Prechtl Neurological Examination (Prechtl, 1977; Prechtl & Beintema, 1964)	Approximatley 52 items + states, postures, spontaneous activity	Gross state of CNS reactivity (motor activity, states) + specific lesional approach; syndromes identified	(+) Extensivley studied, good standardization, provides immediate diagnosis, prognosis, those needing follow-up, behavioral response descriptions; (−) lengthy, perhaps too detailed
Brief Infant Neurobehavioral Optimality Scale (Aylward, Verhulst, & Colliver, 1985)	Reduced version of Revised Prechtl Neurological Examination, 15 items scored in optimal/nonoptimal manner	Screen of CNS intactness (tonus, tendon reflexes, spontaneous activity, some primitive reflexes)	(+) Easily administered, less time-consuming, similar sensitivity and specificity values as Prechtl, summary score; (−) not as much data on states, not as extensive as Prechtl
Parmelee's Neurological Examination (Parmelee, Michaelis, Kopp, & Sigman, 1974)	Divided into two sections—Section I: state observations, 20 items; Section II: crying, activity, tremor, etc.	Active and reflexive muscle tone, primary reflexes, arousal, and spontaneous behavior	(+) Brief—takes 10 minutes to administer, summary score; (−) not as extensive as Prechtl
Graham Behavior Test for Neonates (Graham, Matarazzo, & Caldwell, 1956; Rosenblith, 1974)	Five scales: pain threshold, maturational level, visual responsiveness, irritability, and muscle tension ratings; pain threshold deleted in revision	Originally designed to differentiate normal and brain-injured newborns; motor function (head control, crawl) tactile-adaptive (cotton over nose), visual tracking, auditory responsiveness, irritability rating	(+) Correlations between neonatal data and early infant data, revision had large sample; (−) long-range predictability fair, used infrequently

Age: Infancy		
Gesell Developmental Schedules (Knobloch & Pasmanick, 1974; Knobloch, Stevens, & Malone, 1980).	Items provided at each of key ages, under five groups; can be scored by observation or history	(+) Basis for most examinations of infancy, good screening inventory; (−) not as well standardized as other infant examinations, ratio developmental quotient
Bayley Scales of Infant Development (Bayley, 1969)	Mental Developmental Index (163 items), Psychomotor Developmental Index (81 items), Infant Behavior Record	(+) Well standardized, good overall assessment of child's strengths and weaknesses, most widely used; (−) questionable predictability, very dependent on motor function
Griffiths Mental Developmental Scale (Griffiths, 1954, 1970)	Derived from Gesell, 498 items, most detailed in first 2 years; five areas with several items for each month of age	(+) Used predominantly in Great Britain, rigorous training; (−) many unreliable items
Cattell Infant Intelligence Scale (1940)	Items arranged on an age scale, drawing from Gesell at early ages and Stanford-Binet from 22 months upwards; 2–36 months	(+) Smooth transition from infant to early childhood examination, good for testing older children who function at lower levels; (−) small standardization sample (294), IQ concept questionable, not used frequently
Milani-Comparetti Neuro-Developmental Screening Examination (Milani-Comparetti & Gidoni, 1967)	Assesses spontaneous behavior, postural control, evoked responses; chart provided with age norms in terms of onset and disappearance of responses 0–24 months	Neuromotor abnormalities—head and body control, movement, evoked primitive reflexes, righting, parachute, and tilting reactions; enables detection of cerebral palsy, developmental delay (+) Administered in 5–10 minutes, good screening device that can be used with other examinations; (−) tilting reactions need tilt board, which is often not readily available

(continued)

TABLE 2. (Continued)

Assessment instrument	Description	Information	Comment
Age: Toddler/early childhood Merrill-Palmer Scale of Mental Tests (Stutsman, 1948); Extended Merrill-Palmer Scales (1969)	Verbal, perceptual-motor, and nonverbal items grouped into 6-month age ranges; extended version has 16 tasks—1½–6 years, 3–5 years	Perceptual-motor function; extended version—semantic production and evaluation, figural production and evaluation (verbal expression, comprehension, perceptual-motor, and nonverbal skills)	(+) Can be used in language-delayed children, high interest level for children; (−) norms outdated, heavily loaded with perceptual performance items, should be used as a supplemental test, poor predictive validity
Stanford-Binet (1960; Terman & Merrill, 1972)	Age 2–adult, provides IQ score; grouped at half-year intervals from 2 to 5, yearly thereafter	General intellectual abilities; general comprehension, visual-motor ability, arithmetic reasoning, memory and concentration, vocabulary, judgment and reasoning	(+) Used frequently, good predictive utility; (−) unequal distribution of verbal and nonverbal items at different ages, heavy loading of perceptual/performance items at early ages
Stanford-Binet-Revised (Thorndike, Hagen, & Sattler, 1986)	Items of same type grouped into 15 tests—2–adult	Four areas assessed: verbal, abstract/visual, quantitative reasoning, short-term memory	(+) Differentiates between MR and LD, better reliability, better underlying test theory; (−) new instrument, needs more application
McCarthy Scales of Children's Abilities (McCarthy, 1972)	Eighteen component tests divided into five scales: verbal, perceptual-performance, quantitative, memory, and motor; provides a General Cognitive Index, 2½–8½ years	Five scales + general cognitive (summary of verbal, perceptual-performance, and quantitative); provides good overview of child's general function (verbal and nonverbal) as well as specific strengths and weaknesses; early detection of LD	(+) Age equivalents available for subtests, includes a gross motor component, best in the 3- to 5-year age range, can prorate; (−) LD children score lower on this test, may give underestimate of child's true abilities, of limited utility for older children

not assessed consistently, whereas receptive, expressive, and processing functions are evaluated in depth. Because it requires a great deal of skill to elicit reflexes at this age, observation of neurological function, as evident in gross and fine motor behavior, becomes even more important.

Useful Findings

Neuropsychological indicators in the newborn period that are particularly useful as indicators of dysfunction include Prechtl's syndromes, hypertonicity of the axial musculature and lower extremities, high amplitude-low frequency tremors, nystagmus, clonus, reflex overflow, and aberrant state regulation. Isolated abnormal findings are generally not helpful. In addition, early hypotonia and head lag, subtle asymmetries, mediocre visual tracking, and suspected motor or neurological diagnoses are often transient. During infancy, persistence of primitive reflexes, cortical thumb sign, consistent irritability, persistent dystonia, a very predominant hand preference, stereotyped, repetitive movements, and developmental quotients that are 2 or more standard deviations below average indicate significant problems. Suspect motor or neurological diagnoses are often variable, and most infants tend to improve. In early childhood, many of the functions seen in older children become more apparent. Neuropsychological assessment should focus particularly on emerging temporal-sequential skills (but *not* digits backwards), concentration, word retrieval difficulties, perseverative tendencies (motor and cognitive), activity levels, and gross motor function. Visual-motor skills may be overemphasized during infancy and at this later time period.

DIRECTIONS

The emergence of a discipline of early developmental neuropsychology is timely and meets a need that is expanding in relation to improvements in pediatric health care. This discipline consists of a synthesis of existing developmental and neurological techniques, but it is distinct from developmental neurology or developmental neuropsychiatry. Early developmental neuropsychology includes assessment from the neonatal period to early childhood, an age span that is currently underserved.

It is likely that this chapter includes many concepts and descriptions of assessment instruments that are not familiar to neuropsychologists accustomed to working with older populations. Those who are acquainted with these instruments and concepts constitute a definite minority. There are several reasons for this situation: Assessment in this group has been provided by other disciplines, there are very limited training opportunities in traditional psychology programs, and a lack of acceptance by

TABLE 3. Assessment Instruments and Functions Assessed[a]

Functions	Newborn/neonatal					Infancy					Toddler/early childhood			
	Brazelton	Prechtl	Brief Neurobehavioral Optimality Scale	Parmelee's Neurological Examination	Graham/ Rosenblith	Gesell	Bayley	Griffiths	Cattell	Milani-Comparetti	Merrill-Palmer	Stanford-Binet	Stanford-Binet-R	McCarthy Scales
I. Neurologic functions														
Reflexes	+	+	+	+	+	−	−	−	−	+	−	−	−	−
Asymmetries	+	+	*	+	*	*	*	*	*	*	*	*	*	*
Stereotyped/lateralized postures	+	+	*	+	*	+	+	+	+	+	*	*	*	*
Muscle tone	+	+	+	+	+	+	+	+	+	+	*	*	*	*
Visual tracking/intactness	+	+	−	−	+	+	+	+	+	*	*	*	*	*
L/R discrepancy	−	+	*	+	*	*	*	*	*	*	*	*	*	*
Motor inhibition	+	+	−	−	−	*	*	*	*	*	*	*	*	*
Protective reflexes	+	+	−	+	+	+	+	+	+	+	−	−	−	−
Auditory orientation	+	+	−	−	+	+	+	+	+	*	−	−	−	−
II. Receptive functions														
Visual perception	+	−	−	−	+	+	+	+	+	−	+	+	+	+
Auditory/language	−	−	−	−	−	+	+	+	+	−	+	+	+	+
Spatial relations	−	−	−	−	−	+	+	+	+	−	+	+	+	+
Tactile processing	+	−	−	−	+	+	+	+	+	−	+	*	*	*
III. Expressive functions														
A. Fine motor/oral motor														
Visual/motor integrative	−	−	−	−	−	+	+	+	+	−	+	+	+	+
Language/speech	−	−	−	−	−	+	+	+	+	−	+	+	+	+
Fine motor constructive	−	−	−	−	−	+	+	+	+	−	+	+	+	+
Visual/spatial	−	−	−	−	−	+	+	+	+	−	+	+	+	+
Articulation	−	−	−	−	−	+	+	+	+	−	*	*	*	*

B. Gross motor												
Motility	+	+	+	+	+	+	+	+	+	+	−	+	+
Coordination	+	+	+	+	+	+	+	+	+	+	−	+	+
IV. Processing												
A. Memory												
Temporal-sequential organization (auditory)	+	−	−	+	+	+	+	+	+	+	−	+	+
Anticipatory behaviors	−	−	−	−	−	−	+	+	+	+	−	−	−
Visual memory	+	−	−	−	−	+	+	+	+	+	+	+	+
Visual sequencing	−	−	−	−	−	−	−	+	−	−	−	+	+
Word retrieval	−	−	−	−	+	+	+	+	+	+	+	+	+
B. Thinking/reasoning												
Cognitive/adaptive problem solving	−	−	−	−	−	+	+	+	+	−	+	+	+
Abstracting	−	−	−	−	−	+	+	+	+	+	+	+	+
Seriation/classification	−	−	−	−	−	+	+	+	−	+	+	+	+
Number concepts	−	−	−	−	+	+	+	+	+	−	−	+	+
Imitation	−	−	−	−	+	+	+	+	+	+	+	+	+
Judgment	−	−	−	−	+	+	+	+	+	+	+	+	+
V. Mental activity												
A. Attentional/level of consciousness												
Conceptual tracking/concentration	−	−	−	−	−	*	*	*	−	+	+	+	+
Perseveration	−	−	−	−	−	*	*	*	−	*	+	*	*
Attention/distractability	+	−	*	−	−	*	*	*	−	*	+	*	*
Behavioral states	+	+	*	+	+	−	−	−	*	−	+	−	−
Alertness	+	+	*	+	+	+	−	*	*	*	+	*	*
B. Activity												
Arousal	+	+	*	*	*	+	*	*	*	*	+	*	*
Cognitive	−	−	−	−	−	+	+	*	−	*	+	*	*
Motor	+	+	+	+	+	+	+	+	*	+	+	*	*
Irritability	+	*	*	+	+	*	*	*	*	*	+	*	*

[a] A "+" indicates function is assessed by evaluation instrument; a "−" indicates function is not assessed directly; a "*" means observations of this function can be made but are not scored formally.

other professionals, particularly those in medicine, is prevalent. A significant component of neonatal and infant neurological assessment is behavioral observation; psychologists are specialists in the observation of behavior. Therefore, a major thrust in early developmental neuropsychology is to make examiners better versed in which behaviors to elicit and to observe.

Early developmental neuropsychology requires specific training that is not afforded in traditional clinical or developmental psychology training programs. Training should be allied closely to pediatrics, pediatric neurology, neonatology, genetics, and interdisciplinary clinics. Reading materials should be expanded to include texts such as that of the Committee on Joint Assessment of Prenatal and Perinatal Factors Associated with Brain Disorders (Freeman, 1985). Examiners cannot learn assessment techniques solely from manuals or books; hands-on experience is required under the direction of a variety of professionals. Unfortunately, as is often the case with instruments such as the Bayley Scales, unqualified examiners attempt to pass themselves off as competent in the use of a test. In addition, and perhaps most important, a thorough understanding of normal development is necessary so that the examiner can detect deviations from normality. Concepts and techniques should be structured from fetal development upwards; techniques applicable to adults or even older children cannot be downscaled. Information that is helpful at later ages may be useless in infants and young children, and vice versa.

In early neuropsychological assessment, damage, age, development, and environment form a complex interactive matrix in which cause–effect relationships and models are obscured. The previously mentioned Risk Route concept (Aylward & Kenny, 1979), which takes many of these factors into account, should be considered in any early neuropsychological assessment. A major dilemma facing those involved in this type of assessment is that the probability of detecting subtle damage is greater with increased age; however, the longer the time between an insult and the assessment, the greater is the influence of intervening variables, particularly the environment. Therefore, earlier assessment has a better potential to elucidate potential cause-and-effect relationships, although there are limitations on what can be assessed. At later ages, assessment techniques are better, but cause-and-effect relationships are more muddled, largely owing to environmental influences. A major area for future research is the development of predictive models of dysfunction. The optimum duration of follow-up, and selection of appropriate instruments are two additional research topics that require attention.

There are many limitations in the test instruments that are available currently since many were developed in the 1920s and 1930s (Gesell, 1928; Gesell & Amatruda, 1947). Other tests lack a unifying conceptual base and instead contain unrelated items that children are required to pass at a given age. Better methods are needed to help in scoring behaviors that have not been scored previously. It may be more informative to focus on *how* an infant or a young child achieves a criterion measure rather than *if* the item is passed or not. Further, many functions are linked with test items in a *post hoc* method (e.g., Stanford-Binet), rather than defining a function and devising a task to assess it.

Selection of combinations of items, drawn from existing tests but based on a conceptual framework of functions, is suggested as the best approach. It is advisable to implement the basics of Prechtl's (1980) optimality concept in early neuropsychological assessment. Rather than focusing on the normality or abnormality of a response, the optimality concept provides a measure of deviation (or lack of deviation) from a known optimal neuropsychological response. The problem of weighting different items is circumvented because the optimal responses are summed and divided by the total number of neuropsychological items administered. Cutoff scores (e.g., 75% of the responses were optimal) could be devised to assist in diagnosis. This technique has been used by investigators during the neonatal and earl infancy period with good results (Aylward, Verhulst & Colliver, 1985; Stave & Ruvalo, 1980). This method would be particularly helpful in infancy and early childhood assessment, where combinations of examination instruments and techniques need to be employed. The optimal response for each item could be determined from previous data, and these criteria could then be assembled into a workable assessment battery.

The need for an instrument that would identify infants and young children who have abnormalities of posture, tone, and movement, as well as those with developmental delays, has recently been emphasized. This is because categorical results of developmental assessment instruments often yield low sensitivity (Sciarillo, Brown, Robinson, Bennett, & Sells, 1986). We are currently applying this methodology with the Early Neuropsychological Optimality Rating Scales (ENORS). Different scales have been developed in an *a priori* manner to reflect major developmental acquisitions at several key ages (6, 12, 18, and 24 months). As an example, the 12-month ENORS is found in the Appendix.

The scales are a synthesis of information outlined previously in Tables 1 and 3 and are designed to provide a more thorough assessment by covering functions that would ordinarily be missed with the administration of a developmental or neurological examination in isolation. The scales utilize components of the Bayley, the Milani-Comparetti, and neurological indicators, as well as developmental milestones. Individual items included in the ENORS are not necessarily new; basic reflexes and many expressive and receptive functions are emphasized in pediatric postgraduate training. Similarly, developmental milestones and the Bayley developmental quotients are used by developmental psychologists.

The standard format, the combination of a variety of items into a conceptual framework, and having scoring and interpretation based on the optimality concept are innovations. A short scoring manual to define optimal responses is available for each age scale, and this affords reliability in scoring at different centers.

We are in the process of applying this concept to a sample of 611 babies enrolled in the National Heart, Lung and Blood Institute Antenatal Steroid Study, approximately 70% of whom were followed to 3 years of age. We plan to produce cutoff scores for various ages, based on more long-term sensitivities and specificities, and items that are redundant will be eliminated. This instrument will subsequently be applied to a smaller sample ($n = 100$) of high-risk infants derived from our High Risk Nursery Developmental Continuity Clinic. This approach is a fertile area for subsequent research.

In summary, there is a need for early developmental neuropsychology, particularly in neonatal follow-up and multidisciplinary diagnostic clinics. Acceptance of this discipline will be gained by the continued demonstration of clinical and research competencies.

APPENDIX

Early Neuropsychological Optimality Rating Scale
12 Months

Classification	Optimal	Nonoptimal
I. Basic Reflexes		
Persistence of primitive reflexes (Moro, asymmetric tonic neck, palmar/plantar grasps, etc.)	No	Yes
Asymmetries/marked L-R discrepancy (mirroring, obvious hand preference)	No	Yes
Presence of protective reactions (parachute reactions)	Yes	No
Good head control	Yes	No
Hypotonia/hypertonia—extremities	No	Yes
Absence of stereotyped, repetitive movements and/or cortical thumb sign	Yes	No
II. Receptive Functions		
Appropriate responses to auditory stimuli (orients, turns head)	Yes	No
Appropriate responses to visual stimuli (tracking, lack of nystagmus, etc.)	Yes	No
Follows simple commands	Yes	No
III. Expressive Functions		
A. Fine motor/oral motor		
Neat pincer grasp	Yes	No
Presence of midline behaviors (hands together, transfers, holds two objects simultaneously)	Yes	No
Radial-digital grasp	Yes	No
Babbles/appropriate sounds for age (dada/mama specifically, etc.)	Yes	No
Good eye–hand coordination	Yes	No
B. Gross motor		
Age-appropriate gait/ambulation (no tiptoe walking, no dragging of an extremity)	Yes	No
Uncoordinated movements	No	Yes
Psychomotor Developmental Index ≥ 90	Yes	No
IV. Processing		
Appreciation of object permanency	Yes	No
Imitative abilities	Yes	No
Simple problem-solving skills	Yes	No
V. Mental Activity		
Goal-directed behaviors	Yes	No
Attentive to procedures	Yes	No
Average level of activity for age	Yes	No
Persistant crying/irritability	No	Yes
Mental Developmental Index ≥ 90	Yes	No

Total Optimal _____

Total Nonoptimal _____

$$\text{Neuropsychological Optimality Score} = \frac{\text{Total Optimal }(\ \ )}{\text{Optimal }(\ \ ) + \text{Nonoptimal }(\ \ )} = \_\_\_\_\_$$

REFERENCES

Amiel-Tison, C. (1982). Neurologic signs, aetiology, and implications. In P. Stratton (Ed.), *Psychobiology of the human newborn* (pp. 75–94). New York: Wiley.

Aylward, G. P., Dunteman, G., Hatcher, R. P., Gustafson, N. F., & Widemayer, S. (1985). The SES-Composite Index: A tool for developmental outcome studies. *Psychological Documents, 15*(Ms. No. 2683).

Aylward, G. P., Gustafson, N., Verhulst, S. J., & Colliver, J. A. (1987). Consistency in the diagnosis of cognitive, motor and neurologic function over the first three years. *Journal of Pediatric Psychology, 12,* 77–98.

Aylward, G. P., & Kenny, T. J. (1979). Developmental follow-up: Inherent problems and a conceptual model. *Journal of Pediatric Psychology, 4,* 331–343.

Aylward, G. P., Verhulst, S. J., & Colliver, J. A. (1985). Development of a brief infant neurobehavioral optimality scale: Longitudinal sensitivity and specificity. *Developmental Neuropsychology, 1,* 265–276.

Bayley, N. (1969). *Bayley Scales of Infant Development.* New York: Psychological Corporation.

Bierman-van Eendenburg, M. E. C., Jurgens-van der Zee, A. D., Olinga, A. A., Huisjes, H. H., & Touwen, B. C. L. (1981). Predictive value of neonatal neurological examination. A follow-up study at 18 months. *Developmental Medicine and Child Neurology, 23,* 296–305.

Brazelton, T. B. (1973). *Neonatal behavioral assessment scale.* Clinics in Developmental Medicine, No. 50. Philadelphia: Lippincott.

Cattell, P. (1940). *The measurement of intelligence of infants and young children.* New York: Psychological Corp.

Chess, S., & Thomas, A. (1983). Dynamics of individual behavioral development. In M. D. Levine, W. B. Carey, A. C. Crocker, & R. T. Gross. *Developmental-behavioral pediatrics* (pp. 158–174). Philadelphia: W.B. Saunders.

Coolman, R. B., Bennett, F. C., Sells, C. J., Swanson, M. W., Andrews, M. S., & Robinson, N. M. (1985). Neuromotor development of graduates of the neonatal intensive care unit: Patterns encountered in the first two years of life. *Journal of Developmental and Behavioral Pediatrics, 6,* 327–333.

Davies, P. A. (1984). Follow-up of low birthweight children. *Archives of Disease in Childhood, 59,* 794–797.

Dubowitz, L. M. S., Dubowitz, V., Palmer, P. G., Miller, G., Fawer, C. L., & Levine, M. I. (1984). Correlation of neurologic assessment in the preterm newborn infant with outcome at one year. *Journal of Pediatrics, 105,* 452–456.

Ellenberg, J. H., & Nelson, K. B. (1981). Early recognition of infants at high risk for cerebral palsy: Examination at age four months. *Developmental Medicine and Child Neurology, 14,* 575–584.

Frankenburg, W. K. (1983). Infant and preschool developmental screening. In M. D. Levine, W. B. Carey, A. C. Crocker, & R. T. Gross (Eds). *Developmental-behavioral pediatrics* (pp. 927–937). Philadelphia: W. B. Saunders.

Frankenburg, W. K., & Dodds, J. B. (1967). The Denver Developmental Screening Test. *Journal of Pediatrics, 71,* 181–191.

Freeman, J. (Ed). (1985). *Prenatal and perinatal factors associated with brain disorders* (NIH Pub. No. 85–1149). Washington, DC: U.S. Department of Health and Human Services.

Gesell, A. (1928). *Infancy and human growth.* New York: Macmillan.

Gesell, A., & Amatruda, C. (1947). *Developmental diagnosis* (2nd ed.). New York: Hoeber.

Graham, F. K., Matarazzo, R. G., & Caldwell, B. M. (1956). Behavioral differences between normal and traumatized newborns: II. Standardization, reliability and validity. *Psychological Monographs, 70*(21. Whole No. 428).

Griffiths, R. (1954). *The abilities of babies.* New York: McGraw-Hill.

Griffiths, R. (1970). *The abilities of young children. A comprehensive system of mental measurement for the first eight years of life.* London: Child Development Research Center.

Hack, M., Caron, B., Rivers, A., & Fanaroff, A. A. (1983). The very low birthweight infant: The broader spectrum of morbidity during infancy and early childhood. *Journal of Developmental and Behavioral Pediatrics, 4,* 243–249.

Hanson, R., Smith, J. A., & Hume, W. (1984). Some reasons for disagreement among scorers of infant intelligence test items. *Child: Care, Health, and Development, 10,* 17–30.

Hertzig, M. E. (1983). Temperament and neurological status. In M. Rutter (Ed.). *Developmental neuropsychiatry* (pp. 164–180). New York: Guilford Press.

Hunt, J. V. (1981). Predicting intellectual disorders in childhood for preterm infants with birthweights below 1501 gm. In S. L. Friedman & M. Sigman (Eds.), *Preterm birth and psychological development* (pp. 329–352). New York: Academic Press.

Kalverboer, A. F., Touwen, B. C. L., & Prechtl, H. F. R. (1973). Follow-up of infants at risk of minor brain dysfunction. *Annals of the New York Academy of Sciences, 205,* 173–187.

Knobloch, H., & Pasamanick, B. (1974). Developmental diagnosis (3rd. ed.). New York: Harper & Row.

Knobloch, H., Stevens, F., & Malone, A. F. (1980). Manual of developmental diagnosis. New York: Harper & Row.

Lenard, H. G., von Bernuth, H., & Prechtl, H. F. R. (1968). Reflexes and their relationship to behavioral state in the newborn. *Acta Paediatrica Scandinavica, 57,* 177–185.

Levine, M. D. (1983). The developmental assessment of the school age child. In M. D. Levine, W. B. Carey, A. C. Crocker, & R. T. Gross (Eds.), *Developmental-behavioral pediatrics* (pp. 938–947). Philadelphia: W.B. Saunders.

Lezak, M. D. (1983). *Neuropsychological assessment* (pp. 15–38). New York: Oxford University Press.

Luria, A. R. (1973). *The working brain* (pp. 19–42, 341–344). New York: Basic Books.

McCarthy, D. (1972). *Manual for the McCarthy Scales of Children's Abilities.* New York: Psychological Corp.

Milani-Comparetti, A., & Gidoni, E. A. (1967). Routine developmental examination in normal and retarded children. *Developmental Medicine and Child Neurology, 9,* 631–638.

Oski, F. A., & Honig, A. S. (1978). The effects of therapy on the developmental scores of iron deficient infants. *Journal of Pediatrics, 92,* 21–25.

Ounsted, M., Cockburn, J., & Moar, V. A. (1983). Developmental assessment at four years: Are there any differences between children who do, or do not, cooperate? *Archives of Disease in Childhood, 58,* 286–289.

Parmelee, A. H., & Michaelis, R. (1971). Neurological examination of the newborn. In J. Hellmuth (Ed.), *Exceptional infant 2: Studies in abnormalities* (pp. 3–23). New York: Brunner/Mazel.

Parmelee, A. H., Michaelis, R., Kopp, C. B., & Sigman, M. (1974). Newborn neurological examination. UCLA Infant Studies Project.

Prechtl, H. F. R. (1968). Neurological findings in infants after pre- and parinatal complications. In J. H. P. Jonxis, H. K. A. Vissir, & J. A. Troelestra (Eds.), *Aspects of praematurity and dysmaturity.* Leiden: Stenfert Kroese.

Prechtl, H. F. R. (1977). *The neurological examination of the full-term newborn infant* (2nd ed.). Clinics in Developmental Medicine, No. 63. London: Heinemann.

Prechtl, H. F. R. (1980). The optimality concept. *Early Human Development, 4,* 201–205.

Prechtl, H. F. R. (1984). Continuity and change in early neural development. In H. F. R. Prechtl (Ed.), *Continuity of neural functions from prenatal to postnatal life* (pp. 1–15). Clinics in Developmental Medicine, No. 94. Philadelphia: Lippincott.

Prechtl, H. F. R., & Beintema, D. (1964). *The neurological examination of the full-term newborn infant.* Little Club Clinics in Developmental Medicine, No. 12. London: William Heinemann Medical Books.

Prechtl, H. F. R., Vlach, V., Lenard, H. G., & Grant, D. (1967). Exteroceptive and tendon reflexes in various behavioral states in the newborn infant. *Biologia Neonatorum, 11,* 159–175.

Public Law 94-142. (1975). Education for all handicapped children act. 94th Congress, S.6.

Rosenblith, J. F. (1974). Relations between neonatal behaviors and those at eight months. *Developmental Psychology, 10,* 779–792.

Sameroff, A. J. (1975). Early influences on development: Fact or fancy? *Merrill-Palmer Quarterly, 21,* 267–294.

Sciarillo, W. G., Brown, M. M., Robinson, N. M., Bennett, F. C., & Sells, C. J. (1986). Effectiveness of the Denver Developmental Screening Test with biologically vulnerable infants. *Journal of Developmental and Behavioral Pediatrics, 7,* 77–83.

Siegel, L. S. (1983). Correction for prematurity and its consequences for the assessment of the very low birth weight infant. *Child Development, 54,* 1176–1188.

Stave, V., & Ruvalo, C. (1980). Neurological development in very-low-birthweight infants: Application of a standardized examination and Prechtl's optimality concept in routine evaluations. *Early Human Development, 4,* 229–241.

Stutsman, R. (1948). *Guide for administering the Merrill-Palmer Scale of mental tests.* New York: Harcourt Brace Jovanovich.

Taylor. D. J. (1984). Low birthweight and neurodevelopmental handicap. *Clinics in Obstetrics and Gynecology, 11,* 525–542.

Terman, L., & Merrill, M. (1972). *Stanford-Binet intelligence scale.* Boston: Houghton Mifflin.

Thorndike, R. L., Hagen, E. P., & Sattler, J. M. (1986). *Guide for administering and scoring the fourth edition. Stanford-Binet intelligence scale.* Chicago: Riverside.

Tjossem, T. (1976). *Intervention strategies for high risk infants and young children.* Baltimore: University Park Press.

Touwen, B. C. L. (1973). The neurological development of the human infant. In D. Davis & J. Dobbing (Eds.), *Scientific foundations of pediatrics.* Leiden: University Press.

Touwen, B. C. L. (1978). Variability and stereotyping in normal and deviant development. In J. Apley (Ed.), *Care of the handicapped child.* Clinics in Developmental Medicine, No. 67 (pp. 99–110). London: Heinemannn.

Ulrey, G. (1981). Psychological evaluation. In W. K. Frankenburg, S. M. Thornton, & M. E. Cohrs (Eds.), *Pediatric developmental diagnosis* (pp. 175–183). New York: Thieme-Stratton.

Ulrey, G. (1982). Influences of infant behavior on assessment. In G. Ulrey & S. J. Rogers (Eds.), *Psychological assessment of handicapped infants and young children* (pp. 14–24). New York: Thieme-Stratton.

Ulrey, G., & Schnell, R. R. (1982). Introduction to assessing young children. In G. Ulrey & S. J. Rogers (Eds.), *Psychological assessment of handicapped infants and young children* (pp. 1–13). New York: Thieme-Stratton.

Vohr, B. R., & Hack, M. (1982). Developmental follow-up of low-birthweight infants. *Pediatric Clinics of North America, 29,* 1441–1454.

Wolf, A. W., & Lozoff, B. (1985). A clinically interpretable method for analyzing the Bayley Infant Behavior Record. *Journal of Pediatric Psychology, 10,* 199–214.

Yang, R. K. (1979). Early infant assessment: An overview. In J. D. Osofsky (Ed.), *Handbook of infant development* (pp. 165–184). New York: Wiley.

Questions of Developmental Neurolinguistic Assessment

MICHAEL A. CRARY, KYJTA K. S. VOELLER, and NANCY J. HAAK

INTRODUCTION

It is obvious upon the most casual inspection that children develop language gradually and that there is an apparent temporal sequence to the acquisition of linguistic skills. A basic premise of this chapter is that the order of events of language acquisition reflects, or more pointedly, is dependent upon, a normal sequence of neurological maturation. This seems to be an almost obvious supposition. Yet the clinical evaluation of communicative abilities in children has not, to date, subscribed to a developmental neurolinguistic philosophy. In the following pages the questions of the utility of a developmental neurolinguistic approach to speech/ language assessment will be addressed. It would be preliminary to offer a comprehensive model given present knowledge. Nonetheless, the major purpose is to propose the possibility of such an approach and to identify areas for additional study.

   An oversimplified description of language development might include the sequence from babbling to single words, to word combinations, to increasingly complex grammatic expressions. Additional descriptive subdivisions might include the separation of comprehension of spoken language from the ability to express verbal concepts. There are, however, multiple skill areas that have potential influence upon a developing language system. Included among these attributes are motor performance,

MICHAEL A. CRARY, KYJTA K. S. VOELLER, and NANCY J. HAAK • Departments of Communicative Disorders and Neurology, University of Florida, Gainesville, Florida.

memory, and attending skills. The necessity to evaluate multiple behaviors is complicated further by the fact that the various components change during the course of development. Both of these observations address the need for a dynamic, multidimensional emphasis in any proposed model of developmental neurolinguistic assessment.

The neurological portion of a neurolinguistic evaluation is no less challenging than the linguistic portion. Present approaches to communicative assessment typically begin with descriptions of language behaviors, usually derived from an adult model of language. An attempt is then made to connect these descriptions with underlying psychological functions. The dynamic nature of the developing system(s) is usually overlooked. In this chapter, developmental aspects of language behavior and anatomical features of neurological maturation will be synthesized to formulate a *neurolinguistic systems* model of language development. In this respect, our proposed model of developmental neurolinguistic functions will be based upon facts of neuroanatomical maturation and knowledge of the relative contribution of various developing neuroanatomical systems to the acquisition of linguistic and paralinguistic skills.

Present approaches to language assessment typically address a developmental performance-level model. In this approach, an individual's performance is compared with normative data from groups of children in a similar age range. It is not the intent of this chapter to advocate a massive revision in test procedures, but rather to propose that the interpretation of language test results be referenced to an underlying neuropsychological model of linguistic functions. Such an approach would give equal importance to process and product. Language assessment from this perspective would be an invaluable asset in the interpretation of other neuropsychological test results. Rather than assigning clinical significance to a set of test scores derived solely from a normative basis, a pattern of results would be identified in conjunction with a biological model as well. Using this strategy, both functional and nonfunctional neuropsychological processes would be identified. In short, it is proposed that a common explanatory, neurological model be developed that applies to language as well as other psychological functions.

BASICS OF LANGUAGE DEVELOPMENT

In formulating an approach to developmental neurolinguistic assessment, it is necessary first to specify the significant parameters of language to be accounted for. An explosion of psycholinguistic research in recent years has identified numerous aspects of linguistic development. There have been, however, only a few longitudinal studies and these have evaluated limited numbers of children (e.g., R. Brown, 1973). These studies have described developmental changes that children demonstrate as they acquire the rudimentary skills of verbal language. An additional body of information has focused upon the period of language readiness or prelinguistic stage (e.g., Bates, Benigni, Bretherton, Camaioni, & Volterra, 1979; Halliday, 1975). Work by these and other authors has helped to fill the developmental gap between birth and the formal use of verbal language. From these descriptions of prelinguistic and linguistic development, three general *stages* within the developmental continuum can be constructed that include a prelinguistic stage, a stage of lexical expansion, and a stage of grammatical expansion.

Prelinguistic Communication

The prelinguistic stage extends from birth to approximately 12 months. It is during this time that the child is developing rapidly in a variety of skill areas, with the most obvious being motor skills, social development, and finally the emergence of spoken language. Early behaviors lack intention and might be characterized as reflexive. At this stage, the infant is able to communicate basic biological and social needs via a rudimentary system of movements and vocalizations. Language, as the adult recognizes it, has not yet emerged. However, language foundations are being constructed during this time. For example, there is increasing evidence that infants have a remarkable ability to perceive certain aspects of human communication. Neonates will show excitation to selective people, voices, or objects (Alegria & Noirot, 1978). Also Lieberman (1967) has pointed out that children as young as 3 months will change the pitch of the voice during vocal play depending on the adult with whom they are interacting. Voice pitch is higher if the adult is a female rather than a male. This would indicate that the infant has recognition of certain paralinguistic parameters and is able to exert some control over vocal productions at this early age.

The child's repertoire of preintentional behaviors expands until at about 8 months of age, when the first signs of intentional behaviors are recognized (Bates, 1975). At this time the infant becomes more persistent in communicative signaling. Behaviors give the adult a clear indication of whether responses are appropriate or not, and vocal patterns become increasingly varied. During this stage the interactive system of gestures, facial expressions, and vocalizations becomes so rich that it has been called a "protolanguage" (Halliday, 1975). This pattern of complex behaviors expands and leads to the onset of first words early in the second year of life. The emergence of productions recognized by adults as meaningful words signals the beginning of the lexical stage of language development.

Lexical Expansion Stage

For children and adults words are referents for objects or events occurring in the environment. However, to suggest that a child's word has the same implications as that of the adult would be misleading. From a linguistic perspective, the stage of lexical growth is characterized by increased semantic (meaning) and phonological knowledge (sound organization and production ability). Like the prelinguistic stage, this stage of lexical expansion may be divided into two components. Bloom (1973) and Moskowitz (1980) have suggested that the first 50 words represent broad concepts that serve as independent units of language (holophrases). These productions have been referred to as idioms, and it has been proposed that they emerge outside of the existing phonological system. In support of this contention is Leopold's (1947/1970) depiction of his daughter's use of the word *pretty*. Hildegard used this word with adultlike pronounciation before 1 year of age. By the age of 22 months her production of the word had deteriorated to a point where it was consistent with her general phonological ability. These "advanced forms" may represent the automatic production of a semantic concept that has not yet been integrated fully into the child's linguistic system.

Clark (1973) explains growth in semantic knowledge as a process of semantic feature acquisition. This position states that, although a child may use an adult word-form, the child does not possess a complete adult representation of the meaning of that word. The process of acquiring semantic knowledge is a result of the child assigning more features to the lexical representation of the verbal concept. These "features" are presented as the child's representation of encoded perceptual information. An example offered by Clark involves the word *doggie*. Initially, this label may apply to any four-legged animal. As additional features are acquired—e.g., hoofs, horns, says moo—the child begins to subdivide the larger category or concept into units more closely aligned with adult representation. Acquisition of semantic knowledge then is a function of the child's analyzing the environment and applying increasingly complex feature contrasts to a general set of verbal labels.

Phonological growth is an additional characteristic of this lexical stage of language development. Phonologists also subdivide this stage. Ingram (1976) discusses the phonology of the first 50 words and subsequently the phonology of the simple morpheme. The early stage of phonological growth is limited and tends to coincide with initial vocabulary acquisition. It is at this time that phonological growth *may be* subservient to semantic growth (i.e., advanced forms). Jakobson (1968) described the process of phonological growth as the acquisition of a system of feature contrasts. The child learns contrasts between various sounds of language on the basis of differences in meaning that result from using different sounds. The description of phonological acquisition during this period is similar to the semantic feature acquisition position presented by Clark (1973). Perhaps at this early stage of verbal language growth the child's task is to extract and analyze meaningful perceptions from the environment, and subsequently to attach linguistic significance to these perceptions in terms of semantic and phonological features.

Prosodic variation appears to be an additional device of linguistic contrast during this period of development. As stated above, children are responsive to prosodic aspects of spoken language as early as 3 months of age. During the later part of the stage of lexical expansion children reportedly use prosodic variation to signal linguistic distinctions. Menyuk and Bernholtz (1969) reported that children between 18 and 20 months of age used prosodic variation to signal statements, questions, or emphasis. This variation appears to coincide with the emergence of multiword utterances. Multiword expressions typically emerge at about 18 months of age; however, single-word utterances are dominant in child speech until approximately 2 to 2½ years of age.

The period of growth from 18 months to 2 years represents the second division of the stage of lexical expansion. During this period linguistic changes include a sudden growth in vocabulary, rapid phonological expansion, and the emergence of multiword utterances. The presence of these growth spurts signals the onset of our next general stage of language development—growth in grammatical complexity.

Grammatical Expansion Stage

The emergence of word combinations follows the single-word stage and occurs at about 18 months of age. By 2 years of age the child is demonstrating systematic and consistent increases in the length and complexity of verbal productions. This begins the stage we refer to as the grammatical expansion stage. Chronologically this is the longest stage of language development. Limitations in syntactic knowledge have been demonstrated in children ranging from 5 to 9 years (Chomsky, 1969).

During the years from 2 to 5 the child is demonstrating dramatic growth in all aspects of grammar. Phonological productions become increasingly complex and approximate adult performance by age 6 (Sander, 1972). Systematic increases in the length and complexity of spoken utterances also are observed. R. Brown (1973) has designated five stages of grammatical performance based upon mean length of utterance during this period. His first stage is similar to the end of the lexical expansion stage. The next stage is characterized by the emergence of grammatical morphemes. Subsequent stages are characterized by increasing length and linguistic complexity of spoken utterances. If one uses Brown's observations as a guideline, the onset of the grammatic expansion stage tends to be characterized by a significant increase in multiword utterances and the emergence of morphological grammatical markers. Although the specifics of this stage of grammatical expansion are beyond the scope of this chapter, the central concepts include an increase in the sequential complexity of word order manifested in increased length and syntactic complexity. Also, at this time, the basic phonological system reaches a state of relative maturity.

A COMMENT ON STYLES OF LANGUAGE PROCESSING

Although the order of acquisition of language structures and functions follows a general pattern, there is considerable variability in the rate and *style* of language learning among children. Variations in styles of language learning have been dichotomized by terms such as "*referential vs. expressive*" (Nelson, 1973) and "*analytic vs. gestalt*" (Peters, 1977, 1983). However, as Peters (1983) points out, these labels represent the extreme ends of a continuum of learning strategies used during language development. From a simplified perspective, gestalt/expressive children tend to be more verbal, producing a greater number of multiword utterances at an early age. Analytic/referential children tend to be more conservative, typically speaking in one-word units. Bates (1979) has suggested that the temporal order of emerging cognitive skills might contribute to differences in language-learning strategies. Peters (1983) reviews factors that she feels may influence the strategies used by a particular child and suggests that the child's "individual neurologic endowment" affects the style of language learning (p. 21). The implication of these observations is that variations in the organization of neurolinguistic systems may relate to, or even predict, the style(s) of language learning employed by an individual child.

RELATION OF NEUROLOGICAL MATURATION TO ACQUISITION OF LANGUAGE SKILLS

Neuroanatomic Maturation

There are at least two perspectives regarding maturation of human cortex and the development of functional systems. Traditionally, a hierarchial model of cortical development has been proposed. On the basis of indices such as brain weight, dendritic proliferation, and myelination (Altman, 1967; Conel 1939–1963; Flechsig, 1901; Yakovlev & Lecours, 1967), this model has proposed that the primary sensory and motor projection areas are the first to mature, followed in sequence by secondary (projection-association) areas, and finally by tertiary (association-association) areas.

A typical example of neurological maturation from this perspective is the degree of dendritic proliferation noted in various anatomic subsystems. DeCrinis (cited by Lenneberg, 1967) reported different patterns of dendritic growth for different cortical areas. The first areas to reach dendrogenetic maturity are the primary projection areas of vision and audition and the pre- and post-Rolandic strips for sensory and motor functions. The next areas to mature are the secondary association areas that receive input from the projection areas. These areas mature at approximately 2 years of age. The final stage of maturation begins between the ages of 2 and 4 years. During this time period, parts of the frontal and parietal lobes begin to mature. As with the other cortical regions, primary sensory and motor areas develop first, followed by their peripheral association areas. Regions of interarea association are the last to develop. The primary projection areas develop independently and are connected only when the final stages of this rapid dendrogenesis are complete. This pattern also has been reported by Poliakov (1961).

Recent studies of brain growth in both primates and humans have provided an alternative model for describing cortical development. Rakic, Bourgeois, Eckenhoff, Zecevic, and Goldman-Rakic (1986) examined pre- and postnatal synaptogenesis in five areas of macaque cerebral cortex. Although they expected to identify differential growth patterns supporting a hierarchical model, they instead identified more homogeneous synaptogenesis in all areas and layers of cortex examined. During the last 2 months of gestation, synaptic density increased at a rapid rate in all cortical areas examined, reaching a level equivalent to that of the sexually mature adult macaque. Synaptic density increased to levels much higher than that of the adult during the first 4 postnatal months. Subsequently, a reduction of synapses was noted that was rapid at first and then more gradual. This study suggests that the macaque brain develops as a whole rather than hierarchically and implies that functional subsystems may be an outgrowth of synaptic "pruning" postnatally. Huttenlocher (1979) has demonstrated a similar pattern of synaptic overproduction in the human cortex. The tempting implication of these observations is that in both the human child and the macaque, functional maturation may result from synapse elimination facilitating the development of subsystems to mediate more refined behaviors.

Jason Brown (1979) has suggested a similar model of neurological maturation in explanation of language functions and disorders. He reviews findings concerning neurological maturation in both human and nonhuman species that "are in agreement with the concept of an evolutionary and maturational progression from a diffuse to a focal organization. . ." (p. 143). He contends that focal cortical areas develop out of generalized neocortex. This phylogenetic approach proposed by Brown appears to share points of agreement with the recent findings of Rakic et al. (1986). The resulting model appears to be the converse of the more traditional hierarchical model. However, both views recognize the post-natal development of cortical functional subsystems. In this respect, the two views have similar implications for language development. Both would predict that early behaviors would reflect more diffuse/nonfocal processes and that development of more refined/analytic behaviors would result from maturation of specific subsystems. Thus, although there are questions concerning the precise nature of neurological matura-tion relevant to language development, the functional interpretations may be similar at a simplified behavioral level.

Hemispheric Functions

Another question concerns the role of the right versus the left hemi-sphere in the development of neurolinguistic functions. One approach to this topic is to evaluate the effects of early unilateral lesions on subse-quent language development. Until the early 1970s, it was accepted wide-ly that left hemisphere lesions early in development had little impact on subsequent language acquisition. This position was based on the concept of plasticity or the equipotentiality of the two cerebral hemispheres to process language in the young child. It was assumed that if a child sus-tained left hemisphere damage, the right hemisphere would take over these functions. Lenneberg (1967) stated that lateralization of language to the left hemisphere was a function of development and that plasticity continued until adolescence. However, the concept of plasticity rested on two assumptions and several clinical observations that have not weath-ered the test of time.

The first premise was that the immature brain had a remarkable re-silience to early lesions (Kennard, 1938). Acceptance of the fact that spe-cific early lesions resulted in impaired functioning at maturity in experi-mental animals did not occur until the 1970s, following the work of Goldman and colleagues (Goldman, 1971, Miller, Goldman, & Rosvold, 1973). Working with macaques, these investigators demonstrated that the timing and location of focal brain lesions was critical in determining the extent of behavioral deficits. Early prenatal lesions resulted in little func-tional impairment whereas later lesions (infancy) tended to create pro-found deficits. Also, the appearance of some behavioral deficits was tem-porally distant from the lesion. For example, lesions of dorsolateral frontal cortex did not result in any immediate impairment in a delayed response task. However, at approximately 16 months of age, the time at which this cortical area is believed to become functionally active in the

macaque, behavioral limitations became obvious and increased in severity as the animal matured. Lesion location interacted with timing in producing functional impairments. Specifically, these investigators demonstrated that subcortical lesions (caudate) produced in infancy resulted in
more severe deficits than cortical lesions occuring in the same time
period.

The second premise was that there is no anatomical difference between the cerebral hemispheres. Once it was established that there was a
difference in the size of the right and left planum temporale (Geschwind &
Levitsky, 1968), and that these asymmetries were present in the fetus and
infant (Chi, Dooling, & Gilles, 1977), the morphological basis of plasticity
was undermined. Physiological studies revealing hemispheric asymmetries for many tasks in young children provided further contradictions to
the concept of equipotentiality (Witelson, 1977).

Proponents of plasticity frequently relied upon Basser's (1962)
clinical observations of 102 hemiplegics. Basser reported that, following
left or right hemispherectomies, "speech was developed and maintained
in the intact hemisphere and in this respect the left and right hemispheres
were equipotential" (p. 451). However, Robinson (1981) has pointed out
that the majority of Basser's subjects were either retarded or uncoopera-
tive and untestable. Robinson concluded that "careful reading of his findings in the 30 children whose hemiplegia occurred *after the onset of
speech* does show that those having a right hemiplegia had a greater
impairment in language than those with a left hemiplegia. . ." (p. 380,
italics added). Kiessling, Denckla, and Carlton (1983) evaluated language
outcome in right and left hemiplegic children who had onset of hemiplegia in the pre- or perinatal period. The right hemiplegic group performed poorly on tasks requiring higher-level syntactic awareness and
repetition of semantically coherent materials. Dennis and Whitaker's
studies (1975, 1976) of hemispherectomized infants also indicated that
subjects with left hemispherectomies had residual deficits in processing
linguistic information, especially when it was conveyed by syntactic
conventions.

From these reports, the impression is formed that the left hemisphere
has a special role in mediating certain language functions from birth onward. However, lesions in the right hemisphere of very young infants may
cause residual language problems, and left hemisphere lesions in very
young children do not preclude language development. It should be
pointed out, however, that subtle linguistic deficits may persist in such
cases even when the onset occurs very early (Alajouanine & L'Hermitte,
1965; Woods & Carey, 1979). Vargha-Khadem, O'Gorman, and Watters
(1983) compared the residual effects of left versus right hemisphere lesions acquired at different ages (prenatal, birth to 5 years, and 5 to 14
years). They found no significant deficits in their language measures from

the right hemisphere group, but they did find a significant age effect among subjects in the left hemisphere group. Children who incurred damage later in life presented more severe residual deficits than children who sustained early damage. Yet, even in those cases of prenatal left hemisphere lesions, subtle linguistic deficits persisted.

The collective impression from reports such as those reviewed here is that a modified form of plasticity may apply to the developing neurolinguistic system. Although it appears that the left hemisphere has a special function in language processing from birth, the right hemisphere also is capable of linguistic processing, albeit not as efficiently. With development, the left hemisphere becomes more dominant in the control of linguistic functions. Given these observations, a better understanding of developmental neurolinguistic functions will require information regarding the role of the right hemisphere in language processing and the development of subsystems within the left hemisphere to process different types of language tasks.

Contributions of the Right Hemisphere

Studies with adults have demonstrated a significant contribution from the right hemisphere (RH) to language processing. Zaidel (1979, 1985) reviewed data from split-brain and lesion cases and summarized many of the linguistic capabilities of the right hemisphere. In adults, the RH has substantial semantic comprehension abilities. Notably, it possesses a rich lexical knowledge. The RH also has the ability for auditory discrimination, though this skill deteriorates in noise. This pattern may represent an extention of lexical identification. The RH also has the ability to perform rudimentary syntactic analyses. This ability is limited by increases in the length (limited auditory-verbal short-term memory) and syntactic complexity of verbal stimuli. Zaidel's conclusions indicated that the RH contributes to the semantic analysis of language but has little skill for syntactic or phonological aspects.

Zaidel (1985) pointed out that the adult RH has the linguistic ability of a child between 3 and 6 years of age. This finding was taken to suggest that the RH is highly active in language acquisition up to this point in time but that the left hemisphere becomes more dominant thereafter. Considering the normal progression of language development, this *apparent shift in hemispheric "dominance" may be a phenomenon of the demands of a maturing linguistic system in cooperation with specific neurological growth or change.* As the child enters the stage of grammatical expansion, analytic and sequential processing demands of language increase dramatically. Apparently, the left hemisphere is better suited to perform the types of processing required by more complex grammatic language.

Additional language or paralanguage functions of the RH include pragmatic aspects of language and prosodic abilities. Foldi, Cicone, and Gardner (1983) reported that the adult with RH damage has reduced abilities for nonliteral interpretation and reduced ability to comprehend narratives. In essence, the RH-damaged patient has adequate linguistic interpretation but cannot use contextual information to extract indirect meanings from communications. These investigators suggested that the RH is important for the integration of cues to form a single concept (gestalt). Production and comprehension of prosodic features also are associated with RH functioning. Ross (1981) described dysprosodias susequent to RH damage in a manner similar to descriptions of aphasias resulting from LH damage. Although there has been little systematic assessment of prosodic abilities in children, Voeller (1986) has observed prosodic deviations in 9 of 15 children who had sustained RH damage.

This brief summary of RH language functions suggests that the right hemisphere may have an active role in language acquisition and subsequent language use. The semantic and prosodic abilities of the young infant seem to parallel processing properties designated to the right hemisphere. However, this observation raises questions of early left hemisphere functions and potential developmental interactions between the two hemispheres. Most present knowledge of left hemisphere neurolinguistic function comes from studies of adults who present language impairment subsequent to hemispheric damage.

Left Hemisphere Contributions—Neurolinguistic Subsystems

In adult patients, lesions to different areas of the left hemisphere (LH) are known to result in differential impairment to language processes. A simple method of classifying lesion effects on language is with reference to comprehension, expression, and repetition functions. For example, lesions involving lateral frontal-parietal cortex typically result in a marked reduction in expressive abilities with a less severe reduction in comprehension (Broca aphasia). Damage to posterior temporal cortex typically devastates auditory comprehension but does not interfere with the motoric aspects of speech production (Wernicke aphasia). Lesions that spare perisylvian cortex also spare repetition skills (transcortical aphasias). Whitaker (1971) has formalized observations in this respect into a neurolinguistic representation of the Central Language System. Syntactic/phonological skills are subserved via Broca's area, the arcuate fasciculus, and the anterior portion of Wernicke's area. Semantic functions are subserved by posterior Wernicke's area and portions of the posterior temporal and inferior parietal lobes. Lexical abilities are diffuse without a specific anatomic "home." However, work by Cappa, Cavotti, and Vignolo (1981) has suggested the presence of a lexical-semantic area in posterior temporal-parietal cortex.

In addition to the traditional cortical representations of adult language functions, recent investigations have highlighted subcortical influences. Damage to the thalamus (Mohr, Watters, & Duncan, 1975) and the capsular/striatal system (Naeser et al., 1982) has been shown to produce dysphasias in adults that parallel, but have characteristics distinct from, cortical dysphasia. Although the linguistic significance of these cortical and subcortical mechanisms is not completely understood, they do contribute toward a framework from which to study neurolinguistic functions in adults.

Unfortnuately, language symptoms reported in children with acquired aphasia do not fit a predictable model like those of their adult counterparts. This observation may be due, in part, to the lack of a specific neurolinguistic assessment perspective in those studies that have evaluated children with acquired aphasia. Reports of childhood aphasia typically depict language symptoms as initial muteness followed by nonfluent, telegraphic speech with relatively spared comprehension. There are few reports of posterior LH language symptoms such as paraphasias, fluent speech, and reduced auditory comprehension (Satz & Bullard-Bates, 1981). If auditory comprehension is impaired, it is typically transient (e.g., Hecaen, 1976), or present in children above 9 or 10 years of age (VanDongen, Loonen, & VanDongen, 1985). These reported patterns of linguistic impairment in childhood-acquired aphasia apparently are not helpful in proposing an LH subsystems model of neurolinguistic functions for children.

There is a separate, larger group of language-impaired children, however, who do present different profiles of linguistic impairment at an early age. Examination of subtypes of development language disorder (DLD) may be useful in formulating developmental neurolinguistic subsystems of the LH. Many investigators have proposed different subtypes of DLD from various theoretical positions. A major stumbling block to cross-study interpretation is that different investigators have used different populations and different test protocols to classify subgroups of DLD children. Yet there are often commonalities in the resultant subgroups. For example, Aram and Nation (1975) used standardized clinical tests to examine formulation (expression), repetition, and comprehension of phonological, syntactic, and semantic aspects of language functions. They identified six subgroups of children representing varying combinations of abilities and deficits for the selected tasks. Rapin and Allen (1983) grouped children on the basis of clinical observation, longitudinal results of observation, and clinical testing into seven subgroups. Their criteria for grouping were based upon observations of children's expressive language, interactive behavior, and apparent comprehension. Despite dramatic differences in the techniques of evaluation and data analysis, these two studies did report commonalities in some of their subgroups. There appear to exist robust subgroups of DLD children with impaired phonological and syntactic abilities, but spared comprehension of spoken language. Also, there are children who present a more global deficit of language functions involving both comprehension and expression of all language functions. A somewhat different perspective has been offered by Denckla (1981), who studied language impairment in learning-disabled children. Denckla found six subgroups of language impairment on the basis of evaluation of vocabulary, digit span, memory, and naming tasks. Some of these subtypes were topographically similar to those identified by Aram and Nation (1975). Global impairments were noted as well as more selective impairments of naming, repetition, and comprehension. Also, both of these studies identified a subgroup of language-impaired children with spared repetition ability.

Differences in subject selection, tests employed, and method of data analysis preclude direct comparison of most studies. However, it is important to note two facts. First, despite methodological differences, various studies have identified similar profiles of language impairment in subgroups of DLD children. Second, collectively, the various studies indicate a range of possible language-impairment profiles that approximates that seen in adult aphasia. This observation implicates the presence of developing neurolinguistic subsystems in children who have reached the stage of grammatical expansion. Available information appears to support this implication. Frisch and Handler (1974) compared neuropsychological profiles (Reitan-Indiana) among normal children and two groups of language-impaired children. One of their language-impaired subgroups presented profiles similar to those of adults with LH post-Rolandic lesions. The clinical language profiles of these children would be similar to what Rapin and Allen (1983) call their "phonologic-syntactic syndrome." Such reports support the existence of LH neurolinguistic subsystems in children and suggest that once children reach the stage of grammatic expansion they have the basic components of adult neurolinguistic subsystems. Subsequent neurolinguistic development may be a function of neurological maturation of these subsystems, permitting the gradual increase in grammatical performance that is observed in the child from 2 years onward. If this proves to be a valid assumption, then developmental neurolinguistic assessment during this time must incorporate considerations for the comprehension, repetition, and expression of phonological, syntactic, and semantic aspects of language.

LANGUAGE ASSESSMENT AT PRESENT—WHAT'S COVERED, WHAT'S NOT?

The first step in language assessment is to determine what the goal of the evaluation is to be. Many assessment measures are descriptive in nature and designed to assess the performance level of an individual compared with standardized performance data. If the assessment goal is to portray language strengths/deficits as part of a more global profile, then standardized developmental protocols should be employed. If, on the other hand, a major purpose of the assessment is to identify specific areas of skill or impairment to be addressed in a treatment program, then standardized batteries only begin the task. The practitioner subsequently must employ more qualitative protocols/strategies in order to identify specific intervention targets. A complete assessment battery should include both quantitative and qualitative evaluation. In the following pages a preliminary description is provided for how currently available clinical protocols may be utilized in a developmental neurolinguistic assessment approach.

In evaluating proposed developmental neurolinguistic abilities, both the functions and the content of language must be assessed. The following review of currently available protocols is not meant to be exhaustive. Rather, the intent is to present a representation of what is or is not readily available to assess various language functions and content from a neurolinguistic perspective. Obviously, assessment of prelinguistic communicative functions cannot be approached in the same manner as linguistic abilities. As such, only brief commentary on prelinguistic assessment is warranted.

Prelinguistic Assessment (0 to 12+ Months)

Communicative assessment of the prelinguistic child (both reflexive and intentional) typically is accomplished through application of so-called readiness scales (Thorum, 1981). These may include both parent interview and direct observation of infant behaviors in a variety of low-structure playlike situations. Such scales typically address a range of developmental skill areas, including motor, self-help, emotional, cognitive, and communicative. The general goal of such instruments is to identify global developmental delays or, in the older infant, to assess specific cognitive or language-readiness skills that are thought to be important for subsequent growth in communicative ability. Examples of these scales include the Receptive-Expressive Emergent Language Scale (Bzoch & League, 1971) and the Denver Developmental Screening Test (Frankenburg, Dodds, Fandal, Kazuk, & Cohrs, 1975). Specific communicative functions in the young child may be described using observational guidelines such as those published by Bates (1975) and Halliday (1975). There are few procedures designed to assess specific neurolinguistic functions. However, available research suggests directions for development of new procedures. Given the early maturational lead of the right hemisphere, such protocols may do well to address early communicative functions associated with right hemisphere attributes. For example, face- and voice-recognition procedures, and procedures for evaluating perception and possibly imitation of simple prosodic features, may be of benefit in generating specific neurolinguistic predictions regarding the child's developing linguistic system. These assessments would be most applicable to the child who has reached the intentional stage of language development. By using the global developmental surveys to sample a range of developing behaviors, and with subsequent focus on specific communicative functions (possibly RH in nature), practitioners may find increased ability to predict impending linguistic impairment in the prelinguistic infant.

Lexical Expansion Assessment (12 to 24+ Months)

As the title of this stage implies, assessment of children in this developmental range (12–24 months) should address semantic growth and impending phonological development. As with the earlier stage, there are no standardized tests of language abilities for this young age range. In this respect, many of the readiness scales used for the prelinguistic child also are employed here. Since children in the lexical expansion stage are expected to demonstrate emerging verbal skills, nonverbal scales of language readiness will address only a portion of developing skills in these children. However, several mutlidimensional inventories of early language are available that "sample" a variety of receptive and expressive language functions. Typically, these focus upon early aspects of social communication. The goal of these protocols typically is to arrive at a developmental performance level for receptive versus expressive language functions.

At this stage of growth, it is suspected that the right hemisphere may be actively involved in language processing. As such, an evaluation from a neurolinguistic perspective should include detailed assessment of semantic knowledge, pragmatic functions, and prosodic recognition and production (possibly for both affective and linguistic prosody). Semantic knowledge may be evaluated informally by observing the child's use of single words or word combinations to express concepts. There are no standard estimates of semantic knowledge; however, repeated evaluations will provide the practitioner with information regarding growth in vocabulary and the child's acquisition of semantic features. As word combinations emerge, calculations of the average utterance length and vocabulary growth estimation will provide useful information regarding semantic growth. Pragmatic functions also may be evaluated by observing how the child uses verbal language to manipulate the environment (e.g., requesting, commenting, directing). Although no standard assessments exist in this respect, several authors have proposed formal assessments of pragmatic functions of language (e.g., Bates, 1975; Halliday, 1975). Assessment of prosodic abilities also would seem to be an important aspect of the lexical expansion stage. Menyuk and Bernholtz (1969) reported that children near the end of this stage used prosodic information to signal grammatical distinctions in expressive language. Also, there has been speculation that "normal" prosodic abilities in this age range are extremely important to subsequent grammatical growth (Crystal 1979; Shadden, Asp, Tonkovich, & Mason, 1980). However, there are no formal assessment approaches for prosodic recognition or production at this stage of development. Practitioners may be able to infer information regarding prosodic abilities by evaluating how the child responds to different affective voices (happy, sad, angry) or by using linguistic prosody to signal grammatical distinctions (questions, emphasis).

Another aspect of linguistic growth is the rapid expansion of phonological abilities that occurs near the end of the stage of lexical expansion. Although the child's sound inventory begins to expand during this time, the majority of phonological growth coincides with syntactic development during the stage of grammatic expansion.

Grammatical Expansion Assessment (2 to 4+ years)

The stage of grammatic expansion is marked by dramatic increases in phonology and syntax along with continuing growth in semantic, pragmatic, and prosodic abilities. As mentioned previously, a multitude of tests and procedures are available for evaluation of phonological and syntactic abilities. Semantic abilities in this stage are assessed primarily in association with syntactic skills (it is difficult if not impossible to separate these two aspects) and/or with reference to word knowledge and word use. Given the rapid growth in verbal language skills during this period, the practitioner also is confronted with consideration of paralanguage variables that may influence a child's performance on linguistic tasks. Major focus is given to motor, memory, and attending abilities. The growth of grammatical functions is believed to signal the emergence of the left hemisphere as the "dominant" language hemisphere. Within the left hemisphere there appear to be functional subsystems serving the comprehension, expression (formulation), and repetition of the language content areas. From available knowledge, naming functions appear to be bihemispheric, or at least not localized to a specific area.

Comprehension of Spoken Language

As discussed earlier, both the right and left hemispheres have the ability to comprehend basic linguistic information. The RH, however, is not as sophisticated as the LH, being limited by constraints on short-term memory and specific grammatical knowledge. From this perspective, we would expect that overreliance on RH comprehension strategies and/or deficient LH comprehension abilities would result in language comprehension abilities that differ significantly from those of the normal child. In this respect, it would be necessary to compare a child's comprehension of different language content areas. There are a variety of standardized procedures that permit such comparison. For example, the Test for Auditory Comprehension of Language-Revised (Carrow, 1985) contains three subtests addressing word classes and relationships, grammatical morphemes, and elaborated sentences. It also is possible to evaluate comprehension of various language content areas by using combinations of tests and/or subtests from different protocols. For example, word knowledge might be assessed by the Peabody Picture Vocabulary Test-Revised (Dunn & Dunn, 1981), knowledge of semantic relations might be assessed by the Processing Word Classes Subtests of the Clinical Evaluation of Language Functions (Semel & Wiig, 1980), comprehension of specific syntactic structures might be assessed by the receptive portion of the Northwestern Syntax Screening Test (Lee, 1971), and comprehension of spoken instructions with increasing length and complexity might be assessed by the Token Test for Children (DiSimoni, 1978). The important issue to address is that the comprehension of spoken language may be differentially impaired across language content areas. It is this pattern of differential impairment that permits the practitioner to begin building an explanatory profile of specific neurolinguistic impairment. The assessment strategy is to employ standardized performance tests to ascertain the extent of comprehension deficit, and subsequently to evaluate multiple content areas to delineate the pattern of deficits.

Language Expression/Formulation

Expressive language functions would appear to be predominately within the domain of the left hemisphere, even in the young child. As discussed before, children with expressive language deficits in the presence of relatively good comprehension typically present with both phonological and syntactic deficits. Again, there are multiple clinical procedures available to assess these language areas. Standardized phonological assessments typically follow a developmental sound acquisition orientation, and test for the production of various speech sounds in different positions within a word. Examples of common speech-articulation tests include the Templin-Darley Tests of Articulation (Templin & Darley, 1969) and the Goldman-Fristoe Test of Articulation (Goldman & Fristoe, 1969). Recent application of linguistic theory has emphasized a rule-governed or pattern analysis over the more traditional one-sound-at-a-time approach. Although no standardized protocols exist for these analyses, formal descriptive procedures are available (e.g., Hodson, 1980; Shriberg & Kwiatkowski, 1980). Using both of these approaches permits the practitioner to establish a developmental performance level for phonological ability and to describe major error patterns.

There are numerous procedures available for the evaluation of syntactic formulation. Specific grammatical morphemes are evaluated in procedures such as the Grammatic Closure Subtest of the Illinois Test of Psycholinguistic Abilities (Kirk, McCarthy, & Kirk, 1968) and the Grammatic Completion Subtest of the Test of Language Development (Hammill & Newcomer, 1982). Sentence-formulation skills are assessed in a variety of methods by different protocols. The expressive portion of the Northwestern Syntax Screening Test (Lee, 1971) evaluates syntactic constructions of increasing complexity in a delayed imitation format. The Producing Model Sentences Subtest of the Clinical Evaluation of Language Functions (Semel & Wiig, 1980) provides the child with a stimulus word to be used in a sentence generated by the child. The Carrow Elicited Language Inventory (Carrow, 1974) requires the child to imitate 52 model utterances. Each of these procedures is an example of a performance level assessment of syntactic formulation abilities. Beyond this quantitative analysis, it might be beneficial to evaluate specific syntactic structures used or misused by a particular child. A variety of formal descriptive approaches are available. Miller's (1981) Simple Sentence Analysis provides a format for the analysis of syntactic structure used by children in a conversational sample. Lee (1974) presented an attempt at quantifying a descriptive analysis of conversational language samples in her Developmental Sentence Scoring Procedure. A short and simple way to estimate the grammatical complexity of an utterance is the calculation of mean length of utterances (e.g., R. Brown, 1973).

The collective utilization of procedures evaluating different content areas of language expression from both a performance level and a descriptive perspective will facilitate a more complete depiction of any expressive language deficits noted in the child. As is the case with comprehension, it may be that the pattern of phonological and/or syntactic errors has relevance to a neurolinguistic explanation of language deficits. Unfortunately, this is a poorly investigated area of developmental language impairment in children.

Repetition

Although many clinical protocols use repetition in one way or another, the significance of strengths or deficits in this communicative function has not been explained fully. It would be tempting, for example, to speculate that those children studied by Aram and Nation (1975) or Denckla (1981) who demonstrated good repetition skills represented a developmental transcortical neurolinguistic impairment. However, such an assumption would be highly speculative. Use of repetition tasks has been criticized from the perspective that such tasks overestimate (Maratsos & Kuczaj, 1974; Smith, 1970) or underestimate (Prutting, Gallagher, & Mulac, 1975) language knowledge. It is possible that comparison of language content areas expressed in repetition versus conversation may be a differentiating factor in identifying operational neurolinguistic subsystems in the child in the same way that this comparison is applied to adults with acquired language deficits.

Naming

In both the child and the adult, naming is probably a bihemispheric linguistic task. Thus, the identification of quantitative deficits on naming tasks such as the Boston Naming Test (Kaplan, Goodglass, & Weintraub, 1983) or the Expressive One-Word Vocabulary Test (M. F. Gardner, 1979) may not be useful in differentiating neurolinguistic deficits. Differential patterns of naming impairment across tasks may be more informative in identifying a pattern of selective neurolinguistic deficits.

Pragmatic Language Functions

The child's use of language functions in the social environment may provide an indication of right hemisphere contributions to language deficits. However, the evaluation of pragmatic functions is a relatively recent focus of linguistic assessment in children, and few or no formal protocols exist. Some authors (e.g., Thorum, 1981) consider the use of existing behavioral scales that contain social and interpersonal measures (i.e., Adaptive Behavior Scales, Nihira, Foster, Shelhas, & Leland, 1974). In combination with assessment of other pragmatic functions, such as the ability to extract inferential meanings, social irregularities may have important diagnostic indications for neurolinguistic assessment. Wiig (Wiig, 1982a, 1982b; Wiig & Bray, 1983) has developed a series of checklists for evaluating pragmatic language functions in children 3 years of age and up. For younger children, observation of verbal interactions in a natural setting is recommended. For older children, elicited tasks are employed. Though useful, such checklists focus primarily upon social communicative skills, with little emphasis on other RH pragmatic functions (e.g., indirect meaning, narrative interpretation). Perhaps, as more developmental information regarding pragmatic function/dysfunction is available, more diverse and systematic assessment protocols will emerge.

Prosody

Assessment of prosodic abilities is an additional area that has received limited attention in child populations. The Seashore Tests of Musical Ability (Seashore, Lewis, & Saetveit, 1960) evaluates the perception/discrimination of multiple prosodic features. This procedure is, however, designed for children 9 years of age or older. There has been recent clinical research with younger speech-language-impaired children demonstrating deficits in production of prosodic features. Crary and Tallman (1985) found that children with severe phonological disorders, considered to represent verbal dyspraxia, produced prosodic patterns similar to adults with speech dyspraxia secondary to LH damage. The recent increase in prosodic studies with adult patients (Ross, 1981) may provide neurolinguistic models and subsequent assessment procedures that will make it possible to study prosodic abilities in language-impaired children systematically.

Paralanguage Measures

Three paralanguage areas that may affect a child's performance on language tasks include motor ability, memory, and attending skill. Motor speech ability may affect growth in the child's phonological system. Motor speech performance may be assessed by visual inspection of the speech mechanism and by tests of oral-facial praxis and speech diadochokinesis. There is no formal protocol for assessing facial praxis in the child. Most practitioners use modifications of procedures recommended for adult patients. Motor speech abilities are typically assessed with speech diadochokinetic tasks. In this regard, Fletcher (1978) has published performance data from 6 years to 13 years, and Riley (Riley & Riley, 1985) has provided limited normative data down to 4 years of age.

The child with reduced short-term memory ability may present impaired repetition functions as well as deficient performance in other language areas. There are several memory assessment procedures available. For example, subtests of the Detroit Test of Learning Aptitude (Hammill, 1985) evaluate auditory retention of unrelated words and oral directions. In addition, digit span memory may be assessed using the appropriate subtest from the Illinois Test of Psycholinguistic Ability (Kirk, *et al.*, 1968).

Impaired attending ability has been postulated to contribute to reduced comprehension performance in certain brain-damaged language-impaired children (Campbell & McNeil, 1985). Yet mechanisms of attention, their clinical assessment, and their potential contributions to apparent language dysfunction have received limited investigation. Aside from skilled observations regarding a child's attending ability, there are few available tests that attempt to estimate the potential influence of attention deficits on language performance. Two procedures that evaluate aspects of "auditory attention" are the Goldman-Fristoe-Woodcock Selective Attention Test (Goldman, Fristoe, & Woodcock, 1974) and the Flowers-Costello Tests of Central Auditory Abilities (Flowers, Costello, & Small, 1970). Additional aspects of attention such as concentration or sustained attention may be inferred from tasks such as digit span (forward and backward) or other counting and spelling tasks (e.g., Lezak, 1983). Cancellation tasks, visual closure tasks, and selected subtests from the Wechsler Intelligence Scale for Children-Revised (Arithmetic, Coding, Mazes) also have been suggested for the evaluation of concentration (Gardner, 1979). Gardner (1979) further describes tasks of auditory or visual vigilance (sustained attention) that might be useful for evaluation of attention in language-impaired children. Barkley (Chapter 6, this volume) provides a superb overview of the assessment of attention in children.

Summary of Present Assessment Capabilities

Our brief review identified examples of available protocols or strategies for evaluating language functions for the three general stages of development. An attempt also was made to identify the gaps in available clinical assessment protocols. At present, there is no battery of tests that has been developed or organized from a developmental neurolinguistic perspective. However, it is possible to form testable inferences about neurolinguistic functions in language-impaired children through the use of currently available protocols supplemented with specific clinical observations and "qualitative" assessment. A basic approach to assessment of the language-impaired child should include use of standardized performance tests supplemented by more descriptive procedures, particularly in identified deficit areas. It is important not only to profile basic language functions (comprehension, formulation, repetition, naming) but also to profile abilities in various language content areas (phonology, syntax, semantics, pragmatics). There are multiple clinical procedures available for children across the developmental span in most aspects of language assessment. However, significant gaps exist in the systematic assessment of pragmatic and prosodic functions. Because these communicative aspects may rely heavily upon right hemisphere functions, it would seem important to pursue clinical research leading to the development of valid assessment protocols in these areas. Finally, in addition to a basic communication assessment, it would be valuable to consider a variety of paralanguage factors such as motor, memory, and attention abilities, that may influence a child's linguistic performance.

GUIDELINES AND QUESTIONS REGARDING DEVELOPMENTAL NEUROLINGUISTIC ASSESSMENT

In designing a neurolinguistic assessment approach, considerations must be given not only to language functions (e.g., comprehension, naming) but also to language content (e.g., syntax, morphology, pragmatics).

Additionally, procedures evaluating paralanguage factors must be included (e.g., motor speech, attending, memory). A simplified summation of these factors is presented in Table 1. With a few notable exceptions there are multiple clinical procedures available for evaluating these factors in the developing child. However, considerable diversity in the theoretical basis, method of assessment, test construction, and scoring procedures has been noted for tests within the same function/content area and age range (Thorum, 1981). In addition, various psychometric concerns have been expressed for many protocols, including lack of reported predictive validity, interexaminer reliability, and test-retest reliability (McCauley & Swisher, 1984; Wiig & Semel, 1984). Finally, most available procedures test a specific language function, such as naming or auditory comprehension. The few "batteries" that are available measure an array of content and functions; however, the theoretical basis of measurement may change from one task to the next (Spekman & Roth, 1984).

The fact that no developmental neurolinguistic assessment protocol exists at present does not imply that such an approach to language assessment in children cannot be developed. Rather, the absence of this approach to language assessment appears to be the result of gaps in knowledge and unanswered questions. In this chapter, consistencies between language development and neurological maturation have been discussed. Further, an attempt was made to explain growth in language functions with reference to the roles of the respective cerebral hemispheres and the development of subsystems within the left hemisphere. Table 2 presents a summary model of neurolinguistic development. Although this model is admittedly incomplete in its explanation of neurolinguistic functions, it does permit a systematic approach to questions that must be addressed in

TABLE 1. Summary of Language Functions, Language Content Areas, and Paralanguage Performance Factors

Language functions	Language content	Paralanguage performance factors
Comprehension	Pragmatics	Motor speech Dysarthria Dyspraxia
Expression (formulation)	Semantics	
Repetition	Syntax	Memory functions
Naming	Morphology	Attending abilities
Speech production and → prosody	{ Phonology } { Phonetics }	

TABLE 2. Depiction of Preliminary Model of Developmental Neurolinguistic Functions

Age range	Anatomic subsystem	Hemispheric relations	Language stage	Language mode	Representative skills
0–8 months	Primary projection (sensory and motor)	Primarily subcortical control and/or diffuse cortical systems	Prelinguistic	Reflexive (preintent)	1. S→R crying and cooing 2. Voice and face recognition 3. Prosodic recognition and limitation
8–12 months	Primary projection Growth in corpus callosum Growth in projection association system	Right > left	Prelinguistic	Intent	1. Increased intentional communication (pragmatics) 2. Onset of first words
1–2 years	Projection-association	Right > left or Right = left	Lexical	Semantic (gestalt)	1. Increased vocabulary 2. Preliminary phonological development 3. Initial word combinations
2–4+ years	Association-association	Left > right	Grammatic	Sequential/analytic	1. Phonological growth 2. Syntactic growth 3. Continued growth in all language areas

developing a more comprehensive model and subsequent clinical approaches.

Areas that must be addressed in subsequent research include the consideration of normal aspects of language development, evaluation of neurological dysfunction as it may relate to specific linguistic impairment, and the development of valid clinical neurolinguistic assessment strategies. With respect to normal aspects of language development, there are obvious questions regarding relationships between structure and function at various points along the developmental continuum. Peters (1977, 1983) has asserted that different language-processing strategies can be identified both within and across normal children. Furthermore, she points out that children with language-learning difficulties may differ from normal children in the repertoire of strategies useful to them. For example, Weeks (1974) described a child who had limited strategies for learning language but who was adept at using other learning strategies in compensation of language limitations. These observations raise questions pertaining to the issues surrounding neurological maturation and plasticity. As was pointed out, the hierarchical and holistic views on cortical maturation appear to reach similar ends in the development of functional subsystems. However, the learning strategies available to the child prior to the functional activation of these subsystems would be expected to vary according to specific aspects of neurological maturation. Also, disruption of the anticipated pattern of maturation at various points in development may lead to different compensatory processes available to the child. To address these issues adequately, focus must be given to the processes of language development in relation to neurological maturation. Unfortunately, a great deal of the work currently available addresses product and not process.

In evaluating potential relationships between structure and function in the developing central nervous system, it will be mandatory to have accurate descriptions of structural alterations in those individuals with language impairments. However, until recently, studies of acquired aphasia in children referenced hemispheric involvement by physical symptoms (i.e., right or left hemiplegia). There are several limitations to those studies lacking adequate control for describing areas of brain damage. For example, if the brain injury has occurred pre- or perinatally, diffuse damage secondary to hypoxia is likely. Also, at any age, it will be difficult to control for the possibility of bihemispheric lesions without objective measurement procedures. Delineation of the extent and location of any lesion will require at least application of one of the imaging techniques currently available. Studies that undertake longitudinal evaluation of children with identified brain lesions will be invaluable in defining developing neurolinguistic systems.

Related to the issue of lesion localization is the issue of cortical versus subcortical lesions. Knowledge of the differential effects of these lesions at different points in development would help to clarify the respective roles of cortical versus subcortical systems in language acquisition. It is known that specific subcortical lesions may result in more severe functional impairments than cortical lesions in the young macaque. Also, language impairments subsequent to subcortical lesions have been reported in adults (Naeser *et al.*, 1982). Aram, Rose, Rekate, and Whitaker (1983) have reported two instances of aphasia in older children secondary to capsular/striatal lesions. Aside from these reports, little is known of the potential roles of subcortical mechanisms in language development and disorders.

The development of valid developmental neurolinguistic assessment tools must be an outgrowth of future advances in the aforementioned areas. Most language assessment protocols currently available are oriented toward a developmental level approach. In general, these protocols describe the end result (product) of language processes, but they do not address the processes themselves. Some protocols incorporate tasks from a particular psycholinguistic perspective. However, it is often unclear how the various tasks fit into the specified model or whether the model has useful clinical application. Practitioners attempting a neurolinguistic interpretation from the results of currently available protocols will find a combination of quantitive and qualitative procedures useful in formulating testable clinical hypotheses. Yet significant gaps in areas such as prosodic and pragmatic functions in combination with the traditional focus on product rather than process will limit the ability to make specific conclusions regarding neurolinguistic abilities. To fill these gaps, researchers and clinicians will have to address normal aspects of paralanguage functions as they influence language performance in the developing child. Protocols that attempt to identify underlying processing strategies used by children of different ages also will be helpful. Such research must incorporate large numbers of children and be longitudinal, not cross-sectional. Resulting explanations must be dynamic and multidimensional to account for potential variability in the interaction among developing cognitive processes (e.g., Bates, 1979).

A Concluding Example

Crary (1984) has attempted an initial neurolinguistic interpretation of one group of developmental communication deficits. In evaluating relationships between motor and speech-language limitations, he has proposed a continuum of impairments under the label of developmental verbal dyspraxia. Children with more "executive" dysfunctions would present difficulties in most motor and speech tasks, whereas children with deficits more toward the "planning" end of the continuum would present difficulties in sequential activity with relatively spared executive functions. The proposed neurolinguistic basis for this deficit involves subsystems of the left hemisphere with dysfunction in either frontotemporal regions, temporoparietal regions, or both. Though this position has not been substantiated unequivocally, preliminary supportive evidence has been generated.

The language profiles of these children demonstrated strengths in semantic processing in both comprehension and expression tasks, but pronounced deficits in phonology and syntax. This observation led to the hypothesis that such children are functioning primarily in the lexical stage of language development with better gestalt/simultaneous than analytic/sequential abilities. In evaluating motor ability, an experimental test of facial mimicry revealed deficits associated with the sequential complexity of the task. To evaluate the hypothesis that sequential processing was impaired, six children were administered the Kaufman Assessment Battery for Children (Kaufman & Kaufman, 1983). This procedure compares performance on tasks designed to assess simultaneous versus sequential processing skills. The mean scale score (Mean = 10, Standard Deviation = 3) for simultaneous subtests was 9.5 whereas that for sequential subtests was 8.2. This was not a great difference, but it was in the predicted direction. Four of these children underwent central auditory testing using dichotic procedures in an attempt to identify hemispheric asymmetries. Two children demonstrated a strong left ear advantage (potential left hemisphere deficit). The remaining two demonstrated right ear advantages; however, their scores for the right ear (left hemisphere) were outside of 2 standard deviations of expected normal performance.

Although these observations require replication with larger samples, they support our hypothesis that some children with developmental verbal dyspraxia have left hemisphere dysfunction specifically related to sequential aspects of information planning. These cases may represent children who are "stuck" between the lexical and grammatical stages of linguistic development. Work must continue to address this hypothesis and to formulate neurolinguistic arguments that might help to identify functioning or dysfunctioning subsystems that are limiting the development of the grammatical stage. It is obvious that linguistic assessment or neuropsychological assessment in isolation would be limited in reaching this goal. A collaboration of orientations is necessary.

REFERENCES

Alajouanine, T. H., & L'Hermitte, F. (1965). Acquired aphasia in children. Brain, 88, 635–662.
Alegria, J., & Noirot, E. (1978). Neonate orientation behavior towards the human voice. International Journal of Behavioral Development, 1, 291–312.

Altman, J. (1967). Postnatal growth and differentiation of the mammalian brain, with implications for a morphological theory of memory. In C. Quarton, T. Melnechuk, & F. Schmitt (Eds.), The neurosciences, New York: Rockefeller University Press.

Aram, D. M., & Nation, J. E. (1975). Patterns of language behavior in children with developmental language disorders. Journal of Speech and Hearing Research, 18, 229–241.

Aram, D. M., Rose, D. F., Rekate, H. L., & Whitaker, H. A. (1983). Acquired capsular/striatal aphasia in childhood. Archives of Neurology, 40, 614–617.

Basser, L. S. (1962). Hemiplegia of early onset and the faculty of speech with special reference to the effects of hemispherectomy. Brain, 85, 427–460.

Bates, E. (1975). Acquisition of performatives prior to speech. Merrill-Palmer Quarterly, 21, 205–226.

Bates, E. (1979). The biology of symbols: Some concluding thoughts. In E. Bates, L. Benigni, I. Bretherton, L. Camaioni, & V. Volterra (Eds.), The emergence of symbols: Cognition and communication in infancy. New York: Academic Press.

Bates, E., Benigni, L., Bretherton, I., Camaioni, L., & Volterra, V. (1979). The emergence of symbols: Cognition and communication in infancy. New York: Academic Press.

Bloom, L. (1973). One word at a time: The use of single-word utterances before syntax. The Hague: Mouton.

Brown, J. W. (1979). Language representation in the brain. In H. D. Steklis & M. J. Raliegh (Eds.), Neurobiology of social communication in primates: An evolutionary perspective (pp. 133–195). New York: Academic Press.

Brown, R. (1973). A first language: The early stages. Cambridge: Harvard University Press.

Bzoch, K. R., & League, R. (1971). Receptive-expressive emergent language scale. Gainesville, FL: Tree of Life Press.

Campbell, T. F., & McNeil, M. R. (1985). Effects of presentation rate and divided attention on auditory comprehension in children with an acquired language disorder. Journal of Speech and Hearing Research, 28, 513–520.

Cappa, S., Cavotti, G., & Vignolo, L. A. (1981). Phonemic and lexical errors in fluent aphasia: Correlation with lesion site. Neuropsychologia, 19, 171–177.

Carrow, E. (1974). Carrow Elicited Language Inventory. Austin, TX: Learning Concepts.

Carrow, E. (1985). Test for Auditory Comprehension of Language-Revised. Boston: Teaching Resources.

Chi, J. D., Dooling, E. C., & Gilles, F. H. (1977). Left-right asymmetries of the temporal speech areas of the human fetus. Archives of Neurology, 34, 346–348.

Chomsky, C. (1969). The acquisition of syntax in children from 5 to 10. Cambridge, MA: M.I.T. Press.

Clark, E. V. (1973). What's in a word: On the child's acquisition of semantics in his first language. In T. Moore (Ed.), Cognitive development and the acquisition of language. New York: Academic Press.

Conel, J. L. (1939–1963). Postnatal development of the human cerebral cortex (Vols. 1–6). Cambridge: Harvard University Press.

Crary, M. A. (1984). A neurolinguistic perspective of developmental verbal dyspraxia. Communicative Disorders, 9, 33–49.

Crary, M. A., & Tallman, V. L. (1985, November). Production of propositional prosodic features by speech-language normal and speech-language disordered children. Paper presented at the American Speech-Language-Hearing Association Annual Convention, Washington, DC.

Crystal, D. (1979). Prosodic development. In P. Fletcher & M. Garman (Eds.), Language acquisition. Cambridge: Cambridge University Press.

Denckla, M. B. (1981). Minimal brain dysfunction and dyslexia: Beyond diagnosis by exclusion. In M. E. Blair, I. Rapin, & M. Kinsbourne (Eds.), Child neurology. New York: Spectrum.

Dennis, M., & Whitaker, H. (1975). Hemispheric equipotentiality and language acquisition.

In S. Segalowitz & F. Gruber (Eds.), *Language development and neurological theory.* New York: Academic Press.

Dennis, M., & Whitaker, H. A. (1976). Language acquisition following hemi-decortication: Linguistic superiority of the left over right hemisphere. *Brain and Language, 3,* 404–433.

DiSimoni, F. (1978). *The token test for children.* Hingham, MA: Teaching Resources.

Dunn, L. M., & Dunn, L. M. (1981). *Peabody Picture Vocabulary Test-Revised.* Circle Pines, MN: American Guidance Service.

Flechsig, P. (1901). Developmental (myelogenetic) localization of the cortex in human subjects. *Lancet, October,* 1027–1029.

Fletcher, S. G. (1978). *The Fletcher Time-by-Count Test of Diadochokinetic Syllable Rate.* Tigard, C. C. Publications.

Flowers, A., Costello, M., & Small, V. (1970). *Flowers-Costello Test of Central Auditory Abilities.* Dearborn, MI: Perceptual Learning Systems.

Foldi, N. S., Cicone, M., & Gardner, H. (1983). Pragmatic aspects of communication in brain-damaged patients. In S. J. Segalowitz (Ed.), *Language functions and brain organization* (pp. 51–86). New York: Academic Press.

Frankenburg, W. K., Dodds, J. B., Fandal, A. W., Kazuk, E., & Cohrs, M. (1975). *Denver Developmental Screening Test.* Denver: LADOCA Project & Publishing Foundation.

Frisch, G., & Handler, L. (1974). A neuropsychological investigation of functional disorders of speech articulation. *Journal of Speech and Hearing Research, 17,* 432–445.

Gardner, M. F. (1979). *The Expressive One-Word Vocabulary Test.* Novato, CA: Academic Therapy Publications.

Gardner, R. A. (1979). *The objective diagnosis of minimal brain dysfunction.* Cresskill, NJ: Creative Therapeutics.

Geschwind, N., & Levitsky, W. (1968). Human brain left-right asymmetries in temporal speech region. *Science, 161,* 186–187.

Goldman, P. S. (1971). Functional development of the prefrontal cortex in the infrahuman primate. In C. L. Ludlow & M. E. Doran-Quine (Eds.), *The neurological bases of language disorders in children: Methods and direction for research* (**NINCDS Monograph** (No 22, NIH Publication No. 79-440). Bethesda: U.S. Department of Health, Education and Welfare.

Goldman, R., & Fristoe, M. (1969). *Goldman-Fristoe Test of Articulation.* Circle Pines, MN: American Guidance Service.

Goldman, R., Fristoe, M., & Woodcock, R. (1974). *The Goldman-Fristoe-Woodcock Test of Auditory Discrimination.* Circle Pines, MN: American Guidance Service.

Halliday, M. A. K. (1975). *Learning how to mean: Explorations in the development of language.* London: Edward Arnold.

Hammill, D. D. (1985). *Detroit Tests of Learning Aptitude (DTLA-2).* Austin, TX: Pro-Ed.

Hammill, D. D., & Newcomer, P. L. (1982). *Test of Language Development.* Austin, TX: Pro-Ed.

Hecaen, H. (1976). Acquired aphasia in children and the ontogenesis of hemispheric functional specialization. *Brain and Language, 3,* 114–134.

Hodson, B. (1980). *The assessment of phonological processes.* Danville, IL: Interstate.

Huttenlocher, P. R. (1979). Synaptic density in human frontal cortex: Developmental changes and effects of aging. *Brain Research, 163,* 195–205.

Ingram, D. (1976). *Phonological disability in children.* New York: American Elsevier.

Jakobson, R. (1968). *Child language, aphasia and phonological universals.* The Hague: Mouton. (Original work published, 1941)

Kaplan, E., Goodglass, H., & Weintraub, S. (1983). *The Boston Naming Test.* Philadelphia: Lea & Febiger.

Kaufman, A. S., & Kaufman, N. L. (1983). *Kaufman Assessment Battery for Children.* Circle Pines, MN: American Guidance Service.

Kennard, M. A. (1938). Reorganization of motor function in the cerebral cortex of monkeys deprived of motor and premotor areas in infancy. *Journal of Neurophysiology, 1,* 477–496.

Kiessling. L. S., Denckla, M. B., & Carlton, M. (1983). Evidence for differential hemispheric function in children with hemiplegic cerebral palsy. *Developmental Medicine and Child Neurology, 25,* 727–734.

Kirk, S. A., McCarthy, J. J., & Kirk, W. D. (1968). *Illinois Test of Psycholinguistic Ability* (Rev. ed.). Urbana: University of Illinois Press.

Lee, L. L. (1971). *Northwestern Syntax Screening Test.* Evanston, IL: Northwestern University Press.

Lee, L. L. (1974). *Developmental sentence analysis.* Evanston, IL: Northwestern University Press.

Lenneberg, E. H. (1967). *Biological foundations of language.* New York: Wiley, M.I.T. Press.

Leopold, W. F. (1947). *Speech development of a billingual child: A linguists' record (Vol. 2). Sound learning in the first two years.* Evanston, IL: Northwestern University Press. (Reprinted by AMS press, New York, 1970)

Lezak, M. D. (1983). *Neuropsychological assessment* (2nd ed.). New York: Oxford University Press.

Lieberman, P. (1967). *Intonation, perception and language.* Cambridge, MA: M.I.T. Press.

Maratsos, M., & Kuczaj, S., (1974). Evidence from elicited imitation for productive competence in a grammatical system. *Papers and Reports of Child Language Development.* Palo Alto, CA: Stanford University.

McCauley, R. J., & Swisher, L. (1984). Psychometric review of language and articulation tests for preschool children. *Journal of Speech and Hearing Disorders, 49,* 34–42.

Menyuk, P., & Bernholts, N. (1969). Prosodic features and children's language. *Quarterly Progress Report of Research Laboratory of Electronics* (Vol. 93, pp. 216–219). Cambridge, MA: M.I.T. Press.

Miller, E. A., Goldman, P. S., & Rosvold, H. E. (1973). Delayed recovery of function following orbital prefrontal lesions in infant monkeys. *Science, 182,* 304–306.

Miller, J. (1981). *Assessing language production in children.* Baltimore: University Park Press.

Mohr, J., Watters, W., & Duncan, G. (1975). Thalamic hemorrhage and aphasia. *Brain and Language, 2,* 3–17.

Moskowitz, B. A. (1980). Idioms in phonology acquisition and phonological change. *Journal of Phonetics, 8,* 69–83.

Naeser, M., Alexander, M., Helm-Estabrooks, N., Levine, H., Laughlin, S., & Geschwind, N. (1982). Aphasia with predominantly subcortical lesion sites. *Archives of Neurology, 39,* 2–14.

Nelson, K. (1973). Structure and strategy in learning to talk. *Monographs of the Society for Research in Child Development, 38.*

Nihira, N., Foster, R., Shelhas, M., & Leland, H. (1974). *Adaptive behavior scales.* Washington, DC: American Association of Mental Deficiency.

Peters, A. M. (1977). Language learning strategies: Does the whole equal the sum of the parts? *Language, 53,* 560–573.

Peters, A. M. (1983). *The units of language acquisition.* Cambridge: Cambridge University Press.

Poliakov, G. I. (1961). Some results of research into the development of the neuronal structure of the cortical ends of the analyzers in man. *Journal of Comparative Neurology, 117,* 197.

Prutting, C., Gallagher, T., & Mulac, A. (1975). The expressive portion of the N.S.S.T. compared to a spontaneous language sample. *Journal of Speech and Hearing Disorders, 40,* 40–49.

Rakic, R., Bourgeois, J. P., Eckenhoff, M. R., Zecevic, N., & Goldman-Rakic, P. S. (1986).

Concurrent overproduction of synapses in diverse regions of the primate cerebral cortex. *Science, 232,* 232–235.

Rapin, I., & Allen, D. A. (1983). Developmental language disorders: Nosologic considerations. In U. Kirk (Ed.), *Neuropsychology of language, reading and spelling* (pp. 213–219). New York: Academic Press.

Riley, G., & Riley, J. (1985). *Oral motor assessment and treatment: Improving syllable production.* Tigard, C.C. Publications.

Robinson, R. O. (1981). Equal recovery in child and adult brain? *Developmental Medicine and Child Neurology. 23,* 379–383.

Ross, E. D., (1981). The aprosodias. *Archives of Neurology, 38,* 561–569.

Sander, E. K. (1972). When are speech sounds learned. *Journal of Speech and Hearing Disorders, 37,* 55–61.

Satz, P., & Bullard-Bates, C. (1981). Acquired aphasia in children. In M. T. Sarno (Ed.), *Acquired aphasia* (pp. 399–426). New York: Academic Press.

Seashore, C., Lewis, D., & Saetveit, J. (1960). *Seashore Measures of Musical Talents.* New York: Psychological Association.

Semel, E. M., & Wiig, E. H. (1980). *Clinical evaluation of language functions.* Columbus, OH: Charles E. Merrill.

Shadden, B. B., Asp, C. W., Tonkovich, I. D., & Mason, D. (1980). Imitation of suprasegmental patterns of five-year-old children with adequate and inadequate articulation. *Journal of Speech and Hearing Disorders, 45,* 390–400.

Shriberg, L., & Kwiatkowski, J. (1980). *Natural process analysis.* New York: Wiley.

Smith, C. S. (1970). An experimental approach to children's linguistic competence. In J. R. Hayes (Ed.), *Cognition and the development of language.* New York: Wiley.

Spekman, N., & Roth, F. (1984). Clinical Evaluation of Language Functions (CELF) Diagnostic Battery: An analysis and critique. *Journal of Speech and Hearing Disorders, 49,* 97–100.

Templin, M., & Darley, F. (1969). *Templin-Darley Tests of Articulation,* (2nd ed.). Iowa City: Bureau of Ed. Res. and Services, University of Iowa.

Thorum, A. R. (1981). *Language assessment instruments: Infancy through adulthood.* Springfield, IL: Charles C Thomas.

VanDongen, H. R., Loonen, M. C. B., VanDongen, K. J. (1985). Anatomical basis for acquired fluent aphasia in children. *Annals of Neurology, 17,* 306–309.

Vargha-Khadem, F., O'Gorman, A., & Watters, G. V. (1983, February). *Aphasia in children with prenatal versus postnatal left hemisphere lesions: A clinical and CT scan study.* Paper presented at the International Neuropsychological Society Annual Convention, Mexico City, Mexico.

Voeller, K. K. S., (1986). Right hemisphere deficit syndrome in children. *American Journal of Psychiatry, 143,* 1004–1009.

Weeks, T. (1974). *The slow speech development of a bright child.* Lexington, MA: D. C. Heath.

Whitaker, H. A. (1971). Neurolinguistics. In W. O. Dingwall (Ed.), *A survey of linguistic science.* College Park, MD: Linguistic Program, University of Maryland.

Wiig, E. H. (1982a). *Let's talk: Developing prosocial communication skills.* Columbus, OH: Charles E. Merrill.

Wiig, E. H., (1982b). *Let's talk inventory for adolescents.* Columbus, OH: Charles E. Merrill.

Wiig, E. H., & Bray, C. M. (1983). *Let's talk for children.* Columbus, OH: Charles E. Merrill.

Wiig, E. H., & Semel, E. (1984). *Language assessment and intervention for the learning disabled.* Columbus, OH: Charles E. Merrill.

Witelson, S. F. (1977). Early hemisphere specialization and interhemisphere plasticity. In S. J. Segalowitz & F. A. Gruber (Eds.), *Language development and neurological theory* (pp. 213–289). New York: Academic Press.

Woods, B. T., & Carey, S. (1979). Language deficits after apparent clinical recovery from childhood aphasia. *Annals of Neurology, 6,* 405–409.

Yakovlev, P. I., & Lecours, A. R. (1967). The myelogenetic cycles of regional maturation of the brain. In A. Minkowski (Ed.), *Regional development of the brain in early life* (pp. 3–70). Oxford: Blackwell.

Zaidel, E. (1979). The split and half brain as models of congenital language disability. In C. L. Ludlow & M. E. Doran-Quine (Eds.), *The neurological basis of language disorders in children: Methods and directions for research* (**NINCDS Monograph 22,** pp. 55–89). Washington, DC: U.S. Government Printing Office.

Zaidel, E. (1985). Language in the right hemisphere. In D. F. Benson & E. Zaidel (Eds.), *The dual brain: Hemispheric specialization in humans.* New York: Guilford Press.

Learning Disabilities Subtypes

Perspectives and Methodological Issues in Clinical Assessment

GEORGE W. HYND, ROBERT T. CONNOR,
and NAOMI NIEVES

INTRODUCTION

In a relatively young industrial society such as ours, only about 100 years have elapsed since an inability to learn, retain, and use a symbolic means of communication fluently has been viewed as a learning disability. Prior to the end of the 19th century, the acquisition of reading, arithmetical, and other more demanding cognitive skills was not viewed as essential for a productive life. These abilities are clearly essential today.

Considerable evolution has taken place in how learning disabilities are conceptualized. Approximately a century ago they were considered only insofar as reading abilities were affected. Today, serious deficits cutting across many different domains such as arithmetic or spelling may result in a diagnosis of learning disability. Even in the historically important domain of reading, a variety of studies suggest the existence of many subtypes or subpopulations of disabled readers. Further articulation of these subtypes, more well-controlled research studies, and technologically sophisticated investigations that relate deficient regions of brain activity (e.g., metabolic) to disordered cognitive ability will probably impact on new conceptualizations of learning disabilities and their assessment.

GEORGE W. HYND • Departments of Educational Psychology and Psychology, University of Georgia, Athens, Georgia, and Department of Neurology, Medical College of Georgia, Augusta, Georgia.   ROBERT T. CONNOR and NAOMI NIEVES • Kennedy Institute, Johns Hopkins School of Medicine, Baltimore, Maryland.

Within this context, the purpose of this chapter is to provide some integrative perspective as to how learning disabilities were viewed and diagnosed historically, provide a current critique of subtyping methodologies, and relate assessment practices in clinical child neuropsychology to a neurolinguistic model of cognitive processes known to be important in learning. It should be emphasized that the primary focus will be on reading disabilities since most research efforts have been directed toward this most common of all learning disabilities. In this fashion, the unique clinical problems associated with neurodevelopmental learning disorders and their diagnosis may be addressed productively.

EARLY CONCEPTUALIZATIONS OF LEARNING DISABILITIES

Clinical Case Reports and Observations

Early investigators were struck by the variable visual-perceptual deficiencies seen in patients who had suffered neurological trauma, especially as it related to reading ability. Although the highly variable assessment practices and reporting styles among these investigators were acknowledged as problematic even at that time (Bastian, 1898), these early reports showed an evolving realization of what behaviors characterized learning disabilities.

For example, as early as 1877 Kussmaul used the term "word blindness" to describe a patient who, although not blind, was unable to read words. Subsequently, Hinshelwood and others (Bastian, 1898; Claiborne, 1906; Fisher, 1905; Hinshelwood, 1895, 1900; Jackson, 1906; Morgan, 1896; Stephenson, 1905) published similar cases involving word blindness and related neurological disorders. The reporting of these early cases was obviously important since these cases of acquired learning or behavioral disabilities set the stage for the awareness that learning disabilities could also manifest as a neurodevelopmental or congenital disorder.

Hinshelwood (1900) reported two cases of what he referred to as "congenital" word blindness. The first, a boy of 11 years, had been unable to identify highly familiar words after 4 years of instruction. His auditory memory, however, was excellent; he had been able to learn his lessons without reading the words. He was contrasted with a boy of 10 years who could recognize familiar words but had difficulty with uncommon short words (e.g., tub, rug). Additional case studies were rapidly forthcoming and, in reviewing them, one can see the developing notions regarding differential manifestations according to gender, processes involved, and possible neuroanatomical correlates.

Fisher (1905), for instance, reported yet another case of a girl with reading disabilities. After 2 years of instruction she persisted in mixing her letters, displayed poor arithmetic skills, and misnamed musical notes. Family history revealed that her uncle had reading problems as a young-ster and still experienced difficulty spelling as an adult. Fisher described this case as evidence of a familial condition of impairment in the left angular gyrus; "the visual memory centre for words." These notions con-cerning the possible congenital or genetic etiology continued to attract support, as evidenced by Stephenson's (1905) case of congenital word blindness affecting three generations.

Thus, by 1905 it was already reasonably well established that (1) severe learning disabilities were manifested in children of normal intel-ligence (although no standardized measure of IQ was yet generally avail-able), (2) they affected a greater number of boys than girls, (3) the deficits were manifested variably, impacting differentially on each child's ability to read or perform some cognitive task, (4) the disability was not generally responsive to traditional learning opportunities, (5) it seemed to have a genetic component that expressed itself variably, (6) it could be diagnosed using many different informal and formal clinical assessment practices, and (7) it might be related to some neurodevelopmental pathology in the region of the angular gyrus in the left hemisphere. With the benefit of hindsight, it is remarkable how sophisticated and accurate were the obser-vations made by these early clinicians.

What's in a Name?

By the early part of this century, many different terms had been suggested in attempts to define this syndrome accurately. A representa-tive few include amblyopia, amnesia visualis verbalis, bradylexia, cogeni-tal alexia, congenital word blindness, and later, primary reading retarda-tion, strephosymbolia, and developmental dyslexia (Drew, 1956; Hynd & Cohen, 1983; Pirozzolo, 1979). Each of the investigators who introduced these terms offered his or her own rationale.

However, it was Orton (1928) and his ideas regarding mixed cerebral dominance that seemed to capture the attention of psychologists and edu-cators alike. Historically, he was important, not so much because his theories were well accepted but because he stimulated some five decades of research into the relationship involving laterality, language abilities, and reading acquisition. Overall, Orton estimated that 2 to 4% of the school population had a significant reading deficit that merited special training. After decades of research in which the relationships between laterality and academic or cognitive performance have been examined, it can be concluded firmly that Orton's (1928) ideas have not stood the test of time. Reviews by Benton (1975), Kinsbourne and Hiscock (1981), and Zangwill (1960) support this conclusion. His ideas do, however, continue to attract attention (Geschwind & Behan, 1982). More recent efforts to define specific learning disorders, such as severe reading disability, have, as in the past, generated continued controversy and yet more definitions and research.

DEFINING LEARNING DISABILITIES

It might well be asked, why so much attention on how learning disabilities are defined? A multitude of reasons exist, of course, and include the following: (1) so that the syndrome can be adequately differentiated from other neurological or behavioral syndromes manifesting similar symptoms, (2) for treatment reasons, i.e., differential diagnosis leads to differential treatment, (3) for fiscal planning purposes (how one defines a condition impacts directly on how large a clinical population is and the resulting need for training of teachers and related services), and (4) agreeing, even temporarily, on the definition of a syndrome and how it is diagnosed can aid researchers in their continued efforts to assess the parameters of the syndrome and build further testable hypotheses as to its etiology, manifestation, and treatment. Thus, in this vein, assessment is a vital and dynamic component in clinically identifying children and furthering, through research, our understanding of learning disabilities.

The Public Forum and PL 94-142

Public awareness of the potential impact of having a significant number of children progress through school without profiting from their experience led to a growing realization that special funds needed to be set aside for special education efforts. The neurological perspective continued to be articulated (e.g., Strauss & Kephart, 1955; Strauss & Lehtinen, 1947), and through the efforts of parent and teacher groups (Doris, 1986; McCarthy & McCarthy, 1969), a consensus definition, based considerably on the World Federation of Neurology's definition (Critchley, 1970) and that offered by Kirk and Bateman (1962), evolved. The result of these efforts led in 1975 to the passage of a public law, PL 94-142, that affirmed the rights of all handicapped children, including the learning-disabled, to a public, appropriate, and least restrictive education.

Acknowledging the Neurological Etiology

The impact of PL 94-142's definition was indeed tremendous. With the significant increase in the number of learning-disabled children referred, assessed, and diagnosed, there were concurrent increases in school personnel (e.g., learning disabilities teachers, school psychologists). A vast administrative network now existed for the identification and treatment of children who experienced learning difficulties.

However, a great deal of controversy arose. One issue of particular relevance was the notion that these disorders were of neurodevelopmental etiology. There were those who argued that learning disabilities were a result of inadequate instruction or other nonneurological factors (e.g., Harris & Hodges, 1981; Ross, 1976; Smith, 1978).

Recognizing, however, that a large body of evidence argued for a neurological etiology, the National Joint Committee for Learning Disabilities (NJCLD) published a more complete definition, which, it hoped, would address directly many concerns raised by critics of the definition offered by PL 94-142. The NJCLD defined learning disabilities as "a generic term that refers to a heterogeneous group of disorders manifested by significant difficulties in the acquisition and use of listening, speaking, reading, writing, reasoning or mathematical abilities. These disorders are intrinsic to the individual and *presumed to be due to central nervous system dysfunction*" (Hammill, Leigh, McNutt, & Larsen, 1981).

In the context of the present discussion, the NJCLD committee apparently agreed that "hard evidence of organicity did not have to be present in order to diagnose a person as learning disabled, but that no person should be labelled LD unless CNS dysfunction was the suspected cause" (Hammill *et al.*, 1981, p. 340).

It is in this particular regard and in the belief that learning disabilities have a neurological etiology that the focus of this chapter is offered. To understand fully the literature regarding the neuropsychological subtypes of learning disabilities, a brief overview of over two decades of research will be presented. Then, the supporting evidence as to the distribution of neuropathology in the brains of learning-disabled subjects will be reviewed in an attempt to place the subtyping literature in some neurological perspective. Finally, and most important, implications for clinical neuropsychological assessment of these children will be offered.

MULTIFACTOR RESEARCH

Perspectives on the Single Factor Research

Decades of research investigating unifactorial conceptualizations of the primary perceptual or cognitive deficit underlying developmental dyslexia led down a nonproductive path (Hynd & Cohen, 1983). Single factor research efforts focused on visual perceptual deficits (e.g., Lyle, 1969; Lyle & Goyen, 1968, 1975) and particularly their importance in the early acquisition of fluent reading skills (Jansky & deHirsch, 1972; Rourke, 1976; Satz, Friel, & Rudegeair, 1974; Silver & Hagen, 1971). Dissatisfaction with this perspective and nonsupportive evidence provided by Liberman, Shankweiler, Orlando, Harris, and Brett (1971) and Fischer, Liberman, and Shankweiler (1978) led to a general recognition that the deficits children typically evidenced in these visual-perceptual studies actually resulted from linguistic intrusion errors. These, perhaps, were reflective of deficits in verbal mediation, not visual perception.

Early Subtyping Studies

Concurrent with the popular efforts of many investigators in the 1960s to define the one single deficit underlying learning disorders in children was a growing awareness by some investigators that there existed two, if not more, subtypes of disabled readers.

Kinsbourne and Warrington (1963) clearly should receive the credit for providing the first of some 30 or more published studies in which subtypes have been identified. This study is important for several reasons: First, it has historical significance; second, it clearly represents those approaches that might be considered more "clinical" in nature; and third, unlike many of the multivariate studies published today, that of Kinsbourne and Warrington had a clearly defined hypothesis to examine.

Employing only 13 subjects referred to them because of a history of reading or writing problems, Kinsbourne and Warrington (1963) divided these subjects into two groups. One group of subjects ($n = 6$) had at least a 20-point difference in Verbal and Performance IQ (PIQ > VIQ). The second group ($n = 7$) were characterized as having Wechsler IQs in the reverse direction (VIQ > PIQ). Both groups of subjects received a clinical neurological examination, an achievement test, and tests of finger differentiation. They predicted that if, in fact, "reading backwardness" was due to multiple causes, then their two groups of subjects, divided primarily along a verbal-visual perceptual continuum, might be differentiated on other dependent measures. To this end they found that the subjects who had superior perceptual skills did indeed have marked language disabilities, whereas those characterized as having normal language skills but poor visual-perceptual abilities were remarkably like children with a developmental Gerstmann syndrome (finger agnosia, dysgraphia, dyscalculia, and right–left orientation problems). They suggested that "insofar as the acquisition of reading and writing skill is a complex procedure, involving a variety of cerebral functions, it is not surprising to find that retarded development of one or other of the functions subserved by the cerebral hemispheres may delay this acquisition, and do so in different ways, depending upon the exact nature of the function which is insufficiently developed" (p. 153).

Thus, the stage was set for further investigations. Bannatyne (1966) and particularly Bateman (1968) provided further evidence that at least two, if not three or more, subtypes existed, as suggested by Kinsbourne and Warrington (1963). It remained, however, for Boder (1973) to add to Kinsbourne and Warrington's (1963) findings. She reasoned that reading and spelling were interdependent functions, and thus, by examining reading and spelling patterns, one could elicit a more clear conceptualization as to the nature of the cerebral dysfunction characteristic of developmental dyslexics. Using a diagnostic reading-spelling task she had developed earlier (1971), Boder (1973) administered it to 107 children from 8 to 16 years of age. All were diagnosed as developmental dyslexic. Primarily on the basis of her clinical impressions, she identified three groups of disabled readers.

First, there were those who had difficulty with the phonetic aspects of reading and read words globally using visual gestalt perception. According to Boder, this subtype accounted for approximately 63% of all disabled readers in her sample. The second subgroup Boder identified were the dyseidetic dyslexic or those disabled readers who read laboriously and had a poor visual memory for words. These dyslexics, she believed, accounted for some 9% of the disabled readers in her sample. Finally, a third identifiable pattern of reading-spelling errors emerged in which the children, about 22% of her sample, were severely handicapped, sharing the traits of both the dysphonetic and the dyseidetic dyslexic. This subgroup she referred to as her mixed type, and it was believed that these disabled readers had the poorest educational prognosis.

These two earlier studies have been highlighted because they both adequately represent the contribution that clinical neurology made in delineating the behavioral manifestations of subtypes of disabled learners. In each case, these investigators applied clinical-experimental measures to differentiate the unique behavioral manifestations of each subtype. However, potential issues related to instrument reliability and validity clearly were not a focus of concern.

There quickly followed a number of statistically sophisticated studies. Some, such as Rourke, Young, and Flewelling (1971) were more empirical replications of Kinsbourne and Warrington's (1963) basic study, whereas others (e.g., Mattis, French, & Rapin, 1975) examined related issues pertaining to the presumed degree of neurological involvement. Many of these studies and others that followed are summarized in Table 1.

Some Directions in Subtyping Research: Multivariate Classification Approaches

By the mid 1970s several equally productive lines of research regarding subtypes of learning disabilities were being pursued. Generally, there were those studies that sought, through multivariate techniques, to identify the deficient neuropsychological processes that characterized the subtypes. For example, the study by Petrauskas and Rourke (1979) used a large sample of retarded readers and, applying factor analysis to a large data set, found that three reliable subtypes existed. The first group of

TABLE 1. A Chronology of the Major Subtyping Studies Conducted 1963–1986[a,b]

Author(s)	N	Population	Sex	SES	Matched	Age range (years)	Tests	Type of study	Analysis	General findings
Kinsbourne and Warrington (1963)	13	Nonverbal > verbal by at least 20 points Verbal > nonverbal by at least 20 points	M = 62% F = 38%	N/R	No	8 to 31	1. WISC-R or WAIS 2. Schonell Reading and Spelling 3. Tests of Finger Differentiation	Clinical impressions	Qualitative	P > V clinical tesing revealed signifi-language impairment. V > P failed tests of finger differentiation and had difficulties with arithmetic. Called Group 1, the language-retardation group. Called Group 2, the Gerstmann Group.
Ingram, Mason, and Blackburn (1970)	82	Dyslexics 1. Specific dyslexics = 62 2. General dyslexics = 20	M = 80% F = 20%	N/R	No	7 to 15.11	1. Stanford-Binet 2. Schonell Reading, Spelling, Arithmetic 3. Goodenough Draw-a-Man 4. Neuropsychological Assessment (EEG, lateral dominance) 5. Physical exam	Frequencies	Chi-square	Specifics had a significant higher proportion of boys than girls. Generals had significantly more neurological findings. Specifics had significantly more audiophonic reading errors.
Rourke, Young, and Flewelling (1971)	90	LD 3 groups 1. PIQ > VIQ 2. PIQ = VIQ 3. PIQ < VIQ	M = 80% F = 20%	N/R	No	9 to 14	1. PPVT 2. WRAT 3. Reitan's Category Test 4. Aphasia Screening Test 5. Speech Perception Test Rhythm Test Trails A and B	Differential performance of LD types	Multiple 1-way ANOVAs	HV-LP group was significantly better on those tasks involving verbal, language, and auditory perceptual skills. LP-HV group significantly better on tasks involving visual-perceptual skills.
Naidoo (1972)	98	Dyslexics 1. 56 reading deficits	All males	Middle class	Age + type of school	8 to 12.11	1. WISC 2. Reading, Spelling tests	Differential performance of LD types	Cluster analysis	Dyslexics had a significantly greater family history of

Study	N	Definition/Sample	Sex		Age	Measures		Analysis	Findings
		2. 42 spelling deficits				3. Perceptual tasks (auditory, visual, motor) 4. Social Adjustment Scales			reading problems than controls. No subtypes of dyslexia were identified. Evidence suggests that sequencing disability may underlie reading and spelling retardation.
Boder (1973)	107	Children who met the world federation definition of developmental dyslexia.	M = 86% F = 14%	N/R	8 to 16	Boder Reading-Spelling Pattern Test	Clinical impression	Qualitative	3 subtypes 1. Dysphonetic (63%) 2. dyseidetic (9%) 3. Mixed (22%) Undetermined (6%)
Nelson and Warrington (1974)		Study 1 Reading and Spelling deficits—2 years		N/R	No	8 to 14	1. WISC 2. Schonell Reading and Spelling	Error analysis	Multiple t-tests	Degree of VIQ decrement is much more strongly associated with degree of reading retardation than with spelling retardation.
	39	1. More general verbal retardation by 15 points (WISC)	M = 85% F = 15%						
	82	2. No general verbal retardation	M = 76% F = 24%						
	17	Study 2 1. Reading < 2 years retarded, spelling > 2 years retarded	M = 88% F = 12%	N/R	No	Same as above	Same as above	Error analysis	Multiple t-tests	Spelling and reading retardates had significantly lower VIQ than spelling-only retardates.

(continued)

[a]Abbreviations in this table include (N/R) not reported, WISC-R (Wechsler Intelligence Scale for Children-Revised), WAIS (Wechsler Adult Intelligence Scale), PPVT (Peabody Picture Vocabulary Test), WRAT (Wide Range Achievement Test), PIQ (Performance IQ), VIQ (Verbal IQ), FSIQ (Full Scale IQ), LP (Low Performance IQ), SPA (Spatial factor), CON (Conceptual factor), SEQ (Sequential factor), FTNW (Finger Tip Number Writing), LNNB-CR (Luria-Nebraska Neuropsychological Battery-Children's Revsion), VMI (Developmental Test of Visual Motor Integration), PIAT (Peabody Individual Achievement Test), K-ABC (Kaufman Assessment Battery for Children), P (WISC Performance IQ), V (WISC Verbal IQ), M (males), F (females), EEG (Electroencephalogram), ANOVA (Analysis of Variance), LD (Learning-Disabled), X̄ (Mean), NLD (Non-Learning-Disabled), R-L (Right-Left), WISC (Wechsler Intelligence Scale for Children), EMR (Educable Mentally Retarded), SES (Sociometric Status), ANCOVA (Analysis of Covariance), MANOVA (Multivariate Analysis of Variance), CAT (California Achievement Test), SLDR (Specific Learning Disabled Resource), CBI (Classroom Behavior Inventory), SCAN (Schedule of Classroom Activity Norms), SEARCH (Systematic Evaluation of Reading Criteria for High Risk).

[b]It should be noted that subtypes (auditory, visual, auditory-visual, emotional, and pedagogic) of reading disability were proposed earlier than 1963. For example, Gjessing (1953) noted those listed above a decade earlier than Kinsbourne and Warrington's (1963) report. However, the validating evidence for the existence of these subtypes has only been the focus of researchers during the past 25 years.

TABLE 1. (Continued)

Author(s)	N	Population	Sex	SES	Matched	Age range (years)	Tests	Type of study	Analysis	General findings
	54	2. Reading > 2 years retarded, spelling > 2 years retarded	M = 83% F = 17%							Spelling and reading retardates made more phonetic errors than did spelling-only retardates.
Mattis, French and Rapin (1975)	113	3 groups N = 31 brain-damaged reader N = 53 brain-damaged dyslexic N = 29 Non-brain-damaged dyslexic	Not specified	N/R	No	8 to 18	1. WAIS or WISC 2. Benton Test of Visual Retention 3. Ravens Progressive Matrices 4. Oral language (4) 5. WRAT 6. Motor tasks (3)	Comparisons of group performance	Multiple ANOVAs with Duncan's new multiple range test	Brain-damaged readers PIQ significantly lower than either dyslexic group. Brain-damaged readers significantly better than one or both dyslexic groups on verbal labeling, language comp., and imitative speech. Similarity between the developmental dyslexic and the brain-damaged dyslexic. Then defined 3 patterns and assigned criteria. Accounted for 90% of dyslexics.
Doehring and Hoshko (1977)	65	Reading and learning problems Group R, N = 34 reading problems Group M, N = 31 mixed problems	M = 91% F = 9% M = 68% F = 32%	N/R	No	8 to 17	31 Tests: 9 Reading 8 Visual scanning 7 Visual matching 7 Auditory visual matching	Differential performance of LD types	Q Factor Analysis for Group R, Group M, and combined.	Group R—3-factor solution Group M—3-factor solution Combined—4-factor solution Group R 1. Slow oral word reading 2. Slow aud-vis. letter association 3. Slow aud-vis. as-

Study	N	Sample/Definition	Sex			Age	Measures	Purpose	Analysis	Findings
Smith, Coleman, Dokecki, and Davis (1977)	208	Learning-disabled 1. N = 132 IQ > 75 VIQ & PIQ ≥ 90 2. N = 50 not meeting criteria above 3. N = 26 EMR FSIQ < 75	M = 76% F = 24%	N/R	No	6.3 to 12.1	WISC-R (no digit span given)	Differential performance on the WISC-R	Repeated measures ANOVA, Newman-Keuls	Total sample—SPA > CON > SEQ and acquired knowledge EMR-spatial > than all others. sociation of words and symbols.
Omenn and Weber (1978)	21	Dyslexics—3 groups N = 7 auditory problems, N = 11 visual problems, N = 3 mixed.	Both, but #s not reported	N/R	No	School-aged, but not reported	1. Slingerland 2. WISC 3. Spelling tests 4. Visual and Auditory Evoked Potentials 5. Family history 6. Academic records 7. Handedness	Differential performance of LD types	Chi-square	Evoked potential recording—no significant differences when comparing left and right parietal responses. No asymmetries were seen within subtypes, handedness, or spelling error types for auditory or visual evoked response. Visual dyslexics tend to have families with visual dyslexia and auditory dyslexics have families with auditory dyslexia.
Rourke and Finlayson (1978)	45	Learning-disabled—3 groups 1. Low in reading, math, spelling 2. Low in reading, spelling. Math ok. 3. Low in math, reading, and spelling ok.	M = 87% F = 13%	N/R	No	9 to 14	1. WRAT 2. WISC 3. PPVT 4. Halstead-Wepman Aphasia Screening Test 5. Vocabulary Recognition Task	Comparison of group performances	Multiple 1-way ANOVAs with Tukey comparisons	Group 3 > 2 on all verbal and perceptual measures (except auditory closure) Group 3 VIQ > PIQ PIQ Group 2 > 3 Group 1 & 2 similar Group 1 VIQ < PIQ

(continued)

TABLE 1. (Continued)

Author(s)	N	Population	Sex	SES	Matched	Age range (years)	Tests	Type of study	Analysis	General findings
Sweeney and Rourke (1978)	48	Groups (3) 4th- and 8th-graders 1. Nonphonetic retarded spellers 2. Phonetic retarded spellers 3. Control	M = 63% F = 37%	Middle class	Age + WISC PIQ	4th grade 9.9 to 10.1 8th grade 13.3 to 13.4	1. Auditory tests 2. Verbal tests 3. Reading 4. Visual Closure test	Differential performance of LD types and control	Multiple ANOVAs with Newman-Keuls comparison	Normals significantly greater than phonetically inaccurate spellers only at older age level on all but the simplest of auditory discrimination and immediate auditory-verbal memory measures.
Doehring, Hoshko, and Bryans (1979)	158	3 subtypes Reading problems (n = 34) Mixed problems (n = 31) Combination of reading and mixed problems (n = 62) Controls (n = 31)	N/A	N/R	Age + Sex	8 to 17	31 Tests 9 Reading 8 Visual Scanning 7 Visual Matching 7 Auditory-Visual Matching	Differential performance of LD and controls	1. Q-factor 2. Cluster analysis	Q factor analysis replicated same 3 subtypes when original data pooled with normal readers. Same subtypes remained well defined when reexamined using cluster analysis approach.
Fisk and Rourke (1979)	264	Learning-disabled 3 groups 9–10 years (n = 100) 11–12 years (n = 100) 13–14 years (n = 64)	M = 81% F = 16%	N/R	No	9 to 14.9	1. WRAT 2. Reitan's Neuropsychological Battery	Differential performance of LD types on neuropsychological battery	Q-factor analysis	54% of subjects were classified into subtypes that were "replicated" across 2 or more age levels. Type A-Poor auditory verbal processing and finger localization deficit. Type B-Linguistic deficit. Type C-Poor performance in fingertip number writing perception (may be a variant of Subtype A).

Study	N	Groups	Sex	SES	IQ control	Age	Tests	Purpose	Analysis	Results
Petrauskas and Rourke (1979)	160	2 groups $N = 133$ retarded readers $N = 27$ normal readers	M = 86% F = 14%	N/R	No	7 to 8.9	1. WRAT Reading 2. Reitan 6 skill areas: Tactile, Motor, Visual-Spatial, Auditory-Verbal, Abstract-Conceptual, and Sequencing	Differential performance of normal and retarded readers	Pearson Product-Moment Correlations Factor analysis using iterated principal axes solution	3 reliable subtypes found. 50% of subject sample could be reliably classified. Type 1—Most language disturbances. Type 2—Sequencing deficits. Finger Agnosia. Type 3—Conceptual, motoric, and verbal expressive deficits.
Pirozzolo (1979)	24	Right-handed 3 groups 1. Visual dyslexics 2. Auditory-linguistic dyslexics 3. Normal readers	All males	N/R	Age + Full Scale IQ	$\bar{X} = 11.1$ range not reported	1. 16 three-letter stimulus words 2. Eye movement monitor 3. Gray Oral Reading Test passages	Differential performance of LD and controls	ANOVA with Newman-Keuls comparisons	Auditory-linguistic group showed no lateral asymmetries for word recognition when compared with normals. Visual-spatial group had significant deficits recognizing words presented parafoveally, faster saccadic leftward eye movement, and more return sweep reading inaccuracies when compared with normals.
Lyon and Watson (1981)	150	100 learning-disabled resource 50 controls	M = 90% F = 10%	Middle class	Age + WISC-R FSIQ	11 to 12.5	10 tests 1. Auditory tests 2. Token tests 3. Raven's Coloured Progressive Matrices 4. VMI 5. PIAT (2) 6. Memory for designs 7. Naming Test	Differential performance of LD and controls	Multiple 1-way ANOVA Cluster Analysis *(only on LD subjects) Multivariate discriminant analysis Scheffé post hoc pairwise comparisons	6 homogeneous subgroups for raw and standard scores, accounted for 94% of SLDR subjects. Discriminant analysis between 6 subgroups yielded 2 discriminant functions. 1. Language and vi-

(continued)

TABLE 1. (Continued)

Author(s)	N	Population	Sex	SES	Matched	Age range (years)	Tests	Type of study	Analysis	General findings
										sual-motor integration function 2. An orthogonal visual-motor integration dimension.
Satz and Morris (1981)	325	5th-grade white boys in Florida Longitudinal Project	All males	N/R	No	X̄ = 11 years (range not reported)	WRAT PPVT Neuropsychological Battery SES	Differential performance of white 5th-graders	2 cluster analyses—first one to identify learning disability group, second to subtype the learning-disabled group	5 subtypes 1. Impaired on both language variables. 2. Impaired on verbal fluency only. 3. Impaired on language and perceptual measures. 4. Impaired on perceptual only. 5. No impairment.
Thompson (1982)	83	Spelling and reading-disabled Average IQ 3 age groups	N/R	N/R	No	3 age groups: 8 to 10.11 (n = 29) 11 to 13.11 (n = 29) 14 to 16.11 (n = 24)	1. WISC-R 2. Raven's 3. British Ability Scales 4. Neal's Analysis of Reading Ability	Error analysis	1-way ANOVAs with Tukey multiple comparisons for a repeated-measures design	3 subgroups were defined as basis of reading and spelling errors. A greater number of children with auditory-linguistic deficits than visuo-spatial at all ages. Visuo-spatial group scored less well on speed of information processing, block design level and block design power.
Nolan, Hammeke, and Barkley (1983)	36	a. Normal-WRAT ≥ 40 percentile b. Reading-Spelling ≤ 20 percentile	M = 78% F = 22%	N/R	No	7 to 13	WISC-R, FTNW, Finger Agnosia, LNNB-CR, WRAT	Determine if LD subtypes would exhibit unique neuropsychologi-	1-way ANOVA Scheffé ANCOVA	Partial evidence for notion of unique neuropsychological profiles. The expres-

Author (Year)	N	Sample	Sex		Control	Age	Measures	Purpose	Analysis	Results
								cal profiles		sive speech, writing, and reading scales of LNNB-CR differentiated the poor reading/spelling group from the other 2 groups. Did not differentiate the math deficient group.
		Math ≥ 40 percentile c. Math ≤ 20 percentile, Reading-Spelling ≥ 40 percentile								
Watson, Goldgar, and Ryschon (1983)	65	Children who were referred for LD	M = 77% F = 23%		N/R	No	7 to 14.11	6 skill areas: Reading/Spelling Visual Processing Language Memory Perceptual Organization, VMI/Behavior	Differential performance of children referred for LD	Cluster analysis with K-means iterative partitioning method	3 clusters a. visual processing deficit b. generalized language disorder c. minimal deficit subtype Clusters relatively heterogeneous and may have limited clinical utility.
Meacham and Fisher (1984)	50	4 groups CAT scores Normal readers (n = 20) Reading-disabled in Special Ed. (n = 10) Reading/Language disabled in self-contained LD (n = 10) Scores < 35%ile on CAT—No remediation (n = 10)	M = 54% F = 46%		N/R	No	7.1 to 9.2	CAT SEARCH WRAT	Differential performance of LD types and controls	t tests, Q factor, discriminant analysis	4 subtypes for kindergarten. 3 subtypes for second grade. There was little stability in the subtypes from kindergarten to second grade.
Fletcher (1985)	87	Controls (16), Reading-Spelling LD (10), Reading-Spelling-Arithmetic LD (38), Spelling-Arithmetic LD (10), and Arithmetic LD (13)	M = 58% F = 42%		N/R	No	7.6 to 12 ($\bar{X}$ = 9.94)	WISC-R, WRAT, Verbal and Nonverbal Selective Reminding Task	Differential Performance of LD achievement subtypes on verbal and nonverbal selective reminding task. Influence of IQ also examined.	MANOVA, ANOVA, post hoc comparisons (Tukey)	Relative to controls, Arithmetic-Spelling LD subjects had difficulty on the nonverbal task, the reading, spelling children had difficulty on the verbal

(continued)

TABLE 1. (Continued)

Author(s)	N	Population	Sex	SES	Matched	Age range (years)	Tests	Type of study	Analysis	General findings
										memory task, and Reading-spelling-arithmetic LD subtypes did poorly on both verbal and nonverbal tasks. IQ is not a significant factor. Supports differentiation of LD Children on the basis of patterns of achievement.
Hooper and Hynd (1985)	117	5 groups 30 Normal Readers 32 Nonspecifics 30 Dysphonics 5 Dyseidetics 20 Alexics	M = 55% F = 45%	Middle class	Age, sex, geographic location	8.4 to 12.5	K-ABC Boder	Differential diagnosis of LD subtypes	MANOVA, ANOVA, Duncan Multiple range with harmonic n, discriminant analysis	Sequential processing (K-ABC) was able to distinguish between normals and dyslexics. Simultaneous processing component did not discriminate among subtypes except for matrix analogies subtest.
Snow, Cohen, and Holliman (1985)	106	LD 7 black subjects 99 white subjects	M = 83% F = 17%	N/R	No	$\bar{X} = 10.4$	WISC-R	Differential diagnosis of LD subtypes	Cluster analysis using factor scores derived from the WISC-R. A hierarchical approach was utilized.	A 6-subgroup solution was considered most appropriate discussed in terms of cognitive patterns.
Snow and Hynd (1985)	100	LD 79 resource 21 self-contained	M = 85% F = 15%	N/R	No	8 to 12 ($\bar{X}$ = 10)	LINNB-CR, WISC-R WRAT	Differential diagnosis of LD subtypes	Q factor analysis, ScreeTest MANOVA and t tests	72% subjects classified into distinct subgroups, but all 3 groups probably represented variation of

Study	N	Sample	Sex	Sex + race	SES/Level	Age	Measures	Purpose	Statistical analysis	Findings
Speece, McKinney, and Appelbaum (1985)	129	LD (n = 63); Normal achievers (n = 66)	a. LD M = 76% F = 24%; b. M = 77% F = 23%		All levels represented	LD—X̄ = 7.2; NLD—X̄ = 7.2	CBI SCAN	Differential diagnosis of LD based on ratings of classroom behaviors	Hierarchical cluster Analysis, Ward's Minimum variance, split sampling replication and forecasting, MANOVAs	language-disordered LD. More than 1/3 of LDs did not exhibit maladaptive behaviors. 7 subgroups of LD (85% of non-LD fell into 2 clusters) were identified.
Breen (1986)	90	LD—3 groups a. 30 Math > Reading b. 30 Reading > Math c. 30 Math = Reading	M = 65% F = 34%	No	N/R	a. X̄ = 9.5 b. X̄ = 9.6 c. X̄ = 9.9	Woodcock-Johnson Psycho.-Ed. Battery	Differential diagnosis of LD subtypes	t tests, 1-way ANOVA, multiple regression and discriminant function, Tukey comparisons	Most subtests and clusters differed significantly for at least one comparison. Groups 1 and 2 were comparable and tended to score higher than Group 3. 64% of LD children were correctly classified by subtypes. Inconclusive results in terms of stable cognitive patterns.
Morris, Blashfield, and Satz (1986)	200	Nonclinical normal and reading-disabled males, tested at kindergarten, second, and fifth grades, from the Florida Longitudinal Project	All males	No	N/R	X̄ = 5.6 in kindergarten	13 measures of neuropsychological and cognitive skills. Factor analysis of this battery yielded two major factors, which these 8 measures represented. 1–4. verbal/conceptual 1. PPVT	Longitudinal	1. Outlier identification techniques. 2. Longitudinal cluster analysis 3. Internal validation of useful solutions 4. External validation of	5 developmental subtypes Type A. deficient verbal skills and increasing strength on visual perceptual motor skills with age. Type B. increasing deficits in performance, especially in verbal-conceptual

(continued)

TABLE 1. (Continued)

Author(s)	N	Population	Sex	SES	Matched	Age range (years)	Tests	Type of study	Analysis	General findings
							2. Verbal Fluency 3. Similarities 4. Dichotic Listening 5–8, sensorimotor/perceptual 5. Recognition-Discrimination Test 6. Embedded Figures 7. Beery-Buktenica Developmental Test of Visual-Motor Integration 8. Auditory-Visual Integration Test		useful solutions across nine domains of variables not used for classification (MANOVA + Chi-Square)	skills with age. Type C. below average on all tests and ratings. Type D. average to above average on all tests and ratings. Type E. above average on all tests and ratings.
Spreen and Haaf (1986)	335	LD referrals a. 63-referral group b. 96-IQ > 79 c. 170-Adult subjects (including 46 controls)	Not reported	N/R	Age, Sex SES	a. $\bar{X}$ = 10.14 b. $\bar{X}$ = 9.91 c. $\bar{X}$ = 24.28	PIAT WISC SAIS Sentence Rep., Categories Purdue Pegboard, R-L orient.	Longitudinal study to look at stability of LD subtypes across age	Hierarchical cluster analysis, with Ward minimum variance, Cluster Cubing Criterion, K-means iterative partitioning, Chi-Square, ANOVA, MANOVA	Group 1—6 subtypes Group 2—8 subtypes (similar to Group 1) Group 3—9 subtypes visuospatial and graphomotor were identified but not linguistic subtype.

children suffered language disturbances. The second group of subjects evidenced sequencing deficits and, like Kinsbourne and Warrington's (1963) Gerstmann group, finger agnosia. The third group of subjects was identified as suffering conceptual, motoric, and verbal-expressive deficits. This study was well conceptualized but, as with so many other multivariate studies (e.g., Fisk & Rourke, 1979; Omenn & Weber, 1978), either many potentially important variables were not reported or the study suffered from other flaws that only compromised the results. For example, in not one of Rourke's or his colleagues' studies (Fisk & Rourke, 1979; Rourke & Finlayson, 1978; Sweeney & Rourke, 1978) was any mention made regarding the socioeconomic level of the subjects. This is clearly a significant oversight since considerable evidence suggests this to be an important variable with regard to neuropsychological abilities (e.g., Reynolds & Gutkin, 1979). Further, in studies where previously existing data bases were employed, rarely was an effort made to control for potentially important variables such as SES, IQ, or gender.

In a considerably more sophisticated study in which some of these issues were addressed, Lyon and Watson (1981) examined 100 reading-disabled (diagnosed according to federal guidelines [PL 94-142] employing measures of reading recognition and comprehension) and 50 normal readers matched according to school and chronological age. The normal readers were used primarily to establish local norms for the test variables used. In an effort to identify subtypes, raw scores and standardized scores of the reading-disabled children (using local norms) were cluster-analyzed separately. Six homogeneous subgroups for raw and standard scores were obtained, accounting for 94% of the reading-disabled subjects. Thus, rather compelling evidence from this particular study suggested considerably more discrete subtypes than previously reported.

Other studies (e.g., Satz & Morris, 1981; Watson, Goldgar, & Ryschon, 1983) also have contributed considerably in providing convincing evidence that (1) more than two subtypes exist, and (2) each subtype can be characterized by reliable cognitive profiles. However, these studies do not contribute greatly to our understanding of the linguistic systems involved in fluent or dysfluent reading. A number of these studies have employed neuropsychological tests from the Halstead-Reitan Neuropsychological Battery (e.g., Fisk & Rourke, 1979; Petrauskas & Rourke, 1979; Rourke & Finlayson, 1978; Rourke et al., 1971). Considerable evidence suggests that this test battery is heavily loaded with tasks that assess visual-motor abilities (Crockett, Klonoff, & Bjerring, 1969), and, worse yet, Seidenberg, Giordani, Berent, and Boll (1983) provide evidence that nearly half (6 out of 14) of these measures correlate significantly with IQ. Thus, these tests reveal little beyond the IQ results, and what extra is contributed has little to do with semantic-linguistic processes that typically characterize the disabled learner.

Thus, many of the studies cited in Table 1 are by and large atheoretical (rarely is any specific rationale given for tests employed). A typical multivariate study (in Table 1) utilizes variables that are distantly related to actual reading or achievement. These variables then are clustered to yield "subtypes" that often have little significance in helping us understand why these children cannot learn normally.

Satz and Morris (1981), Taylor, Fletcher, and Satz (1982), and others (e.g., Coltheart, 1980) have argued cogently that subtypes should be defined in terms of actual patterns of deficient learning or reading behaviors and then studied neuropsychologically. This type of approach makes sense for three reasons.

First and foremost, grouping or subtyping children by the actual patterns of errors they make in learning should, through careful error analysis, eventually reveal many of the potential subprocesses directly involved in learning within any specific domain. Thus, neurocognitive theory will be advanced. Second, it should seem obvious that by assessing actual processes involved in fluent reading, the assessment achieves more ecological validity. Thus, the derived subtypes may actually be observed in the clinic setting. Third, and probably most important, if neuropsychologists can delineate competently the actual neurocognitive, especially neurolinguistic, behaviors that characterize these subtypes, direct treatment implications may result.

In fact, Fletcher (1985) provides an excellent example of how such research efforts should be conducted, He examined verbal and nonverbal memory (storage and retrieval) using a selective reminding procedure among four groups of learning-disabled children. These groups were those with (1) reading-spelling disabilities, (2) reading-spelling-arithmetic disabilities, (3) spelling-arithmetic disabilities, and (4) arithmetic-only disabilities. Consistent with his hypotheses, he found that arithmetic- and spelling-arithmetic-disabled children did poorer on the nonverbal tasks whereas the reading-spelling group did worse on the verbal task. Those with the reading-spelling-arithmetic disabilities performed poorly on the storage and retrieval tasks tapping both verbal and nonverbal memory. Thus, Fletcher concluded that there does seem to be validity in subtyping disabled learners on the basis of patterns of academic achievement. With this study in mind, let us now return our attention to reading disorders where some initial progress along this dimension is being made.

Neurolinguistic Subtyping

Frustration with the fact that decades of research on "subtypes" of reading disorders have failed to increase significantly our theoretical understanidng of the linguistic processes by which children access printed material has led to efforts in subtyping these children according to the kinds of reading errors they make. Based on a neuroanatomical-neurolinguistic model of reading (see Hynd & Hynd, 1984, for a review), a number of subtypes may exist in which deficient reading processes can be tied directly to hypothesized neuroanatomical correlates. Basically, several subtypes have emerged.

Deloche, Andreewsky and Desi (1982) have described what they have referred to as the surface dyslexic. The surface dyslexic reads by well-established phonological rules, processes short words better than long words, and has difficulty in semantic access. Whenever words are unfamiliar or irregular, reading becomes difficult. These dyslexics have difficulty with the visual aspects of word recognition, and whereas they have good phonological skills, their comprehension is seriously affected.

Another subtype that has been identified through careful error analyses of reading error patterns is what has been referred to as the deep dyslexic. Deep dyslexics are able to read familiar words well, particularly nouns, but seem to make many semantic paralexias in oral reading (Friedman & Perlman, 1982). They may, for example, see the word *mutton* and say *sheep*. It has been proposed that the deep dyslexic suffers an anomia, and thus, the semantic category is accessed correctly but the incorrect visual-semantic association occurs, resulting in the paralexic response. These readers seem to rely on imageability, concreteness, and word frequency in their reading behavior.

Other neurolinguistic subtypes have been proposed (Marshall & Newcombe, 1973, 1980; Warrington, 1981); however, these studies are relatively few in number, they focus on small numbers of children, and most of the validating evidence as to correlated neuroanatomical structures comes from adult brain-injured patients. Thus, the results from this line of investigation might still be considered as preliminary insofar as identifying subtypes of reading-disabled children is concerned. However, it is clear that this may prove to be a much more fruitful avenue for subtyping research in the areas of reading, spelling, and mathematical disabilities than those studies that have unfortunately typified much of the efforts of researchers to date.

NEUROANATOMICAL–LINGUISTIC PERSPECTIVES

The Wernicke-Geschwind Model

Geschwind (1974) has had a dramatic impact on the development of our understanding of the neurolinguistic-neuroanatomical relationships involved in speech, language, and reading (Mayeux & Kandel, 1985). Largely, his ideas, as well as those advanced by Luria (1980) and others (e.g., Sevush, 1983; Whitaker, 1976), represent an extension of the neu-rolinguistic model of speech and language first formally advanced by Wernicke (1874). This model is of particular relevance, both theoretically and clinically, in that most learning-disabled children have language-related disorders of one kind or another.

One issue should be dealt with at this point. First, it has long been assumed that the brains of children either are organized differently from those of adults, such that most functions have bilateral representation, or that the brain, although organized similarly to that of an adult, has a remarkable capacity for recovery or reorganization (Sandoval & Haapenen, 1981). We assume, however, that the failure of most of the research to document developmental trends in lateralized function (Hynd, Obrzut, Weed, & Hynd, 1979) argues strongly that children's brains are at the least, organized similarly to those of adults and that, with developmental learning problems, the organizational pattern remains as normally preordained but operates less efficiently (Hynd & Willis, 1988; Kinsbourne & Hiscock, 1981). Thus, we would view Denckla's (1973) suggestion as conservative when she proposed that "as localization in the traditional sense is not a reasonable goal, utilization of analogies and critical differences between childhood and adult syndromes sharing similar complaints brings us closer to a clinical classification scheme" (p. 449) for childhood learning disorders.

It is proposed here that validation of cortical dysfunction in the brains of learning-disabled children in the regions predicted by the Wer-nicke-Geschwind model argues that the organizational pattern of these children's brains is similar to that of adults (Duffy, Denckla, Bartels, & Sandini, 1980). Owing to neurodevelopmental abnormalities in these cortical regions (Drake, 1968; Galaburda & Kemper, 1979; Galaburda, Sherman, Rosen, Aboitiz, & Geschwind, 1985), normal cognitive functioning is impaired significantly.

Basically, in terms of the functional system involved in reading, as an example, it would appear that there is a widespread network of subcortical and cortical zones that interact or contribute to fluent reading. Figure 1 illustrates this proposed functional system. For instance, reading aloud a word would involve the image projected to the retina being transferred via the lateral geniculate nucleus to the primary visual cortex (Brodmann's area 17). Low-level feature analysis occurs in the visual association cortex (Brodmann's areas 18 and 19), with imageable words processed better in the right visual association cortex and letter-strings favored in the left visual association cortex. Input from the visual cortex is shared via commissural fibers from the right visual cortex, and via intrahemispheric fibers from the left visual cortex with the angular gyrus (Brodmann's region 39) at the juncture of the left temporal, parietal, and occipital regions. Cross-modal integration (e.g., grapheme-phoneme cor-

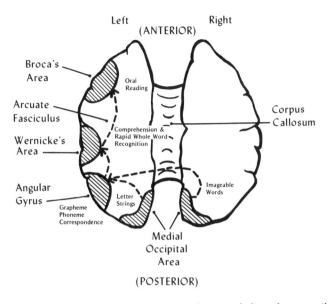

FIGURE 1 A neurolinguistic model of the functional system believed to contribute significantly to fluent reading. (From Hynd & Hynd, 1984, with permission.)

respondence) is thought to result here. This information is then shared with Wernicke's region (Brodmann's area 22) in the left superior posterior temporal cortex. Here auditory-linguistic images are associated with the visual-phonemic stimuli and the word is recognized and comprehended. In oral reading, this comprehended word would be shared with Broca's region via the arcuate fasciculus, where the motor-grammatical images necessary for expressive speech and articulation reside. From here the facial and motor musculature for speech (Brodmann's area 4) would be activated (Hynd & Hynd, 1984; Mayeux & Kandel, 1985; Patton, Sundsten, Crill, & Swanson, 1976).

Knowledge of this model and linguistic processes involved in speech allows one to make accurate predictions about lesion sites involved in aphasia. Also, it is clear that while most linguistic functions are indeed lateralized to the left cerebral cortex, other associated components may be differentially associated with the right hemisphere. Ross (1981), for example, has provided convincing evidence that disturbances of the affective components of language (e.g., intonation or prosody, emotional gesturing, prosodic comprehension, and comprehension of emotional gesturing) are associated meaningfully with the right cerebral hemisphere. As yet, the validation and localization of these functions in children's brains remains a challenge for clinical child neuropsychologists.

Clinical Implications for Process-Based Assessment

From the perspective presented in the preceding two sections on the neurolinguistic systems believed to exist in disabled readers, it should be clear that many, if not most, of the studies summarized in Table 1 relate poorly to any actual processes involved in dysfluent reading. Conceptually, it makes more sense to begin one's organization of a neuropsychological test battery to differentiate subtypes of learning disability by including measures that assess those processes known to be important in the neurolinguistic system involved in reading or achievement in some other domain.

The neurolinguistic model discussed projects that performance on tasks assessing the automatization of basic subskills directly involved in actual performance will distinguish subtypes of learning-disabled children (Sternberg & Wagner, 1982). Therefore, assessment of these children during letter and word recognition tasks, especially on speeded classification tasks (Hayes, Hynd, & Wisenbaker, 1986) makes sense. It also makes conceptual sense to assess not only bisensory perceptual and memory tasks where cross-modal integration is involved (e.g., Obrzut, 1979) but various components of comprehension as well. For instance, different subtypes of learning disability may emerge when different components of comprehension (word, passage, contextual) are assessed. Some other aspects of the neurolinguistic processes thought to be important in reading would also include repetition, fluency, syntactic-pragmatic abilities, and naming. The differentiation of subtypes according to variable performance on tasks assessing these abilities should tell us more about the actual pattern of disabilities and abilities that characterize these learners.

For the clinician, what does this perspective suggest? First, when one considers the neuropathological studies of the brains of dyslexic individuals (Galaburda & Kemper, 1979; Galaburda *et al.*, 1985), it seems reasonable that we should *expect* much psychometric variability among the subtypes. The distribution of the neurodevelopmental abnormalities (focal dysplasias, disordered cortical layering, polymicrogyria), although clustering in the left perisylvian region, is completely distinctive in each case. Thus, it makes conceptual sense that each particular case seen by clinicians should have a qualitatively different porfile of neurolinguistic abilities. Also, it suggests that clinical neuropsychologists should consider refocusing their assessment strategies away from largely redundant neuropsychological batteries (e.g., Luria Nebraska Neuropsychological Battery-Children's Revision; Halstead-Reitan Batteries; Hynd, Snow, & Becker, 1986) and include a wide array of functional skills with more direct measures of actual processes reflected in learning-disabled children. A conceptual model for such an assessment exists (Hynd & Cohen, 1983; Obrzut, 1981).

CONCEPTUAL FRAMEWORK FOR CLINICAL EVALUATION

Obrzut (1981) proposed that neuropsychological assessment of children generally should follow a modification of Johnson and Myklebust's (1967) hierarchy of information processing. As modified further by Hynd and Cohen (1983), this conceptual hierarchy may lead to a more organized, and thus systematic, method for clinical appraisal of children, particularly those with learning disorders. Table 2 presents this conceptual framework.

This framework merely presents a way in which assessment procedures may be related more efficiently to systems important to adequate functioning in children. It also suggests that by carefully selecting various measures, one may assess across the domains of information processing efficiently and in a manner more directly tied to a referral question. Thus, the assessment becomes less time-consuming than traditional neuropsychological batteries, less redundant (see Hynd et al., 1986), and more germaine to the referral question. It also should be pointed out that one must be familiar with a great number of assessment procedures across these domains.

Specifically relevant to the topic of this chapter, however, is the question: What does this hierarchy have to do with diagnosing subtypes of learning disabilities? In light of our knowledge of the research reviewed previously, it can be stated that most learning disabilities are diagnosed on the basis of a significant discrepancy between measured intelligence and academic achievement. Thus, in the context of this hierarchy, tests of cognitive ability and general achievement should be administered to determine (1) if there is such a discrepancy and (2) in what academic area.

Further relying on our knowledge of the literature, and presuming that the disability is documented in the area of reading, it seems reasonable on the basis of Kinsbourne and Warrington's (1963) study to select tests of finger agnosia, laterality, and visual-motor ability. Other research (Petrauskas & Rourke, 1979) suggests a subtype with motoric dysfunction. Thus, the proposed battery also should include measures of motor maturity, such as tests of fine and gross motor coordination, and dysmetria.

Clearly, though, the vast majority of the research in this area suggests that the majority of children with reading disorders have difficulty with auditory-linguistic processing (Pirozzolo, 1979), phonemic segmentation (Liberman, Shankweiler, Liberman, Fowler, & Fischer, 1977), verbal fluency, and comprehension. Their reading errors are often marked by frequent paralexic errors as well (semantic, visual, and auditory) (e.g., Friedman & Perlman, 1982). Thus, the evaluation should include tasks of these sorts drawn from the conceptual hierarchy which in turn are directly tied to the neuroanatomically based neurolinguistic model presented in Figure 1.

TABLE 2. Conceptual Hierarchy and Some Associated Tests/Evaluation Procedures

I. Sensation and Sensory Recognition
  Acuity
    Visual
    Auditory
  Recognition
    Finger Agnosia
    Finger-Tip Number Writing
    Tactile Form Recognition
II. Perception
  Auditory
    Speech Sounds Perception Test
    Seashore Rhythm Test
  Visual
    Bender Gestalt Test
    Beery Visual Motor Integration test
    Benton Visual Retention Test
  Tactile-Kinesthetic
    Tactual Performance Test
III. Motor
  Cerebellar Screening
  Tandem Walking
  Tests for Dysarthria
  Fine Motor Coordination
  Tests for Nystagmus

Lateral Dominance-Motor
  Grip Strength
  Edinburgh Inventory
  Finger Tapping
IV. Psycholinguistic
  Screening Measures
    Aphasia Screening Test
    Fluency Test
    Peabody Picture Vocabulary Test
  Formal Assessment
    Illinois Test of Psycholinguistic Ability
    Boston Aphasia Examination
  Language Asymmetries
    Dichotic listening
    Visual half-field tasks
    Time-sharing tasks
V. Academic
  Comprehensive Battery
    Peabody Individual Achievement Test
    Woodcock-Johnson Psychoeducational Battery
  Reading Tests
    Durrell Analysis of Reading Difficulties
    Gates-McKillop Reading Mastery Tests
    Woodcock Reading Mastery Test

Clinical Measures
  Test for Phonetic Sounds (nonsense words)
  Test for Vowel Principles (nonsense words)
  Syllabication (nonsense words)
  Oral Reading Passages (graded)
  Try-Outs-Diagnostic Teaching
  Phonemic Segmentation
  Flash Vocabulary
VI. Cognitive-Intellectual
  Category Test
  Raven's Coloured Matrices Test
  Kaufman Assessment Battery for Children (K-ABC)
  Wechsler Intelligence Scale for Children-Revised (WISC-R)

Consequently, the neuropsychological battery should (1) be constructed around the tasks that the research literature suggests these children do poorly on, (2) be tied to a valid neurolinguistic model, (3) be flexible such that depending on what the referral suggests, the battery can be individually constructed, and (4) allow the clinician to relate performance back to the subtyping literature such that a diagnosis consistent with this literature, if possible, can be derived.

To carry our example to its final conclusion, suppose we selected an intelligence test (WISC-R), a general achievement battery (PIAT), tests of finger agnosia, laterality, motor functioning, tests for phonetic sounds, vowel principles, and syllabication, an oral reading test in which we would note the kind and type of errors, as well as tests for word knowledge and passage comprehension (Woodcock Reading Mastery Tests). Let us suppose we found that our reading-disabled child had good skills in phonological coding, had poor comprehension, was able to read short words better than long words, but had considerable difficulty in comprehension. No motor or tactile-kinesthetic deficits were noted. It was found, however, that he did poorly on visual-perceptual tasks. This clinical description fits well with what has been referred to by Deloche *et al.* (1982) as the surface dyslexic. Thus, through a carefully selected test battery, a knowledge of the subtyping literature, and an understanding of the neurolinguistic model of reading, a consistent set of data may well emerge. Further, with such a diagnosis, specific intervention strategies may be particularly useful (see Hynd, 1986).

CONCLUSIONS

There has indeed been a long history, first in neurology and more recently in psychology, in attempting to describe the manifestations of learning disabilities in children. What first struck the early clinicians was the similarities between these children's performance and that of brain-damaged adults. Clearly, these disorders have a neurodevelopmental origin remarkably consistent with what was originally proposed by neurologists nearly 100 years ago. Currently accepted definitions reflect this perspective.

Concurrent with the involvement of psychologists in research with these children, there has been a move away from the benefits that careful clinical-observational research provides (e.g., Boder, 1973; Kinsbourne & Warrington, 1963) toward a largely atheoretical multivariate approach. Tests are often included in neuropsychological batteries for no apparent reason, existing populations previously diagnosed as being disabled are often employed without any screening as to the validity of the initial diagnosis, and the resulting subtypes are often characterized by profiles across variables that frequently correlate poorly, if at all, to actual deficiencies on academic tasks.

It is clearly time to use these statistical tools, which indeed are powerful, to evaluate theory, rather than construct *post hoc* explanations that have little ecological validity. Clinically, subtypes should be identified according to actual deficient academic processes, evaluated using a theoretically driven neuropsychological battery. For researchers, groups of children should then be examined statistically as to how the subtypes vary on neurolinguistic and neurocognitive variables deemed important in cognitive maturation. Only in this fashion will researchers in this area provide results that are meaningful to the clinicians who must work with these children.

REFERENCES

Bannatyne, A. (1966). The etiology of dyslexia and the color phonics system. In J. Money (Ed.), *The disabled reader: Education of the dyslexic child*. Baltimore: Johns Hopkins Press.

Bastian, H. C. (1898). *Aphasia and other speech defects*. London: H. K. Lewis.

Bateman, B. (1968). *Interpretation of the 1961 Illinois Test of Psycholinguistic abilities*. Seattle: Special Child Publications.

Benton, A. L. (1975). Developmental dyslexia: Neurological aspects. In W. J. Friedlander (Ed.), *Advances in neurology* (Vol. 2). New York: Raven Press.

Boder, E. (1973). Developmental dyslexia: A diagnostic approach based on three atypical reading patterns. *Developmental Medicine and Child Neurology, 15*, 663–687.

Breen, M. J. (1986). Cognitive patterns of learning disability subtypes as measured by the Woodcock-Johnson Psychoeducational Battery. *Journal of Learning Disabilities, 19*, 86–90.

Claiborne, J. H. (1906). Types of congenital symbol amblyopia. *Journal of the American Medical Association, 47*, 1813–1816.

Coltheart, M. (1980). Deep dyslexia: A review of the syndrome. In M. Coltheart, K. Patterson, & J. C. Marshall (Eds.), *Deep dyslexia*. Boston: Routledge & Kegan Paul.

Critchley, M. (1970). *The dysexic child*. London: William Heinemann Medical Books.

Crockett, D., Klonoff, H., & Bjerring, J. (1969). Factor analysis of neuropsychological tests. *Perceptual and Motor Skills, 29*, 791–802.

Deloche, G., Andreewsky, E., & Desi, M. (1982). Surface dyslexia: A case report. *Brain and Language, 15*, 12–31.

Denckla, M. B. (1973). Research needs in learning disabilities: A neurologist's point of view. *Journal of Learning Disabilities, 6*, 44–50.

Doehring, D. G., & Hoshko, I. M. (1977). Classification of reading problems by the Q-technique of factor analysis. *Cortex, 13*, 281–294.

Doehring, D. G., Hoshko, I. M., & Bryans, B. N. (1979). Statistical classification of children with reading problems. *Journal of Clinical Neuropsychology, 1*, 5–16.

Doris, J. (1986). Learning disabilities. In S. J. Ceci (Ed.), *Handbook of cognitive, social, and neuropsychological aspects of learning disabilities* (pp. 3–54). Hillsdale, NJ: Erlbaum.

Drake, W. E. (1968). Clinical and pathological findings in a child with a developmental learning disability. *Journal of Learning Disabilities, 1*, 486–502.

Drew, A. L. (1956). A neurological appraisal of familial congenital word blindness. *Brain, 79*, 440–460.

Duffy, F. H., Denckla, M. B., Bartels, P. H., & Sandini, G. (1980). Dyslexia: Regional differences in brain electrical activity by topographic mapping. *Annals of Neurology, 7,* 412–420.

Federal Register (1976). *Education of handicapped children and incentive grants programs* (Vol. 41, p. 46977). Bethesda, MD: U.S. Department of Health, Education and Welfare.

Fisher, J. H. (1905). Case of congenital word-blindness (Inability to learn to read). *Ophthalmic Review, 24,* 315–318.

Fisher, W. F., Lieberman, I. Y., & Shankeiler, D. (1978) Reading reversal and developmental dyslexia: A further study. *Cortex, 14,* 496–510.

Fisk, J. L., & Rourke, B. P. (1979). Identification of subtypes of learning disabled children at three age levels: A neuropsychological, multivariate approach. *Journal of Clinical Neuropsychology, 1,* 289–310.

Fletcher, J. M. (1985). Memory for verbal and nonverbal stimuli in learning disability subgroups: Analysis by selective reminding. *Journal of Experimental Child Psychology, 40,* 244–259.

Friedman, R. B., & Perlman, M. B. (1982). Underlying causes of semantic paralexias in a patient with deep dyslexia. *Neuropsychologia, 20,* 559–568.

Galaburda, A. M., & Kemper, T. L. (1979). Cytoarchitectonic abnormalities in developmental dyslexia: A case study. *Annals of Neurology, 6,* 94–100.

Galaburda, A. M., Sherman, G. F., Rosen, G. D., Aboitiz, F., & Geschwind, N. (1985). Developmental dyslexia: Four consecutive patients with cortical anomalies. *Annals of Neurology, 18,* 222–233.

Geschwind, N. (1974). Anatomical foundations of language and dominance. In C. L. Ludlow & M. E. Doran-Quine (Eds.), *The neurological basis of language disorders in children: Methods and direction for research* (NIH Publication No. 79-440). Bethesda, MD: U.S. Department of Health, Education, and Welfare.

Geschwind, N., & Behan, P. O. (1982). Left handedness: Association with immune disease, migraine, and developmental learning disorders. *Proceedings of the National Academy of Sciences, 79,* 5097–5100.

Hammill, D. D., Leigh, J. E., McNutt, G., & Larsen, S. C. (1981). A new definition of learning disabilities. *Learning Disability Quarterly, 4,* 336–342.

Harris, T. L., & Hodges, R. E. (Eds.). (1981). *A dictionary of reading and related terms.* Newark, NJ: International Reading Association.

Hayes, F. B., Hynd, G. W., & Wisenbaker, J. (1986). Learning disabled and normally achieving college students on reaction time and speeded classification tasks. *Journal of Educational Psychology, 78,* 39–43.

Hinshelwood, J. (1895). Word-blindness and visual memory. *Lancet, 2,* 1564–1570.

Hinshelwood, J. (1900). Congenital word-blindness. *Lancet, 1,* 1506–1508.

Hooper, S. R., & Hynd, G. W. (1985). Differential diagnosis of subtypes of developmental dyslexia with the Kaufman Assessment Battery for Children (K-ABC). *Journal of Clinical Child Psychology, 14,* 145–152.

Hynd, C. (1986). Educational intervention in children with developmental learning disorders. In J. E. Obrzut & G. W. Hynd (Eds.), *Child neuropsychology: Clinical practice* (pp. 265–297). New York: Academic Press.

Hynd, G. W., & Cohen, M. (1983). *Dyslexia: Neuropsychological theory, research, and clinical differentiation.* New York: Grune and Stratton.

Hynd, G. W., & Hynd, C. R. (1984). Dyslexia: Neuroanatomical/neurolinguistic perspectives. *Reading Research Quarterly, 19,* 482–498.

Hynd, G. W., Obrzut, J. E., Weed, W., & Hynd, C. R. (1979). Development of cerebral dominance: Dichotic listening asymmetry in normal and learning-disabled children. *Journal of Experimental Child Psychology, 28,* 445–454.

Hynd, G. W., Snow, J. H., & Becker, M. G. (1986). Neuropsychological assessment in clinical child psychology. In B. B. Lahey & A. Kazdin (Eds.), *Advances in clinical child neuropsychology* (Vol. 9). New York: Plenum.

Hynd, G. W., & Willis, W. G. (1988). Pediatric neuropsychology. Orlando, FL: Grune and Stratton.

Ingram, T. S., Mason, A. W., & Blackburn, I. (1970). A retrospective study of 82 children with reading disability. Developmental Medicine and Child Neurology, 12, 271–281.

Jansky, J., & deHirsch, K. (1972). Preventing reading failure—Prediction, diagnosis, and intervention. New York: Harper & Row.

Jackson, E. (1906). Developmental alexia (congenital word blindness). American Journal of Medical Science, 131, 843–849.

Johnson, D. J., & Myklebust, H. R. (1967). Learning disabilities: Educational principles and practices. New York: Grune and Stratton.

Kinsbroune, M., & Hiscock, M. (1981). Cerebral lateralization and cognitive development: Conceptual and methodological issues. In G. W. Hynd & J. E. Obrzut (Eds.), Neuropsychological assessment and the school-age child: Issues and procedures. New York: Grune and Stratton.

Kinsbourne, M., & Warrington, E. K. (1963). Developmental factors in reading and writing backwardness. British Journal of Psychology, 54, 145–156.

Kirk, S. A., & Bateman, B. (1962). Diagnosis and remediation of learning disabilities. Exceptional Children, 29(2), 73–78.

Kussmaul, A. (1877). Disturbance of speech. Cyclopedia of Practical Medicine, 14, 581.

Liberman, I. Y., & Shankweiler, D., Orlando, L. Harris, K. S., & Bertt, F. B. (1971). Letter confusion and reversal of sequence in the beginning reader: Implications for Orton's theory of developmental dyslexia, Cortex, 7, 127–142.

Liberman, I. Y., Shankweiler, D., Liberman, A. M., Fowler, C., & Fischer, W. F. (1977). Phonetic segmentation and recoding in the beginning reader. In A. Reber & D. Scarborough (Eds.), Toward a psychology of reading. Hillsdale, NJ: Erlbaum.

Luria, A. R. (1980). Higher cortical functions in man (2nd ed.). New York: Basic Books.

Lyle, J. G. (1969). Reading retardation and reversal tendency: A factorial study. Child Development, 40, 833–843.

Lyle, J. G., & Goyen, J. (1968). Visual recognition developmental lag and stephosymbolia in reading retardation. Journal of Abnormal Psychology, 73, 25–29.

Lyle, J. G., & Goyen, J. (1975). Effects of speed of exposure and difficulty of discrimination on visual recognition of retarded readers. Journal of Abnormal Psychology, 8, 673–676.

Lyon, R., & Watson, B. (1981). Empirically derived subgroups of learning disabled readers: Diagnostic characteristics. Journal of Learning Disabilities, 14, 256–261.

Marshall, J. L., & Newcombe, F. (1973). Patterns of paralexia: A psycholinguistic approach. Journal of Psycholinguistic Research, 2, 175–197.

Marshall, J. C., & Newcombe, F. (1980). The conceptual status of deep dyslexia: A historical perspective. In M. Coltheart, K. Patterson, & J. C. Marshall (Eds.), Deep dyslexia (pp. 1–21). Boston: Routledge & Kegan Paul.

Mattis, S., French, J. H., & Rapin, I. (1975). Dyslexia in children and young adults: Three independent neuropsychological syndromes. Developmental Medicine and Child Neurology, 17, 150–163.

Mayeux, R., & Kandel, E. R. (1985). Natural language, disorders of language, and other localizable disorders of cognitive functioning. In E. R. Kandel & J. H. Schwartz (Eds.), Principles of neural science (2nd ed., pp. 688–703). New York: Elsevier.

McCarthy, J. M. (1975). Children with learning disabilities. In J. J. Galagher (Ed.), The application of child development research to exceptional children. Reston: Council for Exceptional Children.

McCarthy, J. J., & McCarthy, J. F. (1969). Learning disabilities. Boston: Allyn Bacon.

Meacham, M. L., & Fisher, G. L. (1984). The identification and stability of subtypes of disabled readers. International Journal of Clinical Neuropsychology, 4, 269–274.

Morgan, W. P. (1896). A case of congenital word-blindness. British Medical Journal, 2, 1378.

Morris, R., Blashfield, R., & Satz, P. (1986). Developmental classification of reading-disabled children. Journal of Clinical and Experimental Neuropsychology, 8, 371–392.

Naidoo, S. (1972). *Specific dyslexia*. New York: Wiley.

Nelson, H. E., & Warrington, E. K. (1974). Developmental spelling retardation and its relation to other cognitive abilities. *British Journal of Psychology, 65*, 265–274.

Nolan, D. R., Hammeke, T. A., & Barkley, R. A. (1983). A comparison of the patterns of the neuropsychological performance in two groups of learning disabled children. *Journal of Clinical Child Psychology, 12*, 22–27.

Obrzut, J. E. (1979). Dichotic listening and bisensory memory skills in qualitatively diverse dyslexic readers. *Journal of Learning Disabilities, 12*(5), 24–33.

Obrzut, J. E. (1981). Neuropsychological assessment in the schools. *School Psychology Review, 10*, 331–342.

Omenn, G. S., & Weber, B. A. (1978). Dyslexia: Search for phenotypic and genetic heterogeneity. *American Journal of Medical Genetics, 1*, 333–342.

Orton, S. T. (1928). Specific reading disability—Strephosymbolia. *Journal of the American Medical Association, 90*, 1095–1099.

Patton, H. D., Sundsten, J. W., Crill, W. E., & Swanson, P. D. (1976). *An introduction to basic neurology*. Philadelphia: Saunders.

Petrauskas, R., & Rourke, B. P. (1979). Identification of subgroups of retarded readers: A neuropsychological multivariate approach. *Journal of Clinical Neuropsychology, 1*, 17–37.

Pirozzolo, F. J. (1979). *The neuropsychology of developmental reading disorders*. New York: Praeger Press.

Reynolds, C., & Gutkin, T. B. (1979). Predicting premorbid intellectual status of children using demographic data. *Clinical Neuropsychology, 1*, 36–38.

Ross, A. O. (1976). *Psychological aspects of learning disabilities and reading disorders*. New York: McGraw-Hill.

Ross, E. D. (1981). The aprosodias. *Archives of Neurology, 38*, 561–569.

Rourke, B. D. (1976). Issues in the neuropsychological assessment of children with learning disabilities. *Canadian Psychological Review, 17*, 89–102.

Rourke, B. P., & Finlayson, M. A. J. (1978). Neuropsychological significance of variations in patterns of academic performance: Verbal and visual-spatial abilities. *Journal of Abnormal Child Psychology, 6*, 121–133.

Rourke, B. T. Young, G. C., & Flewelling, R. W. (1971). The relationships between WISC verbal-performance discrepancies and selected verbal, auditory-perceptual, visual-perceptual, and problem-solving abilities in children with learning disabilities. *Journal of Clinical Psychology, 27*(4), 475–479.

Sandoval, J., & Haapanen, R. M. (1981). A critical commentary on neuropsychology in the schools: Are we ready? *School Psychology Review, 10*, 381–388.

Satz, P., Friel, J., & Rudegeair, F. (1974). Differential changes in the acquisition of developmental skills in children who later became dyslexic. In D. G. Stein, J. J. Rosen, & N. Butters (Eds.), *Plasticity and recovery of function in the central nervous system*. New York: Academic Press.

Satz, P., & Morris, R. (1981). Learning disability subtypes: A review. In F. J. Pirozzolo & M. C. Wittrock (Eds.), *Neuropsychological and cognitive processes in reading* (pp. 109–141). New York: Academic Press.

Seidenberg, M., Giordani, B., Berent, S., & Boll, T. J. (1983). IQ level and performance on the Halstead-Reitan Neuropsychological Test Battery for Older Children. *Journal of Consulting and Clinical Psychology, 51*, 406–413.

Sevush, S. (1983, February). *The neurolinguistics of reading: Anatomic and neurologic correlates*. Paper presented at the annual meeting of the International Neuropsychological Society, Mexico City.

Silver, A., & Hagen, R. (1971). Memory and attention factors in specific learning disabilities. *Journal of Learning Disabilities, 4*, 94–106.

Smith, F. (1978). *Reading without nonsense*. New York: Teachers College Press.

Smith, M. D., Coleman, J. M., Dokecki, P. R., & Davis, E. E. (1977). Recategorized WISC-R scores of learning disabled children. *Journal of Learning Disabilities, 10*, 444–449.

Snow, J. H., Cohen, M., & Holliman, W. B. (1985). Learning disability subgroups using cluster analysis of the WISC-R. *Journal of Psychoeducational Assessment, 4,* 391–397.

Snow, J. H., & Hynd, G. W. (1985). A multivariate investigation of the Luria-Nebraska Neuropsychological Battery-Children's Revision with learning disabled children. *Journal of Psychoeducational Assessment, 3,* 101–109.

Speece, D. L., McKinney, J. D., & Appelbaum, M. I. (1985). Classification and validation of behavioral subtypes of learning disabled children. *Journal of Educational Psychology, 77,* 67–77.

Spreen, O., & Haaf, R. G. (1986). Empirically derived learning disability subtypes: A replication attempt and longitudinal patterns over 15 years. *Journal of Learning Disabilities, 19,* 170–180.

Stephenson, S. (1905). Six cases of congenital word blindness affecting three generations of one family. *Ophthalmoscope, 5,* 482–484.

Sternberg, R., & Wagner, R. K. (1982). Automatization failure in learning disabilities. *Topics in Learning and Learning Disabilities, 2,* 1–11.

Strauss, A. A., & Kephart, N. C. (1955). *Psychopathology and education of the brain-injured child* (Vol. 2). New York: Grune and Stratton.

Strauss, A. A., & Lehtinen, L. E. (1947). *Psychopathology and education of the brain-injured child* (Vol. 1). New York: Grune and Stratton.

Sweeney, J. E., & Rourke, B. A. (1978). Neuropsychological significance of phonetically accurate and phonetically inaccurate spelling errors in younger and older retarded spellers. *Brain and Language, 6,* 212–225.

Taylor, H. G., Fletcher, J. M., & Satz, P. (1982). Component processes in reading disabilities: Neuropsychological investigation of distinct subskill deficits. In R. N. Malatesha & P. G. Aaron (Eds.), *Reading disorders: Varieties and treatments* (pp. 121–147). New York: Academic Press.

Thomson, M. E. (1982). The assessment of children with specific reading difficulties (dyslexia) using the British Ability Scales. *British Journal of Psychology, 73,* 461–478.

U.S. Department of Education, Office of Special Education and Rehabilitative Services (1983). *Fifth annual report to Congress on the implementation of PL 94-142: The Education of All Handicapped Children's Act.*

Warrington, E. K. (1981). Concrete word dyslexia. *British Journal of Psychology, 72,* 175–196.

Watson, B. U., & Goldgar, D. E., & Ryschon, K. L. (1983). Subtypes of reading disability. *Journal of Clinical Neuropsychology, 5,* 377–399.

Wernicke, C. (1874). *Der aphasiche symptemkomplex.* Breslaw: Cohn and Weigert.

Whitaker, H. A. (1976). Neurobiology of language. In E. R. Carterette & M. P. Friedman (Eds.), *Handbook of perception* (Vol. 7). New York: Academic Press.

Zangwill, D. L. (1960). *Cerebral dominance and its relation to psychological function.* Edinburgh: Oliver & Boyd.

The Prediction of Learning Disabilities in the Preschool Child

A Neuropsychological Perspective

STEPHEN R. HOOPER

INTRODUCTION

Although neuropsychological measures have not been developed specifically for the preschool child, the early identification and prediction of learning problems are major challenges for the child neuropsychologist. Working with such young children presents any array of problems, including measurement difficulties, interpretive issues, and developmental questions. This latter concern is particularly important given that even a group of children having the same chronological age, gender, and ethnic background will show a wide range of "normal" developmental variation (Wolff, 1981). Assessment methods will need to be guided by a neurodevelopmental theoretical framework if the study of brain–behavior relationships in this age group is to be advanced.

Assuming that an assessment technology can be advanced that has strong neurodevelopmental underpinnings, what services or treatment linkages will be available to meet the needs of learning-disabled children and their families? The Education for All Handicapped Children Act (PL 94-142) mandated that a free and appropriate education be provided to all handicapped children from birth to 21 years of age, but it has been only recently that infant and preschool services have come to the forefront with respect to public school services. Funding issues notwithstanding, it

STEPHEN R. HOOPER • Department of Psychiatry, University of North Carolina School of Medicine, and Clinical Center for the Study of Development and Learning, University of North Carolina, Chapel Hill, North Carolina.

is no accident that this area has not been advanced sooner owing to its significant complexity.

Further compounding the difficulties confronted in the preschool population, some investigators have taken the stance that disability labels, such as learning disability, should be used sparingly with young children, if at all, owing to the negative expectations that can arise (Algozzine, Mercer, & Countermine, 1977; Foster, Schmidt, & Sabatino, 1976; Foster & Ysseldyke, 1976). For example, preschoolers experiencing only a temporary developmental delay may be misdiagnosed, and those working with the child may begin to hold negative expectations of the child's potential. This could create secondary problems of adjustment for such children, confusion in their families, and self-fulfilling prophecies in the form of actual learning difficulties. Given these concerns, it will be important for developmentally appropriate, reliable, and valid neuropsychological measures to be developed for this population. Such tools will prove useful for the early identification and prediction of learning problems, and in obtaining accurate descriptive accounts of a preschool child's strengths and weaknesses in academic readiness.

This chapter will discuss the prediction of learning problems in the preschool child from a neuropsychological perspective. Initially, the importance of this area to child neuropsychology is presented, and this is followed by a review of the literature addressing this question. Given Aylward's discussion of the application of a neuropsychological perspective in infancy and early childhood (Chapter 9, this volume), this chapter will be confined to children from approximately age 3 to age 5. Finally, the literature is integrated to underscore important directions for neuropsychologists working with preschool children and to shed some light on issues relevant to the early prediction of learning disabilities.

THE IMPORTANCE OF EARLY PREDICTION OF LEARNING DISABILITIES

There are several major reasons that make the early identification and prediction of learning disabilities important to the field of child neuropsychology. First, the extent of the problem is such that it cannot be ignored by professionals working with preschoolers. Second, these children appear to be at greater risk for a continuing downward spiral of learning and perhaps social-emotional difficulties. However, it is reasonable to assume that early identification and intervention can contribute to eliminating or lessening the severity of later learning, emotional, and behavioral difficulties that might arise. In conjunction with this viewpoint, evidence also has been presented that timely, early intervention actually may capitalize on sensitive neurodevelopmental periods during the preschool years, thus maximizing the possibilities for a child to develop adaptive coping strategies. These various reasons for early identification will be discussed in turn.

Extent of the Problem

Learning disabilities represent one of the major areas of study for the child neuropsychologist (Rourke, 1983). However, advances in the field of learning disabilities have been hindered by various definitional issues. More generally, Behr and Gallagher (1981) have proposed that a more flexible definition of what constitutes a handicap is needed for preschool children with special needs, one that involves not only the *extent* of a developmental variation but the *type* of variation. With respect to learning disabilities, recent efforts to clarify definitions have conceptualized learning disabilities as a heterogeneous group of neurologically based disorders (Hammill, Leigh, McNutt, & Larsen, 1981). Obviously, the difficulties encountered in arriving at an accepted definition have contributed to added problems in the understanding of learning disabilities and their epidemiology.

Despite these definitional difficulties, the study of learning disabilities has seen tremendous growth, particularly over the past 25 years. This growth has been fueled by legislative action as well as by the increased survival rates of many medically high-risk infants. Although not surprising, the bulk of this study has occurred with the school-age child and has not addressed the needs of the preschool population as intensely. However, figures from the U. S. Department of Education (1984) revealed that children with learning disabilities represented about 8.3% of all preschool special education recipients, making them second only to speech-impaired students in terms of categorical dysfunction. When all children receiving special education services are considered, learning-disabled children become the number one handicapped group receiving services in the public schools (Doris, 1986). These figures support the need for appropriate identification and prediction procedures for learning disabilities in the preschool population.

Given the extent of this problem, the National Joint Committee on Learning Disabilities (NJCLD, 1986) has put forth a list of recommendations for addressing the needs of preschool children. Specifically, the NJCLD outlined personnel training recommendations, testing bias concerns, and family needs. Suggestions also addressed concerns regarding the need for systematic identification programs, appropriate assessment technology and procedures, development of early intervention programs and, generally, the need for more research to gain a better understanding of learning dysfunction in preschoolers. These concerns are consistent with a child neuropsychological perspective and they reflect issues relevant to the accurate prediction of learning disabilities in the preschool child.

Minimizing Educational Failure

A second major reason why this area is important to child neuropsychology is the potential that a comprehensive neuropsychological evaluation has for guiding interventions aimed at arresting continued academic decline. The hypothesis is that the earlier a child showing learning impediments can be identified, and the more detailed the profile description, the greater is the possibility that an intensive intervention program will be able to address the child's needs in an adequate manner.

Support for this thinking has been mixed, but a significant positive trend has been asserted. White (1986), in a meta-analysis of the early intervention literature, concluded that early intervention has definite positive effects for most children, but that there was no evidence of superiority for any one kind of intervention program. In another meta-analysis, Casto and Mastropieri (1986) supported these findings and further noted that children participating in the longer, more intensive programs showed the most improvement. However, these investigators found inconclusive evidence regarding the benefits of various factors, including early program initiation (i.e., there actually was a surprising trend for better prognosis to be associated with later entry), the importance of parental involvement, and the degree of program structure (although there was a trend that favored more structured programs).

Despite these generally positive findings, Schonhaut and Satz (1983) found equivocal evidence for the notion that early identification and treatment of learning disabilities improves prognosis. In their review of follow-up studies in the learning disability area, they noted that the academic prognosis is generally poor for children with early learning problems, and that many learning-disabled children continue to experience learning difficulties as adults, even if they are occupationally or educationally successful.

Although more research is needed in this area, it appears that early intervention programs do have a positive effect for most learning-disabled children. By providing a detailed profile of a preschooler's cognitive, sensorimotor, and preacademic strengths and weaknesses, a comprehensive neuropsychological evaluation could provide a solid foundation for the development of an intervention plan designed to address the child's specific educational needs. Conceivably, this should contribute to lessening the possibility of continued educational failure.

Minimizing Social–Emotional Difficulties

Bryan and Bryan (1986) asserted that learning-disabled children are at greater risk for social adjustment difficulties than their normal achieving peers. Other researchers have suggested that these children are at greater risk than normal learners for developing secondary emotion-al/behavioral disorders and dropping out of school (Rutter, Tizard, Yule, Graham, & Whitmore, 1976; Spreen, 1978). Children with learning defi-cits also have been shown to have a higher incidence of delinquency and psychopathology, although these data remain strictly correlational and are not as yet conclusive (Schonhaut & Satz, 1983). Nonetheless, the logic for early identification of learning problems remains the same. If a child's specific learning problems can be addressed comprehensively and inten-sively at an early age, the better are the chances that the child will develop a more positive self-image and show a healthy personality development.

Social-emotional difficulties can exert a pervasive effect on a child's functioning. Where these difficulties are sparked by learning problems, it would be important for early identification procedures to address a child's learning needs accurately to minimize the potential for social-emotional difficulties that may arise from repeated failure and frustration. Certain kinds of neuropsychological profiles might carry a greater risk for developing psychopathology, and planning for these difficulties may help the child's adjustment. In this regard, some evidence has surfaced in the school-age population showing potential relationships between particular patterns of behavioral maladjustment and specific neuropsychological profiles (Nussbaum & Bigler, 1986; Porter & Rourke, 1985; Speece, McKin-ney, & Appelbaum, 1985; Strang & Rourke, 1985). Although these rela-tionships have not been replicated in a preschool population, these find-ings do underscore the potential contributions that a neuropsychological perspective may have for identifying children at risk for social-emotional difficulties.

Effects of Environmental Influences

A fourth important reason for child neuropsychologists to be in-volved in the early identification of learning problems comes from the evidence suggesting that children may be more sensitive to positive change during early developmental periods. Currently, there are two ma-jor lines of thinking on this issue.

One viewpoint suggests that relatively immature brain regions may subserve functions that typically would be managed by other brain re-gions when these are disrupted by an insult (i.e., neural reorganization). The second line of thinking views the less crystallized brain systems in the younger child as being more susceptible to environmental influence and, subsequently, positive behavioral change (Rourke, Bakker, Fisk, & Strang, 1983). Evidence for these suppositions has surfaced from both animal (Bennett, 1976; Coss & Globus, 1978; Walsh, 1981) and human research (Bakker, Moerland, & Goekoop-Hoefkens, 1981; Zihl, 1981). Re-gardless of the processes involved in the acquisition or reacquisition of function, the implication that optimal learning periods exist provides a potential therapeutic window for the child neuropsychologist who is working with the preschool child (Rourke *et al.*, 1983).

Summary

The above discussion highlighted the importance of learning disability prediction to the child neuropsychologist. The extent of the problem, the possibility of minimizing learning and emotional difficulties, and the potential for making a valuable contribution to the treatment programming of children at risk for learning disabilities all argue for more active efforts with preschoolers on the part of child neuropsychologists. The next section will provide a review of the current status of the field with respect to research on the early prediction of learning problems.

THE PREDICTION OF LEARNING DISABILITIES: CURRENT STATUS

There have been hundreds of studies that have addressed the prediction of learning problems during the preschool years. For over two decades researchers have attempted to find the "best" predictor, or groups of predictors, for identifying the preschool child with a learning problem. Needless to say, this search has turned up a wide variety of "effective" predictors, numerous assessment strategies and, characteristic of the learning disability field in general, findings that are contradictory in nature. These contradictory data have served to demonstrate the complexity of the prediction process. This section will discuss several recent literature reviews related to the preschool prediction of learning disabilities. Several exemplary studies also will be presented that have made major contributions to the early prediction efforts.

Recent Reviews of the Literature

To date several major reviews of the literature in this area have been put forth. Most of these have focused on predicting learning problems (de Hirsch, Jansky, & Langford, 1966; Horn & Packard, 1985; Jansky, 1978; Mercer, Algozzine, & Trifiletti, 1979; Simner, 1983), and others have addressed the prediction of learning in the preschool child more broadly (Barrett, 1965; Tramontana, Hooper, & Selzer, 1988). Examining the more recent reviews reveals an inconsistent set of conclusions with respect to the early identification literature.

Mercer *et al.* (1979) reviewed early prediction studies extending from 1966 to 1977 that employed single and multiple predictor procedures.

Although 70 studies were reviewed, only 15 were deemed appropriate for their matrix analysis of classification hit rates. For single measures, such as the Reading Subtest of the Wide Range Achievement Test, the Bender Visual-Motor Gestalt Test, and an unusual birth history, Mercer *et al.* found a median hit rate of 73%. For multiple instrument batteries (e.g., de Hirsch Index) the median overall hit rate was slightly increased to 79%. Mercer *et al.* noted that teacher ratings tended to predict later learning difficulties best (i.e., approximately 84%), especially if the teachers were provided with checklists containing items directly related to academic learning.

These reviewers also stated that the literature supported the inclusion of preacademic skills (e.g., letter recognition) in the preschool assessment since these tasks accurately identified at-risk learners more often than other predictor measures. Further, they noted that the timing of the initial screening was potentially important, with administration during the winter or spring of the kindergarten year having predictive advantages over testing during the fall (e.g., allowing for the child's adjustment to formal schooling and increased time for teacher observation). However, the conclusions of this review were difficult to evaluate because no descriptions were provided of the studies included, thus leaving any methodological concerns unknown but crucial elements.

Simner (1983) discussed the potential warning signs of school failure in the kindergarten child. Selectively reviewing about 18 studies conducted from 1966 to 1982, Simner concluded that gross or fine motor coordination, peer acceptance, basic language skills, and drawing/ copying errors were not effective predictors of later learning problems. However, attention/distractibility. verbal skills, and printing errors did seem to be effective predictors of later school failure. Despite these findings, Simner's review was limited in that it tended to focus on univariate predictors. Global measures (e.g., IQ) and test batteries were omitted from consideration with respect to their comparative effectiveness. Other important issues also were neglected, such as multivariate prediction, variation as a function of the academic criterion predicted, time of assessment, prediction interval, and demographic factors.

In a well-designed meta-analysis, Horn and Packard (1985) conducted a review of 58 studies predicting reading achievement during the elementary school years. Most of the studies included in the meta-analysis were conducted between 1960 and 1980. They found that the best single predictors of reading achievement in grades 1 and 3 were measures of general cognitive functioning, language, attention/distractibility, and internalizing behavioral problems. Horn and Packard's review suggested that measures tapping sensory-perceptual functions and soft neurological signs (e.g., gross motor skills) were less effective predictors of later reading problems.

Horn and Packard were cautious to note that predicting school success or failure is a complex process, and that it is unreasonable to think that a single predictor could account for all of the variance in school achievement. They noted that even the best early predictors accounted for less than 36% of the variance in elementary school reading achievement. Nonetheless, as with the two previous reviews, the focus of the meta-analysis was on univariate prediction, with only token consideration being given to how various measures might be combined effectively to increase prediction of learning difficulties. Also, like many of the early identification and prediction studies, the Horn and Packard review focused solely on reading problems and did not address other academic areas. Further, the studies included in their review were not limited to pre-first-grade prediction efforts. Finally, although the meta-analysis was well done, this procedure likely masked the vast heterogeneity across studies due to the nature of the technique (i.e., the need to compare the investigations on a common metric) (Wilson & Rachman, 1983).

More recently, Tramontana et al. (1988) provided a comprehensive examination of the preschool prediction of later academic achievement. This review focused on 74 studies conducted since approximately the inception of PL 94-142 and included only studies in which the predictor measures were administered prior to first grade. In general, effective predictors spanned a wide range of variables, which included cognitive, verbal, sensory-perceptual, perceptual-motor, behavioral, and demographic domains. Further, the authors noted that predictive relationships tended to vary according to the specific criterion variable being assessed.

Measures of letter naming, general cognitive ability, language, visual-motor skills, and finger localization were found to be accurate predictors of reading in grades 1 through 3. However, these findings can only be viewed as preliminary because very few of the studies examined reading in terms of its component parts (e.g., recognition, comprehension). The one study that did examine reading more precisely found a differential predictive pattern, with IQ being the best predictor of reading vocabulary and the Bender-Gestalt being the best predictor of reading comprehension (Wallbrown, Engin, Wallbrown, & Blaha, 1975). To complicate matters, developmental factors seemed to contribute to an apparent shift in the predictive power of a set of predictors. Satz, Taylor, Friel, and Fletcher (1978) demonstrated this by noting the importance of visual perceptual factors in the prediction of early reading recognition, but the relatively greater importance of verbal abilities as children progressed through elementary school.

The Tramontana et al. review found that math was predicted about as well as reading, although it was not studied as extensively. Effective predictors included IQ, visual-motor skills, memory, attention, and auditory comprehension of language. As with the reading criterion, selective components of mathematics rarely were considered. None of the studies included in the review devoted primary emphasis to the preschool prediction of mathematics achievement.

The Tramontana *et al.* review concluded that the research to date had succeeded in providing a general set of preschool measures that allow for a gross discrimination of children falling at the extremes of academic ability during the early elementary school years. However, these measures lack sensitivity in the identification of the child who initially appears to be functioning normally but later develops a learning impediment.

Exemplary Studies

Although the early identification literature extends back as far as the 1920s (Smith, 1928), the interest in this area exploded during the 1960s. Despite the large number of studies in this area, there have been only a few exemplary works that have set the stage for current endeavors, particularly from a neuropsychological vantage point.

One of the first longitudinal efforts in the early prediction of reading problems was initiated by de Hirsch et al. (1966). These investigators examined the effectiveness of a battery of tests containing linguistic and perceptual measures in the prediction of later reading achievement. Children were tested at the end of their kindergarten year and re-evaluated at the end of second grade. Jansky and de Hirsch (1972) reported that their Screening Index accurately identified 79% of children with reading problems, although there was a large number of false-positive prediction errors (i.e., 25%). Specific variables that were most predictive of second-grade reading problems included letter naming, picture naming, word matching, copying, and sentence memory. Generally, these authors stressed the importance of language factors (e.g., verbal retrieval) as major predictors of reading success.

Silver and Hagin (1972) also presented data from one of the first longitudinal investigations on early identification. As early as 1960, Silver and Hagin postulated that the perceptual dysfunction typically observed in reading disability was an extension of deficits in spatial and temporal organization (e.g., deficits in visual discrimination, auditory sequencing problems, right–left confusion, finger agnosia). These investigators speculated that these deficits were associated with a lack of cerebral dominance for language and/or they resulted from poorly modulated interhemispheric transfer of information.

Silver and Hagin evaluated beginning first-grade students with a battery measuring neurological, psychiatric, psychological, social, and achievement areas. A factor analysis of their battery was performed, and five factors emerged that accounted for approximately 61% of the total prediction variance. These factors were Auditory Association, Visual-

Neurological, Psychiatric Impairment, Chronological Age, and General Intelligence. Working from their theoretical position, measures from the top two factors, Auditory Association and Visual-Neurological, were combined to form one predictive battery, the SEARCH (Silver & Hagin, 1976). Not only has this screening battery been successful in predicting reading problems at the end of second grade, but it has been the diagnostic foundation for a prescriptive intervention program, TEACH (Hagin, Silver, & Kreeger, 1976). Although the Silver and Hagin work was conducted with entry-level first-graders, their investigations were noteworthy for specifying underlying factors of early identification instrumentation, establishing a theoretical perspective involving neurocognitive processing abilities, and demonstrating efforts to validate a systematic intervention approach based upon specific assessment technology.

A third early identification and prediction project, the Florida Longitudinal Project (Satz et al., 1978), represented one of the most comprehensive longitudinal efforts in the early identification literature. Satz and co-workers conceptualized that specific precursors to reading were related to maturational factors affecting readiness. Reading problems were described as initially reflecting delays in the early development of sensory-perceptual processes and, subsequently, delays in conceptual-linguistic skills. Generally, these delays were postulated to be related, in part, to lagged maturation of the cerebral cortex (Satz & van Nostrand, 1973).

Satz and colleagues employed a broad-based, multivariate approach to prediction using multiple follow-up points and numerous cross-validation studies. Their project was based on an original sample of 497 white male kindergarten students in the Alachua County Public School System in Florida. The predictor battery consisted of 22 measures, 16 of which were grouped empirically into three factors. These included factors measuring skills in the Sensory-Motor-Perceptual, Conceptual-Verbal, and Verbal-Cultural domains. Taken together, these factors accounted for approximately 60% of the variance in reading prediction. Criterion measures included tests of reading recognition and teacher ratings of reading. These investigators found about an 84% correct classification rate, with finger localization, recognition-discrimination tasks, and alphabet recitation being the best predictors of reading outcomes in second grade. At the end of grade 5, a 76% correct classification rate was obtained, with the Peabody Picture Vocabulary Test, the Developmental Test of Visual-Motor Integration, alphabet recitation, and finger localization emerging as the best predictors.

However, when these results were scrutinized more closely, it was noted that although these measures were quite good at predicting the severely disabled and the superior readers, the correct classification rates fell significantly for the middle ranges of functioning. False negative rates (i.e., children who were functioning adequately in kindergarten, but who later "grew into" deficits) ranged from about 5% in grade 1 to about 26% in grade 5. This is disappointing, given that this was based on one of the best sets of screening procedures that the field has to offer at the present time. Despite these difficulties, the Florida Longitudinal Project represents one of the most extensive efforts to date in the early identification and prediction of learning problems.

In addition to the three studies above, two other efforts deserve mention. Stevenson, Parker, Wilkinson, Hegion, and Fish (1976) conducted a well-designed study and follow-up (Stevenson & Newman, 1986) in isolating a differential set of predictors for reading and mathematics. Using a comprehensive battery of cognitive, perceptual, memory, and academic tasks, these investigators found the best kindergarten predictors of reading to be letter naming, visual-auditory paired associates, Horst reversals, and verbal categorization. The best predictors of math included verbal recall, visual-auditory paired associates, perceptual learning, and coding. This pattern of predictors was relatively stable for first-, second-, third-, fifth-, and tenth-grade follow-up points. Not only is this study important for describing a differential pattern of predictors for reading and mathematics, but it also has one of the longest follow-up intervals reported to date.

Finally, the last study to be discussed is important largely because of its direct application of standard neuropsychological methods. Although several studies have employed a neuropsychological perspective (e.g., the Florida Longitudinal Project), Teeter (1985) used an established neuropsychological battery to predict first-grade achievement. Using the McCarthy Scales of Children's Abilities and portions of the Reitan-Indiana Neuropsychological Battery, Teeter predicted first-grade achievement with 57% and 61% accuracy, respectively. Generally, Teeter found the Reitan-Indiana variables to be slightly more predictive than the McCarthy for spelling, reading, and mathematics scores on standardized achievement testing.

Summary

There is an extensive literature dealing with studies that were designed to obtain the best predictor, or set of predictors, for later learning difficulties. However, it appears that this has been too simplistic a goal, given the complexities of the learning process and its underlying neuropsychological mechanisms. The child neuropsychologist investigating the early identification and prediction of learning disabilities during the preschool years will need to address a more complicated series of questions. For example, a more sophisticated question might be: What combination of measures, administered during specific times, are effective in predicting specific outcomes for specific types of children at specific points in their subsequent development? Future efforts in the early identification area should address such questions more thoroughly.

Previous work has laid the foundation for exploring the complexities of this area, but these complexities are rapidly beginning to confront practitioners in the preschool domain. Recent legislation (i.e., PL 99-457, the Education of the Handicapped Act Amendments of 1986) directly addressing some of the service needs of the preschool population also will drive increased efforts in this area. The literature does suggest the presence of broad neuropsychological constructs that could be incorporated into a predictive preschool battery, but their specific predictive accuracy will require further study. Also, the field would benefit from a greater reliance on neurodevelopmental theory in the development of neuropsychological assessment technology.

ISSUES AND DIRECTIONS

Although there have been efforts to apply neuropsychological assessment methods to the preschool prediction of learning disabilities, the bulk of the literature is not unique to the field of neuropsychology. In fact, aside from the use of the Reitan-Indiana Neuropsychological Battery with 5-year-old children, even the instrumentation is not exclusive to the field. In this regard there are few, if any, instruments specifically designed to assess brain–behavior relationship in this population. Consequently, then, what are the advantages of using a neuropsychological assessment model over more traditional psychological or psychoeducational procedures?

The advantages do not seem to be associated with particular instrumentation, although further development certainly is needed with respect to this, but more with the perspective that can be employed in planning measurement strategies and organizing assessment findings around specific neuropsychological constructs. The literature has begun to provide a comprehensive list of broad-band neuropsychological constructs for this population, but the assessment of these constructs in a developmental fashion will require more than just the use of age-appropriate measures having adequate normative bases. Any instrumentation must be sensitive to how a child's abilities are increasing and changing (e.g., flexibility in problem solving) and provide information relative to the normal and aberrant development of specific behaviors over time (e.g., academic precursors)—even if a child is at a satisfactory level. The assessment also must be grounded within a theoretical framework consistent with what is known about preschool brain–behavior relationships.

Neurodevelopmental Theory

It will be crucial for work in the area of early prediction to be guided by theoretical conceptualizations. Knowing that a specific predictor–criterion relationship exists is not enough; it also is necessary to know *why* such a relationship exists. Although the efforts of Luria (1980), Rourke *et al.* (1983), Satz *et al.* (1978), Silver and Hagin (1972) and, more recently, Levine (Blackman, Levine, Markowitz, & Aufseeser, 1983; Levine & Schneider, 1982) have set the stage for employing a neurodevelopmental theoretical perspective, it is surprising that this has not been developed more extensively. This is especially the case with learning disabilities, given that current definitions of learning disabilities require at least the suspicion of underlying neuropathology (Hammill *et al.*, 1981). Some work already has been advanced noting neuroanatomical (Hier, LeMay, Rosenberger, & Perlo, 1978) and neurophysiological (Duffy, Denckla, Bartels, & Sandini, 1980) anomalies as correlates of learning disabilities. These anomalies have been implicated in contributing to the academic deficits in learning-disabled children as well as underlying their deviant information processing.

Despite the promise of these findings, certain aspects of neurodevelopment are better substantiated and should be incorporated into a neuropsychological perspective with this population. For example, it has been argued that cerebral lateralization of function does not "develop," but that it is present at birth (Kinsbourne & Hiscock, 1978). Indirect evidence for this supposition has been provided by Gilbert and Climan (1974), Ingram (1975), and Marcotte and LaBarba (1985) using dichotic listening paradigms with preschoolers as young as 2½ years of age. Anatomical asymmetries, favoring the left hemisphere, also have been reported in the neonate (Witelson & Pallie, 1973). These data suggest that left hemisphere language lateralization exists from the outset, and thus set the stage for the interpretation of hemispheric specialization and functional systems in the preschooler.

At present there are at least two major neurodevelopmental conceptualizations that attempt to account, at least in part, for the later emergence of a learning disability. The first model proposes a maturational lag in cortical functioning (Satz & van Nostrand, 1973), and the other suggests that the area of deficit is always present, but that deficiencies are manifested only when specific demands challenge the processing capabilities of the involved brain region (Rourke *et al.*, 1983). This latter position also is consistent with the neurodevelopmental model espoused by Luria (1980).

The model put forth by Satz (Satz & van Nostrand, 1973) provided much of the theoretical guidance for the Florida Longitudinal Project (Satz *et al.*, 1978), which investigated the precursors to later reading problems. This theory predicted delays in brain maturation that differentially affected skills that were in primary ascendancy at different chronological ages. Skills that develop during the preschool years, such as visual-perceptual abilities and cross-modal sensory integration, were speculated to be delayed because of immaturity in the cortical regions associated with those skills and, consequently, to interfere with early aspects of reading acquisition. Although these visual-perceptual deficiencies eventually would resolve, skills that develop ontogenetically later in childhood and at a slower rate (such as linguistic skills and formal operations) would be delayed in immature older children and would continue hindering reading development. Although this theory is noteworthy for its incorporation of neurodevelopmental processes in the understanding of reading difficulties, the concept of maturational delays in cortical development does not address several important issues adequately in the prediction of learning-disabled children.

First, if the underlying premise is that of developmental delays in cortical maturation, then a child should be expected eventually to "catch up" with chronological-aged peers, or at least to narrow the gap in ability–achievement discrepancies over time. Present research would suggest that this is not the case (Schonhaut & Satz, 1983). Although learning-disabled children do show gains in their skills and abilities, they rarely demonstrate an adequate level of academic functioning, and this is inconsistent with the concept of neuromaturational delay.

Second, if a child's specific learning problems are due to developmental delays, then one should expect a relatively normal (albeit slow) pattern of skill acquisition. However, evidence has surfaced that suggests that not only are these children delayed in their skill acquisition, but they manifest aberrant information processing styles as well (Aram & Nation, 1975). A model of neuromaturational lag does little to explain the deviant processing abilities evidenced by many learning-disabled children. It does not reflect the number and kinds of deficits that a child can exhibit at a particular age.

Finally, the model does not provide any explanation for why many "normal" children appear to "grow into" a deficit during later childhood. Indeed, the data from the Florida Longitudinal Project support this contention, in that by fifth grade the false-negative rate (i.e., children initially described as "normal" in kindergarten) climbed from 5% in grade 1 to about 26% by grade 5. Despite the difficulties inherent with a neuromaturational lag hypothesis, it has provided insights into some of the kindergarten precursors to reading.

A second major position, proposed by Rourke et al. (1983), suggests that the deficits seen in learning-disabled children are not due to neuromaturational delays but are always present and remain "silent" until the affected region or functional system is challenged by environmental demands. It is at this time that the selective deficits associated with the brain lesion or structural anomaly are manifested. This theory would begin to account for the observation that a large percentage of "normal" functioning preschoolers (about 26% in the Florida Longitudinal Project) later show learning impediments. This theoretical position also would not limit the identification of early deficits mainly to visual-perceptual abilities and, consequently, would be more consistent with recent heterogeneous conceptualizations of learning disabilities than a neuromaturational-delay model.

The implications for neuropsychological assessment based on this theoretical model provide guidance in the search for neurodevelopmental precursors to learning problems. It broadens the number of potential neuropsychological constructs that may be relevant to the preschool child and would provide an explanation for the large number of "effective" predictors that have been asserted. It also would explain why a measure seemingly unrelated to academics, such as finger localization, has been consistently predictive of later reading difficulties (Lindgren, 1978; Satz et al., 1978).

Specifically, finger localization is felt to represent a measure of parietal lobe functioning (Reitan & Davison, 1974). Structures directly associated with the parietal lobe, such as the angular gyrus, have been directly linked to reading skills (Gaddes, 1985). These tertiary cortical regions are slower to mature and hierarchically are dependent upon intact functioning of the modality-specific primary and secondary cortical zones (Luria, 1980). Finger localization, which is a secondary-level parietal function, may forecast a child's readiness to engage in tertiary-level functions, such as reading, although little is known about its predictive value for specific aspects of reading dysfunction or perhaps other kinds of academic deficits (e.g., math).

Given the neurodevelopmental perspective offered by Rourke et al. (1983), it will be important for the field to begin to evolve new instrumentation and procedures. This goes beyond establishing normative data for a set of tasks and extends into describing more accurately the neurocognitive underpinnings of learning and achievement precursors. Although debates will continue regarding when a child's brain becomes fully functional, it is clear that there is a developmental sequence in brain development that can be tapped by behavioral tasks during the preschool years. It is suspected that the more accurately these underlying neurodevelopmental processes can be assessed, the better the prediction of later learning and behavioral outcomes will become.

For example, with respect to the development of behaviors associated with the frontal lobes, Luria (1959) demonstrated that 3-year-old children typically are unable to inhibit their behaviors using overt verbal mediation, but that by age 4 this would emerge and later evolve into internal verbal regulation of behavior. This was replicated in a well-designed study by Tinsley and Waters (1982). Similar studies have begun to examine normal developmental expectations for other neurocognitive functions. Using Luria's (1980) model of neurodevelopment, Passler, Isaac, and Hynd (1986) and Becker, Isaac, and Hynd (1988) found evidence for a developmental progression of frontal lobe development in subjects ranging from about 5 to 12 years of age. Heverly, Isaac, and Hynd (1986) noted a similar progression in normal children with respect to tactile-visual discrimination functions associated with parietal lobe development. These kinds of theoretically driven neurobehavioral tasks hold promise for improving the predictability of later academic difficulties and the description of specific brain–behavior relationships in this population.

These efforts are noteworthy with respect to understanding the neurodevelopmental sequences of various cognitive functions, but they will require further refinements if indeed they are to be applied clinically to the preschool child. Evidence with respect to their predictive validity for later academic functioning also will need to be demonstrated. This latter point will be important not only for predicting the extremes of functional outcomes but for charting their false-positive and false-negative prediction rates.

Finally, with respect to neurodevelopmental theory, it is important to remember that learning problems are not totally inherent to the child. Other variables, such as socioeconomic status, family climate, and nursery school experiences, should be evaluated in tandem with specific neurodevelopmental variables so as to better gauge their interactive complexities. Although highly important, neurodevelopmental variables only account for a portion of the variance of later academic successes and difficulties.

Neuropsychological Constructs and Preschool Prediction

Wilson (1986) conjectured that child neuropsychology is about 25 years behind adult neuropsychology, and perhaps this gap becomes even wider when one considers the status of the neuropsychological assessment of the infant, toddler, and preschooler. Although predicting learning outcomes is not a simple matter, and no universal set of techniques has been established, there are important clues that have emerged from the existing prediction literature.

The evidence generated to date would not indicate an overall preference for linguistic abilities, perceptual skills, or any other broad classification of functions in the prediction of learning problems. However, consistent with the mainstream of neuropsychological testing, assessment of a wide array of functional domains would appear most useful for the clinician at this time. The addition of maturationally sensitive tasks also would provide the foundation for determining predictive brain–behavior relationships in preschool children from a neurodevelopmental perspective.

In this regard there have been several general (Deysach, 1986; Hartlage & Telzrow, 1982; Wilson, 1986) and specific (Korkman, 1987; Reitan & Davison, 1974; Satz & Fletcher, 1982) clinical neuropsychological assessment models proposed for use with the preschooler. Structured neurodevelopmental examinations also have been developed that purport to measure a broad range of functional areas in this population (Blackman et al., 1983; Levine & Scheider, 1982). Generally, these models espouse the assessment of abilities covering auditory processing and language, memory, preacademic skills, adaptive behavior, behavioral ratings, motor functions, and sensory-perceptual abilities. It is perhaps the measurement of these latter two functional domains that distinguishes neuropsychological assessment from other types of testing. However, with the exception of the study by Teeter (1985) and the work of Satz in the Florida Longitudinal Project, there is no evidence regarding the validity of any of these neuropsychological assessment models in predicting later learning problems.

For example, how well do Reitan's four methods of inference (i.e., level of performance, pattern of performance, pathognomonic signs, left/right differences) apply to the preschool population, particularly given this population's increased performance inconsistencies? Is one of these methods of inference more related to accurate prediction than another? Although models currently exist for the neuropsychological assessment of the preschool child, their applicability in predicting later learning difficulties remains to be addressed empirically.

Factor-analytic work with preschool assessment batteries has produced factors that are remarkably similar to the areas of functioning generally included in a neuropsychological assessment. Jansky (1970) identified five factors in her factor analysis of 19 kindergarten tests. These included Oral Language (A and B), Pattern Matching, Pattern Memory, and Visual-Motor Integration. Silver and Hagin (1972) also identified five factors from their preschool battery that included Auditory Association, Visual-Neurological, Psychiatric Impairment, Chronological Age, and General Intelligence. The Silver and Hagin factors are notable for their psychiatric factor suggesting that there also may be social-emotional precursors to later academic problems. Satz et al. (1978) identified three factors in their work, which largely assessed skills in the Snesory-Motor-Perceptual, Conceptual-Verbal, and Verbal-Cultural domains. These studies have found precursors of later learning difficulties, and the inclusion of skills assessed by these factors would prove useful for a preschool neuropsychological battery designed for predicting learning outcomes.

Taken together, the clinical and empirical studies support the development of a predictive neuropsychological assessment model covering a wide array of lower as well as higher cognitive functions. It is suggested that such a battery include specific neurodevelopmental tasks (e.g., Passler *et al.* 1986) that will provide behavioral indicators of brain development and, ultimately, clues to better prediction of learning problems. Needless to say, a preschool neuropsychological battery designed to predict later learning difficulties also should include a comprehensive medical, family, and developmental history. This will contribute to delineating social-cultural difficulties as well as possible brain-based learning deficits in the assessment and prediction of learning disabilities.

Related Issues in the Prediction of Learning Disabilities

In addition to constructing a neuropsychological assessment battery designed to predict later learning impediments, several related issues should be addressed. First, the literature has focused largely on reading as the criterion variable. The need to extend predictive relationships to other academic criteria is obvious. Further, it will be important for predictive relationships to examine specific components of a criterion area such as reading comprehension. The few studies that have addressed these concerns revealed a differential pattern of results, not only among reading components but between reading and mathematics (Stevenson *et al.*, 1976; Wallbrown *et al.*, 1975). Efforts in the further refinement of criterion variables also will provide evidence with respect to the neurocognitive underpinnings of specific component skills and perhaps contribute to improved treatment linkages.

A second issue is related to when the initial assessment or screening should occur. Is there an optimal time for this evaluation? At present, the available literature suggests that late kindergarten is the optimal time for the initial assessment to occur. In many of the studies reviewed by Tramontana *et al.* (1988), this time period minimized the interval between predictor and criterion measurements. More important, however, it seems that late kindergarten is optimal largely because of the increased stability of prerequisite skills, abilities, and response tendencies in the preschooler. The later assessment time also allows the child to become more comfortable with the kindergarten setting, thus minimizing the effects of adjustment to the novel preschool situation. However, the timing of initial screening may be limited by current assessment technology. Using instrumentation developed around neurodevelopmental factors might allow for an earlier, yet reliable, prediction of learning disabilities. This question will become even more important as legislation begins to require the early identification of handicapped youngsters (i.e., PL 99-457).

Another issue to be addressed is the need for the child neuropsychologist to employ multiple points for follow-up testing. The work by Satz and colleagues amply illustrates how many children could be missed if multiple assessment points were not instituted. There are many children who appear to "grow into" learning problems despite functioning within a normal range on a kindergarten screening battery. It would be useful for the child neuropsychologist to institute additional planned follow-up points so as to monitor the children who fall in the middle ranges of functioning during the preschool years. This would serve to identify children who may be primed to become immersed in an insidious academic decline secondary to neurodevelopmental anomalies, particularly if such testing were designed to occur simultaneously with the shifting pattern of academic demands. This type of ongoing assessment/screening process recognizes the dynamic and complex aspects of learning. It would allow for the incorporation of external variables into the assessment process, such as teacher variables, classroom behaviors, psychosocial issues (e.g., family), and socioeconomic factors. With the development of more sophisticated methods for the neuropsychological assessment of the preschool child, it also may prove fruitful for tracking the topographical continuity of various learner subtype patterns with respect to their evolvement, prognosis, and treatment.

It is surprising, given the contradictory predictive findings currently generated and the interactive complexities of the learning process itself, that predictors of specific learning disability subtypes have not emerged. Rourke (1983) noted that the subtyping of learning disabilities may be the most pressing issue at this time in the learning disability field, and its downward extension to preschoolers is only logical. This will surface undoubtedly once assessment technology and neurodevelopmental underpinnings are better integrated, and their predictive accuracy substantiated.

CONCLUSIONS

This chapter has attempted to establish the importance of viewing the early identification of learning disabilities within a neuropsychological perspective. From the literature reviewed, it seems that the complex issues regarding the prediction of learning problems during the preschool years have only begun to be addressed. Noteworthy efforts by Satz et al. (1978), Silver and Hagin (1972), and others have set the stage for future research in this area. However, it is clear that the field needs to receive theoretical direction and, given the recent conceptualization of learning disabilities as having a neurological basis, a neuropsychological perspective appears logical. In addition, a neuropsychological perspective would be consistent with the concerns recently outlined for the learning-disabled preschooler by the NJCLD (1986), particularly with respect to the need for reliable diagnosis and prediction.

Currently, clinicians and researchers should assess a wide variety of abilities, including sensory and motor functions, within the context of theoretically driven assessment model. Investigators also should be striving to develop new instrumentation as well as refining traditional methods so as to increase our ability to delineate brain–behavior relationships in the preschool population. Criterion measures should be more focused and refined as well. The prediction of learning disabilities during the preschool years is complex and, consequently, any neuropsychological assessment strategy must be dynamic and multifaceted. If learning and learning disabilities were to be viewed in a more dynamic fashion, systematic and aggressive follow-up testing of all children could be pursued in an effort to minimize the number of children who seemingly "grow into" a deficit (false-negatives) as well as those who initially show deficits but later "catch up" (false-positives). This also will permit the optimal time for performing initial predictive assessments to be determined more accurately, and perhaps contribute to lowering the age of initial assessment. Addressing these concerns will permit investigators to identify future learning problems more effectively.

REFERENCES

Algozzine, B., Mercer, C. D., & Countermine, T. (1977). The effects of labels and behavior on teacher expectations *Exceptional Children, 44,* 131–132.

Aram, D. M., & Nation, J. E. (1975). Patterns of language behavior in children with developmental language disorders. *Journal of Speech and Hearing Research, 18,* 229–241.

Bakker, D. J., Moerland, R., & Goekoop-Hoefkens, M. (1981). Effects of hemisphere-specific stimulation on the reading performance of dyslexic boys: A pilot study. *Journal of Clinical Neuropsychology, 3,* 155–159.

Barrett, T. C. (1965). Relationship between measures of prereading visual discrimination and first grade reading achievement: Review of the literature. *Reading Research Quarterly, 1,* 51–76.

Becker, M. G., Isaac, W., & Hynd, G. W. (1988). Neuropsychological development of nonverbal behaviors attributed to frontal lobe functioning. *Developmental Neuropsychology*

Behr, S., & Gallagher, J. J. (1981). Alternative administrative strategies for young handicapped children: A policy analysis. *Journal of the Division for Early Childhood, 2,* 113–122.

Bennett, E. R. (1976). Cerebral effects of differential experience and training. In M. R. Rosenzweig & E. L. Bennett (Eds.), *Neural mechanisms of learning and memory* (pp. 279–287). Cambridge, MA: M.I.T. Press.

Blackman, J. A., Levine, M. D., Markowitz, M. T., & Aufseeser, C. L. (1983). The pediatric extended examination at three: A system for diagnostic clarification of problematic three-year-olds. *Developmental and Behavioral Pediatrics, 4,* 143–150.

Bryan, T., & Bryan, J. (1986). *Understanding learning disabilities* (3rd ed.). Palo Alto: Mayfield.

Casto, G., & Mastropieri, M. A. (1986). The efficacy of early intervention programs: A meta-analysis. *Exceptional Children, 52,* 417–424.

Coss, R. G., & Globus, A. (1978). Spine stems on tectal interneurons in jewel fish are shortened by social stimulation. *Science, 200,* 787–790.

de Hirsch, K., Jansky, J., & Langford, W. (1966). *Predicting reading failure.* New York: Harper & Row.

Deysach, R. E. (1986). The role of neuropsychological assessment in the comprehensive evaluation of preschool-age children. *School Psychology Review, 15,* 233–244.

Doris, J. (1986). Learning disabilities. In S. J. Ceci (Ed.), *Handbook of cognitive, social, and neuropsychological aspects of learning disabilities* (pp. 3–54). Hillsdale, NJ: Erlbaum.

Duane, D. D. (1979). Toward a definition of dyslexia: A summary of views. *Bulletin of the Orton Society, 29,* 56–64.

Duffy, F. H., Denckla, M. B., Bartels, P. H., & Sandini, G. (1980). Dyslexia: Regional differences in brain electrical activity by topographic mapping. *Annals of Neurology, 7,* 412–420.

Foster, G., Schmidt, C., & Sabatino, D. (1976). Teachers' expectancies and the label "learning disabilities." *Journal of Learning Disabilities, 9,* 58–61.

Foster, G., & Ysseldyke, J. (1976). Expectancy and halo effects as a result of artificially induced teacher bias. *Contemporary Educational Psychology, 1,* 37–45.

Gaddes, W. (1985). Learning disabilities and brain function: A neuropsychological approach (2nd ed.). New York: Springer-Verlag

Gilbert, J. H. V., & Climan, I. (1974). Dichotic studies in two and three year olds: A preliminary report. *Speech Communication Seminar, Stockholm* (Vol. 2). Upsala: Almquist & Wiksell.

Hagin, R. A., Silver, A. A., & Kreeger, H. (1976). *Teach.* New York: Walker Educational Book Corporation.

Hammill, D. D., Leigh, J. E., McNutt, G., & Larsen, L. C. (1981). A new definition of learning disabilities. *Learning Disability Quarterly, 4,* 336–342.

Hartlage, L. C., & Telzrow, C. F. (1982). Neuropsychological assessment. In K. Paget & B. Bracken (Eds.), *Psychoeducational assessment of preschool children* (pp. 295–320). New York: Grune and Stratton.

Heverly, L. L., Isaac, W., & Hynd, G. W. (1986). Neurodevelopmental and racial differences in tactile-visual (cross-modal) discrimination in normal black and white children. *Archives of Clinical Neuropsychology, 1,* 139–145.

Hier, D. B., LeMay, M., Rosenberger, P. B., & Perlo, V. P. (1978). Developmental dyslexia: Evidence for a subgroup with a reversal of cerebral asymmetry. *Archives of Neurology, 35,* 90–92.

Horn, W. F., & Packard, T. (1985). Early identification of learning problems: A meta-analysis. *Journal of Educational Psychology, 77,* 597–607.

Ingram, D. (1975). Cerebral speech lateralization in young children. *Neuropsychologia, 13,* 103–105.

Jansky, J. J. (1970). *The contribution of certain kindergarten abilities to second grade reading and spelling achievement.* Unpublished doctoral dissertation, Columbia University, New York.

Jansky, J. J. (1978). A critical review of "Some developmental and predictive precursors of reading disabilities." In A. L. Benton & D. Pearl (Eds.), *Dyslexia. An appraisal of current knowledge* (pp. 377–394). New York: Oxford University Press.

Jansky, J. J., & de Hirsch, K. (1972). *Preventing reading failure—prediction, diagnosis, intervention.* New York: Harper & Row.

Kinsbourne, M., & Hiscock, M. (1977). Does cerebral dominance develop? In S. J. Segalowitz & F. A. Gruber (Eds.), *Language development and neurological theory* (pp. 171–191). New York: Academic Press.

Korkman, M. E. (1987, February). *NEPSY—A neuropsychological test battery for children, based on Luria's investigation.* Paper presented at the Fifteenth Annual Meeting of the International Neuropsychological Society, Washington, DC.

Levine, M. D., & Schneider, E. A. (1982). *Pediatric Examination of Educational Readiness. Examiner's manual.* Cambridge, MA: Educators Publishing Service.

Lindgren, S. D. (1978). Finger localization and the prediction of reading disability. *Cortex, 14,* 87–101.

Luria, A. R. (1959). The directive function of speech in development and dissolution. *Word, 15,* 341–352.

Luria, A. R. (1980). *Higher cortical functions in man* (?nd ed.). New York: Basic Books.

Marcotte, A. C., & LaBarba, R. C. (1985). Cerebral lateralization for speech in deaf and normal children. *Brain and Language, 26,* 244–258.

Mercer, C. D., Algozzine, B., & Trifiletti, J. J. (1979). Early identification: Issues and considerations. *Exceptional Children, 46,* 52–54.

National Joint Committee on Learning Disabilities, The. (1986, February). *A position paper of the National Joint Committee on Learning Disabilities.* Baltimore, MD: Orton Dyslexia Society.

Nussbaum, N. L., & Bigler, E. D. (1986). Neuropsychological and behavioral profiles of empirically derived subgroups of learning disabled children. *International Journal of Clinical Neuropsychology, 8,* 82–89.

Passler, M., Issac, W., & Hynd, G. W. (1986). Neuropsychological development of behavior attributed to frontal lobe functioning in children. *Developmental Neuropsychology, 1,* 349–370.

Porter, J. E., & Rourke, B. P. (1985). Socioemotional functioning of learning-disabled children: A subtypal analysis of personality patterns. In B. P. Rourke (Ed.), *Neuropsychology of learning disabilities: Essentials of subtype analysis* (pp. 257–280). New York: Guilford Press.

Reitan, R. M., & Davison, L. A. (1974). *Clinical neuropsychology: Current status and applications.* New York: Wiley.

Rourke, B. P. (1983). Outstanding issues in research on learning disabilities. In M. Rutter (Ed.), *Developmental neuropsychiatry* (pp. 564–574). New York: Guilford Press.

Rourke, B. P., Bakker, D. J., Fisk, J. L., & Strang, J. D. (1983). *Child neuropsychology.* New York: Guilford Press.

Rutter, M., Tizard, J., Yule, W., Graham, P., & Whitmore, K. (1976). Research report: Isle of Wight studies, 1964–1974. *Psychological Medicine, 6,* 313–332.

Satz, P., & Fletcher, J. M. (1982). *Florida Kindergarten Screening Battery.* Odessa, FL: Psychological Assessment Resources.

Satz, P., Taylor, H. G., Friel, J., & Fletcher, J. M. (1978). Some developmental and predictive precursors of reading disabilities: A six year follow-up. In A. L. Benton & D. Pearl (Eds.), *Dyslexia: An appraisal of current knowledge* (pp. 315–347). New York: Oxford University Press.

Satz, P., & van Nostrand, G. K. (1973). Developmental dyslexia: An evaluation of a theory. In P. Satz & J. Ross (Eds.), *The disabled learner: Early detection and intervention* (pp. 121–148). Rotterdam: Rotterdam University Press.

Schonhaut, S., & Satz, P. (1983). Prognosis for children with learning disabilities: A review of follow-up studies. In M. Rutter (Ed.), *Developmental neuropsychiatry* (pp. 542–563). New York: Guilford Press.

Silver, A. A., & Hagin, R. A. (1960). Specific reading disability: Delineation of the syndrome and relationship to cerebral dominance. *Comparative Psychiatry, 1,* 126–134.

Silver, A. A., & Hagin, R. A. (1972). Profile of a first grade: A basis for preventive psychiatry. *Journal of the American Academy of Child Psychiatry, 11,* 645–674.

Silver, A. A., & Hagin, R. A. (1976). *Search.* New York: Walker Educational Book Corporation.

Simner, M. L. (1983). The warning signs of school failure: An updated profile of the at-risk kindergarten child. *Topics in Early Childhood Special Education, 17,* 17.

Smith, N. B. (1928). Matching ability as a factor in first grade reading. *Journal of Educational Psychology, 19,* 560–571.

Speece, D. L., McKinney, J. D., & Appelbaum, M. I. (1985). Classification and validation of behavioral subtypes of learning disabled children. *Journal of Educational Psychology, 77,* 67–77.

Spreen, O. (1978). *Learning-disabled children growing up* (Finale report to Health and Welfare Canada, Health Programs Branch). Ottawa: Health and Welfare Canada.

Stevenson, H. W., & Newman, R. S. (1986). Long-term prediction of achievement and attitudes in mathematics and reading. *Child Development, 57,* 646–659.

Stevenson, H. W., Parker, T., Wilkinson, A., Hegion, A., & Fish, E. (1976). Longitudinal study of individual differences in cognitive development and scholastic achievement. *Journal of Educational Psychology, 68,* 377–400.

Strang, J. D., & Rourke, B. P. (1985). Adaptive behavior of children who exhibit specific arithmetic disabilities and associated neuropsychological abilities and deficits. In B. P. Rourke (Ed.), *Neuropsychology of learning disabilities: Essentials of subtype analysis* (pp. 302–328). New York: Guilford Press.

Teeter, P. A. (1985). Neurodevelopmental investigation of academic achievement: A report of years 1 and 2 of a longitudinal study. *Journal of Consulting and Clinical Psychology, 53,* 709–717.

Tinsley, V. S., & Waters, H. S. (1982). The development of verbal control over motor behavior: A replication and extension of Luria's findings. *Child Development, 53,* 746–753.

Tramontana, M. G., Hooper, S. R., & Selzer, S. C. (1988). Research on the preschool prediction of later academic achievement. *Developmental Review, 8,* 89–147.

U. S. Department of Education, Division of Educational Services. (1984). *Sixth annual report to Congress on the implementation of Public Law 94-142: The Education for All Handicapped Children Act.* Washington, DC: Author.

Wallbrown, J. D., Engin, A. W., Wallbrown, F. H., & Blaha, J. (1975). The prediction of first grade reading achievement with selected perceptual-cognitive tests. *Psychology in the Schools, 12,* 140–149.

Walsh, R. (1981). *Towards an ecology of brain.* Lancaster, PA: MIP Press.

White, K. R. (1986). Efficacy of early intervention. *Journal of Special Education, 19,* 401–416.

Wilson, B. C. (1986). An approach to the neuropsychological assessment of the preschool child with developmental deficits. In S. B. Filskov & T. J. Boll (Eds.), *Handbook of clinical neuropsychology* (Vol. 2, pp. 121–171). New York: Wiley.

Wilson, G. T., & Rachman, S. J. (1983). Meta-analysis and the evaluation of psychotherapy outcome: Limitations and liabilities. *Journal of Consulting and Clinical Psychology, 51,* 54–64.

Witelson, S. F., & Pallie, W. (1973). Left hemisphere specialization for language in the newborn: Neuroanatomical evidence of asymmetry. *Brain, 96,* 671–696.

Wolff, P. H. (1981). Normal variation in human maturation. In K. J. Connolly and H. F. R. Prectl (eds.), Maturation and development: Biological and psychological perspectives. *Clinics in Developmental Medicine, 77–78.* Philadelphia: Lippincott.

Zihl, J. (1981). Recovery of visual functions in patients with cerebral blindness. *Experimental Brain Research, 44,* 159–169.

Electrophysiological Assessment in Learning Disabilities

GRANT L. MORRIS, JOEL LEVY, and FRANCIS J. PIROZZOLO

INTRODUCTION

This chapter will explore some of the nonbehavioral neurodiagnostic assessment techniques that were introduced in Chapter 3 of this volume. These techniques include neuroimaging techniques, such as computerized tomography (CT) and magnetic resonance imaging (MRI), electroencephalography, and evoked potentials. To illustrate the potential of these tehcniques for assessment in child neuropsychology we have chosen to focus specifically upon learning disabilities (LD).

The subtle and uncertain symptoms that characterize learning disabilities provide a challenge to both conventional psychometric assessment techniques and those nonbehavioral techniques that we will be reviewing in this chapter. As new neuropsychological assessment tools are introduced, often one of the first problems with which they are tested is LD. For this reason, and despite the relatively short time that some of these techniques have been around, considerable research already exists using both neuroimaging and electrophysiology in the assessment of learning disabilities.

Learning disabilities typically are not associated with any known neuropathology or trauma. However, LD symptoms often appear consistent with localized dysfunction in at least one brain system. Conse-

GRANT L. MORRIS • Department of Psychology, University of Northern Colorado, Greeley, Colorado.   JOEL LEVY • Department of Psychology, Texas Institute for Rehabilitation and Research, Houston, Texas   FRANCIS J. PIROZZOLO • Department of Neurology, Baylor College of Medicine, and Houston VA Medical Center, Houston, Texas.

quently, learning disabilities have long been suspected as having a neurological basis. This presumed etiology was not made explicit in the definition of LD found in Public Law 94-142. The definition of LD subsequently published by the National Joint Committee for Learning Disabilities addressed this question: "These disorders are intrinsic to the individual and presumed to be due to central nervous system dysfunction" (Hammill, Leigh, McNutt, & Larsen, 1981). At the same time, individual learning-disabled children show such a variety of specific behavioral anomalies that assessment often ends with cataloging the problem behaviors rather than attempting to discover the underlying neurological dysfunction.

Some of the purposes potentially served by electrophysiological and neuroimaging techniques in the assessment of LD include the following (also see John, 1977; Otto et al., 1984):

1. *Providing insight into the neurological bases of LD.* Numerous models of aberrant brain function in LD point to problems in specific systems or regions of the brain. Will there be support from electrophysiological and neuroimaging findings, or will the suspected multiple etiologies of LD be confirmed by neurological correlates as variable as the behavioral dysfunctions themselves?
2. *Differential diagnosis of learning disabilities with neurological involvement.* Being able to confirm or exclude organic involvement in a child's learning difficulties has clear implication for therapy.
3. *Early detection.* This may lead to therapeutic intervention at the onset or even prior to formal schooling rather than after the learning disability has manifested itself behaviorally.
4. *Culture-fair assessment.* This is a promise that follows from the presumption that neuroimaging and electrophysiology are measures of brain status and functioning that are not heavily affected by the child's cultural experience and achievement.
5. *Assessment of the course of the disorder and effect of therapy.* An assessment can be made to the extent that the disorder is the result of, or at least correlated with, neurological status.

Anatomical Correlates of Learning Disorders

The roots of theorizing about anatomical bases of learning disorders began with the observations of Broca (1861) and Wernicke (1874) on aphasia. Later, Hinshelwood (1895) found areas of cerebral cortex to be damaged in patients with acquired reading disorders. However, it was left for Morgan (1896) to suggest that these areas probably were underdeveloped in children with developmental reading difficulties. Fisher (1910) proposed specifically that underdevelopment of the left angular gyrus might be responsible for developmental dyslexia. Orton (1937) subsequently hypothesized that dyslexia in children might result from a "reversal of cerebral dominance." Little further investigation into the presence of a neurostructural abnormality associated with learning disorders was carried out until the 1960s. In 1968, Geschwind and Levitsky called attention to a statistically normal hemispheric asymmetry in the temporal lobe, just posterior to the primary auditory projection zone, an area referred to as the planum temporale. This area is roughly equivalent to Wernicke's area. Geschwind and Levitsky found the planum temporale to be larger on the left than on the right in autopsied adults. Witelson and Pallie (1973) confirmed this asymmetry in young children from autopsy specimens. Neuroimaging markers of this asymmetry have been reported by LeMay and Kido (1978) and LeMay (1982) using computed tomography (CT) scans, and by Kertesz, Black, Polk, and Howell (1986) using magnetic resonance imaging (MRI).

This asymmetry appears to be a normal structural marker for dominance. Kertesz reported that these anatomical measures classify subjects for handedness with better than 95% accuracy. Departures from this asymmetry may be markers for structural anomalies associated with learning disorder, and as such, they may constitute modern support for Orton's (1937) original premise. Several autopsy reports (Drake, 1968; Galaburda & Kemper, 1979; Galaburda, Sherman, Rosen, Aboitiz, & Geschwind, 1985) on learning-disabled patients have described deviations from the normal left-greater-than-right asymmetry of the planum temporale and, in some cases, cytoarchitectonic anomalies. They have found either that the planum temporale was equal in size across hemispheres or that there was a reversal of the asymmetry, with the right side being larger. Hier, LeMay, Rosenberg, and Perlo (1978) examined the CT images from 24 developmental dyslexics and found that 42% had a reversal of the expected asymmetry. This neuroanatomical finding also correlated with lower mean verbal IQ. Symmetry or reversal-of-expected asymmetry has been observed in at least three subsequent studies. Denckla, LeMay, and Chapman (1985), on the other hand, found only 20% of CT scans to be abnormal, despite the presence of neurobehavioral evidence of lateralized dysfunction.

Taken together, these studies do support a neuroanatomical basis for learning disabilities. The ability to correlate structural abnormalities with neuropsychological assessment will enrich our understanding of structure–function relationships and perhaps lead to new directions for assessment and intervention in these disorders. What is needed is a comfortable, safe, precise, and preferably noninvasive method for neuroimaging. Some of the currently available methods are discussed below.

Neuroimaging Methods

CAT Scans

The now conventional CAT or CT scan is an X-ray technique that technically should be referred to as X-ray transmission tomography. This is because CT only stands for computed tomography, and a tomographic image can be derived from different sources, including X-ray absorption by tissue, the emission of internally administered radioactive substances, or magnetic resonance.

In X-ray transmission tomography, the patient's head is placed in a large doughnut-shaped housing. Inside this housing, a movable X-ray emitter is positioned, with a detector aligned to oppose it on the other side of the ring housing. This configuration revolves around the patient's head in small stepwise increments. It also moves up and down the long axis of the patient's body to make images every centimeter from the top of the head to the base of the skull. As the scanner moves around the head, measurements of the amount of X-radiation absorbed by the tissue between emitter and detector are made and converted to numerical density data. Each point in the head is scanned from at least two directions. The image is based on the principle that the cerebrospinal fluid absorbs less radiation than brain white matter, which absorbs less than gray matter, which in turn absorbs about 1/20th of the amount that bone does. Flowing blood absorbs an amount that overlaps both gray and white matter ranges; therefore, to visualize intracranial circulation or defects in the venous system (e.g., hemorrhage or thrombosis), a radiation-opaque contrast medium is usually injected intravenously.

The radiation absorption values are stored in a computer, which reconstructs an image of the brain and skull after the scans have been completed. It is important to remember that the scan is not like a direct visual X-ray film but is the transaxial absorption data translated into a TV-type picture. The most recent scanners can resolve about a 1 mm X 1 mm area of tissue. The technique involves approximately the same dose of radiation as a standard skull radiograph. Inaccuracies or artifacts in the image are sometimes produced by the beam hitting bony structures and producing a shadow. However, these shadows actually may hide small brain lesions. Other inaccuracies include failure to distinguish some types of hemorrhages or tumors from normal brain tissue. However, this is not typically a consideration in brain volumetric studies such as would be proposed for an LD evaluation. Risks associated with this procedure include allergic reactions that some people experience to the contrast media. The exposure to radiation and the infusion of contrast material make X-ray transmission tomography perhaps the most invasive neuroimaging procedure.

Positron Emission Tomography

Positron emission tomographs, or PET scans, also utilize radiation, but they derive this energy source from radioactively labeled compounds that are injected into the bloodstream. Rather than imaging only static structures, PET scans image the dynamic, physiological function by detecting radioactively labeled glucose usage in the tissue. The standard compound used is fluorodeoxyglucose. This compound competes with the normal sugar in blood that the brain needs to fuel its activity. It thus concentrates in brain areas that are undergoing increased energy utilization. This compound is a positron-emitting source that, upon encountering an electron, annihilates it with a release of electromagnetic energy. This energy is detected with arrays of sensors that translate these data into an image that reflects the localization and concentration of the radioactive material in the brain.

Once again, this is not a direct radiation-exposed film image, but a two-dimensional reconstruction of the energy data by means of computer processing. The advantage of this technique is its visualization of energy usage in the brain, which can be correlated with cognitive or motor activity. The disadvantages are the high cost of producing and using the radioactive compounds, the necessity of introducing these compounds into the bloodstream, the length of time necessary to transport and utilize these compounds in the tissue under study (which requires a sustained cognitive or motor activity because the scan is not sensitive to transient motor or cognitive events), and the limits of spatial resolution of the scan.

To date, PET represents strictly a research rather than a diagnostic tool for the evaluation of learning disorders. Future investigators may be able to use PET to diagnose LD subtypes on the basis of functional data profiles, even in the absence of clear structural anomalies reported by CT.

Regional Cerebral Blood Flow

In much the same way that positron emission tomography is accomplished, regional cerebral blood flow (rCBF) detects blood-borne compounds that emit radiation. The principle here is that areas of the brain that are involved in intensive specific cognitive function require increased blood flow to deliver nutrients for that functioning. The compound frequently used in this technique is 133-Xenon, which typically is inhaled. Sensors detect the radiation from this gas in the blood as it flows through different regions in the brain. The gas then quickly diffuses out of the body via exhalation from the lungs. The major advantages of this technique are the speed of scanning and the correlation of blood flow with cognitive activity. The disadvantages of the method are the limited resolution of the image and the use of a radioactive material, although the 133-Xenon gas is thought to be relatively innocuous.

Like PET, blood flow studies remain at the investigational stage for assessment of childhood cognitive disabilities. Normative studies on inter- and intrahemispheric blood flow have been reported (Hynd, Hynd, Sullivan, & Kingsbury, 1987), and limited data are now available on hemispheric asymmetry. Despite the lower resolution for rCBF, increased left hemisphere blood flow has been correlated with verbal test performance, whereas performance on a nonverbal perceptual test was found to be associated with increased right frontal and parietal flow. In one of the first blood flow studies on dyslexic children, Hynd et al. (1987) found that there was less cerebral blood flow in the dyslexic groups, for both resting and activation states, than for matched controls. Increased blood flow during reading occurred in the left perisylvian and right parietooccipital regions for the normal controls.

As the technology advances and resolution of structures becomes more refined, this methodology offers the same promise as PET for diagnosis of subtypes of learning disabilities because it traces active function and directly relates it to structure. Unlike PET, however, the ease of using inhalable tracer compounds appears to be more comfortable and suitable for young children.

Magnetic Resonance Imaging

Nuclear magnetic resonance imaging is a relatively new technique for obtaining images of internal body structures. This method is now more commonly known as magnetic resonance imaging (MRI) to dispel any misconception that it involves subjecting patients to nuclear or ionizing radiation. In MRI the body is exposed to a strong, encompassing magnetic field. Atoms with odd numbers of protons, neutrons, or both will align themselves like bar magnets when placed in a magnetic field, although the atomic nucleus continues to spin like a top, with some wobble. This wobble has a certain characteristic frequency, the "magnetic resonance" frequency, which depends on the magnetic strength and mass of the nucleus. When the nucleus is then pulsed with more magnetic energy, via radio waves at the same resonant frequency, the nucleus "rings." The radio wave pulse is tuned to the frequency of the atom under investigation, usually hydrogen because it is part of most chemical structures found in the body, and the pulse times are adjusted to maximize the signal from the nuclei. The "ringing" can be detected with receiving coils.

Two terms commonly involved in MRI are T1 and T2. These denote the times when (a) the nucleus dissipates the ringing with respect to the direction of alignment to the external, large magnetic field (T1), and (b) the nucleus stops ringing coherently with the other hydrogen nuclei around it (T2). These two types of resonance also are called spin-lattice and spin-spin, respectively. Another term used frequently is inversion recovery. This is when the radio wave pulse is directed through the tissue from the opposite direction immediately after the initial pulse so as to enhance the "ringing" even further. This method provides the sharpest detail for differentiating between gray and white matter.

Very striking images that rival anatomical drawings for detail can be obtained from MRI. Tumors, hemorrhages, ischemic regions, and demyelination sites all stand out more distinctly than with X-ray tomography because MRI capitalizes on the subtle differences in chemical structure between these types of tissue. MRI has the added advantages that no radiation is applied to the body, no contrast material is injected, and scans may be done frequently without radiation risk. Further, structures do not cause shadow artifiacts as they do in CT scans. No known risk to health or cognitive function has been associated with exposure to magnetic fields of the strength used in MRI. The only disadvantages now known are the current expense of the procedure, the long times required for the scanning during which the body must remain motionless or distortion artifact occurs, and reports of claustrophobia from having to spend such long times in the scanner.

Recent advances in this method allow for tuning of the device to different molecules so that information on metabolism can be detected, much like the PET scan but without the radiation involved. In our laboratory, we have undertaken a study of six children, referred to us from speech pathologists, diagnosed with developmental dysphasia (Pirozzolo *et al.* 1985). These children underwent neuropsychological testing, audiometric assessment, and neurostructural imaging by MRI. The children, ranging from the low-average to the high-average range of intellectual functioning, demonstrated decreased performance in verbally based cognitive functions (e.g., vocabulary and comprehension), cognitive set shifting, and arithmetic achievement. Abnormalities were found in the auditory evoked responses (in the middle latency or late vertex wave forms) consistent with central auditory dysfunction. Results of MRI scanning in five of the six children revealed reversal of temporal structural asymmetry consistent with CT and microscopic cytoarchitectural findings previously reported. MRI provides a safe and precise means for identifying these structural anomalies.

ELECTROPHYSIOLOGICAL TECHNIQUES AND FINDINGS

Electroencephalography

Basic Description

Electroencephalography (EEG) is a technique for amplifying and recording the variations in the electrical potentials detectable on the scalp. Exclusive of artifact generated by muscle activity (electromyographic artifact) in the vicinity of scalp electrodes, these potentials have their origins within the brain. This cortical activity is measured either as the difference in potential seen at two scalp electrodes (bipolar recording) or the activity at a single site referred to some other part of the body presumed to be electrically inactive insofar as EEG is concerned (referential recording). Bipolar recordings are especially useful in localizing abnormal EEG activity, e.g., associated with a tumor site. Referential recordings are of less use in localizing abnormal EEG activity, but they are sensitive to EEG activity whose origin lies at some distance from the active electrode (so-called far-field recording). The signal itself is a complex wave form that appears to have an unstable frequency and amplitude. However, under constant conditions of recording site and arousal, a stable dominant frequency can be seen. The dominant frequency of EEG may vary from 0.5 to more than 50 Hz. Most EEG amplitudes lie within a range of 5 to 50 microvolts. Much of the research employs a band-pass classification scheme that labels specific frequency ranges. These typically include delta (0.5–4 Hz), theta (5–7 Hz), alpha (8–12 Hz), beta (13–30 Hz), and gamma (30–50 Hz).

A "montage" is a description of a specific set of electrode locations. Until the establishment of the standard International 10/20 system of electrode placement (Jasper, 1958), variations in electrode placements confounded attempts at replications and comparisons among laboratories. The letters of the 10/20 system refer to the major area of the brain over

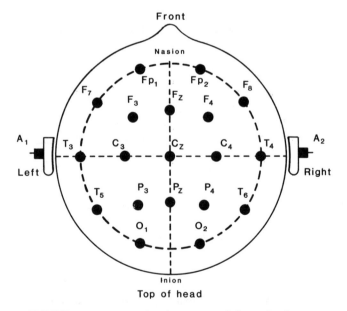

FIGURE 1. International 10/20 system of electrode placement.

which the electrode is placed: occipital (O), parietal (P), central (C), frontal (F), and temporal (T). The subscript associated with each letter denotes laterality, with odd numbers indicating left hemisphere placements, and even numbers placement over the right hemisphere. The magnitude of the number indicates the degree of displacement from the midline of the brain, which is designated as zero (z). Although this convention is widely followed, particular experiments may use different placements. However, these unique placements typically are described in terms of their relation to the 10/20 system. Figure 1 illustrates the 10/20 system for electrode placement.

EEG Analysis Methods

Traditionally, analysis of the frequency and amplitude composition of a paper EEG record was accomplished by visual inspection. This type of summary analysis is typically accompanied by the examiner's report of any anomalous EEG patterns or wave forms, such as the classic "spike and dome" pattern associated with a petit mal epilepsy. Such laborious manual methods of analysis must, of necessity, use only a small fraction of the information in an EEG record, and consequently they are heavily dependent upon the training and experience of the individual examiner.

Advances through Computerized EEG Data Analysis. In recent years EEG methodology has been refined by the use of computer-based analytic techniques. These techniques aim for the spectral decomposition of the complex EEG signal through techniques such as fast-Fourier transformations (FFTs) or digital filtering, and the comparison of EEG activity among various electrode sites through techniques such as coherence analysis. The results from these efforts at measuring EEG from various electrode sites and under different behavioral conditions in LD children have been promising (see John, 1977).

The analogue voltage changes of the EEG are recorded on magnetic tape for later analysis, or fed on line into an analogue-to-digital (AD) converter. This device converts the continually varying voltages into a series of numbers whose values are directly proportional to the instantaneous EEG voltages. The output of the AD converter is then fed into a computer that can store or analyze these numeric equivalents of the original EEG. Fourier transformations and digital filtering quantify the proportion of the total power of the EEG wave form that lies within prespecified ranges of frequencies or band passes.

Spectral analysis is the result of Fourier transformations or digital filtering as described above. The frequency and power composition of spontaneous EEG can be defined as a function of electrode site, task, and diagnostic group of the participant. Further analyses include measurement of coherence and asymmetry of power among various electrode sites. Coherence is a reflection of the similarity of EEG being produced at the two electrode sites being compared. As such, coherence is essentially the correlation of the instantaneous EEG voltage being produced at these two sites. Asymmetry is usually expressed as the ratio of the EEG power occurring at two sites within a particular frequency band pass. Typically, homotopic electrode sites are used in coherence and asymmetry analysis. Homotopic sites are the bilateral companion sites such as O_1 and O_2 or T_3 and T_4.

Differences in methodology among studies often are responsible for the conflicting results in electrophysiological research:

> ... the study of EEG and AEP (averaged evoked potentials) characteristics of learning-disabled children has not yielded consistent results over the last 30 years. This variability has arisen from problems both in the behavioral specification of what set of variables characterizes learning disabilities, and from the absence of a uniform system for acquisition and quantification of electrophysiological data. It is not surprising that inconsistent and unreliable protocols in either domain will negate any attempts at brain–behavior correlation, regardless of which domain is inconsistent or unreliable, and regardless of how carefully the statistical analysis is carried out. (Kaye, John, Ahn, & Prichep, 1981, p. 16)

The variability in method for acquiring and analyzing electrophysiological data from LD children, combined with the large amount of data generated by these techniques, has nearly overwhelmed our capacity to comprehend and assimilate the results. Consequently, the most helpful approaches with learning-disabled children have been those that either have offered methods for standardizing data collection protocols, such as the neurometrics approach (John et al., 1977; Kaye et al., 1981) or have developed new methods for graphically summarizing and presenting the data, such as the brain electrical activity mapping (BEAM) technique (Duffy, Denckla, Bartels, & Sandini, 1980; Duffy, Denckla, Bartels, Sandini, & Kiessling, 1980).

The neurometrics approach consists of a battery of electrophysiological measures, including spontaneous EEG along with auditory, somatosensory and visual evoked potentials. Evoked potential stimuli range from the rather simple, such as taps or flashing panels of light, to those that are intended as significant probes ("challenges") of brain function, such as different geometric shapes and letters. This effort also is commendable for the establishment of large normative data from normal and special populations, including learning-disabled children.

The BEAM technique deals with the problem of extensive tables filled with the numerical results of power or coherence analysis by representing these data as varying colors or textures that represent value as a function of cortical area on a graphical representation of the head. (An example of this technique of data presentation can be found in Chapter 3).

EEG in LD Children

Results of Analysis of EEG through Visual Inspection. In 1978, John Hughes summarized work over the preceding two decades that looked at EEG in hospitalized nondyslexic children as well as dyslexic children. These studies used visual inspection to detect significant anomalies in the EEG records. Ten of the reviewed studies involved a total of over 900 nondyslexic subjects. Across all of these studies, nearly half of the nondyslexic subjects were identified as having significant EEG anomalies. In another ten studies during the same time period, a slightly smaller proportion of dyslexic children were identified as having abnormal EEGs. Clearly, the probability of false negatives and false positives was high. Conners (1978), critiquing the studies covered in the Hughes review, noted that the diagnostic category of subjects was often known to the EEG reader, and thus the reliability of the EEG evaluation was questionable. Conners found that the definition of dyslexia varied across studies, and rarely was any attempt made to screen out possible associated behavioral or neurological conditions. He observed that experimental procedures, such as matching control and experimental subjects, were often poor or absent, especially in the earlier studies. As experimental method improved in the more recently reviewed studies, significantly less abnormality tended to be reported. He found that there was no consistent relationship across studies in terms of the locus or type of EEG abnormality, and that there was often an inverse relationship between the degree of behavioral impairment and the degree of severity of EEG abnormality. In those few studies that employed a follow-up, the EEG contributed nothing to the prediction of outcome.

Until that time the studies analyzing EEG through visual inspection seemed to offer little consistent evidence to support a general conclusion of an association between EEG abnormality and dyslexia. Although many of the problems raised in the Hughes review have not been systematically addressed by more recent studies, the use of automatic data analysis has at least begun to address the problems presented by the visual inspection technique.

Computerized EEG Findings in LD Children. Sklar, Hanley, and Simmons (1973) conducted one of the first computerized EEG studies with dyslexic children. In the place of visual inspection of paper EEG records, the data were collected using frequency-modulation (FM) recorders and magnetic tape. Later, these data were digitized and then read into the minicomputer for Fourier analysis. This permitted reliable quantification of the proportion of the power in the raw EEG within any frequency band.

Twelve dyslexic and 13 normal children matched for age and sex participated. EEGs were recorded from both groups during various mental tasks and rest situations. The spectral vectors derived from the Fourier transformations were used as predictor variables in a stepwise discriminant analysis. This analysis permitted the identification of the variables most disparate between the two groups. The most distinctive differences appeared in the parietooccipital region during the resting-with-eyes-closed condition. The dyslexic subjects, on the average, had more energy in the 3- to 7-Hz (theta) band and the 16- to 32-Hz (beta) band, whereas the normals exhibited the greatest energy within the 9- to 14-Hz (alpha) band. However, during the reading tasks, the spectral disparity between the two groups was reversed at 16 to 32 Hz, with the normals tending to show greater energy in this band.

During reading, the coherences of broad spectrum EEG among various scalp leads were the most prominent discriminating feature. Within the same hemisphere coherences between leads were higher in dyslexics than in normals. However, between symmetrical regions across the midline of the head (i.e., between homotopic electrode sites) coherence tended to be higher in normals. Thus, Sklar et al. were able to differentiate between dyslexic and normal age- and sex-matched children on the basis of spectral estimates and coherence of their EEGs. However, their findings did not fit well into any model that might predict cortical immaturity in the dyslexic group, as reflected by general slowing of EEG, or a lack of hemispheric specialization, which would predict less, rather than greater, interhemispheric coherence in the normal group.

Rebert, Wexler, and Sproul (1978) undertook an EEG study to determine if the left and right hemispheres of LD children responded differently to changing cognitive demands. The children included 11 residents of a school for neurologically handicapped who were diagnosed as having dyslexia. The other 11 participants were characterized as severely handicapped in oral language and were designated as dysphasic. Unfortunately, normal control subjects were not available. The bilateral electrode placements were at locations that were intended to overlie the angular gyrus in the parietal region, and the planum temporale in the temporal region. The average and peak powers within the theta and alpha bands were computed for the monitored sites. Subjects were tested in five conditions, which included eyes closed-relaxed, eyes opened-relaxed, reading by child, reading to child with child's eyes open, and while performing a drawing task.

In the absence of an appropriate control group, the authors were unable to assess the EEG maturation level of the participatns, but they felt that there was a great deal of theta activity, and that the theta band was most responsive to experimental manipulations. The Matousek and Petersen (1973) age-based norms clearly suggest that theta power declines throughout childhood and adolescence, and that its greater-than-normal presence in any age group is indicative of neurological immaturity. Changes in EEG asymmetry among certain recording conditions distinguished the two diagnostic groups. A complex task, power, and diagnostic group relationship (as reflected in right and left parietal theta) was most pronounced at the angular gyrus. A significant interaction with groups led to the conclusion that the dyslexics had more left than right power during reading-by-child that became less marked during drawing. A discriminant analysis on theta power correctly classified 20 of the 22 children. An abundance of left theta during eyes open-relaxed and a slight decline of that frequency during reading is consistent with Witelson's (1977) supposition that dyslexics have a dysfunctional left hemisphere.

Fein et al. (1983) recorded resting eyes-closed and eyes-open EEG in normal and dyslexic 10- to 12-year-old boys. The EEG was recorded bilaterally from the central, parietal, and midtemporal regions. Two segments of EEG were recorded which were separated by approximately a 4- to 5-hour interval. Test-retest reliabilities were computed for each band and for the entire spectrum, and reliabilities were assessed separately for each condition and for absolute power and relative power. High reliability was observed in the normal reading group. Reliabilities for the dyslexic group were slightly lower but still were judged acceptable. No systematic EEG differences were reported between the two groups. However, the authors concluded that excellent reliability of both absolute and relative power for the passive eyes-closed and eyes-open conditions can be obtained from dyslexic children, and that this supports the utility of EEG power spectra as a reliable index of brain functioning in studies of normal and learning-disabled children.

The BEAM recording technique has been used to study a group of pure dyslexic subjects and their age-matched controls (Duffy, Denckla, Bartels, & Sandini, 1980; Duffy, Denckla, Bartels, Sandini, & Kiessling, 1980). These researchers found significant differences in patterns of EEG activity between the two groups. Discrete brain areas that have been classically associated with speech and reading were identified in the dyslexics as being significantly different from the control subjects. The dyslexic children exhibited EEG anomalies in Broca's area and in the region of intersection of the left temporal and parietal lobes, including the angular gyrus and Wernicke's area.

Kaye et al. (1981), using the neurometrics battery, evaluated the differences in EEG and average evoked potential (AEP) characteristics of 50 children who were of normal IQ but who were underachievers either in verbal academic performance, in arithmetic performance, or in both (mixed). These underachievers were compared with matched controls who were adequately achieving. They built the EEG portion of their neurometrics battery around electrode sites and eyes-closed EEG relative power age-related norms published by Matousek and Petersen (1973). The EEG was recorded from four bilateral, bipolar locations, which included the central, temporal, parietooccipital, and frontotemporal regions. Relative spectral EEG densities were derived for the delta, theta, alpha, and beta frequency bands while eyes were closed. Age-normed and Z-transformed measures of delta, theta, alpha, and beta wave shape coherence and amplitude symmetry were available for each region.

In comparison with the matched controls, the poor verbal achievers showed significant deviations only in temporal coherence and symmetry. The poor arithmetic achievers exhibited marked deviations in several bilateral regions across several of the frequency bands. The mixed underachievers showed yet another pattern of differences in comparison with the controls. Their pattern included a larger number of left hemisphere frontotemporal, temporal, and parietooccipital differences, and marked frontotemporal incoherence and asymmetry. Kaye et al. were successful at replicating these findings with a larger sample of 215 children. These highly variable patterns of group-specific EEG anomalies support the presumption of multiple etiologies of learning disability. Further, they also may form the basis for significant discrimination between LD and normal subjects, and among the subcatagories of LD.

In an earlier presentation of LD data using this approach, John (1977) discussed the problem of unreliable, anecdotal, or psychometric diagnosis of learning disability when attempting to determine the electrophysiological correlates of this disorder. Based upon the presumption of accurate anecdotal diagnosis, or "prediagnosis" made by the teacher or referring clinician, discriminant analysis of LD and normal children was conducted using either a battery of psychometric instruments or the EEG data collected as part of the neurometrics battery. Instruments found to contribute to the multiple discriminant function included subscales of the Wechsler Intelligence Scale for Children, the Wide Range Intelligence Test, and the Peabody Picture Vocabulary Test. Overall accuracy of classification of normal and LD children based on the psychometric battery was 71%. Selected EEG measures from the neurometric battery yielded a 77% accuracy in classification.

At that point, John had classifications of all subjects into normal or LD categories based upon three independent criteria: the original classifications or "prediagnoses," the assignment to group by the psychometric battery, and the group assignment by the EEG discriminant function. By comparing the concordance of classification by the three schemes for each child, John proposed some details of various etiologies. Children who were classified as normal by prediagnosis and EEG measures, but classified as LD by psychometric criteria, were presumed normal; in these cases, the psychometric-based LD classification was viewed as the result of cultural factors or bias in the psychometric instruments. These accounted for 5% of his sample. An additional 6.5% of his sample were classified as normal by prediagnosis and psychometrics but were classified as LD by the neurometrics EEG. Although none of the children in his study was initially prediagnosed as normal and subsequently classified as LD by both psychometrics and neurometric EEG, a total of 11.5% of prediagnosed normal children were classified as LD by one of the two batteries. The 13% of his sample who were prediagnosed as LD, but classified as normal by the other two measures, were presumed to be neurologically normal, with their learning difficulties stemming from emotional problems. The 9% who were classified as LD by the prediagnostic and EEG criteria, but normal by psychometric criteria, were presumed to be LD and to have been missed on the psychometric criteria because of the narrow scope of functions assessed.

The neurometrics approach has seen mixed reviews. Yingling, Galin, Fein, Peltzman, and Davenport (1986) reported that the neurometrics EEG tests, supplemented with a subset of evoked potential tests, were not able to discriminate dyslexics from controls. This failure was attributed to the stringent screening applied to both groups in the study, designed to ensure that all subjects were of normal intellectual, neurological, sensory, and emotional status. They concluded that pure dyslexia is not associated with neurological anomalies detectable by the neurometric battery, and that earlier indications to the contrary were artifactual.

Lubar et al. (1985) conducted a study with boys classified as learning-disabled according to the Tennessee state definition of this disorder. A bipolar electrode montage was used bilaterally in the frontal-temporal, temporal, and occipital-parietal regions. The EEG was recorded in each of seven different conditions, which included baseline (relaxed, eyes open), two levels of reading, two levels of math, and hard and easy puzzles. The fast-Fourier transformation analysis produced percent and power values of the EEG broken down into seven frequency bands of 4-Hz width from 0 to 28 Hz. It was found that learning-disabled children had more power in the theta band (4–8 Hz), the high-theta/low-alpha bands (6–10 Hz), and in the high-beta band (20–28 Hz).

The theta and high-theta low-alpha bands generally distinguished normal from LD children, but other EEG frequencies did not. An EEG recorded during the puzzles task provided the greatest discrimination between the diagnostic groups. For the measure at the frontal-temporal locations F7-T5 and F8-T6 the analysis identified 79.2% of the normals and 75.6% of the LDs correctly. For central locations the discrimination was lower. Correct classification in the study was 68.8% for the normals and 64.4% for the LD children. An EEG from the occipital locations correctly classified the normals 71% of the time and the LDs 75% of the time. These results indicated that the frontal-temporal data provided slightly better group discrimination than posterior data, and that significant slowing of EEG frequency seemed to characterize the LD subjects. The neurometric data, by contrast, suggested that EEG slowing in the occipital region is most discriminative of LD (John, 1977).

Summary

Recent reanalysis of the Matousek and Petersen (1973) developmental EEG changes in normals further confirms that there is an age × cortical area × frequency interaction, with the modal EEG frequency moving progressively upward with age. This frequency-shift process (i.e., maturation) occurs earliest and most rapidly in the occipital region, but it is considerably delayed in the frontal-temporal region in normals. At all electrode sites the pattern of change seen within the EEG frequency spectrum is a progressive decline of delta and theta power accompanied by an increase in alpha and beta between birth and age 19 to 20 years (W. H. Hudspeth, personal communication, June 1987). Alpha is the dominant frequency in more developmentally mature individuals when resting with eyes closed. In normals, alpha has replaced delta-theta as the dominant frequency band in the pareitooccipital region by age 8 years.

Much of the research reviewed in this section is consistent with the concept of cortical immaturity in LD as revealed by a "slowing" of EEG activity. This is most frequently seen as higher-than-normal theta band power for a given age. This finding is most stable during the recording of eyes-closed spontaneous EEG in the posterior region (Lubar et al., 1985; Rebert et al., 1978; Sklar et al., 1973). The Lubar et al. (1985) findings also suggested that, while engaged in an activity, the theta EEG from the frontal region permits considerable classification accuracy of LDs.

Rebert et al. (1978) and Duffy, Denckla, Bartels, and Sandini (1980) reported specific lateralized differences in LDs in the areas of the left temporal-parietal cortex associated with language and reading skills, particularly during tasks that would activate these areas. Although the fact of general cortical EEG "slowing" seems established, the more intriguing findings of lateralized temporoparietal anomalies in LD children await replication and further definition.

Evoked Potentials

Basic Description

An evoked potential (EP) is the electrical indication of the brain's reception of, and response to, an external stimulus. Typically, EPs are not visible during the ongoing EEG recording. This is because of the relatively low amplitudes of most EPs (0.1–20 microvolts) and their presence within normal spontaneous EEG from throughout the brain and other artifacts (such as electromyographic activity) that may be as much as several hundred microvolts in amplitude. Separation of the buried EP wave forms from these unwanted artifacts is accomplished by computer signal averaging. It is assumed that the electrical response of the brain to the stimulus (the EP) always comes at the same interval of time after the stimulus, and thus has a constant latency. It also is assumed that the other electrical activities present are not coupled to the stimulus and may be considered random. Because these assumptions appear to be valid, computers (signal averagers) can be used to isolate the evoked potential from the temporally random background activity. Stimuli are given repetitively, and the computer averages the new data acquired after each stimulus (random EEG plus EP) with the averaged results from previous stimuli stored in its memory. This averaging process is continued until the random EEG and other artifacts have been reduced to an acceptably low level, and the desired evoked potential has "grown" by virtue of the summation of its constant temporal characteristics relative to the eliciting stimulus over many trials (Chiappa, 1983). When averaged in this manner, visual, auditory, and somatosensory stimuli are seen to evoke a series of discrete electrophysiological responses or "peaks" of characteristic latency for a given set of stimulus parameters. In their early (short latency) stages, these peaks reflect the progress of the stimulus-evoked neural response through the series of synaptic junctions within the anatomical pathway of the stimulated modality. As the latency of these peaks extends past 100 msec, and their loci shift from peripheral or brain stem sites to the cortex, the peaks become more variable in latency and amplitude, more diffuse in terms of anatomic origin, and more sensitive to cognitive state and attention.

Exogenous Evoked Responses. Up to a latency of approximately 100 msec after the presentation of the eliciting stimulus, there is a relatively clear linkage between the characteristics of the evoked response and the specific sensory pathway. Further, most researcners are reasonably comfortable with assigning the origin of the various components of evoked responses to specific anatomical regions along the sensory pathway followed by that specific modality. These qualities of the short latency components of an evoked response have led to their being characterized as "exogenous" (John, 1963). They are highly stimulus/modality/anatomic pathway-specific and independent of factors such as state of consciousness and attention. The clinical utility of these early components lies in their ability to reflect the integrity and functioning of the neuroanatomical pathway they follow. "Changes in latency or amplitude, or the lack of distinct waves, reveal the malfunctioning of that receptor, pathway, or brain area which the particular component represents" (Rockstroh, Elbert, Birbaumer, & Lutzenberger, 1982, p. 3). Although both visual and auditory stimuli have been used to study middle- and long-latency evoked responses in dyslexic children, exogenous evoked response work with this population has employed auditory stimuli almost exclusively.

BSER. Brain stem evoked responses (BSER) are classified as exogenous evoked potentials. BSERs are the series of polyphasic voltage changes that occur within the first 10 msec after the presentation of a

brief, discrete auditory stimulus. The measured potentials are time-locked
to the presentation of a stimulus and require computer averaging to observe clearly the small discrete electrical responses from the brain. More
specifically, the evoked electrical activity is often recorded from a set of
four electrodes placed externally on the subject's scalp. One electrode is
located on the vertex (reference site), one electrode is located on each of
the subject's earlobes (active site), and the fourth electrode (ground) is
placed on the forehead. The electrophysiological response can be evoked
by simple auditory signals (e.g., clicks) or more complex auditory stimuli

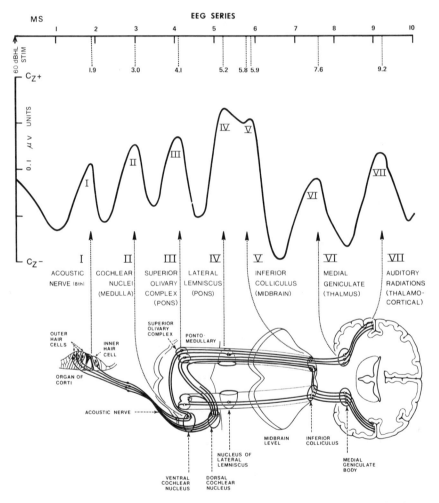

FIGURE 2. Far-field recording of auditory brain stem responses latencies measured in human
subjects. Proposed functional–anatomical correlations.

such as phonemes. This is amplified for each test run, with the response to the auditory stimulus being averaged over trials. Stimuli may be presented either monaurally or binaurally.

BSERs are thought to be the far-field reflection of sequential electrical events at successively higher levels in the brain stem auditory pathway. Depth recordings and lesion experiments in the feline suggest that the approximate neural generators of waves I, II, III, V, and VI of the BSER are the acoustic nerve, cochlear nuclei, superior olives, inferior colliculi, and medial geniculate nuclei, respectively (Picton, Hillyard, Krausz, & Galambos, 1974). The origin of other components of the polyphasic BSER are less clear, but some authors speculate that late components have their origins in the thalamic nuclei and auditory cortex (Stockard & Rossiter, 1977). However, Chiappa (1983) concluded that the origins of peaks V, VI, and VII are still very much in doubt, and because waves VI and VII are unreliable in appearance, they are not used in clinical interpretation. These proposed functional-anatomical associations are illustrated in Figure 2.

Until recently, BSERs were evoked by bilateral auditory stimulation. This practice has been criticized on the clinical grounds that a lateralized dysfunction might be masked through blending the abnormal BSER from the affected side with the BSER from the unaffected side (Chiappa, 1983). Consequently, it is now standard practice to elicit BSERs with monaural stimulation. This practice also opens the door to the discovery of any asymmetry, normal or anomalous, that may exist in an individual's monaural BSERs. An asymmetry would be any significant difference in the latency or amplitude of the corresponding peaks in the BSERs of the two ears. To date, only a few attempts at specifically assessing BSER symmetry have been made. These reveal a controversy over the existence of symmetry in neurologically normal persons (Chiappa, Gladstone, & Young, 1979; Levine & McGaffigan, 1983) and characteristic asymmetry in patients with various neurological diseases (Chiappa & Norwood, 1977) and in stutterers (Decker & Howe, 1981). The limited research looking at evoked response symmetry in LD populations has focused upon abnormalities in lateral asymmetry in the cerebral cortex rather than in the brain stem.

Endogenous Evoked Responses. As the components in the evoked response reach increasingly longer latencies (50–500 msec), both their dependence upon the eliciting stimulus and independence from the prevailing state of consciousness or cognitive state undergo progressive reversal. "Endogenous" components, then, appear to reflect perceptual, cognitive, and perhaps anticipatory motor actions of the central nervous system (Rockstroh et al., 1982). "Endogenous ERPs" (event-related potentials) "are frequently triggered by external stimulus events, but their waveform and timing are determined by the particular cognitive processes activated by the stimulus rather than by its modality or physical properties" (Hillyard & Woods, 1979, p. 346).

The method for recording middle and late components of the visual and auditory evoked potentials is similar to that used for the short-latency or exogenous components, except that the interval of EEG sampling following the presentation of the eliciting stimulus may be as long as 600 msec. The conventions for labeling the various components use a P to designate positive voltage shifts at the active recording site relative to the reference site, and an N for negative voltage shifts. Some researchers differentiate among components of the same polarity by specifying the typical latency in milliseconds at which this component occurs. For example, P_{300} refers to a positive peak (usually measured at the vertex) that is typically seen around 300 msec after the presentation of the eliciting stimulus. Other researchers follow the convention of sequentially numbering the various major positive and negative peaks in the order in which they occur temporally. For example, Fried, Tanguay, Boder, Doubleday, and Greensite (1981) identified their auditory evoked component P1 as a positive component with a latency of approximately 80 msec, N1 as a negative component with a latency of around 120 msec, and P2 as a positive component peaking at around 180 msec. The latency, amplitude, and occurrence of these components vary significantly depending upon modality of the stimulus, concurrent task, attention, and perceptual processing dysfunction. A review of recent research with middle and late components appears in Donchin (1984), and the interested reader is referred there for further discussion. Figure 3 presents an example of an endogenous ERP.

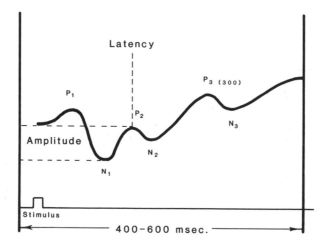

FIGURE 3. Endogenous (middle- and late-latency) evoked potential components.

Probe-Elicited Event-Related Potentials. Galin and Ellis (1975) developed the probe-ERP paradigm. Their intent was to combine the major advantages of the EEG and ERP methods. In their original procedure, task-irrelevant visual stimuli were presented at 3-second intervals while subjects performed writing and block design tasks. These tasks were selected to produce left and right hemisphere activation, respectively. They noted that probe-ERP asymmetry, like EEG alpha, was task-dependent. They observed differential suppression of the probe-elicited response in the hemisphere currently activated by the specific task in which the subject was engaged. They concluded that a brain region is less responsive to the probe stimulus when that region is engaged by the concurrent task. Johnston (1982) also presented data showing that the amplitude of modality-specific components (e.g., auditory N_{100} and visual P_{100}) is most attenuated by a task in the same modality.

Exogenous Evoked Potentials in LD Children

Although the literature on LD and BSERs contains a limited number of studies, the application of BSERs to assist in the diagnosis of LD appears to be promising. Lenhardt (1981) presented a single-case study using audiometry, dichotic listening, and BSERs. Click stimuli were presented monaurally to both ears. A standard vertex referred to the right and left ear montage was employed. At a variety of click intensities and interstimulus intervals the subject displayed missing ipsilateral and contralateral waves II and VII when stimuli were presented to the right ear.

Greenblatt, Bar, Zappulla, and Hughes (1983) described a child with a specific auditory learning disorder and central auditory dysfunction. Pure tone testing revealed hearing to be within normal limits bilaterally, and spectral analysis on the child's EEG was normal when referenced to age-specific norms (Matousek & Petersen, 1973). Visual evoked responses were found to be symmetrically distributed throughout the cortex and within normal limits. Endogenous auditory evoked responses were well defined in the vertex leads and were symmetrical for the central and temporal areas. Monaural BSERs were recorded from each ear ipsilateral and contralateral to the side of stimulation and referenced to the vertex. Clicks were delivered at 60 dB above threshold. BSER latencies for ipsilateral peaks I and V and for contralateral peak V were within normal limits for their laboratory. However, BSERs showed an absence of the contralateral peak III for both left and right ear stimulation.

The authors acknowledge that absence or attenuation of the contralateral peak III does occur in normals. However, they had not previously observed an instance in normals or other populations where the contralateral peak III was absent on stimulation of both ears, as demonstrated in this case. Unfortunately, marked individual variations on the occurrence and symmetry of bilateral peaks seem to be common. Consequently, the report of such a variation in a single subject must await replication before any assessment significance can be attributed to this finding.

Piggott and Anderson (1983) compared two groups of 10 children matched for age and sex on BSER patterns. One child in each pair had evidence of a central language disturbance as determined by neuropsychological testing. All subjects had hearing and IQ scores that fell in the normal range. The results indicated that the children with central language disturbances showed longer latencies and interwave transmission time than did the controls. The segments in which the differences reached significance did not extend past wave III. The findings indicated that BSERs were useful in demonstrating that children with central language disabilities may have auditory stimuli transmission disturbances below the level of the olivary nuclei. This suggests that some presumed central disturbances may actually have their origin, if not their entire basis, in dysfunction in the early stages of the peripheral sensory input system.

Unfortunately, these rather clear-cut findings have been difficult to replicate. Tait, Roush, and Johns (1983) compared absolute and interwave BSER latencies between school-defined LD children and an age-matched group of normal children. BSERs to monaural 70-dB clicks were recorded from the mastoid of the test ear referenced to the vertex. Left and right ears were alternated between subjects during data collection. Findings from this study did not demonstrate any evidence of abnormality in auditory BSERs of LD children. Furthermore, psychoeducational performance as measured by the Woodcock-Johnson Psychoeducational Battery (Woodcock & Johnson, 1977) was not related to BSER latency in these children. The authors concluded that conventional BSER test procedures employing monaural click stimuli do not appear to provide an effective means of differentiating LD groups from age-matched normal controls. In a follow-up study with another sample of LD and normal children, Roush and Tait (1984) again did not find auditory BSERs to be significantly different between the two groups.

Summary. Exogenous BSERs have not yet provided any useful diagnostic schema for the various subtypes of LD, nor have they been shown to be consistently useful in a broad pathognomic sense (i.e., being able to separate normal from LD children). This may well reflect the lack of consistent attention paid to the selection and classification of subjects in these studies. Nevertheless, the occurrence of anomalous BSERs in this population as reported in several studies should encourage further research using this technique. Unlike middle- and late-latency evoked responses, BSERs are a mature clinical tecnhique in audiology and neurology, and extensive norms across developmental periods and for numerous disorders exist (Chiappa, 1983). Learning disabilities appear to have multiple etiologies, and no reason exists at present for excluding peripheral sensory involvement in these disorders. In the evaluation of a child, BSERs have, at the very least, a role to play in permitting the assessment or exclusion of peripheral auditory processing difficulty as contributing to the problem (see Obrzut, Morris, Wilson, Lord & Caraveo, 1987).

Endogenous Evoked Potentials in LD Children

Cohen and Breslin (1984) compared normal readers and dyslexic children on the hemisphere-specific endogenous components of their visual evoked responses. The stimuli were three- or four-letter words and a blank light flash. Data were collected from 10 lead positions, which included bilateral frontal, central, parietal, occipital, and midtemporal. For the two stimulus types, the normal group had a faster P2 occipital area response latency than the dyslexic group. Across all recorded areas, the P3 responses to the flash stimuli tended to have longer latencies and were less positive in the dyslexic group than in the average reading group. In normals, the activity of the right and left hemispheres was dissimilar during reading. However, the interhemispheric activity was quite similar during word reading in dyslexic children. The authors concluded that significant group differences existed in the way that the two hemispheres processed visual information.

The goal of the research conducted by Holcomb, Ackerman, and Dykman (1985) was to determine whether specific dyslexic subgroup differences were apparent in late ERP components, especially P3, recorded from multiple electrode sites. In addition to P3, Pc (a slow positive component that peaks between 700 and 1100 msec) was discovered to be sensitive to diagnostic group differences in this study. Several different visual stimuli were presented to 24 reading-disabled children and 24 normal controls. Electrodes were attached F_{pz}, F_z, C_z, P_z, and O_z, a midline referential montage that is not sensitive to lateralized asymmetries. The reading-disabled children were found to have significantly smaller overall bilateral P3s than age-matched controls. Further, the reading-disabled children showed reduced P3 and Pc amplitudes to three-letter words in contrast to nonalphanumeric symbols, whereas controls had equivalent amplitudes for these two stimulus types. P3 latency data revealed further differences between the two groups. Controls had earlier P3 peaks than the reading-disabled group and made faster behavioral responses to the presented stimuli.

Researchers in the area of endogenous EP components in dyslexia have been, as a group, more sensitive to the need to distinguish among subcategories of dyslexia. In regard to this distinction, Pirozzolo, Dunn, and Zetusky (1983) stated that the evidence compiled during the last two decades has rendered untenable the hypothesis that dyslexia represents a single neuropsychological or educational entity. Further, contemporary evidence overwhelmingly supports the existence of at least two subtypes of developmental dyslexia. These findings are the result of several clinical studies employing differential diagnosis of the cognitive deficits observed in large populations of reading-disabled children (see Chapter 12, this volume).

Fried et al. (1981) concurred that treating the dyslexic population as homogeneous has been a major problem. Their classification included a subgroup composed of individuals having serious impairments in auditory-verbal decoding, auditory sequencing, and symbol manipulation (i.e., dysphonetic), whereas the other subgroup showed deficits in visuospatial organization and visual-motor performance (i.e., dyseidetic). Dysphonetic dyslexics have great difficulty in reading and spelling words phonetically, which may be conceptualized as a defect in auditory processing of speech sounds. In contrast, dyseidetic children have good auditory perception and memory. Their handicap is primarily deficient visual processing. The alexic dyslexics are considered to be a mixture of both dysphonetic and dyseidetic types.

In their investigation Fried et al. (1981) applied ERP techniques to study auditory information processing in the left and right hemispheres of dyslexic subjects classified into subgroups. Dyslexic subjects were 2 or more years delayed in reading and spelling as measured by the Wide Range Achievement Test (Jastak, Bijiou, & Jastak, 1965). Through Boder's (1973) Diagnostic Screening Test for Developmental Dyslexia, five of the dyslexic subjects were classified as dysphonetic, six as dyseidetic, and two as alexic. Dyslexic subjects were age- and sex-matched with normal controls, all of whom were right-handed. Electrodes were placed at left and right frontal locations (F_7, F_8) and temporoparietal sites (midway between T_5 and C_3, and midway between T_6 and C_4, and labeled W_1 and W_2, respectively). Recording was referential. Auditory evoked potential stimuli were voiced words Do and Go, and strummed chords A7 and D7. The word and musical chord stimuli were delivered to each subject binaurally at 70 dB.

The ERP wave form lying between 50 and 400 msec after stimulus onset was chosen as the most likely time in which endogenous ERP activity relating to stimulus processing would occur. The normal and dyseidetic subjects exhibited the expected larger ratio ERP wave form amplitudes to words over chords in the left hemisphere and a differentially smaller ratio in the right hemisphere. However, the dysphonetic subjects did not exhibit this ERP asymmetry to stimulus type by hemisphere. "The lack of greater word-musical-chord ERP waveform differences over the left hemisphere in the dysphonetic group suggests that the left hemisphere of dysphonetic dyslexics may not have a fully developed capacity to process auditory information in a normal manner" (Fried et al., 1981, p. 20).

Auditory and visual evoked potential measures also were used in the Kaye et al. (1981) Neurometrics study reported above with children who were underachieving in verbal, arithmetic, or mixed areas. Auditory evoked potentials were evaluated for signal-to-noise ratio, wave shape coherence, and amplitude symmetry. They reported major differences among the underachieving groups in comparison with the matched normals and, with respect to each other, on the grand averages of both auditory and visual evoked responses. In comparison to the AEP peak latency values observed in the controls, the poor verbal achievers showed primarily scattered left hemisphere latency deviations, whereas the poor arithmetic achievers showed scattered left but consistent right hemispheric latency deviations. The mixed (arithmetic and verbal) underachievers showed almost no right hemisphere problems, but consistent left hemisphere latency deviations. Although these diagnostic group × cortical area deviations do not fit easily into conventional models of hemispheric or regional functional specialization, they do support the importance of these diagnostic subtypes by showing their linkage to functional cortical anomalies.

An attempt has been reported to remediate dysphonetic and dyseidetic subgroup specific asymmetry differences. Training involved practice at a task designed to appeal to the hemisphere in which in ERP anomalies occurred (Bakker & Vinke, 1985). They concluded that their training reduced these hemisphere-specific asymmetry anomalies, and that this reduction was correlated with changes in measures of reading accuracy and speed.

Summary. A number of investigators have found that differences exist between normal children and those with LD. However, it is becoming increasingly evident that it is unwise to think of LD children as having homogeneous disabilities. The subtyping of LD allows for the analysis of specific disabilities in terms of endogenous evoked potentials. The research thus far allows for the conclusion that ERPs can discriminate among LD subtypes; however, it is premature to utilize these data for routine clinical assessment. A major effort at evaluating infants for ERPs in response to phonetic stimuli and then following those children through early schooling to validate the use of ERP in the early prediction of developmental language difficulties is under way (Molfese & Molfese, 1986). The preliminary results of this major longitudinal effort are very encouraging and appear consonant with respect to ERP findings to date.

Probe-Elicited Event-Related Potentials in LD Children

Johnstone et al. (1984) found a difference between dyslexic and control children in regional response to an irrelevant visual probe during reading. While the children performed complex verbal and spatial tasks, light flashes irrelevant to their task were presented and subsequent visual-event related potentials (VERPs) were recorded. VERPs were recorded from central, parietal, midtemporal, and linked-ears leads referred to vertex. Although the dyslexics showed a significant amplitude decrease in the 250- to 350-msec range while reading difficult material, the normal readers did not. The authors believed this to be the result of a complex change in latency of the different components of the VERP that normally occurs during this interval. Therefore, a complete description of VERP effects in dyslexics must include not only regional differences but also a description of the latency of individual components for the VERP within a specific region.

Shucard, Cummins, and McGee (1984) used another variation on the probe-ERP method by presenting irrelevant tones to normal and disabled readers while they were engaged in two reading-related visual tasks. One task (sounding out letters) was designed to activate the left hemisphere differentially, whereas the other (matching letter patterns) was intended to activate the right. The pattern of auditory-event-related potentials (AERPs) was the opposite for the two groups. During both tasks, lower right hemisphere response amplitude was seen in the disabled readers in comparison with the normals. The left hemisphere amplitude also was significantly higher than that of the normals during the task requiring sounding out letters. The authors concluded that the opposing pattern of asymmetries in the two groups suggested that the tasks require different cortical processes in these two populations.

Summary. In terms of hemisphere relevant probes, special techniques are necessary to find differences between normals and LD children. Specifically, it is suggested that the analysis of data should include latency components as well as regional differences. Further, and perhaps more important, there appear to be differential cortical process requirements between LDs and normals.

CONCLUSIONS

Most studies have used only a small portion of the range of neuroimaging and electrophysiological techniques we have surveyed. Overall, the results of these studies are promising, with many of them finding structural or electrophysiological anomalies in the parietooccipital region where receptive speech systems are involved. Several studies also have reported global electrophysiological anomalies, especially in modal EEG frequency. Relatively few of these studies have been sensitive to the need to distinguish among the various subtypes of learning disability. Those that were seem to have found considerable accuracy of classification into those subtypes based upon the functional and structural neurological evidence.

The most successful efforts have been those using a battery of electrophysiological measures combined with clear classification of subjects according to useful subcatagories of learning disability, and involving a healthy sample size (e.g., Kaye et al., 1981). These desirable features of method arc not unique to this area of research, and they have long been recognized as sine qua non in the establishment of the research foundation for any useful clinical assessment tool.

Computerized methods of neuroimaging and electrophysiology are easily able to generate massive quantities of data. It is a temptation, when applying new methods, to employ an atheoretical or "shotgun" approach, rather than restricting the sphere of observation. Over a decade of computerized investigation of EEGs and EPs in learning-disabled children has yielded a large body of provocative, but scattered and inconsistent, results. An effort at consolidation would be helpful. This consolidation needs to take the form of systematic theory and model testing, simultaneously employing as many of the complementary methods as possible. Researchers committing themselves to a well-defined—and therefore risky—explanation of the neurological basis of learning disabilities may be confident, along with Sir Francis Bacon, that truth arises more readily from error than from confusion.

The techniques described in this chapter hold all of the allure and fascination of a possible technological breakthrough for a difficult assessment problem. To be significant, however, neuroimaging and electrophysiological procedures must demonstrate that they offset their high cost and demand for specialized training. They must yield useful diagnostic information about learning disabilities beyond that more cheaply and easily gathered by conventional psychometric and clinical methods.

REFERENCES

Bakker, D. J., & Vinke, J. (1985). Effects of hemisphere-specific stimulation on brain activity and reading in dyslexics. *Journal of Clinical and Experimental Neuropsychology, 7,* 505–525.

Boder, E. (1973). Developmental dyslexia: A diagnostic approach based on three atypical reading-spelling patterns. *Developmental Medicine and Child Neurology, 15,* 663–687.

Broca, P. (1861). Remarques sur le siège de la factulé du language articule, suivi d'un observation d'amphémie. *Bulletin de la Société Anatomique de Paris, Series 2, 6,* 330–357.

Chiappa, K. H. (Ed.). (1983). *Evoked potentials in clinical medicine.* New York: Raven Press.

Chiappa, K. H., Gladstone, J., & Young, R. (1979). Brain stem auditory evoked responses: Studies of waveform variations in 50 normal human subjects. *Archives of Nuerology, 36,* 81–87.

Chiappa, K. H., & Norwood, A. E. (1977). Brainstem auditory evoked responses in clinical neurology: Utility and neuropathological correlates. *Electroencephalography and Clinical Neurophysiology, 43,* 518.

Cohen, J., & Breslin, P. W. (1984). Visual evoked responses in dyslexic children. *Annals of the New York Academy of Sciences, 425,* 338–343.

Conners, C. K. (1978). Critical review of "Electroencephalographic and neurophysiological studies in dyslexia." In A. L. Benton & D. Pearl, (Eds.), *Dyslexia: An appraisal of current knowledge* (pp. 253–261). New York: Oxford University Press.

Decker, T. N., & Howe, S. W. (1981). Auditory tract asymmetry in brain stem electrical responses during binaural stimulation. *Journal of the Acoustical Society of America, 69,* 1084–1090.

Denckla, M. B., LeMay, M., & Chapman, C. A. (1985). Few CT scan abnormalities found even in neurologically impaired learning disabled children. *Journal of Learning Disabilities, 18,* 132–135.

Donchin, E. (1984). *Cognitive psychophysiology: Event-related potentials and the study of cognition* (Vol 1). Hillsdale: NJ: Erlbaum.

Drake, W. E. (1968). Clinical and pathological findings in a child with a developmental learning disability. *Journal of Learning Disabilities, 1,* 486–502.

Duffy, F. H., Denckla, M. B., Bartels, P. H., & Sandini, G. (1980). Dyslexia: Regional differences in brain electrical activity by topographic mapping. *Annals of Neurology, 7,* 412–430.

Duffy, F. H., Denckla, M. B., Bartels, P. H., Sandini, G., & Kiessling, L. F. (1980). Dyslexia: Automated diagnosis by computerized classification of brain electrical activity. *Annals of Neurology, 7,* 421–428.

Fein, G., Galin, D., Johnstone, J., Yingling, C. D., Marcus, M., & Kiersch, M. E. (1983). Electroencephalogram power spectra in normal and dyslexic children: 1. Reliability during passive conditions. *Electroencephalography and Clinical Neurophysiology, 55,* 399–405.

Fisher, J. H. (1910). Congenital word blindness: Inability to learn to read. *Transactions of the Ophthalmological Society, 30,* 216–225.

Fried, I., Tanguay, P. E., Boder, E., Doubleday, C., & Greensite, M. (1981). Developmental dyslexia: Electrophysiological evidence of clinical subgroups. *Brain and Language, 12,* 14–22.

Galaburda, A. M., & Kemper, T. L. (1979). Cytoarchitectonic abnormalities in developmental dyslexia: A case study. *Annals of Neurology, 6,* 94–100.

Galaburda, A. M., Sherman, G. F., Rosen, G. D., Aboitiz, F., & Geschwind, N. (1985). Developmental dyslexia: Four consecutive patients with cortical anomalies. *Annals of Neurology, 18,* 222–233.

Galin, D., & Ellis, R. (1975). Asymmetry in evoked potentials as an index of lateralized cognitive processes: Relation to EEG alpha asymmetry. *Neuropsychologia, 13,* 45–50.

Geschwind, N., & Levitsky, W. (1968). Human brain: Left-right asymmetries in temporal speech region. *Science, 161,* 186–187.

Greenblatt, E. R., Bar, A., Zappulla, R. A., & Hughes, D. A. (1983). Learning disability assessed through audiologic and physiologic measures: A case study. *Journal of Communication Disorders, 16,* 309–313.

Hammill, D. D., Leigh, J. E., McNutt, G., & Larsen, S. C. (1981). A new definition of learning disabilities. *Learning Disability Quarterly, 4,* 336–342.

Hier, D. B., LeMay, M., Rosenberg, P. B., & Perlo, V. P. (1978). Developmental dyslexia: Evidence for a subgroup with reverse asymmetry. *Archives of Neurology, 35*, 90–92.

Hillyard, S., & Woods, D. (1979). Electrophysiological analysis of human brain function. In M. Gazzaniga (Ed.), *Handbook of behavioral neurobiology* (Vol. 2, pp. 345–378). New York: Plenum Press.

Hinshelwood, J. (1895). Word-blindness and visual memory. *Lancet, 2*, 1564–1570.

Holcomb, P., Ackerman, P. T., & Dykman, R. A. (1985). ERPs: Attention and reading deficits. *Psychophysiology, 22*, 656–667.

Hughes, J. R. (1978). Electroencephalographic and neurophysiological studies in dyslexia. In A. L. Benton & D. Pearl (Eds.), *Dyslexia—An appraisal of current knowledge* (pp. 205–240). New York: Oxford University Press.

Hynd, G., Hynd, C., Sullivan, H., & Kingsbury, T. (1987). Regional cerebral blood flow (rCBF) in developmental dyslexia: Activation during reading in a surface and deep dyslexic. *Journal of Reading Disabilities, 20*, 294–300.

Jasper, H. H. (1958). The ten-twenty electrode system of the International Federation. *Electroencephalography and Clinical Neurophysiology, 10*, 371–375.

Jastak, J., Bijiou, S. W., & Jastak, S. R. (1965). *Wide Range Achievement Test.* Wilmington, DE: Guidance Associates.

John, E. R. (1963). Neural mechanisms of decision making. In W. S. Fields & W. Abbott (Eds.), *Information storage and neural control* (pp. 243–282). Springfield, IL: Charles C Thomas.

John, E. R. (1977). *Neurometrics: Clinical applications of quantitative neurophysiology.* Hillsdale, NJ: Erlbaum.

John, E. R., Karmel, B. Z., Corning, W. C., Easton, P., Brown, D., Ahn, H., John, M., Harmony, T., Prichep, L., Toro, A., Gerson, I., Bartlett, F., Thatcher, R., Kaye, H., Valdes, P., & Schwartz, E. (1977). Neurometrics. *Science, 196*, 1393–1410.

Johnston, J. (1982). *Probe event-related potentials during language processing in children: A comparison of resource allocation and stimulus set models of attention.* Unpublished doctoral dissertation, University of California, San Francisco.

Johnstone, J., Galin, D., Fein, G., Yingling, C., Herron, J., & Marcus, M. (1984). Regional brain activity in dyslexic and control children during reading tasks: Visual probe event-related potentials. *Brain and Language, 21*, 233–254.

Kaye, H., & John, E. R., Ahn, H., & Prichep, L. (1981). Neurometric evaluation of learning disabled children. *International Journal of Neuroscience, 13*, 15–25.

Kertesz, A., Black, S. E., Polk, M., & Howell, J. (1986). Cerebral asymmetries on magnetic resonance imaging. *Cortex, 22*, 117–127.

LeMay, M. (1982). Morphological aspects of human brain asymmetry: An evolutionary perspective. *Trends in Neurosciences, 5*, 273–275.

LeMay, M., & Kido, D. K. (1978). Asymmetries of the cerebral hemispheres on computed tomograms. *Journal of Computer Assisted Tomography, 2*, 471–476.

Lenhardt, M. L. (1981). Childhood central auditory processing disorder with brain stem evoked response verification. *Archives of Otolaryngology, 107*, 623–625.

Levine, R. A., & McGaffigan, P. M., (1983). Right-left asymmetries in the human brain stem: Auditory evoked potentials. *Electroencephalography and Clinical Neurophysiology, 55*, 532–537.

Lubar, J. F., Bianchini, K. J., Calhoun, W. H., Lambert, E. W., Brody, Z. H., & Shabsin, H. S. (1985). Spectral analysis of EEG differences between children with and without learning disabilities. *Journal of Learning Disabilities, 18*, 403–408.

Matousek, M., & Petersen, I. (Eds.). (1973). *Automation of clinical electroencephalography.* New York: Raven Press.

Molfese, D. L., & Molfese, V. J. (1986). Psychophysiological indices of early cognitive processes and their relationship to language. In J. E. Obrzut & G. W. Hynd (Eds.), *Child neuropsychology* (Vol. 1, pp. 95–115). New York: Academic Press.

Morgan, W. P. (1896). A case of congenital word-blindness. *British Medical Journal*, 2, 1378.

Obrzut, J. E., Morris, G. L., Wilson, S. L., Lord, J. M., & Caraveo, L. E. (1987). Brain stem evoked response in the assessment of learning disabilities. *International Journal of Neuroscience*, 32, 811–823.

Orton, S. T. (1937). *Reading, writing and speech problems in children.* London: Chapman & Hall.

Otto, D., Karrer, R., Halliday, R., Horst, R. L., Klorman, R., Squires, N., Thatcher, R. W., Fenelon, B., & Lelord, G. (1984). Developmental aspects of event-related potentials. *Annals of the New York Academy of Sciences*, 425, 319–337.

Picton, T. W., Hillyard, S. A., Krausz, H. I., & Galambos, R. (1974). Human Auditory evoked potentials: I. Evaluation of components. *Electroencephalography and Clinical Neurophysiology*, 36, 179–190.

Piggott, L. R., & Anderson, T. (1983). Brain stem auditory evoked responses in children with central language disturbance. *Journal of the American Academy of Child Psychiatry*, 22, 535–540.

Pirozzolo, F. J., Dunn, K., & Zetusky, W. (1983). Physiological approaches to subtypes of developmental reading disability. *Topics in Learning and Learning Disabilities*, 3, 40–47.

Pirozzolo, F. J., Jerger, J., Jerger, S., Morris, G., Levy, J., Goldman, A., & Handel, S. (1985). Neuropsychological electrophysiological and NMR studies of developmental aphasia. *International Neuropsychological Society Bulletin*, 15, 16.

Rebert, C. A., Wexler, B. N., & Sproul, A. (1978). EEG asymmetry in educationally handicapped children. *Electroencephalography and Clinical Neurophysiology*, 45, 436–442.

Rockstroh, B., Elbert, T., Birbaumer, N., & Lutzenberger, W. (1982). *Slow brain potentials and behavior.* Baltimore: Urban and Schwarzenberg.

Roush, J., & Tait, C. A. (1984). Binaural fusion, masking level differences and auditory brain stem responses in children with language-learning disabilities. *Ear and Hearing*, 5, 37–41.

Shucard, D. W., Cummins, K. R., & McGee, M. G. (1984). Event-related brain potentials differentiate normal and disabled readers. *Brain and Language*, 21, 318–334.

Sklar, B., Hanley, J., & Simmons, W. W. (1973). A computer analysis of EEG spectral signatures from normal and dyslexic children. *IEEE Transactions on Bio-Medical Engineering*, 20, 20–26.

Stockard, J. J., & Rossiter, V. S. (1977). Clinical and pathologic correlates of brain stem auditory response mechanisms. *Neurology*, 27, 316–325.

Tait, C., Roush, J., & Johns, J. (1983). Normal ABR's in children classified as learning disabled. *Journal of Auditory Research*, 13, 56–62.

Wernicke, C. (1874). *Der aphasiche symptemkomplex.* Breslaw: Cohn and Weigert.

Witelson, S. F. (1977). Developmental dyslexia: Two right hemispheres and none left. *Science*, 195, 309–311.

Witelson, S. F., & Pallie, W. (1973). Left hemisphere specialization for language in the newborn: Neuroanatomical evidence of asymmetry. *Brain*, 96, 641–646.

Woodcock, R. W., & Johnson, M. B. (1977). *Woodcock-Johnson Psycho-Educational Battery.* Hingham, MA: Teaching Resources Corporation.

Yingling, C. D., Galin, D., Fein, G., Peltzman, D., & Davenport, L. (1986). Neurometrics does not detect "pure" dyslexics. *Electroencephalography and Clinical Neurophysiology*, 63, 426–430.

IV

Comment

Problems and Prospects in Child Neuropsychological Assessment

MICHAEL G. TRAMONTANA

The chapters in this volume have addressed a variety of issues pertaining to the neuropsychological assessment of children. These included a consideration of the implications for assessment that stem from our current knowledge of neurodevelopmental disorders (Risser and Edgell), the unique contributions of neuropsychological assessment in evaluating the brain-impaired child (Bigler), the relative merits of different modes of neuropsychological inference (Willis), as well as the general issue of linking assessment and treatment from a neuropsychological perspective (Lyon, Moats, and Flynn). Special consideration was given to the assessment of key aspects of child neuropsychological functioning, including attention (Barkley), memory (Boyd), functional laterality (Gray and Dean), and language (Crary, Voeller, and Haak). There also was special emphasis on infant and early childhood assessment (Aylward)—an area that has received relatively little attention in child neuropsychology, and on the assessment of learning disabilities—an area that, by contrast, has been the subject of intensive neuropsychological inquiry. Learning disabilities were addressed specifically in terms of the analysis of subtypes (Hynd, Connor, and Nieves), the early identification of developmental precursors (Hooper), and the application of electrophysiological methods in assessment (Morris, Levy, and Priozzolo). Many important topics were covered, and a synthesis of this material in terms of major themes and recommended directions is now in order.

Perhaps the single most prominent theme throughout this volume has been the emphasis on assessing the *component processes* that underlie

MICHAEL G. TRAMONTANA • Bradley Hospital and Department of Psychiatry and Human Behavior, Brown University, East Providence, Rhode Island.

complex functions in children. A global construct like attention was conceptualized in terms of more specific skills and processes, including
arousal and alertness, selective or focused attention, sustained attention
or vigilance, and span of apprehension, as well as the search strategies or
rules used while attending. Deficits in attention were seen as taking a
variety of forms including distractibility, impulsivity, and, less commonly, hemi-inattention or neglect. Likewise, memory was viewed as a
multifactorial construct, with key dimensions involving episodic versus
semantic and strategic versus nonstrategic memory processes. Neurolinguistic assessment was seen as requiring not only a differentiation of basic
language functions (comprehension, formulation, repetition, naming) but
also various aspects of language content (phonology, syntax, semantics,
pragmatics), as well as prosodic features and paralanguage factors (motor
speech, attention, memory). There also was an emphasis on the multifactorial assessment of functional laterality, and the importance of differentiating specific patterns of lateral preference according to coordinated
systems of cerebral function. To varying degrees, the specific component
processes underlying a complex function were conceptualized as being
mediated by different neural substrates, vulnerable to disruption by different etiologies, following different developmental courses, and possibly
responsive to different forms of intervention. Their differentiation in assessment was seen as an essential prerequisite to the identification of
more homogeneous patterns or subtypes of disability.

There is no question that crude, undifferentiated constructs such as
attention or memory are of little value, and that progress in child neuropsychology will depend greatly on the ability to provide a more precise,
multidimensional specification of these aspects of a child's functioning.
However, there is a critical question concerning the proper *level* of analysis, and the point beyond which the specification of component processes
ceases to have clinical utility. As Rourke, Fisk, and Strang (1986) have
pointed out, the use of homogeneous, narrow-band tests—although internally consistent and permitting a precise assessment of a particular ability—may be of little use in assessing the child's capacity to meet complex
everyday demands. This, instead, requires an appreciation for the complex interplay of abilities and their integrated operation in performing
meaningful tasks. A reductionistic approach, if carried to an extreme,
would yield only a fragmented view of the functions in question and have
little meaning in relation to everyday functioning. Thus, in examining
component processes, the emphasis must be on balancing the goals for
specificity with considerations of ecological validity.

Likewise, efforts to identify subtypes of functional disability must be
grounded in a meaningful differentiation of the ways in which various
classes of disabled children actually perform. Important lessons in this
regard can be learned from the neuropsychological research on learning

disabilities, the area in which the study of subtypes is most advanced. As pointed out by Hynd *et al.* in Chapter 11, much of this work has been characterized by the use of multivariate statistical methods for the purpose of distinguishing subgroups of learning-disabled children on the basis of their profiles of neuropsychological performance. However, this often has been done in a *post hoc* fashion, without a clear rationale for the inclusion of various tests in a neuropsychological battery, and with many of these correlating poorly, if at all, with the actual areas of academic deficiency in question. Moreover, academic deficiencies typically have been defined rather crudely (based, for example, on the presence of an achievement lag in a general area like reading), without a more precise specification of the actual deficiencies involved. Hynd *et al.* are quite right in arguing that it would make better conceptual sense to base the definition of subtypes on the identification of *actual error patterns* in academic processes, and then to evaluate these using a theoretically driven test battery to assess those neuropsychological functions known to be important to the academic processes involved. Such an approach emphasizes the use of statistical methods to evaluate theory, rather than to construct subtypes of learning disability that may have little ecological validity. It also emphasizes the assessment of neuropsychological processes that have greater direct relevance to learning disabilities, thereby promoting a stronger foundation for meaningful linkages between assessment and treatment.

Lyon *et al.* (Chapter 5) have provided a thoughtful analysis of the various issues involved in bridging the gap between neuropsychological assessment and treatment. At present, little is known regarding the prescriptive significance of different patterns of neuropsychological data that would be pertinent in the actual selection or design of treatments. This certainly is a critical frontier for child neuropsychology that is greatly in need of systematic inquiry that could link assessment and treatment more directly. Whatever directions these efforts take, it is imperative that treatment prescriptions be considered within the wider context of the child's psychosocial environment. Brain–behavior relationships never operate in isolation but instead are influenced by environmental factors that serve to compound or mitigate any observed functional deficits. For example, the presence of behavioral disturbance in seizure-disordered boys has been found to depend not only on IQ and seizure-related variables but on the degree of parental cohesion with respect to issues of childrearing (Curley, Delaney, Mattson, Holmes, & O'Leary, 1987). Also, as discussed by Barkley in Chapter 6, environmental contingencies have been shown to play an important role in the manifestation of attention deficits. If one ignores these, and focuses exclusively on the task parameters that influence attention, any attempts at intervention outside of the testing situation may be completely ineffective. All of this underscores the value of a *bio-*

psychosocial perspective in the development of treatment-oriented approaches to neuropsychological assessment. This is quite consistent with the major emphasis given to issues of ecological validity by various authors in this volume.

Another point of emphasis has been the need for a coherent framework of developmental brain–behavior relationships to help guide the assessment process and the evaluation of assessment results. As noted in Chapter 1, this requires an understanding of how brain functions develop normally, as well as under various pathological conditions. Such a framework would indicate not only *what* areas of function should be assessed in evaluating the effects of childhood brain injury but *how* these should be assessed at different points in development. It requires, quite frankly, a more complete and dynamic understanding of neuropsychological development than currently exists.

This is not to say that existing knowledge in this area is useless in guiding assessment, because this clearly is not the case. The fact is that more is known about the neuropsychology of the developing brain than is reflected in current assessment practices. There is a complex interplay of factors that can influence the developmental patterns of children who suffer early brain damage (Chelune & Edwards, 1981), and systematic knowledge regarding the developmental significance of different types of early lesions has begun to emerge (e.g., Dennis, 1985). Risser and Edgell (Chapter 2) have provided an excellent overview of much of the work in this area, focusing especially on insults to normal brain development occurring through the first 2 years of life. Although much remains to be learned, there are important implications for how neurodevelopmental disorders are conceptualized and assessed from what already is known.

For example, there is little basis for an unqualified acceptance of Kennard's (1940) principle concerning the enhanced potential for (re)acquisition of function after injury that supposedly characterizes the immature brain. There apparently are definite limits to the extent and type of (re)organization of function that can occur, even for brain injuries sustained very early in life. The available evidence suggests that such injuries often are associated with some degree of deficit and less-than-optimal functioning, *provided that these are assessed appropriately.* Crary et al. (Chapter 10) addressed this point in relation to the specialized role that the left cerebral hemisphere plays in the development of language functions right from birth. Early unilateral injury to the left hemisphere may result in a takeover of language functions by the right hemisphere, but usually at some expense to nonverbal abilities (Bigler & Naugle, 1984). Moreover, although deficits in language functions may not be apparent when assessed simply in terms of Verbal IQ, a careful neurolinguistic assessment will reveal subtle inefficiencies in various aspects of higher-level language processing (Kiessling, Denckla, & Carlton, 1983).

The overall impression from reports such as these is that the young child who sustains brain injury may benefit to some extent from cerebral plasticity. However, any compensatory organization of function is apt to be ineffecient because it would tend to go against the grain of the intrinsic avenues for neural specialization that normally would unfold. Consequently, residual deficits of some significance generally should be expected. These sometimes can be missed unless the assessment strategy is geared to revealing the more subtle features of neuropsychological functioning normally mediated by the injured brain region(s).

Existing evidence also would call into question the purported role of maturational delays in the manifestation of neurodevelopmental disorders. The concept of maturational lag usually has been invoked to account for the fact that some children, including those with learning disabilities, may show significant difficulties in neuropsychological functioning in the absence of a documented history of brain injury. Presumably, these difficulties simply may reflect a slower rate of maturation of an otherwise normal brain (Satz, Taylor, Friel, & Fletcher, 1978). One problem with this idea is that there is no evidence that the brains of children with significant performance lags are immature or "unfinished" with respect to morphological features (Rodier, 1984). Rather, investigations such as the detailed cytoarchitectonic studies of the brains of dyslexics at autopsy (e.g., Galaburda & Kemper, 1979) indicate that brain morphology is truly abnormal. Hynd *et al.* (Chapter 11) have interpreted this work to suggest that abnormalities in cell migration during later periods of fetal development (resulting in assorted defects of the left perisylvian region such as focal dysplasias, disordered cortical layering, and polymicrogyria) constitute the neurodevelopmental basis for many learning disabilities.

Another problem with the concept of maturational lag is that it implies that the child with functional delays eventually will "catch up" and exhibit normal abilities. However, this generally is not the case, as shown in the follow-up literature on children with learning disabilities (Schonhaut & Satz, 1983). Although disabled readers may improve over time, they typically continue to show inefficiencies in their reading skills (Rutter, Tizard, Yule, Graham, & Whitmore, 1976). Moreover, with the exception of the position taken by Boyd (Chapter 7), the general consensus among the authors in this volume is that the processing strategies utilized by disabled learners cannot be compared to those of a younger child. Their functioning is not simply delayed but deviant. These children are delayed in the sense that their inefficiencies result in lower performance levels on age-normed tests, but the kinds of processing strategies that they utilize are uncharacteristic of normal functioning at any age.

Thus, it appears that the concept of maturational lag has little meaning in current conceptualizations of neurodevelopmental disorders. Use of the term should be limited to those instances in which there is a genuine delay in the normal timing or rate of skill acquisition without parallel evidence of aberrations in existing processing abilities. This requires the differentiation of process and product in assessment, and also has important implications for how developmental precursors to learning problems are identified. If functions are not organized differently in learning-disabled children but instead operate less efficiently (as suggested by Hynd et al.), then learning disabilities should be forecast by dysfunction involving the brain regions that normally are preordained to mediate academic skills. Hooper (Chapter 12) has discussed the challenge that this perspective poses for early identification research, given that deficits of this type ordinarily are considered to be "silent" until relatively late in the preschool period.

Some concepts in child neuropsychology, like neuromaturational lag, grew out of an era when it generally was not possible to obtain precise information regarding brain structure and physiology in children with functional handicaps. Just as inadequacies in neuropsychological assessment sometimes resulted in an overestimation of recovery of function or cerebral plasticity in brain-injured children, so too inadequacies in diagnostic tools for assessing brain pathology may have led to false (or at least premature) conclusions concerning the apparent absence of brain anomalies in certain neurodevelopmental disorders. Earlier researchers did not have the benefit of the powerful methods now available for brain imaging and the in vivo study of dynamic neurophysiological processes, which were discussed in detail by Bigler (Chapter 3) and Morris et al. (Chapter 13). The availability of this new generation of neurodiagnostic tools promises to have an unprecedented impact on the advancement of knowledge in child neuropsychology, especially with respect to the neural side of brain–behavior relationships. Full advantage should be taken of the new avenues for investigation that these methods have opened, but without losing sight of the unique contributions that child neuropsychology can make in assessing and conceptualizing the behavioral aspects of various brain anomalies. A clearer understanding of developmental brain–behavior relationships cannot be obtained solely through technical advances in diagnosing brain pathology but will depend also on parallel advances in the development of more precise and ecologically valid tools for assessing neuropsychological functioning.

At this point, there are a number of serious limitations associated with all-purpose or omnibus approaches to the neuropsychological assessment of children. Neuropsychological assessment is becoming increasingly specialized and geared more toward the evaluation of component processes and their impact on a child's everyday functioning. There is a growing appreciation for the need to tailor the assessment process, as well as the constructs that are assessed, according to the clinical questions and specific populations involved. An assessment strategy that is quite useful in one context may be useless in another. Also, new knowledge in developmental neuropsychology is evolving rapidly, and undoubtedly will have an ongoing impact on how the assessment process is conducted and conceptualized. An omnibus test battery would tend to lack the specificity and flexibility necessary in meeting the varied and ever-widening objectives of assessment in child neuropsychology.

However, as noted in Chapter 1, a fixed or standard battery of tests does have the advantage of helping to assure a consistently broad sampling of neuropsychological functioning that is not biased by either referral complaints or the child's initial presentation. There is a need for a core set of test procedures that could provide a consistent frame of reference in making screening decisions regarding those areas of function that require a more in-depth, process-oriented assessment through a flexible selection of tests. The use of a core battery also promotes a greater comparability of finding across different times, patient groups, and research settings. The trouble is that there currently is little agreement within the field as to what procedures should constitute core components in a comprehensive neuropsychological assessment. Existing examples of standardized test batteries for children take much too long to administer to be practical for the purpose of routine neuropsychological screening. Moreover, the information that they yield is often redundant with the results of intelligence testing (Tramontana, Klee, & Boyd, 1984).

What is needed is a core battery of procedures, tailored to children of different ages, which is brief but nonetheless spans key dimensions of neuropsychological functioning. A more coordinated effort in this direction among different groups of investigators would be a very positive step for the field, and it is long overdue. Such an effort would permit a much wider-scale standardization of various measures and a more rapid accumulation of validation data than could be achieved by any single group of investigators working alone. Divergent methods naturally would continue to be used, both in exploring specific questions and as a matter of personal preference, but it is critical for there to be some consensus on the core features of assessment that could serve as general standards for practice. These obviously would be subject to periodic review and revision as new knowledge unfolds and as better instruments become available. This kind of collaboration would not be easy to achieve, and indeed may be unrealistic, but its potential benefits should be recognized and promoted actively by the professional organizations within the field. This ultimately would be more constructive than all of the rhetoric and energy devoted to debates concerning the purported superiority of one assessment approach or another, often with no data to support the claims.

A major objective of this volume has been to emphasize the need for further developments in various aspects of child neuropsychological assessment. The coverage was not exhaustive but was focused instead on certain key areas, including assessment of the younger child. The intent has been to balance the appraisal of present shortcomings with the outlining of worthwhile directions for future work. Innovations and refinements certainly are needed, but progress could be achieved in the meantime by drawing selectively upon some of the methods already available. The contributing authors in this volume have gone "out on a limb," so to speak, in providing informed opinions as to what methods appear to hold particular promise in assessing various aspects of neuropsychological functioning. These recommendations undoubtedly will require change as new knowledge in developmental neuropsychology is obtained, but the judicious use of existing tools will be necessary in order for the knowledge base to grow. Much like its subject of inquiry, the field of child neuropsychology is growing, differentiating, and undergoing dynamic change. It will be essential that our assessment methods both promote and keep pace with the exciting developments that lie ahead.

REFERENCES

Bigler, E. D., & Naugle, R. I. (1984). Case studies in cerebral plasticity. *International Journal of Clinical Neuropsychology, 7*, 12–23.

Chelune, G. J., & Edwards, P. (1981). Early brain lesions: Ontogenetic-environmental considerations. *Journal of Consulting and Clinical Psychology, 49*, 777–790.

Curley, A. D., Delaney, R. C., Mattson, R. H., Holmes, G. L., & O'Leary, K. D. (1987). *Determinants of behavioral disturbance in boys with seizures.* Paper presented at the 95th Annual Convention of the American Psychological Association, New York.

Dennis, M. (1985). Intelligence after early brain injury: I. Predicting IQ scores from medical variables. *Journal of Clinical and Experimental Neuropsychology, 7*, 526–554.

Galaburda, A. M., & Kemper, T. L. (1979). Cytoarchitectonic abnormalities in developmental dyslexia: A case study. *Annals of Neurology, 6*, 94–100.

Kennard, M. A. (1940). Relation of age to motor impairment in man and subhuman primates. *Archives of Neurology and Psychiatry, 44*, 377–397.

Kiessling, L. S., Denckla, M. B., & Carlton, M. (1983). Evidence for differential hemispheric function in children with hemiplegic cerebral palsy. *Developmental Medicine and Child Neurology, 25*, 727–734.

Rodier, P. M. (1984). Exogenous sources of malformations in development. In E. S. Gollin (Ed.), *Malformations of development: Biological and psychological sources and consequences* (pp. 287–313). New York: Academic Press.

Rourke, B. P., Fisk, J. L., & Strang, J. D. (1986). *Neuropsychological assessment of children: A treatment-oriented approach.* New York: Guilford Press.

Rutter, M., Tizard, J., Yule, W., Graham, P., & Whitmore, K. (1976). Research report: Isle of Wight studies, 1964–1974. *Psychological Medicine, 6*, 313–332.

Satz, P., Taylor, H. G., Friel, J., & Fletcher, J. M. (1978). Some developmental and predictive precursors of reading disabilities: A six year follow-up. In A. Benton & D. Pearl (Eds.), *Dyslexia: An appraisal of current knowledge* (pp. 313–348). New York: Oxford Press.

Schonhaut, S., & Satz, P. (1983). Prognosis for children with learning disabilities: A review of follow-up studies. In M. Rutter (Ed.), *Developmental neuropsychiatry* (pp. 542–563). New York: Guilford Press.

Tramontana, M. G., Klee, S. H., & Boyd, T. A. (1984). WISC-R interrelationships with the Halstead-Reitan and Children's Luria Neuropsychological Batteries. *International Journal of Clinical Neuropsychology, 6*, 1–8.

Index

Academic achievement
  learning disability and, 316, 349
  psychological assessment, 84
  See also Learning disability
Actuarial models, 97–102
  base-rate considerations in, 98–100
  clinical models contrasted, 94–96
  methods, 97–98
  stability and generalizability of rules in, 101–102
  validity of criteria in, 100–101
ADD-H Comprehensive Teacher Rating Scale (ACTeRS), 159
Adults
  brain-behavior differences with children, 4
  Halstead-Reitan Neuropsychological Battery and, 6, 10
  learning disabilities, 302
  memory assessment, 177
  treatment linkages, 116–117
Age level
  age specificity and, 31
  attention and, 150
  brain development and, 51–53
  conceptual issues and, 227–234
  Halstead Neuropsychological Test Battery, 9–10
  language development and, 254–261
  learning disabilities, 326–328
  pediatric neurological exam, 68
  See also Infancy and early childhood
Age specificity, 31
Attention, 145–176
  ADD-H Comprehensive Teacher Rating Scale (ACTeRS), 159
  assessment of, 153–169
  behavioral conceptualization of, 151–152

Attention (*Cont.*)
  behavior rating scales, 153–159
  cancellation tasks, 163–164
  Child Behavior Checklist (CBCL), 156
  Children's Embedded Figures Test (CEFT), 164
  components of, 148–149
  Conners rating scales, 154–155
  Continuous Performance Tasks (CPT), 161–163
  defined, 145–146, 148
  developmental issues, 150–151
  direct observational measures of, 167–169
  Direct Reinforcement of Latency (DRL) tasks, 165–166
  Edelbrock Child Assessment Profile (CAP), 156–157, 158
  Freedom From Distractibility (FFD) Factor (WISC-R), 167
  Goldman-Fristoe-Woodcock (GFW) Selective Attention Test, 166
  importance of, 146–148
  Laboratory Measures, 159–167
  Matching Familiar Figures Test (MFFT), 165
  Mazes, 164–165
  measures of, 147–148
  Preschool Behavior Questionnaire (PBQ), 158–159
  psychometric tests/laboratory measures of, 159–167
  Reaction Time (RT) tasks, 160–161
  Revised Behavior Problem Checklist (RBPC), 157
  Span of apprehension test, 166
Attention deficit disorder, 146. *See also* Attention
Auditory-Verbal Learning Test, 183, 184

Bakker Research Program, 131–132
Base-rate considerations, 98–100
Bayesian analysis, 106
BEAM. See Brain Electrical Activity Mapping (BEAM) technique
Behavioral state, 228
Behavior rating scales, 153–159
Bender Visual-Motor Gestalt test, 84
Benton Revised Visual Retention Test, 183, 184
Birth
  brain development, 47
  brain injury, 56
Boder Test of Reading-Spelling Patterns (BTRSP)
  developmental issues, 136
  treatment linkages, 133
Boston Process Approach, 18
Brain
  infancy, 230
  language skills, 254–261
  laterality assessment, 205–223
  learning disabilities, 301–304
  learning disabilities (electrophysiological assessment), 337–366
Brain-behavior relationship
  child-adult differences, 4
  infancy, 226
  treatment linkages, 115–116, 118
Brain damage
  treatment linkages, 113
  See also Localization
Brain development, 4, 41–65
  abnormalities in, 51–56
  neuropsychological implications of, 56–59
  overview of, 41–42
  principles of, 42–51
  treatment linkages, 118
Brain Electrical Activity Mapping (BEAM) technique
  described, 82
  learning disabilities, 346, 349
Brain injury localization. See Brain damage; Localization
Brain stem evoked potentials, 353–355. See also Evoked potentials

Cancellation tasks, 163–164
Category Test, 118
CAT scan, 340

Central nervous system
  infancy, 230
  language skills, 254–261
  See also Brain
Child Assessment Profile (CAP), 156–157, 158
  See also Edelbrock Child Assessment Profile (CAP)
Child Behavior Checklist (CBCL), 156
Child neuropsychological assessment.
  See Neuropsychological assessment
Children's Embedded Figures Test (CEFT), 164
Classification systems, 231–232
Clinical models, 102–107
  actuarial models contrasted, 94–96
  debiasing techniques, 105–106
  design and decision rules, 106–107
  interpretive strategies, 103–104
Cluster analysis, 97, 98
Cognition, 233, 234
Cognitive approach. See Functional profile approach
Coloured Progressive Matrices (CPM), 85
Communication. See Neurolinguistic assessment; Language development
Computed tomography, 337, 340–341.
  See also Neuroradiological tests
Conners rating scales, 154–155
Continuous Performance Tasks (CPT), 161–163
Cranial nerve function, 69

Data-diagnosis contingency, 94–95
Debiasing techniques, 105–106
Denman Neuropsychological Memory Scale, 183, 184
Detroit Tests of Learning Aptitude (DTLA), 179, 181
Developmental issues
  attention, 150–151
  language skills, 254–261
  learning disabilities, 325–328
  memory, 185–195
  psychological assessment, 84–85
  treatment linkages, 118, 121–122, 136–137
  See also Brain development
Developmental neurolinguistic assessment.
  See Neurolinguistic assessment

Developmental Test of Visual-Motor
  Integration, 85
Diagnostic models, 94–96
  data consideration in, 95–96
  data-diagnosis contingency, 94–95
  data importance in, 96
Dichotic listening
  Bakker Research Program, 131–132
  laterality assessment, 207–209
Differentiation (neural), 44–47
Direct observation
  attention assessment, 167–169
  infancy, 233
Direct Reinforcement of Latency (DRL)
  tasks, 165–166
Discriminant analysis, 97
Draw-A-Person test, 84
DSM-III, 106–107
Dynamic assessment, 137–138
Dynamic phase, 8
Dyslexia
  laterality assessment, 216
  See also Learning disability; Reading
    disability

Early childhood. See Infancy and early
  childhood
Eclectic test batteries
  critique of, 19–20
  described, 17
Ecological validity, 8
Edelbrock Child Assessment Profile
  (CAP), 156–157, 158
  See also Child Assessment Profile
Edinburgh Handedness Inventory, 212
Education for All Handicapped Children
  Act, 4
  infancy and, 227
  learning disabilities and, 284, 313, 338

EEG. See Electroencephalography
Electrodiagnostic tests, 80–83. See also
  Electrophysiological assessment
Electroencephalography, 343–352
  analysis methods in, 345–346
  described, 343–345
  fast-Fourier Transformation (FFT), 345

  laterality assessment, 210–211
  learning disability, 337, 347–352
  montage, 334

Electroencephalography (Cont.)
  neuropsychological assessment, 80–81,
    82, 83
  See also Evoked potentials
Electrophysiological assessment, 80–83,
    343
  laterality assessment, 210–211
  learning disabilities, 337–366
Embryonic development, 42–51
Endogenous evoked responses
  described, 355–356
  learning disabilities, 359–361
  See also Evoked responses
Environment
  infancy, 231
  learning disabilities, 317–318
Evoked potentials, 352–362
  described, 352–357
  electroencephalography, 346, 349
  learning disabilities, 337, 357–362
  neuropsychological assessment, 81–82
  See also Electroencephalography
Exogenous evoked responses
  described, 353
  learning disabilities, 357–359
  See also Evoked potentials
Expressive functions, 233

Fast Fourier Transformation, 345
Fetal development, 42–51
Fixed-battery approaches, 9. See also en-
    tries under names of specific test
    batteries
Flynn Research Program, 132–135
Freedom From Distractibility (FFD) factor
    (WISC-R), 167
Functional laterality. See Laterality
    assessment
Functional profile approach, 6–8

Gait disturbance, 68
Genetic disease, 55–56
Gestational age, 45
Goldman-Fristoe-Woodcock (GFW) Selec-
    tive Attention Test, 166
Grammatical expansion stage, 253–254,
    264–269

Halstead-Reitan Neuropsychological Test
    Battery

Halstead-Reitan Neuropsychological Test Battery (*Cont.*)
    critique of, 12–13
    described, 9–13
    historical perspective on, 6
    Luria-Nebraska compared, 14, 15
    memory assessment, 179, 182
    treatment linkages, 119–122
Handedness, 211–214. *See also* Laterality assessment
Head injury, 22–23
Hemiinattention, 149

Impulsivity
    attention, 148
    cancellation tasks, 163
Infancy and early childhood, 225–248
    assessment instruments, 234–239
    conceptual issues in, 227–234
    current status, 225–227
    future directions, 239–244
Information-processing models, 186–188
Intelligence testing
    Halstead-Reitan Neuropsychological Test Battery, 12
    learning disabilities, 286
    localization, 11
    memory, 179
    neuropsychological assessment compared, 86–87
    psychological assessment, 84
    systemic illness, 23–24
    treatment linkages, 117–118

Kaufman Assessment Battery for Children, 87
    memory assessment, 181
    treatment linkages, 122–123

Language development, 250–254
    grammatical expansion stage, 253–254
    lexical expansion stage, 252–253
    prelinguistic communication, 251
    See also Neurolinguistic assessment
Language-impaired children, 215–218
Laterality assessment, 205–223
    brain, 205–206
    clinical implications, 218–219
    dichotic listening methods, 207–209
    electrophysiological measures of, 210–211

Laterality assessment (*Cont.*)
    lateral preference measures, 211–214
    learning disabilities and, 215–218
    methods of, 206–215
    unimanual performance measures, 214–215
    visual half-field procedures, 209
Lateral preference measures, 211–214
Learning
    infancy, 233–234
    memory and, 177, 178, 188–192
    See also Intelligence testing; Memory
Learning disability, 281–312
    assessment applications, 26–27
    Bakker Research Program, 131–132
    conceptual framework for evaluation of, 305–307
    definitions, 284–285
    Flynn Research Program, 132–135
    Halstead-Reitan Neuropsychological Test Battery, 11
    historical perspective on, 7, 282–284
    laterality assessment and, 215–218
    Lyon Research Program, 125–131
    multifactor research in, 285–301
    neuroanatomical-linguistic perspectives on, 301–304
    overview of, 281–282
    prediction of, 313–335
    remediation, 124
    treatment linkages, 114
Learning disability (electrophysiological assessment), 337–366
    anatomical correlates in, 338–339
    CAT scans, 340
    electroencephalography, 343–352
    evoked potentials, 352–362
    magnetic resonance imaging, 342–343
    overview of, 337–338
    positron emission tomography, 341
    regional cerebral blood flow, 341–342
Learning disability prediction, 313–335
    current status of, 318–324
    importance of, 314–318
    issues and directions in, 324–331
    neurodevelopmental theory and, 325–328
    overview of, 313–314
    preschool prediction, 328–330
    related issues in, 330–331
Levels-of-processing model, 187–188

Lexical expansion
  assessment of, 263–264
  described, 252–253
Localization, 10–11
Luria-Nebraska Neuropsychological Test
    Battery, 9
  critique of, 15–16
  described, 13–16
  memory assessment, 179, 182
  qualitative approaches, 18
  treatment linkages, 122
Lyon Research Program, 125–131

Magnetic resonance imaging
  learning disabilities, 337, 342–343
  See also Neuroradiological tests
Matching Familiar Figures Test (MFFT),
    165
Mazes, 164–165
McCarthy Scales, 179, 181
Memory, 177–204
  clinical relevance of models of, 199–
    200
  current status of assessment of, 179–
    185
  developmental models, 185–195
  format suggestions for battery assess-
    ing, 195–196
  infancy, 233–234
  information-processing models of, 186–
    188
  interactionist models of, 188–195
  task type suggestions for battery assess-
    ing, 196–199
  tests for assessment of, 180–183
Memory for Designs Test, 183, 184
Mental activity (infancy), 234
Migration (neural), 43–44
Montage, 334
Motor function, 68–69
Multiaxial system (DSM-III-R), 106–107
Multiple regression, 97
Multistore model (memory), 186–187
Muscle tone, 68–69
Myelination, 47–49

Naming, 267
National Joint Committee for Learning
    Disabilities (NJCLD), 285, 315, 338
Neglect. See Hemiinattention

Neonate, 235. See also Infancy and early
    childhood
Neuroanatomical-linguistic perspective
    (learning disabilities), 301–304
Neuroimaging techniques. See Neu-
    roradiological tests; entries under
    specific procedures
Neurolinguistic assessment, 249–279
  current status of, 261–269
  guidelines/questions regarding, 269–
    274
  language development, 250–254
  language processing styles, 254
  maturational factors in, 254–251
  overview of, 249–250
  See also Language development
Neurolinguistic subtyping, 300–301
Neurological disorder, 21–23
Neuropsychological assessment
  actuarial models of, 97–102
  applications of, 21–28
  attention, 153–169
  brain development, 41–65
  clinical models, 102–107
  conceptual/practical issues in, 28–32
  current interest in, 3–5
  diagnostic models of, 94–96
  eclectic test batteries, 17
  electrodiagnostic tests, 80–83
  fixed-battery approaches, 9
  Halstead-Reitan Neuropsychological
    Battery, 9–13
  historical trends in, 5–9
  infancy and early childhood, 225–248
  intelligence testing compared to, 86–
    87
  laterality assessment, 205–223
  learning disabilities, 26–27 (See also
    Learning disability)
  Luria-Nebraska Neuropsychological
    Battery-Children's Revision, 13–16
  memory, 177–204
  neurolinguistic assessment, 249–279
  neurological disorders, 21–23
  neuroradiological tests, 75–80
  pediatric neurological exam, 68, 75
  problems/prospects in, 369–376
  process-oriented approaches, 18–19
  psychiatric disorders, 24–26
  psychological assessment and, 84–87
  qualitative approaches, 17–18
  rehabilitation of function, 27–28
  special-purpose measures, 20–21

Neuropsychological assessment (Cont.)
  systemic illness, 23–24
  treatment linkages with, 113–142
Noncompliance, 229

Observational measures. See Direct
  observation
Oncology, 24

Paralanguage measures, 268–269
Peabody Individual Achievement Test
  (PIAT), 126–127
Pediatric neurological exam
  anomalous physical development
    markers, 70–73
  cranial nerve function, 69
  findings in, 70
  "hard" versus "soft" findings in, 73–
    74
  mental status characteristics, 74
  motor function, 68–69
  neuropsychological assessment and, 68,
    75
  sensory-perceptual function, 69–70
  station/gait, 68
Personality, 84
Positron emission tomography, 341
Prediction
  infancy, 229–230
  learning disabilities, 313–335
Prelinguistic assessment, 251, 262–263
Preschool Behavior Questionnaire (PBQ),
  158–159
Probe-elicited event-related potentials
  described, 357
  learning disabilities, 362
Processing, 233–234
Process-oriented approaches critique of,
  19–20
  described, 18–19
Proliferation (neural), 43–44
Prosody, 267–268
Psychiatric disorders, 24–26
Psychological assessment, 84–87
Psychometric tests, 159–167
Public Law 94-142. See Education for All
  Handicapped Children Act

Qualitative approaches
  critique of, 19–20
  described, 17–18

Radiology. See Neuroradiological tests
Reaction time tests, 160–161
Reading disability
  Bakker Research Program, 131–132
  Flynn Research Program, 132–135
  historical perspective on, 282–284
  Lyon Research Program, 125–131
  See also Learning disability
Receptive functions, 233
Reflexes, 233
Regional cerebral blood flow, 341–342
Rehabilitation
  assessment applications, 27–28
  treatment linkages, 116
  See also Treatment linkages
Reitan Evaluation of Hemispheric Abili-
    ties and Brain Improvement Training
    (REHABIT), 120–121
Remediation
  responses to, 124
  treatment linkages, 116
  See also Treatment linkages
Repetition, 266–267
Revised Behavior Problem Checklist
    (RBPC), 157

Sensory-perceptual function, 69–70
Sex differences, 146
Single-test approach, 5–6
Social functioning
  attention, 150–151
  learning disabilities, 316–317
Span of apprehension
  attention assessment, 166
  defined, 149
Special-purpose measures, 20–21
Stanford-Binet test, 179, 180
Statistical methods, 97–102
Stimulants, 152
Sustained attention
  defined, 148–149
  developmental issues, 150
Systemic illness, 23–24

Temperament, 228
Test battery/lesion-specification stage, 6
Tetrahedral model (memory), 188–192
Trauma, 282
Treatment linkages, 113–142
  assessment and, 113–142
  Bakker Research Program, 131–312
  classification research needs, 138–139

Treatment linkages (*Cont.*)
developmental issues, 136–137
dynamic issues, 137–138
Flynn Research Program, 132–135
Halstead-Reitan Neuropsychological Test Batteries, 119–122
Kaufman Assessment Battery for Children (K-ABC), 122–123
Luria-Nebraska Battery–Children's Revision, 122
Lyon Research Program, 125–131
models for, 119
overview of, 113–142
professional preparation and experience, 135–136
purposes/measurement characteristics, 115–119
studies in, 123–124

Unimanual performance measures, 214–215

Validity
actuarial models, 100–101
cancellation tasks, 163
Visual half-field procedures, 209

Wechsler Intelligence Scale for Children-Revised, 118
Freedom From Distractibility factor, 167
memory assessment, 179, 180
neuropsychological assessment, 86–87
systemic illness, 23–24
Wechsler Memory Scale, 178
Wernicke-Geschwind model, 301–304

Yale Neuropsychoeducational Assessment Scales-Stigmata schedule, 70–73